Vizcaya on
the Eve of Carlism

BOOKS IN THE BASQUE SERIES

A Book of the Basques
by Rodney Gallop
In A Hundred Graves: A Basque Portrait
by Robert Laxalt
Basque Nationalism
by Stanley G. Payne
Amerikanuak: Basques in the New World
by William A. Douglass and Jon Bilbao
Beltran: Basque Sheepman of the American West
by Beltran Paris, as told to William A. Douglass
The Basques: The Franco Years and Beyond
by Robert P. Clark
The Witches' Advocate: Basque Witchcraft and the
Spanish Inquisition (1609–1614)
by Gustav Henningsen
Navarra: The Durable Kingdom
by Rachel Bard
The Guernica Generation: Basque Refugee Children
of the Spanish Civil War
by Dorothy Legarreta
Basque Sheepherders of the American West
Photographs by Richard H. Lane
Text by William A. Douglass
A Cup of Tea in Pamplona
by Robert Laxalt
Sweet Promised Land
by Robert Laxalt
Traditional Basque Cooking: History and
Preparation
by José María Busca Isusi
Basque Violence: Metaphor and Sacrament
by Joseba Zulaika
Basque-English Dictionary
by Gorka Aulestia
The Basque Hotel
by Robert Laxalt
Vizcaya on the Eve of Carlism: Politics and Society,
1800–1833
by Renato Barahona

The Basque Series

RENATO BARAHONA

Vizcaya on the Eve of Carlism

Politics and Society, 1800–1833

UNIVERSITY OF NEVADA PRESS

Reno and Las Vegas

Basque Series Editor: William A. Douglass

The paper used in this book meets the requirements of
American National Standard for Information Sciences—
Permanence of Paper for Printed Library Materials.
ANSI Z39.48-1984. Binding materials were chosen for strength
and durability. ⊗

This book was published with the support of the Program for
Cultural Cooperation Between Spain's Ministry of Culture and
United States' Universities.

A Spanish-language version of this book is being published in
Spain by Editorial Critica, Barcelona.

Library of Congress Cataloging-in-Publication Data
Barahona, Renato, 1944–
Vizcaya on the eve of Carlism : politics and society, 1800–1833 /
Renato Barahona.
p. cm. — (The Basque series)
Bibliography: p.
Includes index.
ISBN 0-87417-122-9 (alk. paper)
1. Vizcaya (Spain)—Politics and government.   2. Spain—
Politics and government—19th century.   3. Social conflict—
Spain—Vizcaya—History–19th century.   4. Government,
Resistance to—Spain—Vizcaya—History—19th century.
5. Carlist War, 1833–1840—Causes.   I. Title.   II. Series.
DP302.V49B37   1989
946'.072—dc20   89-14638
                                                              CIP

University of Nevada Press
Reno, Nevada 89557 USA

Printed in the United States of America
Designed by Kaelin Chappell

Para Iris y Carlos
Con todo mi amor y agradecimiento

Contents

Acknowledgments xi

Preface xiii

CHAPTER 1 Introduction: Structures and Antecedents 1

CHAPTER 2 Restoration, Reform, and Civil War
(1814–1823) 31

CHAPTER 3 In Search of the Old Order: Conservatism
and the Fueros 71

CHAPTER 4 The State and Vizcaya During the
Ominous Decade 99

CHAPTER 5 Instruments of Counterrevolution:
The Police and the Brigadas de Paisanos
Armados 136

CHAPTER 6 Economic Crisis, Reform, and Class Conflict 167

CHAPTER 7 Carlists, Liberals, and the October 1833
Uprising 201

CHAPTER 8 Conclusion 222

Abbreviations 227

Notes 229

Selected Bibliography 305

Index 319

Acknowledgments

Writing these acknowledgments is a thankless and nearly impossible task. There are countless imperative debts which, regrettably, must be addressed briefly and, of course, inadequately. There is clearly no way to do justice to all the contributions that have made their way directly or indirectly into this work. In one form or another this manuscript has benefited from the assistance, encouragement, and inspiration of the following professors and colleagues: Abilio Barbero, Martin Blinkhorn, Fernand Braudel, Antonio Domínguez Ortiz, William A. Douglass, John H. Elliott, Josep Fontana Lázaro, Juan Pablo Fusi, Manuel González Portilla, Davydd J. Greenwood, Richard Kagan, Emmanuel Le Roy Ladurie, Clara Lida, Vicente Llorens, Nicolás Sánchez-Albornoz, Jerrold Seigel, Barbara Stein, Joan Connelly Ullman, Pierre Vilar, and Iris Zavala.

A most special appreciation goes to Dr. Stanley J. Stein, my doctoral thesis director. Through many years he guided my work, providing me with endless constructive comments and criticisms. Never one to shy from tedious work, Stanley carefully and patiently plowed through unwieldy and awkward drafts, showing me the historical importance or irrelevance of documentation that I had become so attached to after long periods of collecting information, revising my writing, questioning my assumptions, and opening new paths of interpretation. In the process, inevitably, my work was vastly improved, and for this I remain deeply grateful. In all, it was an excellent professional apprenticeship and one that will be remembered fondly.

I also wish to acknowledge the unswerving support of my colleagues at the Latin American Studies Program of the University of Illinois at Chicago—in particular Otto Pikaza, Mary K. Vaughan, and Marc Zimmerman. Through the years they have loyally stood by me, well above and beyond the call of duty. By now, I am certain that they have tired of hearing me talk about this quasi-mythical work, about Basques, and about Carlism. Their tolerance and forbearance alone deserve my sincerest gratitude.

I also wish to single out the superb work of Cindy Wood, this manuscript's chief editor. That she was able to unravel my garbled prose, decipher its intent, and come up with a vastly more legible product are all ample testimony of her skills. However, I alone of course must bear full responsibility for the book's content.

On a more personal and closing note, I extend my profoundest thanks to those closest to me: my family (in Euskadi, México, and the United States) and Kathy. Without their love, sustenance, confidence, and stimulus, it would not have been possible for me to complete this work.

Preface

This book, as indeed most of its kind, has a long and involved history. Initially, the project was an extremely ambitious (and perhaps unrealistic) one; namely, the study of key interrelated facets of Basque socioeconomic history for the period 1700–1850, in an attempt to explain the preeminent position of the region within its peninsular and colonial contexts during the final stages of the *ancien régime.* In other words, the original intention was an enterprise akin to the *longue durée* structural analyses inspired by the *École des Annales.* Secondarily, a goal of the proposed work was to cast light on the origins of Basque Carlism, a much-written and talked about topic which, unfortunately, has hardly received the careful attention and consideration it warrants. However, the original project quickly ran into difficulties upon the author's belated discovery that several investigators in the Basque provinces had been working for some time on similar and related topics, particularly in the areas of socioeconomic and demographic history.[1] Accordingly, so as not to duplicate advanced research in progress, it became necessary to adjust the aims and, in reality, redefine the focus of the proposed study. Several changes and adaptions were therefore made.

For example, the focus of the work was narrowed to more strictly social and political matters. Much to my satisfaction, some archives —both local and national—proved veritable mines of untapped historical information.[2] Chronologically as well, the investigation was limited to the last quarter of the eighteenth century and the first third of the nineteenth—still a sizable time period that would be reduced even further later on. Geographically, the decision was made to concentrate primarily (if not exclusively), on the Basque province of Vizcaya.

More significantly with regard to subject, the basic intent of the work shifted considerably. Rather than an analysis of the crucial mutations of Basque society in the final stages of the ancien régime and its transition from a protofeudal, precapitalist society to one incipiently anchored in bourgeois liberalism, this study instead became a historical examination of the background and general origins of the First Carlist War in Vizcaya. In effect, the initial manuscript's secondary design became the primary one. Given both the proximity and relation of these subjects to Carlism proper, some readers might inadvertently assume that the intent of this work is to trace the genesis and development of Carlism as an organized political force (or party) in Vizcaya. However, that is not this book's purpose. Instead, what follows is a historical examination and reflection of a wide range of factors in the province between 1814 and 1833—social, political, economic, ideological, and religious—that shaped and prepared the way for the severe conflicts of the 1830s. In sum, rather than a history of Vizcayan Carlism proper, the aim of this manuscript is to present the regional and provincial bases— underpinnings, conditions, and causes—that facilitated the growth and consolidation of local conservatism and traditionalism. These potent sociopolitical currents were eventually connected in a tenacious struggle against liberalism and reform and, in turn, became attached to Don Carlos's cause in the late 1820s and early 1830s.

Still, in light of the abundant bibliography on some of these questions (in particular Carlism, one of the region's best-known political movements), at first blush, my plan might well have appeared repetitive at best or stubbornly quixotic at worst. In short, what fresh historiographic contributions could I possibly make to a seemingly already-crowded field?[3] Nevertheless, strongly in my favor was the fact that much of the subject matter had been approached rather formally from almost strictly political, ideological, and legal perspectives—and, at times, not even very successfully. For instance, extraordinarily heavy emphasis had been placed by historians on the tendencies, aspirations, and aims of dynastic legitimism that had purportedly given rise to the first (and perhaps the only real) Vizcayan Carlists.[4] This narrow vision, in my view, had resulted in important socioeconomic—and, strangely enough, even political—historical omissions. Several brief examples (among many that could be cited) of such regrettable gaps can perhaps best illustrate the point.

First, despite occasional and often vague allusions to certain traditional aspects of Basque and Vizcayan society, institutions, and laws, surprisingly little attention had been devoted (until recently) to their socioeconomic structures and foundations (chapter 1). In essence, this meant that key elements of Carlism's infrastructural roots at the regional and provincial levels had been almost entirely ignored.[5] By extension, I quickly became convinced that this neglect had also resulted in the oversight of substantial class conflict, both overt and covert, in Basque society (chapter 6).

Second, it soon likewise became painfully clear that few scholars had examined the many-sided conflictive relations of the Basque region with the Spanish central government at the end of the ancien régime. Given the abundance of excellent source material all along the geographic and political spectrum, this seemed a stunning and nearly unforgivable failing. In fact, in the very initial stages of the investigation, considerable documentary evidence immediately convinced me of deep and persistent disagreements between the Basques and the royal administration during the late eighteenth and early nineteenth centuries. More specifically, as each side defended exclusive interests and prerogatives, dissensions erupted across a broad range of issues and problems—conflicts that were in great measure the result of changing historical circumstances on both sides of the Atlantic, shifting political and class relations in the province, and policy differences toward the Basques on the part of government administrators and personnel. Given their proximity to the First Carlist War, it was of course especially telling (and far from coincidental) that some of the sharpest tensions between the Basque provinces and the Spanish government had occurred during the so-called Ominous Decade of 1823–1833 (chapter 4). This counterrevolutionary era followed the overthrow of the constitutionalist regime, putting an end to the Liberal Triennium's important reform experiment of 1820–1823 (chapter 2).

Third, the crucial local political achievements of the Ominous Decade, such as the creation by the provincial leadership of an efficient Vizcayan police and the organization of peasant and artisan militias—conservative instruments designed to preserve the status quo and forestall a liberal comeback—had also received virtually no attention (chapter 5). Often mired in controversy, both bodies—but in particular the paramilitary corps—were the target of liberals' complaints throughout the 1823–1833 decade. At the end of Ferdinand VII's reign, by the time that a revitalized Vizcayan liberalism was sufficiently strong and confident to mount a concerted political and administrative attack to abolish the militias, it was far too late. An active and able provincial leadership had already managed to integrate the corps' conservative outlook into the fabric of local political life, at once reinforcing the period's political reaction and laying the foundation for important elements of Carlism.

Fourth, although numerous authors have repeatedly referred to the extraordinary importance of the Basque fueros, our understanding of their precise role in the region, as well as their relation to the central government, has remained embarrassingly weak. In view of the Vizcayan liberties' centrality to a broad array of local and national matters, there clearly appeared to be ample room for elucidating obscure historical areas (chapter 3).

Fifth, and finally, relatively little has been known concerning the October 1833 Carlist revolt in Vizcaya—e.g., what preceded it, how it originated and was carried out, the causes and aims of the insurrection, and how Don Carlos was declared king after his allies' successful seizure of Bilbao.[6] Again, as in other instances, I have attempted to fill some of these subjects' more salient voids (chapter 7). In conclusion, a bonanza of primary sources, along with fundamental historical gaps and weighty unanswered questions, combined neatly to suggest important new lines of investigation and scholarly contribution.

A final note: this study, limited in time and space, is admittedly an exercise in regional microhistory—ironically, an anathema to some of the teachers who inspired this work. However, I strongly believe that much of this manuscript's significance would be lost if it were regarded merely (or solely) as Vizcayan or Basque history. Hopefully, larger scholarly and academic purposes are served by the following pages. In a wider context, this study should provide useful parallels and points of comparison for those delving into the formation of nation states (in Europe or elsewhere) during the eighteenth and nineteenth centuries: more specifically, for historians and social scientists who seek to account not only for the growth of the central governments' power and authority at the regions' expense, but also for the latter's resistance to incorporationist and centralist trends.[7] As is well known, the persistence of regional affinities in numerous nations has had important consequences in those countries' processes of political, administrative, and economic unification or, as the case may be, the lack thereof. In the case of Spain, regionalism has been an extremely significant factor in that nation's inability to achieve full-fledged unification until recently, and even now this is still in some doubt given the profoundly nationalist and separatist tendencies manifested in many of the Basque provinces. Even though the mentor I most admired instructed me well regarding the dangers of historical analogies—he disdained them as anachronisms—perhaps this work, despite its limitations, can suggest a comparative perspective for center-periphery relations in Spain over a period of two centuries. If so, and if there are indeed any historical lessons to be learned from the Spanish, Basque, and Vizcayan pasts that are relevant in the present, might my abandonment of the longue durée approach be at least partly forgiven.

CHAPTER 1

Introduction: Structures and Antecedents

After the Basque farmer discovered the way to fertilize the country's naturally weak lands through the use of lime and repeated cultures, [the laborer's] ambition has gained ground, without being discouraged by the soil's ingratitude, and without being intimidated by the harsh situation of the most rugged precipices, burning pasture-grounds and briers, pulling out vines and wild plants, tearing away groves and brambles.

—Reflexiones sobre el sistema agricultor del país bascongado, *"Extractos de las Juntas Generales Celebradas por la Real Sociedad Bascongada de los Amigos del País en la Ciudad de Vitoria por Setiembre de 1777."*

I. GENERAL DESCRIPTION, POPULATION, AND SOCIAL STRUCTURE

Crossing over from Castile into the Spanish Basque region, Henry Swinburne, a late eighteenth-century English traveler, enthusiastically observed: "Every thing round us now assumed a different appearance; instead of the bare, depopulated hills, the melancholy, despondent countenances, the dirty inns, and abominable roads, that our eye had been accustomed to for so many months; we were here revived by the sight of a rich, studied culture, a clean-looking, smiling people, good furniture, neat houses, fine woods, good roads, and safe bridges."[1] Some twenty years later Alexandre de Laborde was no less lavish in his praise of these territories and peoples. In an extremely idealized vein, an obviously

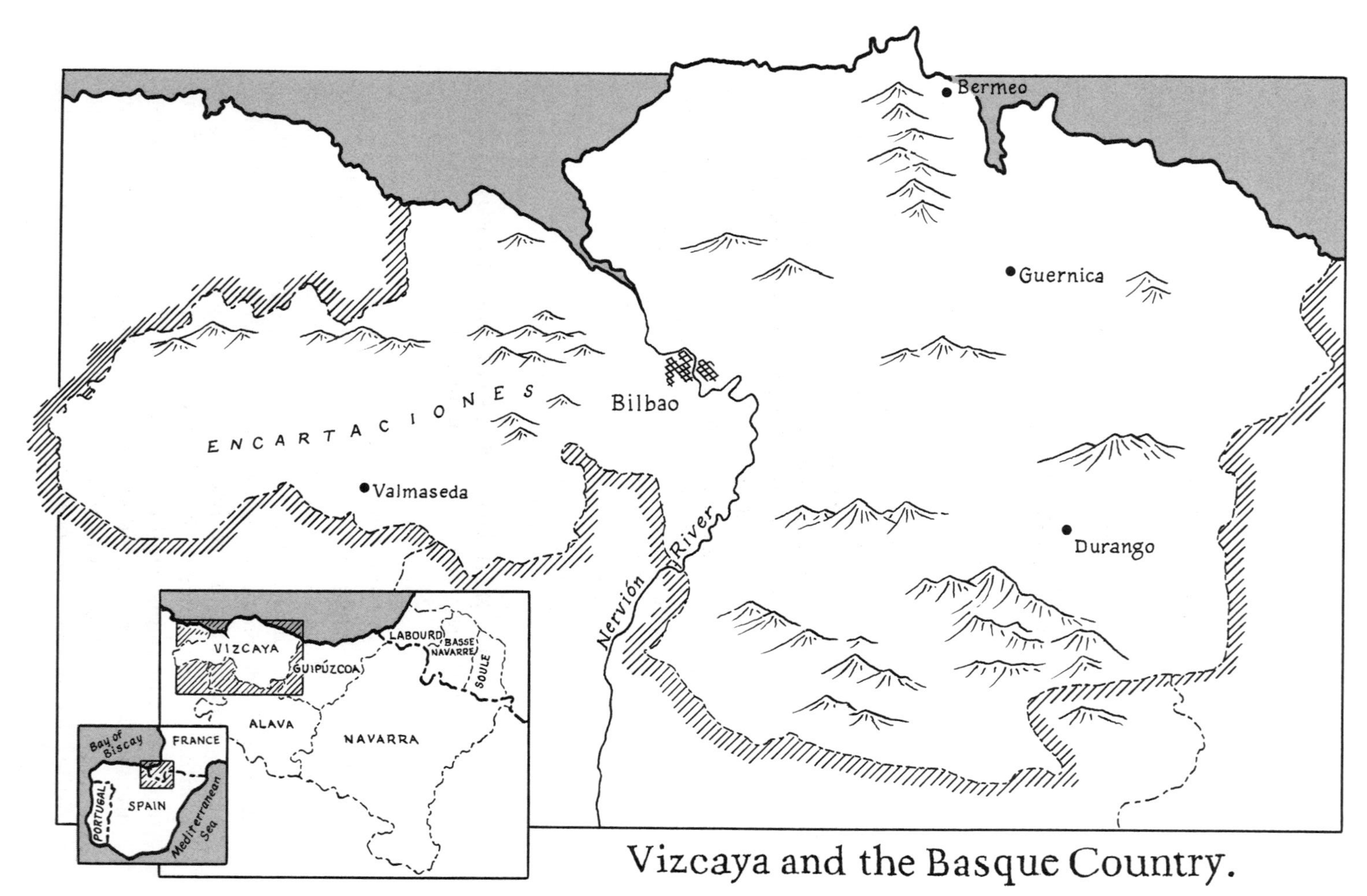

Vizcaya and the Basque Country.

moved Laborde wrote of Vizcaya proper: "The lordship of Biscay still presents in many places a singular, striking, and respectable picture of ancient manners, the affecting simplicity of which inspires a sentiment of veneration."[2] Clearly, this region's extraordinary attractiveness and uniqueness were not lost on its visitors—both foreign and national.

Vizcaya is not a large province. Its area, just over 800 square miles, is roughly two-thirds the size of Rhode Island, the smallest state in the United States. Historically a part of Spain, Vizcaya is on the northern Iberian Peninsula, at the southwestern corner of the Pyrenees. It is nestled between an imposing Cantabrian Sea on the north, and Old Castile and La Rioja on the south. Around 1800, the *Señorío de Vizcaya*'s lush valleys, mountainous terrain, and rocky coastline —until the present a stunning natural setting treasured by its proud inhabitants—harbored a population slightly in excess of 110,000.[3] Vizcaya in the eighteenth century, particularly in the second half, showed unmistakable signs of population pressure. However, the upward trend was checked in the 1790s, and demographic growth leveled off considerably until 1815.[4] A number of reasons accounted for this.

Abundant evidence, for example, points to a profound socioeconomic crisis lasting from the late 1780s until the century's end. During this critical cycle poor crops, harsh weather conditions, and finally, wars and the gamut of hardships associated with them, effectively prevented population increase. A subsistence crisis, starting in 1787–1788 and continuing for nearly a decade with varying intensity, had lasting effects upon local society. The terrible winter of 1789, notoriously known as the "year of hunger," was remembered for generations.[5] War and its effects cannot be underestimated. In the 1794–1795 campaigns close to two-thirds of all Vizcayan males enlisted to oppose the French. While war's ravages were not as extensive as they would be later during the Napoleonic invasion, war's side effects proved extremely damaging. The absence of so many farmers furthered a precarious situation and worsened the existing subsistence crisis. Likewise, the depletion of artisans from key industries (such as iron) naturally hurt both their families and the regional economy. Not until after the War of Independence (1808–1813) would the province begin a sustained and unbroken demographic climb.

Travelers passing through Vizcaya in 1800 encountered an overwhelmingly rural population dispersed throughout an attractive countryside. There were no major cities except for Bilbao and, significantly, its total inhabitants in 1787 numbered less than 10,000.[6] Yet Bilbao's population of 9,600 was more than double that of Vizcaya's second largest city, Bermeo, which barely reached 4,200. In fact, most Vizcayans lived in or around small villages that seldom exceeded a few hundred inhabitants. And many of them lived in *caseríos*, the traditional Basque farm dwellings that usually housed one or more families and which, given their isolation, were largely self-sufficient socioeconomic units.

The population, however, was not evenly distributed throughout the territory. Demographic concentration was heavier along the province's northwest-southeast axis that followed the course of the Nervion-Ibaizabal river system from the sea, past Bilbao, and into the interior. Attracted by economic opportunity, over time the population had grown steadily along both sides of the chief commercial route of the Señorío de Vizcaya (Seigniory of Vizcaya). Although the evidence is inconclusive, it is possible that this gain was achieved partly at the expense of Vizcaya's interior regions—areas that apparently suffered tangible demographic setbacks in the late eighteenth century. Conversely, many of the coastal towns experienced a marked increase. At many levels, both commerce and the sea exerted a powerful influence on Vizcayans and their habitat.

As noted earlier, at the outset of the nineteenth century Vizcaya was a predominantly agrarian society. In other words, consistent with the socioeconomic structures of the ancien régime, the rural classes—in particular the peasantry—made up the bulk of the population. Yet in one essential respect Vizcayan society differed remarkably from most of its European counterparts: Vizcayans possessed the privilege of "universal nobility."[7] Unofficially through the Middle Ages, this status had finally been conferred de jure in the early sixteenth century. This fact alone contributed more than any other to the strong sense of egalitarianism that pervaded much of the local society. Nevertheless, it is important to emphasize that Vizcayan general nobility served to mask deep-rooted inequalities and, in the process, palliate class conflict.

Around 1800 at least 75 to 80 percent of the population derived its subsistence from agriculture. However, it would be a gross mistake to view the Vizcayan countryside as monolithic since there were clearly distinct rural classes. The most basic differentiation was between the landowners and the landless. According to the 1797 census there were in Vizcaya 5,342 landowners (*propietarios*), or 25.3 percent of the rural population.[8] The landless—74.7 percent of the total—fell primarily into two groups: (1) tenants (*arrendatarios*) numbering 13,733, or 64.9 percent; and (2) wage-laborers (*jornaleros*) totaling 2,076, or 9.8 percent. While many of the tenancies probably amounted to virtual ownership, the figures conclusively show that nearly 75 percent of the Vizcayan rural classes made their living cultivating land that they did not legally own. Moreover, for some time the percentage of landholders had been steadily declining, a trend that continued well into the first half of the nineteenth century when no more than 15 to 20 percent of the rural population owned land. In fact, the combination of higher rents (jacked up by the local gentry and absentee urban landlords), disentailment's effects, enclosure, encroachment upon commons, and other socioeconomic developments, worsened the condition of much of the Vizcayan rural world and probably pushed some local inhabitants into wage-earning categories through well-known processes of proletarianization.[9]

Part of the difficulty in analyzing the rural strata, in particular the lower echelons, stems from the fact that during the ancien régime a peasant—even if a landowner—was seldom only a farm laborer. Seasonal employment was a necessity for many, and Vizcayan peasants (in particular, males) often worked in nonagricultural endeavors. For instance, during winters a peasant might toil in the famous local forges and iron-processing centers, gather wood for charcoal, work as a *carbonero* (charcoal maker), and occasionally even enlist in a merchant ship or double as a fisherman.[10] It was also common for peasants to seek part-time employment as artisans, muleteers or teamsters, or perhaps practice the considerably more lucrative trade of smuggling, an important occupation in the region.

If a true noble sector existed in the countryside it was best exemplified by the wealthier *mayorazgos* (entail holders), of whom there were 221 in 1800. Yet even they did not fit the traditional mold of opulent and aristocratic wealth. As Julio Caro Baroja has argued, the region's upper nobility was somewhat similar to the English gentry in lifestyle. A case in point: Instead of relying solely on subsistence agriculture and conventional methods of land use, enterprising landowners, who were associated in some instances with the "enlightened" *Sociedad Vascongada de Amigos del País*, experimented extensively with new crops and techniques. Vizcayans also turned certain limitations and liabilities into valuable assets. For example, in accordance with Castilian law, land in Vizcaya was transmitted through a strict system of primogeniture. This procedure, as is well known, resulted in the exclusion of *segundones* (children other than the first-born) from land inheritance. However, many well-educated "rejects" found their way into every corner of the monarchy, where they became successful entrepreneurs, landowners, royal administrators, clerics, and military men. Together, they formed the backbone of the Vizcayan diaspora, a tight network of personal, family, and regional ties, possessing vast socioeconomic power and political influence.[11] Obviously, powerful forces and interests projected the local countryside well beyond traditional socioeconomic functions and boundaries.

Worth emphasizing as well, certain absentee landlords lived in Bilbao and elsewhere, leaving their estates' management to administrators. Some of these propietarios were not primarily landowners but, in fact, wealthy merchants who had speculated heavily in land. This penetration of the countryside was yet another factor in an age-old conflict that had set Bilbao in opposition to the rural areas.[12] However, the main points of contention between town and country were far larger and stemmed primarily from the relentless advance of an ascendant commercial bourgeoisie in the process of completing its domination over Vizcaya's economic life.

Even with a reduced population, Bilbao was the uncontested motor of the provincial economy. Specifically, Vizcayan economic power was concentrated in the hands of Bilbao's wealthy business community. Pointedly, in 1800—with less than 9 percent of the total population—Bilbao comprised 90 percent of all Vizcayan merchants, 71 percent of the manufacturers, and approximately 45 percent of all traders and shopkeepers. The city also far outdistanced the rest of the province in other important social categories. Over 25 percent of the artisans, 60 percent of the students, nearly 30 percent of the lawyers and attorneys, and over 17 percent of the notaries public and scribes resided there. In addition, over 27 percent of all domestic servants lived in Vizcaya.[13] More than a mere outpost of the Vizcayan bourgeoisie, Bilbao was synonymous with it.

The number of Vizcayan regular and secular clergy was not overwhelming: probably 1,758 in 1787 and only 1,760 ten years later—i.e., no more than 1.5 percent of the population.[14] However, these low figures belie the Vizcayan clergy's importance. In the midst of a deeply religious society, the influence of both the regular and secular clergy was enormous. Always active and meddlesome, the clerics participated at every level of society. In fact, the clerical establishment involved itself openly in local political affairs, and some ecclesiastics seized arms and led struggles whenever change threatened the social order. Such was the case in 1793–1795, 1808–1813, 1820–1823, and 1833–1839, eras in which the Vizcayan clergy overwhelmingly sided with the sociopolitical status quo against reforms and innovations.

Admirers of Vizcaya—veritable apologists at times in view of written attacks from detractors against the province—have been quick to stress the positive aspects of the province's egalitarianism: general nobility, absence of socioeconomic extremes, and participation in local political life. Yet much evidence of significant inequality has been consistently ignored. It is common to find deep socioeconomic stratification such as that described in a 1765 lawsuit comparing the "poor laborer" to the "distinguished and powerful gentleman."[15] A rich source for the study of social attitudes and class conflict can be found in countless lawsuits in which tenants opposed proprietors regarding the right to vote in municipal elections. Discrimination against, and disenfranchisement of, the lowly tenants and wage laborers by landowners and local magnates was a fact of political life. In 1830, several inhabitants of the village of Sondica bitterly opposed an allegedly unfair tax apportionment. The thrust of their suggestive arguments was that those who had proposed the levy had not made the proper distinction "between the rich, those of medium capabilities, and the poor, classifying them all into the same category."[16]

Vizcaya's admirers have also stressed the apparent absence of mendicity and other forms of marginal and deviant behavior in the province. Travelers' accounts would seem to confirm this to some extent, but their evidence (the result of swift journeys) was often extremely superficial. In point of fact, as local and provincial ordinances repeatedly show, both vagrancy and begging were far from unusual. In 1804, amidst a widespread grain crisis, circulars were sent to the local authorities by the Vizcayan Diputación, instructing them to expel "outsiders" searching for handouts and refuge. And again in 1828 and 1833 ordinances against vagrancy and mendicity were circulated throughout the province.

Nor was criminality absent from the territory. For example, following the destabilizing effects of the war against the French of the 1790s, the Vizcayan authorities drafted a harsh criminal code in 1799 to deal with an alarming crime wave.[17] The province's supreme court at Valladolid is studded with records involving banditry and other violent occurrences. Vizcaya at the end of the eighteenth century was not the haven of a quiet and harmonious people. Unrest and social conflict, overt and covert, kept Vizcayan society in a high degree of turmoil. Inter- and intraclass rivalries put the soundness of the social edifice to the test, threatening to upset delicate balances. In conclusion, the deepening contradiction between Bilbao and the countryside, combined with the endless squabbles over taxation, representation, and a host of other problems, represented the tensions of a traditional ancien régime society caught in the throes of rapid change.

II. THE ECONOMIC FOUNDATIONS: AGRICULTURE, MANUFACTURES, AND TRADE

In 1777 the *Sociedad Vascongada de Amigos del País* (Basque Society of Friends of the Country) voiced amazement at the progress of the region's agriculture, noting that its increase was "unbelievable."[18] And in 1786, Corregidor Josef Colón de Larreátegui exuberantly remarked that Vizcayan agriculture had reached "the highest level of perfection."[19] Indeed, to awed contemporaries the eighteenth century was the culmination of an arduous process aimed at reclaiming lands from nature—and humanity?—and placing them under the plow. In fact, it was estimated in 1777 that the arable land in Vizcaya had increased by a third in the course of that century alone.[20] An anonymous local writer described in 1795 how population pressure had forced Vizcayans to clear and till the very summits of mountains.[21] Agricultural progress aside, however, such extensive clearing—necessitated largely by land scarcity—may well have taken its toll on the lumber and charcoal industries.[22]

Partly because of the reduced size of landholdings, adequate farming areas were rare in Vizcaya. Moreover, the soil was not of the best quality or conducive to high yields. Not surprisingly therefore, the territory had never become self-sufficient in essential grains and wines.[23] At best, the province could only produce roughly half of its total grain requirements, yet the huge deficits were easily covered by national and international imports. Vizcaya was geographically blessed with an ideal location: in close proximity to the Castilian breadbaskets near Navarra and with direct and convenient sea access to foreign grain.

Corn, by far the main staple, may well have surpassed wheat 2 to 1 or 4 to 1 in terms of total grain production.[24] Other common grains, such as barley, oats, or rye, were rarely grown in the province. Probably introduced as early as the 1550s, Indian corn (maize) became a popular staple in the Basque Country—a region whose humid, rainy weather was perfectly suited for its cultivation. Nonetheless, it was ultimately the availability of wheat in Vizcaya, which could be imported quickly and cheaply, that accounted for the remarkable absence of widespread hunger (at least until the late 1780s) while other parts of Spain periodically experienced food crises and social unrest. Even the Vizcayan counterpart of the famous 1766 Motín de Esquilache was extraordinarily limited in geographic scope and degree of violence. And in the critical decade of the 1790s, the local authorities and Bilbao merchants worked vigorously to bring about massive foreign grain imports and thus offset some of the more damaging effects of the crisis.

Despite poor pastures, high feeding costs, and the absence of substantial lowland valleys, Vizcayans were extremely adept at ox breeding, cattle raising, and sheep herding. These animals were essential for field work, transportation, and nourishment. Goats, pigs, and other small animals comprised the typical livestock on most farms. However, animal husbandry was generally underdeveloped and unable to meet local demand. Not uncommonly, French livestock and salted meats from other countries were imported, along with hardy mules from Navarra and Aragon for transportation purposes.

Throughout the eighteenth century, *chacolí* (a light Vizcayan wine) had steadily gained popularity and begun to challenge the more conventional beverages such as apple cider. Moralists of the Sociedad Vascongada voiced alarm and displeasure, but the favored wine spread its vineyards relentlessly along the coast. Chacolí was profitable for both growers and middlemen. A limited supply, local protection, and an exaggerated demand put a premium on its price —especially when harvests fell below par.[25] The balance of the consumption was made up primarily of Navarran, Castilian, and Riojano wines which were generally cheap and plentiful. The affluent classes also consumed Port wines, Bordeaux, and other foreign eauxde-vie. In short, Vizcaya was heavily dependent on farm imports to supplement a primary sector that had never become self-supportive.

Iron and its derivatives were unquestionably the territory's chief manufactures.[26] Even though the Vizcayan *ferrerías* (ironworks) enjoyed a legendary reputation, by the second half of the eighteenth century stagnation had clearly begun to set in. Many factors contributed to the ferrerías' problems: the expansion of agriculture, high duties on Vizcayan iron in the peninsula and colonies and, most importantly, foreign competition. Notably, English and Swedish imports hurt domestic production as Bilbao merchants shifted to them upon realizing that the high cost of local iron could never hope to compete with the more competitive foreign finished and semifinished goods. Consistent with this practice, there is evidence that wealthy merchants, who lent considerable sums to iron producers and administrators (*ferrones*), withdrew their investment at the century's end, thereby compounding the crisis of the local iron industry. Obviously, when it came to iron, city and country were once again in opposition.

Since it was the local industry's export par excellence, it is difficult to overstate iron's importance for Vizcaya. From mine to manufacture to shipping, several thousand people were involved at every stage of production and commercialization. Many could, for example, find summer work in the mining and transportation of iron-ore from the extraordinarily rich (and equally poorly exploited) Somorrostro complex to the coastal towns and Bilbao. From there the ore (*vena*) was shipped by sea to the local ferrerías and other important national manufacturing centers. Interestingly, notwithstanding stern prohibitions, considerable amounts of iron-ore reached England as well. Large numbers of Vizcayans were also involved in the production and transportation of charcoal to the ironworks. Even though several of the jobs involved back-breaking labor, fuel-related occupations attracted many people. Outsiders frequently came to the province to toil in charcoal making on a seasonal basis.

Once at the ferrerías, both iron-ore and charcoal were processed into raw or pig iron. On the average, each ironwork employed six to eight workers during the six months of production. Quite primitive and powered by water, most ferrerías could only function in winter and spring. Around 1800, Vizcaya may have had up to 160 ironworks, although by 1807–1808 possibly as many as 25 of them were already inoperative. This decline was sharply accelerated by the Napoleonic invasion, the coup de grâce from which the ferrerías never fully recovered. A postwar testimony asserts that by 1815 only about 50 ironworks might have been in operation, with total production dropping steadily.[27]

In addition to the ferrerías proper, there were numerous workshops in Bilbao, Zorroza, Durango, Elorrio, Ochandiano, and others where pig iron was transformed into finished products. Indiscriminately described as *talleres, fábricas, martinetes, fanderías,* and *fraguas,* to name a few, these small and dispersed manufacturing centers produced a wide array of mining and agricultural tools: implements for sugar mills and plantations, kitchen utensils and cutlery, railings and grills, anchors, hardware, firearm parts, and numerous other instruments. A substantial portion of these products was shipped to America through an efficient network of Vizcayan and Basque entrepreneurs.

However, the commercialization of Vizcayan iron was not easy. Both at home and abroad, smuggling practices raised suspicions among royal officials that the goods were refabrications or reexports of foreign productions and not, as Vizcayans claimed, domestically produced. Hence, to counter possible fraud, the central government in the late 1770s imposed duties on Vizcayan manufactures—primarily iron—upon their entrance into other parts of the peninsula and colonies. The treatment of Vizcayan iron as a foreign product became a major point of contention, causing profound resentment and tension on both sides.[28]

Nor were iron manufactures the only Vizcayan products subject to, and hurt by, tariffs. Others that suffered included leather, chairs, paper, copper goods (from Valmaseda), cordage and rope, hats, and even refined sugar and wheat flour. The Vizcayan Diputación repeatedly demanded the rescission or reduction of the duties. But as long as the specter of smuggling—protected by the province's privileges (fueros)—continued to haunt the government's financial experts, Vizcayans could expect no relief from Madrid. By the start of the nineteenth century some of Vizcaya's most enlightened minds were well aware that the liberties and tariffs (and related government prohibitions) constituted fundamental barriers to local industrial development, and that change was crucial.

Whatever the difficulties, nothing could challenge Bilbao's supremacy on the northern coast. The city was the hub of an extensive system of commercial affiliations spanning the Old World and the New. There were five basic components to Bilbao's trade. One, an English connection, enabled Basque iron and Castilian wool to be exchanged for other products and consumer items. Two, a northern route linked Vizcaya to the North Sea, allowing the province to obtain grain, salted fish (particularly cod), and consumer goods. Three, from another overseas circuit, and in return for Vizcayan iron, local merchants obtained products from North and South America. These so-called colonial goods came to Vizcaya legally via Cádiz, Santander, Bayonne, and Bordeaux, but often illegally as well through multiple smuggling channels. Four, an essential overland nexus linked Bilbao to the Spanish heartlands, including Aragon and Navarra. Five, Bilbao was the key focus of an intra-Basque regional trade that extended far beyond the province.

Yet, for all their stunning accomplishments and success, Bilbao's entrepreneurs remained merely middlemen of a vast commercial system, exhibiting in some crucial respects the typical characteristics of a *comprador* (buyer) bourgeoisie. Given the Vizcayan market's limitations—a small population and the reduced buying power of an austere peasantry—along with the immense (and lucrative) possibilities of internal-external commerce, Bilbao's bourgeoisie naturally fought economic restrictions and sought unlimited free trade. This held true even in cases where it proved detrimental to domestic manufactures. These attitudes and policies, it must be emphasized, were facilitated by the province's objective role as a free trade area. Already in the late eighteenth century, however, a division could be seen among members of this bourgeoisie—a split between merchants whose profits were derived exclusively from trade and others whose holdings and enterprises included some manufactures.

Though far from perfect, French inquiries into the wealth of the Basque provinces in 1810 showed that total income in Vizcaya was distributed in the following manner:

Land rents (*propiedades particulares*)	54 %
Commerce (*comercio*)	33 %
Clergy (*clero*)	9 %
Towns (*propios de pueblos*)	4 %
TOTAL	100 % [29]

With considerably heavier primary sectors and greater clerical revenues, the economies of Guipúzcoa and Alava appeared, by comparison, less dynamic:

	Guipúzcoa	*Alava*
Land rents	69 %	66 %
Commerce	10 %	10 %
Clergy	12 %	21 %
Towns	9 %	3 %
TOTAL	100 %	100 %

In terms of the overall wealth of the three provinces, still measured on the basis of rents, the French arrived at the following breakdown:

Province	*Percent of Basque Population* *1787 Census*	*Percent of Basque Income* *1810 Calculations*
Vizcaya	38	47
Guipúzcoa	39	30
Alava	23	23
TOTAL	100	100

In conclusion, these figures certainly suggest that Vizcayan economic success was due primarily to the advanced state of its commerce. When all this is viewed within the context of a restless manufacturing environment—however limited despite its enormous potential—a precociously modernizing picture emerges from the province's otherwise traditional and fundamentally agrarian economic structures.

III. THE PROVINCIAL INSTITUTIONS: DIPUTACIÓN AND CONSULADO

Almost without exception, Vizcayan institutions were praised by contemporaries as models of good government and agents of social progress. Much of the acclaim was reserved for the executive branch of the Vizcayan government known as the *Diputación General del Señorío*, or simply as the Diputación General or Diputación. Elected every two years during the meeting of the Vizcayan general assembly (*juntas generales*)—held under the watchful eye of the crown's representative, the corregidor—the Diputación was the only body to enjoy permanent continuity at the provincial level. There was no legislature proper, except perhaps for the biennial juntas which usually disbanded quickly after a brief two-week summer work period. During the meeting, decrees for the government of the province were enacted, royal orders were reviewed and acted upon, and elections were held for the coming term. Two delegates (*junteros* or *apoderados*) were generally designated or elected by each voting district and given a mandate (*poder*) to represent their constituency at the juntas. However, there was seldom any open or real debate at these parleys. Nearly all decisions, in particular the important and controversial ones, were made behind closed doors in intensive give-and-take. Most differences were ironed out in conference deliberations and, not strangely, a carefully orchestrated consensus existed by the time official business finally reached the assembly's floor. But this had not always been the case. Until approximately the 1730s–40s the juntas had been truly open, often generating a great deal of participation. But fear of disorders and unruliness—real or imaginary—had apparently induced the dominant provincial oligarchies to restrict attendance and hold the sessions in private.

Powerful rural magnates traditionally controlled the juntas, in which corruption and improprieties were common. Outraged central government officials, notably the *corregidores*, denounced the abuses and called for sweeping reforms.[30] However, their recommendations clashed head-on with entrenched local interest groups bent on preserving their influence and power. And so, despite repeated protests, vote buying and fraud continued unabated during the era of the juntas. The monarch's representatives weren't the only ones dissatisfied with what was ostensibly the centerpiece of Vizcayan democracy and representative government. Bilbao's interests were greatly disadvantaged by the juntas' numerical composition. With only two votes, Bilbao had exactly the same voting power as any other township or community—however large or small, rich or poor. In other words, even if that city's delegates were to commit widespread bribery and vote fraud (not a rare occurrence) it was still extremely difficult for them to control the assembly or unduly influence its decisions. Hemmed in politically by a largely rural constituency, the economic powerhouse of Bilbao had good reason to look warily upon the juntas. This was yet another important dimension of Bilbao's persistent conflicts with the Vizcayan countryside.

In terms of the provincial government, the range of the juntas' attributes was virtually unlimited. The assemblies determined taxation, selected public works projects, devised statutes for a wide array of public matters, organized military defenses, drew up ordinances for policing the territory, and engaged in other important activities.

Barring objections from the corregidor (who, after all, presided over the juntas) the assemblies' accords (*acuerdos*), once passed, acquired the force of law throughout Vizcaya. The central government had the ultimate—if rarely ever used—authority to strike down decisions deemed detrimental to national or state interests. Nevertheless, in practice the juntas possessed sufficient autonomy to do largely as the Vizcayan leadership pleased.

The Vizcayan Diputación was primarily in charge of the province's day-to-day government, a duty it shared with a small but influential royal administration.[31] At the helm of the Diputación were two co-equal general deputies (*diputados generales*), elected for two-year terms at the juntas. As chief policymakers, they were unquestionably the two most powerful Vizcayan political leaders during their terms in office. Below them in rank were the second and third deputies, whose basic role was that of replacing the first in the event of illness, absence, or death. In turn, below the deputies were anywhere from four to six aldermen or officials (*regidores capitulares*). However, despite their apparent proximity to the top of the hierarchy, the regidores were not normally a part of the inner circle of power. Their tasks included work on specific missions (delegated from above) and/or the drafting of reports for the Diputación. In other words, seldom were they involved in crucial decision making. In addition, there were two magistrates (*síndicos procuradores*) who were elected to act as general advisers to the provincial government. Finally, it was customary to elect one or two secretaries. However, by the late eighteenth century these posts had become permanent and were carried over from one term to the next. Belying its seemingly lowly status, the Diputación's secretariat was an extremely important office.

Two other men held posts of great significance in the Vizcayan government: the general counsel (*consultor*) and the treasurer (*tesorero*). Since the consultor was the watchdog of the Vizcayan privileges (fueros), the position required an individual expertly grounded in local law and tradition. Perhaps the consultor's single most important responsibility was that of judging the constitutionality of incoming royal documents in relationship to, and as a function of, the provincial liberties. In essence, the consultor could veto or delay acceptance of orders felt to be contrary to the fueros. This office became permanent during the 1770s when the Diputación decided that it was more important to ensure continuity than to risk constant squabbles over election to the coveted post. By making the general counsel immovable, the Diputación succeeded in making him less subject to the habitual political and economic pressures—both internal and external.

Finally, the provincial finances were largely in the hands of a treasurer appointed by the Diputación. The treasury was an important though thankless and somewhat unattractive office. Moreover, stringent checks from others in official positions made embezzlement risky and highly improbable. The post was often handled by an influential merchant or financier whose entrepreneurial know-how was essential in the administration of substantial public funds.[32]

The *Consulado de Bilbao* (Merchant Guild of Bilbao) was to the city and its merchant community what the Diputación was to Vizcaya as a whole and its rural sectors in particular.[33] Founded in 1511 and formed in direct opposition to its Burgos counterpart, the Consulado had come to represent the city's prosperous merchant community. The guild, however, had only really come into its own in the early stages of the eighteenth century. At that time, the Consulado and the city of Bilbao had purchased from the crown (on an even basis) the so-called right of the *prebostad,* an important privilege that enabled its owners to collect a naval duty (*avería*) on three categories of incoming goods: food, drink, and fuel. The prebostad—generally from 1.5 to 2.5 percent of the value of the incoming product—proved a tremendously lucrative revenue for both the municipality and the merchant guild, a fact that over time came to be profoundly resented by the royal administration.[34]

All Spanish-born merchants residing legally in Bilbao were eligible for membership in the corporation. From this general pool, elections were held annually to choose officers. At the head of the Consulado were two priors (*priores*) whose functions and attributes were roughly equivalent to the Diputación's general deputies. Below the priores were four officials known as consuls (*consules*) whose tasks were analogous to the Vizcayan government's aldermen (*regidores*). In addition, the guild had a counsel (*síndico*) and a secretary. The latter two posts had become somewhat permanent and, not infrequently, their holders had long tenures. Not very different from the elections of the Diputación, *grosso modo,* voting in the Consulado was a tricky two-step process of co-optation and chance. This had the advantage of enabling the electors to first eliminate the less desirable and then choose the guild's officers from a more selected group. While these elections hardly qualified as models of democracy, they nevertheless seem to have spread the opportunities and benefits of office to a large number of merchants.

The conduct of the Consulado was based on a charter known as the *Ordenanzas*. First published in the sixteenth century, the corporation's constitution was updated and republished numerous times. The guild's copious and well-kept records eloquently attest to the competency and meticulousness of its successive staffs. Unquestionably, the Consulado's best years were in the eighteenth century, especially after Bilbao merchants wrested control of trade from foreigners in the 1730s–40s. During its golden age the corporation wielded enormous power and influence in Vizcaya.

Whatever the faults and shortcomings of these institutions, service in them was motivated less by the quest for material benefits and monetary gains than by other types of rewards—notably, status, prestige, and honor. A sense of duty and commitment probably accounted for the seemingly high degree of honesty among Vizcayan office holders. Significantly, corruption and scandal were remarkably rare. And those in the Diputación and Consulado, while faithfully obedient to their respective class interests and constituencies, managed to serve honorably and responsibly. Hence, the population's attachment to, and respect for, its public establishment. In sum, overall these institutions appear to have served Vizcaya well. Royal officials, however, were far less enamored than Vizcayans themselves.

Corregidores complained, for example, that the Diputación and Consulado withheld vital economic information (from them and the central government) in order to conduct policy independently, and, perhaps, arbitrarily. So extensive was Vizcayan autonomy in this crucial area that some corregidores (such as Luis Marcelino Pereyra in the early nineteenth century) voiced dismay and openly declared themselves unable to report accurately on pertinent matters because of insufficient and unreliable data. Pointedly, since there was no royal tax-collection bureaucracy in Vizcaya, the crown was forced to rely —much to its dissatisfaction—on the Diputación for calculations of rents, revenues, population, and other information. The central government's access to Vizcayan finances and other statistics constantly remained a serious point of contention.

The institutional arrangement and workings of the province were patently unsatisfactory to central authority. The royal administration's limited power of intervention there, coupled with the extensive Vizcayan privileges, left most effective authority in the hands of local magnates. The reform attempts of the Bourbon Era, including greater uniformity and centralization, were therefore bound to clash with provincial elites who were stubbornly determined to maintain their economic and political monopolies. The inevitable antagonisms took several forms: tension between the corregidor and the Vizcayan executive, incessant petitioning by the Diputación, occasional (and at times harsh) reprimands from the state, and provincial disobedience and procrastination—especially in the case of royal projects viewed in Vizcaya as plans to modify the province's institutional prerogatives and laws.

IV. THE FUEROS

The legal backbone of the Vizcayan system of government was a wide-ranging series of important privileges, liberties, exemptions, and franchises known as the fueros. Initially compiled in the late fifteenth century, the fueros were first published in 1528.[35] Their main provisions concerned key aspects of local governance as well as Vizcaya's rights and freedoms—e.g., freedom from direct central government taxes, freedom from military conscription, freedom from the imposition of customs duties on imports consumed locally, and freedom from the establishment of crown monopolies such as stamped paper, salt, and tobacco. Theoretically, Vizcaya contributed funds to the state through voluntary donation and not by compulsion or command. The same was true for military service. Moreover, all royal demands for men, money, and support were subject to the approval of the juntas.

There were other significant provisions in the fueros. For instance, since all Vizcayans were considered nobles, none could suffer cruel or demeaning punishment. Furthermore, when charged with criminal activities outside the native territory, Vizcayans had the prerogative of requesting to be tried before the province's chief magistrate (*juez mayor*) who was appointed by the crown and, as noted earlier, presided over the *Sala de Vizcaya* at the Chancilleria de Valladolid (Chancery of Valladolid). Another important privilege related to the fueros was the so-called *pase foral* (or *pase* as it was commonly known). The pase was a procedure that enabled the Diputación to obey—but not put into effect pending appeal—a royal order thought to contradict the freedoms. Armed with this weapon, the Vizcayan ruling elites demonstrated an extraordinary propensity to resist purportedly unconstitutional royal commands and policies.

Firmly convinced that Vizcaya had never been subjugated militarily—part of a deeply rooted if contrived warrior myth—and equally persuaded that the territory had relinquished its political independence voluntarily to attach itself to the Castilian crown in the fourteenth century, Vizcayans regarded their bond to the monarch as contractual. As part of the mutual duties incumbent upon such feudal agreements and in return for Vizcaya's obedience and loyalty, all Castilian monarchs since the Middle Ages had been asked by the Diputación to take an oath pledging to abide by, and uphold, the fueros. After all, one should not forget that according to the terminology of the ancien régime, the monarch was the lord-master (*señor*) of the Seigniory (Señorío) of Vizcaya. Even though Vizcayans never phrased the alleged covenant in thoroughly reciprocal terms, they nevertheless zealously defended their union with the crown as a special and privileged partnership. And with good reason too, since as long as the monarchs recognized the fueros' validity by honoring them, Vizcaya was certain to preserve the numerous benefits derived from the liberties' existence. In short, most Vizcayans linked their own well-being to the preservation of the fueros.

V. THE STATE AND VIZCAYA

Clearly then, it is evident that relations between the state and Vizcaya were not always harmonious.[36] More specifically, contributions to the troubled interaction included the following: Vizcaya's independent behavior, the fueros' strength, the corregidores' numerous conflicts with the Vizcayan Diputación, and the province's potent lobby at court.

First, while part and parcel of the Spanish monarchy, Vizcaya showed a remarkable bent and capacity to act as a separate and quasi-sovereign political entity. Endowed with considerable home rule at many significant levels, the province was in the enviable position of being able to negotiate certain matters of government with the crown on a nearly equal basis. In fact, Vizcaya's autonomy was so extensive that, as in the case of its manufactures, the province ironically found itself treated by Madrid as a totally foreign territory. Giving rise to much confusion and misunderstanding, this ambivalent state of affairs was a fertile field for conflict between the state and Vizcaya.

Second, the central government had to be careful not to infringe upon the regional liberties. Time and again Hapsburgs and Bourbons found themselves unable to effectively enforce policies on account of the fueros. Pointedly, two famous Vizcayan social movements of the seventeenth and eighteenth centuries—the 1631–1634 Salt-Tax Revolt and the 1718 peasant Machinada—had occurred in reaction to governmental violations of the privileges.[37] Fundamentally, the liberties hampered royal authority in Vizcaya.

Third, as noted before, the corregidor and his staff were often at odds with the provincial authorities over substantive issues of government. Moreover, the corregidor's office was set in the framework of a consistently distrustful and occasionally hostile environment. Eager to safeguard its prerogatives, the Diputación did not always readily cooperate with royal representatives, despite the fact that in theory the corregidor and the provincial executive jointly formed the cornerstone of local government. Clearly, the size and extent of the royal presence in Vizcaya were inadequate to fulfill the central government's objectives. Nor could the crown readily hope to use direct military pressure (or even the threat thereof) to force compliance with its policies, since no permanent troops were stationed in Vizcaya.

Four, a powerful lobby of the province's native sons at court compounded the state's perennial difficulties in dealing with Vizcaya. The lobby was two-pronged: first, there were the paid commissioners (*agentes*) of the Diputación, Consulado and municipality of Bilbao, who acted as the official agents of their employers; second, there were the numerous Vizcayan royal functionaries and ecclesiastic officials, who acted informally as a kind of *vizcaíno*—and also at times as a Basque—party. Together at court, both groups formed an imposing political aggregation. A combination of directives from employers, money, local pride, regional affinity, ethnic reflex, kinship, and a common heritage were all used resourcefully by the Vizcayan lobby in defense of provincial interests and the fueros. Subject to the natural flow of time and circumstance, as might be expected,

the lobby was considerably more influential when prominent Vizcayans reached high positions in government. Constituting a kind
of "fifth column" within the royal administration, these individuals
were ideally placed to temper, sidetrack, or even scuttle initiatives
deemed contrary to Vizcaya's well-being.

In essence, if the state ever hoped to impose its will completely
upon Vizcaya it would have to (1) strengthen its representation in
the province (by firming up the *corregimiento* and/or by creating
new royal posts there); (2) whittle down the fueros' influence (by introducing basic modifications in them); (3) incorporate Vizcaya more
fully into the monarchy's central administration; (4) reform the provincial institutions and system of government; and (5) neutralize the
Vizcayan lobby (perhaps by threatening to move against some of the
province's native-born functionaries). However, it would be equally
true that no fundamental state gains would ever be achieved without
a strong backlash and prolonged Vizcayan resistance.

VI. THE RECENT POLITICAL PAST AND WAR OF INDEPENDENCE (1795–1814)

In 1795, upon conclusion of the war with France,
serious charges of treason and collaboration with the enemy surfaced against the leaderships of the Basque provinces, in particular Guipúzcoa.[38] With Spanish troops still in the region, Francisco
de Zamora—a member of the Royal Council and Manuel Godoy's
personal envoy—hoping to make gains from the region's precarious
political situation, suggested a major and ambitious departure from
tradition by calling for a tighter union of the Basque provinces with
the central government.[39] Though the propositions were tempting,
the all-powerful minister of Charles IV (Godoy) downplayed them,
and eventually gave them up as untimely and impolitic. Significantly, during that same year Godoy also vetoed the publication of a
manuscript by Juan Antonio Llorente—canon of Calahorra, member
of the Sociedad Vascongada de Amigos del País, and future prominent historian-critic of the Spanish Inquisition.[40] Llorente, a keen
advocate of the supremacy of royal authority, had written a polemical work allegedly aimed at clarifying the fueros' historical and legal
foundations. The opus' central theme was that the Basque liberties

were largely the result of grants from successive monarchs. Hence, by right of royal authority, what could be given by monarchs could also be reclaimed by them. Godoy may have felt that to publish Llorente at this juncture would further alienate the inhabitants of a region whose allegiance to the crown had proven questionable. But Godoy's rule was—and would remain—largely to blame for Basque and Vizcayan wariness. In future years, despite continual protests from the Diputación that its fueros were being violated, Godoy's ministry would pressure Vizcaya into concessions. Given the persistent requests for men, money, and materials that the war (then with England) imposed during the first years of the nineteenth century, the so-called ministerial despotism of Godoy's era came to be profoundly resented by most Vizcayans. However, fundamental changes were still to take place under Godoy.

The possibility of significantly modifying Vizcayan institutions finally materialized as a result of a brief but politically important revolt that erupted in Bilbao in 1804.[41] The uprising, known to posterity as the Zamacolada—after its prime instigator, Simón Bernardo Zamacola—occurred after years of intense controversy between the city and Consulado on one side, and the Diputación and the central government on the other, over the creation of a new Port of Peace (named after Godoy, the "Prince of Peace"). The proposed facility, to be located between Bilbao and the sea, would considerably reduce the city's trade. The rebellion, a noisy and confusing affair, was swiftly quelled. More importantly, the episode provided Godoy with an ideal opening to carry out what from Madrid's perspective were undoubtedly long-overdue changes in the province. Seizing the occasion in the movement's wake, in May 1805 the central government quickly abolished the mayoralty of Bilbao and the corregimiento of Vizcaya. These posts were then replaced with an *alcalde mayor* and a *comandante general*, respectively. Even though the two new posts were roughly equivalent to those that had been abrogated, the shift was far from academic. It signaled the state's unequivocal intention of radically altering the relations between the royal and the local authorities, as well as the latter's attributes. Constitutionally, the alcalde mayor was totally subordinate to the comandante general who, in turn, became the province's supreme authority. Two related developments also broke sharply with tradition: first, the new high command was primarily a military office, and second, the Vizcayan right of assembly was severely curtailed and left to the discretion of the comandante general.

Not coincidentally, at about the same time, Llorente (with royal support) finally began publishing the famous *Noticias históricas*, a massive work calling into question crucial aspects of the Basque fueros.[42] Nor was this all: complementing Llorente's work (and vice versa), in 1807 Godoy ordered a full-scale investigation into the liberties' legitimacy.[43] Taken as a whole, these actions clearly signaled a marked turning point in royal policy vis-à-vis Vizcaya. Not strangely, the political demise of the "Prince of Peace" in March 1808 (Riot of Aranjuez), was greeted with loud cheers in the province. Quite naturally, Godoy's tenure left a profound resentment among a broad cross section of Vizcayan society. However, despite the deeply troubled political climate, the confirmation of the Vizcayan fueros by the young Ferdinand VII in April 1808 (in Vitoria on his way to Bayonne) at last seemed to presage happier times for the province's inhabitants.[44] In addition to unequivocally ratifying the liberties, Ferdinand VII returned the traditional institutional arrangement and mode of governance to Vizcayans. These benevolent actions would be long remembered by the local population during the innumerable ordeals of the ensuing years.

In the spring of 1808 French troops poured daily into Spain and a de facto military occupation was fast taking shape. Throughout June–July of that year Vizcayan attention was concentrated on the proceedings of the Assembly of Bayonne, a gathering of Spanish notables convened by Napoleon to replace the Bourbons in Spain and give the nation its first constitution. Gabriel Benito de Orbegozo and Juan José María de Yandiola represented the Consulado of Bilbao and the Vizcayan Diputación, respectively, at the famous Assembly. Little is known about Orbegozo's activities there. On the other hand, there is a relative wealth of information concerning Yandiola's work on the Señorío's behalf, whose privileges he lobbied hard to preserve.[45] Yandiola, the newly appointed Vizcayan general counsel, coordinated his efforts closely with the Alavese, Guipúzcoan, and Navarran delegations—as well as with those of Mariano Luis de Urquijo, a Vizcayan *ilustrado* minister under Charles IV and soon thereafter an *afrancesado* one under Joseph I. Against the centralizing and leveling projects of the French, Urquijo and the others skillfully emphasized their native provinces' uniqueness and the liberties' value. In the end, despite the provinces' powerful enemies at Bayonne—foremost among them their old nemesis, Llorente—Urquijo's recommendations prevailed. Perhaps only a temporary reprieve, but nonetheless a significant one, Article 144 of the new

Spanish Constitution (enacted on 7 July 1808) expressly preserved the status quo of the fueros of Navarra and the Basque provinces until the first gathering of the *Cortes* (Parliament).[46] Meanwhile the new king of Spain, Joseph Bonaparte, prepared to leave for that country. Joseph and his afrancesado administration were about to find out that, Bayonne notwithstanding, most Spaniards remained fiercely loyal to Ferdinand VII. Vizcaya was certainly no exception.

News of the momentous May 1808 events in Madrid, along with word of the uprisings in Asturias and Santander, handily served those Vizcayans predisposed to proclaim Ferdinand VII king and openly oppose Joseph I and the French. A reservoir of accumulated tension finally erupted into public disorder in August 1808, leading to the formation in Bilbao of a "Patriotic Junta" attached to the cause of the Bourbon heir.[47] In a sense, the episode marked Vizcaya's formal entrance into the conflict—an unwilling one at that since many in the upper classes feared imminent retaliation from the French. But, as elsewhere in the peninsula, the middle and lower classes forced the hands of the powerful, eliminated their options, and compelled them to take sides at once. To the loyalists' dismay, the Patriotic Junta would not last long. In fact, on 16 August French regulars attacked Bilbao and easily routed a small but defiant insurgent force. In the extensive pillage that followed, General Merlin's troops reportedly looted some 6 million reales from the city's wealthy inhabitants.[48] Adding further misery to the plight of the beleaguered community, the commander swiftly levied an additional forced contribution of 1 million. The harsh reality of war had arrived in Vizcaya.

For the remainder of 1808, French and Spanish regulars—the latter mostly under the command of generals Blake and La Romana—took turns occupying Bilbao while jockeying for position in the western part of Vizcaya and the Santander-Montaña region. However, by year's end it had become evident that the badly equipped and poorly trained Spanish soldiers were no match in open battle for the well-disciplined imperial forces. By early 1809 the French settled in for what they hoped would be a comfortable military occupation of the Vizcayan territory. Bilbao was garrisoned under the command of General Avril, and smaller detachments were eventually deployed strategically at Valmaseda, Durango, Orduña, and elsewhere. The policy of establishing *cantonnements* (quarterings) in the smaller cities went unchallenged at first and assured the French substantial control over the countryside. Eventually, these regulars were bolstered with those of the French *gendarmerie,* a kind of rural police. The *gendarmes'* commander in the Basque provinces, General Buquet, distinguished himself for his hawkish approach to peace keeping—a fact that greatly contributed to the local population's alienation and fanatical hatred of the French occupiers. Also in early 1809, the French administration felt politically secure enough to demand that all local authorities pledge full and formal allegiance to Joseph I. This was done throughout Vizcaya but, as several French commanders reported, seldom in good faith.[49] Grass-roots support for the new ruler and dynasty was virtually nonexistent. In fact (as elsewhere in Spain), to most Vizcayans Joseph I commanded little respect, and was nothing more than an "Intruder King." Designed to try "acts of banditry," an Extraordinary Military Tribunal was created in Bilbao in the spring of 1809, and a few months later a police force was established.[50] In essence, from mid-1809 on, repression by the French and their Vizcayan collaborators grew in direct proportion to stiff popular resistance.

At first, the French military administration was careful not to encumber Vizcayans with too many requests, but leniency soon gave way to a more insistent policy as the occupation's cost and the occupants' needs escalated sharply. Accordingly, the semblance of legality was quickly overshadowed by numerous forced loans, requisitions, quarterings at the occupied's expense, and other measures that, in turn, incensed the population and caused Vizcayans to take up arms. In late 1809, however, only small insurgent bands (some of them fragments of the regular corps) roamed the countryside, demanding rations and arms, and taking fresh recruits with them. Over time, under the able leadership of *guerrillero* commanders such as Longa, Renovales, Porlier, Mina, and others, these partisan bands became effective corps. They were motivated and organized, with excellent intelligence systems built around a sympathetic population, and often armed by the British.[51]

As the conflict progressed it widened and became generalized, inevitably bringing in greater numbers and resources on both sides. And given the enormous stakes, the war was fought with savage determination. Against the mighty imperial corps, the insurgents fought a stubborn guerrilla warfare (*partidas* or *guerra de partidas*), making excellent use of a terrain ideally suited to these martial tactics. Moreover, in the insurgent camp there were frequently few distinctions between the military and civilians. Thus, as Albert J. M.

Rocca—a French military officer and historian of the war—wrote after the conflict, "The French could only maintain themselves in Spain by terror."[52] Perhaps terror was the only "logical" method of fighting a war against a defiant local population. But that method engendered retaliation by the populace and counterretaliation by the French, thereby fanning implacably the flames of a bloody spiral of violence and cruelty.

Godoy's Vizcayan reforms, severe as they might have appeared to contemporaries, were mild in comparison to the drastic institutional overhaul carried out by the French during the Napoleonic domination.[53] In February–March 1810, the imperial administration abolished the corregimiento and completely scrapped the Diputación, replacing the Vizcayan government with a handpicked puppet regime modeled after some French institutions. Further, the three Basque provinces were amalgamated into a single district—the so-called Government of Biscay. The district's governor, General Thouvenot, was granted all effective political, military, and administrative powers.[54] To the dismay of Joseph I's Vizcayan adherents, as well as to that of the monarch himself, his rule there was clearly nominal.

The draconian measures of the French were prompted in large part by the rapidly deteriorating financial and administrative situation in northern Spain. By early 1810, Napoleon had finally decided to place a greater part of the occupation's costly burden on the local population. General Thouvenot proved a remarkably dynamic and demanding administrator. After the system of voluntary supplies and contracts with local entrepreneurs had broken down, Thouvenot instituted (in an unprecedented move) compulsory taxation on the Basques—the largest share of which fell on the wealthiest of the three provinces, Vizcaya. In fact, in the first eighteen months of his tenure Thouvenot taxed the Basque provinces more than 40 million reales, an astronomical sum under any circumstance but even more so to a population customarily exempt from the fisc.[55] At first the taxes were paid with some degree of regularity, but the oppressive system broke down completely by early 1811. This, in turn, brought about another round of French reprisals: incarcerations in houses of detention, hostage taking and deportations, and forced requisitions.[56] Coercion was widely practiced in the countryside, where French regulars swept through small communities, securing payments, grain, and livestock. However, by late 1811–early 1812 the loyalist insurgency was making headway in the rural areas, and

Thouvenot's administration found itself increasingly hard-pressed to meet its obligations. In a crucial turnabout, the insurgents had essentially become masters of the countryside by building an effective politico-military organization, collecting taxes, and securing much-needed supplies and recruits.

Short-term necessities also prompted the formation of other policies that contributed to the unpopularity of the French. Significantly, each of them adversely affected one or more sectors of Vizcayan society. For instance, Thouvenot established customs offices by the sea, seized forbidden imports in accordance with the continental blockade (then burnt or resold the goods to ex-owners), took over large chunks of church properties without compensation, and encouraged the sale of commons by communities to meet their tax allotments.[57] These decisions backfired on two counts: first, seldom were the desired objectives fulfilled and, second, these decisions visibly alienated key parts of commerce, the peasantry and the clergy. Finally, to most Vizcayans the new highly centralized French administration meant a total loss of their autonomy and the fueros. With an ever-increasing political sophistication, the insurgents effectively capitalized on the existent widespread discontent.

General Gabriel de Mendizabal's 1810 arrival in the north, to take charge of the rebel army's Seventh Corps, marked a new era in the insurgents' fortunes. With emissaries and orders from Cádiz turning up in larger numbers and more frequently in Vizcaya and Guipúzcoa, and having firmly seized part of Santander-Montaña-Burgos region as a base of operations, Mendizabal began a tireless campaign to organize a parallel rebel administration. The surge of this counter-political power would have profound influence on the course of the war from 1811 on. As soon as the politico-military organization was strong enough, Mendizabal moved rapidly to restore the region's traditional local institutions. For example, in the Montaña-Vizcaya territory Mendizabal convened juntas to review the general situation and, in early to mid 1812, he created an insurgent Vizcayan Diputación that even included a corregidor.[58] However, the traditionalist orientation would be forced to coexist—admittedly precariously at times—with clear-cut nationalist positions. Pointedly, even in regionalist Vizcaya, to many the war was primarily a national common cause to rid the peninsula of the so-called Napoleonic vermin. By 1812, in fact, the first overt signs of conflict in the Vizcayan loyalist camp had surfaced. Pitted against one another were nationalists (generally liberals) and traditionalists (for the most part conservatives). The former admired the reform-minded Cortes of Cádiz; the latter distrusted them because of the Spanish Parliament's alleged animosity toward the fueros.

At various moments during the war the French entertained the idea of annexing the Basque provinces—ironically, partly as compensation for the emperor's sizeable expenses in pacifying the northern Spanish regions.[59] A full-fledged annexation might have actually been attempted had it not been for the disastrous turn of events for the French that took place in mid-1812. Suddenly, with the insurgency gaining ground steadily, the once mighty imperial forces found themselves unable to control anything except the main urban centers. Meanwhile, an itinerant Vizcayan junta was meeting in the Encartaciones, Valley of Mena, Old Castile, and Vizcaya. To the loyalists' triumphant joy, the French even abandoned Bilbao in August 1812, the first of many evacuations and reoccupations that occurred until the final French departure in the spring of 1813. At the October 1812 Vizcayan juntas at Bilbao (the first that were held under any semblance of normality since the war's start), the main point on the agenda was the acceptance of the recently promulgated Constitution of Cádiz. General Mendizabal, though a mild sympathizer of reform, in the interest of unity attempted to steer a pragmatic middle course between constitutionalists who demanded an unconditional adherence to the "code," and traditionalists who insisted on the preservation of the fueros and the Vizcayan system of government.[60] An impatient guerrilla leader, Mariano de Renovales, threatened the use of military might against the juntas to force Vizcayan compliance with the constitution. General Mendizabal, however, preempted the menace by quietly moving Renovales to Salamanca. It was a victory (albeit a temporary one) for the liberties' defenders since Vizcayans were ordered to pledge unconditional allegiance to the constitution at a secret session of the Cortes held on 5 April 1813.[61]

As French fortunes in the peninsula declined rapidly under the combined weight of Anglo-Spanish forces, Mendizabal was emboldened to attack the occupiers' entrenched garrison at Bilbao. He launched a general attack on 12 April 1813 with some 5,000 men and, although the head-on assault failed to dislodge the French, the end was clearly in sight for both sides.[62] The final liberation of Vizcaya occurred only a month after Mendizabal's daring attack, but elation over the newly gained independence contrasted starkly with the province's ravaged condition. As in the rest of the nation, by war's end Vizcaya was devastated. Much of the countryside was abandoned, farms were run down, and many ferrerías and other manufactures lay in ruins and totally deserted. Indebtedness was the norm for many of the rural classes and village communities, and trade was stagnant and disorganized after years of truncated relations with the rest of the peninsula and colonies. In addition, the Señorío's finances were in chaos, and new demands were constantly being made upon the province's resources by the several thousand outside troops in the area. A torrent of petitions seeking relief poured out of Vizcaya in 1813–1814.[63] This was, in short, the extraordinarily difficult setting for the province's first constitutional experience.

From the outset, the Constitution of Cádiz met with stern resistance in Vizcaya. In accordance with the code, a Diputación *Provincial*—not a *General*—had been named on 28 September 1813. However, as late as November 1813, several Vizcayan towns were reporting that no such body had yet been established. Many of the local officials, who remained suspicious of the constitution and its effects upon the fueros, were obviously dragging their feet. Finally, under direct pressure from the Cortes, a Diputación Provincial was established on 13 November 1813.[64] Apart from a small group of vocal sympathizers who published some fifty issues of the liberal newspaper *El Bascongado*, the Constitution of Cádiz generated little grass-roots support in Vizcaya.[65] Not only was there much confusion over what it signified but, more importantly, there was a marked unwillingness—even among some of the more forward-looking minds —to break with tradition and established forms of government. In other words, local liberalism was still largely in the incipient stages of formation.

The constitutional Diputación lasted approximately six months (13 November 1813–20 May 1814) although, significantly, this body's records show a conspicuous gap from 16 March 1814 on. By mid-May, Ferdinand VII's famous Valencia decrees—abolition of the constitution and return of things to their state at the start of the War of Independence in 1808—were widely known in Vizcaya. The waiting was over and at long last Vizcayans could rejoice in the Desired One's triumphant return. Without skipping a beat, the Vizcayan oligarchy replaced the Diputación Provincial with the traditional Diputación General. The omens were indeed excellent. With Ferdinand VII in full command, Vizcaya had entered the First Restoration.

In conclusion, quickly discarding the French and Spanish reforms, the Basque political leaderships returned the region in 1814 to its traditional institutional structures and modes of government. However, beyond the short-term or immediate consequences, the war and occupation had acted as potent agents of change, leaving in their wake far-reaching and complex legacies. Among the most significant were the following: (1) hastening of the loss of the American colonies; (2) socioeconomic transformations through the transfer of clerical properties and town commons to private ownership; (3) sharp divisions in local political life; and (4) an armed mobilization and preparation of the peasantry for guerrilla warfare. (In fact, unwittingly but no less effectively, the conflict had provided an ideal training ground for the combatants of the 1820–1823 and 1833–1839 civil wars.) For all of these reasons—as well as those outlined earlier—it is impossible to overstate the profound significance of the Napoleonic invasion of the Basque provinces. Far more than a historical episode or series of events, the convulsions of 1808–1813 proved of long-lasting importance, helping to shape and determine the course of events during the next quarter century and beyond. Though contemporaries may not have been fully aware of it, the ancien régime had already begun to fracture, giving way in the process to the formation of a foundation for a new society. Despite vigorous attempts by the local ruling elites to restore the old order, in essence, the world that Basques had known prior to 1808 was hopelessly and forever lost.

CHAPTER 2

Restoration, Reform, and Civil War (1814–1823)

I. THE FIRST RESTORATION IN VIZCAYA (1814–1820)

The minister, the bureaucrat, the Direction of Revenue and the Council of Finance all have an identical opinion of our fueros and privileges in relation to the general system of finance. This opinion is that they should not exist and that we should be brought into uniformity with the other provinces.

Letter to the Consulado of Bilbao from its agent in Madrid, José de Inunciaga, 22 December 1817.

Foremost in the priorities of the Vizcayan elite and its newly reinstalled Diputación General was the confirmation of the fueros, the foundation of the province's system of government and its official legislation.[1] Through the intense lobby of Miguel de Antuñano, its agent in Madrid, the Vizcayan executive sought a swift resolution. The efforts were finally rewarded with the ratification and official royal confirmation of the Vizcayan privileges on 29 July 1814.[2] Moreover, Ferdinand VII issued another royal order, dated 7 August 1814, confirming the franchises and liberties of the three Basque provinces.[3] Once on the verge of losing what one prominent Vizcayan called "our political existence and the most valuable patrimony of our forefathers," the province had at last regained its fundamental laws.[4]

Meanwhile, the Diputación was besieged by a host of problems. As noted earlier, the postwar period was fraught with difficulties. By March 1814 the authorities were already warning of widespread food shortages.[5] Wheat prices skyrocketed in 1814–1815 to levels known only during the crisis-ridden 1789–1790 years.[6] With local agriculture suffering from the devastating effects of war, and lines of communication into the Castilian wheatlands still precarious, numerous troops stationed in Vizcaya strained the grain supply. Partly because of this, the Vizcayan authorities requested the demobilization of the so-called Vizcayan Battalions as well as the departure of all non-Vizcayan troops from the province. On the first score, the Diputación observed that it had been necessary to arm en masse the male population between the ages of seventeen and forty, "leaving agriculture unattended, or more precisely, abandoned, and in the hands of the elderly."[7] The struggle for demobilization finally succeeded in June 1814. The Minister of War, General Eguía, an influential Vizcayan, communicated a royal resolution to the Diputación that ordered "the men of the corps from the Basque Country be able to attend to the labors of sowing and reaping of their fruits, without being hindered."[8] Despite repeated pleas, Vizcaya would not be nearly as fortunate in securing the evacuation of outside military corps. In fact, the central government stationed troops in Bilbao and other points well into October 1818 and possibly even later. This situation created widespread discontent in the province. For instance, a November 1816 joint petition from the townships of Elorrio and Durango to the Diputación clearly expressed the misgiving that even in time of peace the garrisons would become permanent.[9] And so, the issue of non-Vizcayan troops in the señorío and the burden they placed on the population would long remain a sensitive issue.

Another key concern of the Vizcayan authorities was public order. In ways strikingly reminiscent of the explosion of banditry in the mid-late 1790s after the war against the French Convention, Vizcaya witnessed a menacing wave of lawlessness in 1813–1815 following the struggle for independence. When peace was reestablished, some guerrilleros of the Napoleonic era simply turned the remains of their units into bands of marauding brigands. In February 1814, a Vizcayan circular spoke alarmingly of "all types of robberies and excesses on the roads and (in) the towns of the province."[10] In October 1814 the Diputación, by its own admission, was forced to draw up a tough new ordinance to meet the rising tide of criminality.[11] And significantly, as the authorities attempted to curb criminal activities in general and highway robberies in particular, the province's 1799 *Reglamento Criminal* was reprinted in 1815.[12] By March 1815 the Diputación voiced the hope that it was finally winning the battle

against the "misguided individuals who, for a thousand reasons related to a devastating war, have been corrupted and now afflict the
peaceful inhabitants of this province with their thefts."[13] Yet despite
the Vizcayan executive's optimism, strong evidence suggests that
various forms of banditry continued to threaten public safety in later
years.[14]

Morality and mores were two other mildly troublesome aspects
of public life with which the authorities were now forced to cope.
For Vizcayan traditionalists, the previous years' upheavals had corrupted public morals and posed threats to the social fabric. Heightened sensitivity to alleged libertinage and vice, in fact, had even
led the Diputación to petition the crown in September 1814 for
the Jesuits' return.[15] The provincial executive's request stressed the
advantages that this order's religious teachings would bring to the
"unruly youth." The governing body may well have felt the need to
neutralize powerful cosmopolitan influences—particularly French
revolutionary currents—in lifestyles, thought, and politics. Significantly, the demand for the reinstatement of the Jesuits underscored
the "divergence in the opinions of the fundamental maxims of politics" in the province.[16]

Fragmenting the increasingly fragile political and ideological consensus that had dominated the ancien régime, the events of 1808–
1814 had led to the formation of protopolitical groupings in Vizcaya.
Not yet political parties in the formal or accepted sense, the main
camps can best be described as reformist and traditionalist. The first
was the less homogenous (and smaller) of the two. It included afrancesados and *gaditano* constitutionalists politically bound by progressive ideals of reform. During the First Restoration, its factions would
gradually coalesce into the nucleus of the Trienio's liberal party. The
second side was a staunchly conservative royalist sector that saw
itself as the rightful guardian of monarchical legitimacy and Vizcayan institutions. Whereas the reformist group primarily included
urban merchants, professionals, and property owners, the social base
of the second was fundamentally rooted in the countryside among
the peasantry and landowners, the regular and secular clergy and, to
some extent, the artisan classes in the cities.

In 1814, as soon as the political reaction surfaced, Vizcayan conservatives moved swiftly to squelch dissenting political tendencies,
in particular those of reformers. The liberal newspaper *El Bascongado* was summarily shut down in the spring of 1814 and its pub-

lishers (or promoters), Ildefonso de Sancho and Toribio Gutierrez de Cabiedes—both enthusiastic constitutionalists—were accused of insulting the authorities. Although they eventually acquitted themselves favorably after a long hearing, the charges against them caused them to be banned from public office.[17] Certain afrancesado members of the former Government of Biscay were not much more fortunate than the constitutionalists during the early stages of the 1814 Restoration. For example, some of those who had fled abroad with the French were sharply rebuked when applying for reentry, and other collaborators were excluded from holding office.[18] However, to the conservatives' dismay, some afrancesados proved remarkably resilient and resourceful. According to their former leader, General Thouvenot, at least some afrancesados were quickly able to "purify themselves . . . with monetary sacrifices." He noted that, once rehabilitated, they were able to live peacefully and even be employed by the newly restored Vizcayan administration.[19] The more radical Vizcayan elements of the movement for political change proved considerably more uncompromising in later years. When the war hero Mariano Renovales conspired in 1818 to proclaim the Constitution of Cádiz, Bilbao was one of the focal points of the planned uprising. In fact, numerous plotters there were rounded up and jailed in the wake of the ill-fated revolt.[20] Also during the 1817–1819 period, foreign secret agents with strong ties to formerly pro-French local administrators probably proselytized actively in Vizcaya on behalf of international freemasonry and seriously conspired against Ferdinand VII.[21] Notwithstanding these and other contemporary political challenges, the gravest problems confronting the authorities, indeed all Vizcayans, were socioeconomic.

In December 1815 the Diputación painted a decidedly gloomy general picture of the province. The litany of difficulties included allusions to the agricultural hardships that had resulted from the previous years' "enormous sacrifices," to the "towns' misery" due to indebtedness and, of course, to the "most downtrodden" condition of the ironworks "due to the continued obstruction of their production for the Americas."[22] In sum, the Señorío was in a "deplorable state." Even if dramatic, the provincial executive's description was hardly overstated. For example, with curious unanimity, immediate postwar accounts invariably depict agriculture as beset with severe problems. High rents and taxes, forced requisitions by the warring factions and, above all, the absence of young and able rural laborers, had reduced production and depleted existent stocks. Seeking to maintain reasonable prices and adequate grain supplies, in the ensuing years the Diputación followed an effective interventionist policy, doing so at least until early 1818 when Vizcayan agriculture finally appears to have undergone a tangible recovery.[23] However, urgent difficulties in the rural sector (with far-reaching consequences) persisted in other ways.

The war's frequent tax assessments and contributions had led to extensive public and private indebtedness in Vizcaya. To fulfill pressing obligations to their creditors, numerous villages and villagers were forced to sell their lands, pastures, forests, buildings, other properties, and rights. In fact, from 1814 on there was an extraordinary proliferation of land sales by the towns. This resulted in widespread disentailment, sizeable land transfers, and considerable hardship for the marginal or less fortunate—in particular those heavily reliant on the advantages and resources of communal ownership.

However, despite the headlong rush to liquidate annoying debts via the sale of property, some towns found—to their dismay—that transactions of this kind were not always a simple affair. Erecting itself as a defender of communal interests, the Diputación objected to some of the sales on the grounds that the villages could find themselves "entirely stripped of public lands and belongings."[24] The lawyer for one town seeking permission for a sale angrily objected to these obstacles and underscored that "every day the towns find themselves forced to sell communal properties to meet similar needs arising from similar causes."[25] Bowing to the necessity of the transfer, and with many contemporary precedents in full view, a resigned Diputación (and corregidor) eventually consented to the sale.[26] Examples of the Restoration's later years (1818–1819) strongly indicate that it had become considerably less troublesome for towns to dispose of property. For instance, sales conducted by Galdácano and Lemona suggest that the authorities were willing to grant licenses for land transfers after summary and largely proforma hearings—i.e., without the previous years' legal complications.[27] Though little is known about the specific buyers and the new beneficiaries of these lands, there is evidence—based on Fernández de Pinedo's solid studies—that they belonged to the more affluent rural and urban classes, always eager to expand holdings in a region of limited land availability and extremely high rents.[28] In sum, by pushing many entities and individuals to relinquish their assets, the war had acted as an agent of change.

Equally hard hit by the war were Vizcaya's manufactures, in particular its ferrerías. Clearly, all aspects of iron production were in crisis. Openly seeking assistance from the monarch and warning of adverse consequences, the Diputación underlined this plight: "The ironworks are reaching the nadir of their decline, and are near total abandonment, which will ruin the property-holders, the tenants, and the only industry of your Señorío."[29] Valmaseda, famous for its iron and copper production, now found its factories at a near standstill, and the small forges and ateliers at Ochandiano, Ubidea, and Villaro—producers of hardware, nails, and other tools—saw activity dwindle to some of the lowest levels in memory.[30] Apart from those causes directly related to the war, other important considerations contributed to the decline of local iron: foremost among them were increased foreign competition, unfavorable governmental policies, and the loss of colonial markets. Each one effectively accelerated the ferrerías' decline.

First, so serious was the problem of foreign competition that in 1815 the Vizcayan Diputación created a special commission to study the phenomenon. This body's findings, presented in July 1816, were far from reassuring. Said the commission, "The foreign iron which comes into Vizcaya by sea does not pay . . . tariff duties, and . . . this is a powerful incentive for merchants to fill up the country with it."[31] Not surprisingly, the commission concluded that unless strong measures were taken such competition would surely destroy the ironworks. Accordingly, in a protectionist vein it recommended that the provincial government seek from the crown the "absolute prohibition" of foreign iron imports in Vizcaya. This was considerably less than what the Diputación felt was necessary, namely, a total ban in the peninsula. However, as a sort of consolation prize, in April 1817 the executive finally secured and enforced a prohibition that applied to Vizcaya. Word of this decision was immediately communicated by the Diputación to the Consulado so that it would inform the district's merchants not to import foreign iron.[32] Yet even if highly desirable to some, the ban was not without unfavorable repercussions. In fact, some of the province's internal contradictions became quickly apparent. Nor were *bilbaíno* merchants the only ones to oppose the new measures. In 1818, for example, Vizcayan artisans and other specialists dependent on iron imports strongly protested the Diputación's policies.[33]

Second, following the policies of earlier periods, during 1814–1820 the royal administration objectively treated Vizcayan iron products as foreign commodities—in part, admittedly, to curb smuggling. In other words, surcharges were regularly imposed on the region's iron upon its entrance into any of the inland Spanish (or "Contributing") provinces and the colonies. Naturally, nobody was more keenly aware of these problems than the iron producers. In December 1819 a group of them from the area of Arratia accurately noted that as long as Basque products were not regarded in the same manner as all national ones, "the industry and factories will never be able to prosper" in the region.[34] Oblivious to Basque objections, the central government made an extremely unpopular ruling in August 1819 that reaffirmed its tariffs on the region's pig iron upon its arrival in the tax-paying provinces.[35] Although the Vizcayan Diputación predictably protested the royal order, it was nonetheless obliged to honor its content.

Third, the last factor (perhaps the most significant one) involved in the slump of Vizcayan iron production was the loss of Spain's colonies which were historically the province's chief marketplace. The Napoleonic wars and the American liberation movements had ruptured traditional communications and relations between the metropolis and the colonies. The ferrerías' owners and the Vizcayan leadership were deeply aware of the heavy impact that the political and economic situations across the Atlantic were already having on local iron.[36] Unable to recover the overseas possessions by force—an idea which was not altogether popular to Vizcayans, and indeed most Basques—there was painfully little the region could do except to seek favorable treatment from the central government and improve home iron production for greater competitiveness. Commissions (some of them "permanent") were created to study ways to reform iron manufactures but, on the whole and for reasons not entirely clear, these efforts proved grossly inadequate and disappointing to the Vizcayan political leadership.[37]

Intimately related to the catastrophic state of the ferrerías was the no less disastrous condition of Vizcayan mines, in particular those of Somorrostro which contained the richest iron-ore deposits in northern Spain. Specialists who visited there in 1818–1819 reported on how hard-hit the mines were by the war. In fact, some of the visitors even pointed to 1808–1813 as the beginning of the mines' abandonment and decline. However, it was also equally evident that the traditional (and undoubtedly obsolete) methods of exploitation had hurt the mining area's otherwise gigantic potential.[38]

During the First Restoration other Vizcayan manufactures suffered as well. In July 1818 a group of leather manufacturers ruefully observed that their industry was "on the verge of being extinguished once and for all."[39] At about the same time, Hilarión José de Ugarte, the owner of a chord manufacture, described the pitiful impoverishment of numerous workers and their families as a result of his factory's closing.[40] Vizcayan entrepreneurs consistently blamed the manufacturing slump on the war, foreign competition, and the central government's tariff policies.[41] Compounding the region's economic difficulties, Bilbao was still not legally enfranchised (*habilitado*) for direct colonial trade, a problem that also hurt local products. At least some Vizcayans, those familiar with domestic economic affairs, were convinced that the port's enfranchisement would prove vastly beneficial to the manufacturing community.[42] Still, such an eventuality would be certain to split ranks in the province, pitting traditionalists—who feared the establishment of customs houses by the sea in violation of the fueros—against hard-pressed producers looking for desperately needed outlets. Ironically, this split would occur at precisely the time when some colonial markets were starting to close once and for all to the metropolis. In essence, as long as the Diputación adhered strongly to tradition and the fueros remained in place, Vizcaya could expect few concessions from the state on matters of trade.

In September 1814, following repeated Vizcayan requests, the royal administration returned the customs houses to their pre-Napoleonic locations on the right bank of the Ebro, a move that for many signaled the end of the uncomfortable reformist experience undertaken by the French. Yet the same royal order noted that the measure "should be understood in an interim manner . . . until the final resolution of His Majesty."[43] As far as Vizcaya was concerned, the phrasing suggested that at best Ferdinand VII was undecided on the matter, and at worst he was perhaps toying with the politically sensitive idea of reforming the customs administration in the Basque region and, by extension, in Vizcaya. Otherwise, it is difficult to explain the monarch's motives in issuing a measure that was sure to unsettle his usually restless Vizcayan subjects.[44] However, if significant changes were afoot they did not become apparent during the following years and in fact at the end of the First Restoration, by virtue of the interim order, matters remained as they were in September 1814. Despite this victory, Vizcaya still took exception with the central government's stand on many crucial matters. Indeed, the province found itself beset by a phalanx of new charges, and on the defensive in a number of fronts from 1815 on.

Many of the difficulties for Vizcaya emanated from the so-called *Junta de reforma de abusos de Real Hacienda en las Provincias Vascongadas*, a body created by a royal order on 6 November 1815.[45] This junta was specifically mandated to investigate smuggling in the region. Adding to the Vizcayan authorities' concern, Francisco de Campuzano (head of the bureau of royal finance and customs administration in the Basque provinces) was named to the junta. Campuzano was an alleged sworn enemy of the region's privileges. From his post at Vitoria, he had fought against and denounced the voluminous illicit trade that purportedly made its way through the Basque provinces and into the Spanish heartland. Said one of Campuzano's bitter Vizcayan critics: "In his mouth everything is fraud, contraband, scorn for the central government, and a thousand other infamies which he heaps upon the laws and uses" of the Basque provinces.[46] Although the Vizcayan Diputación frantically tried to contest Campuzano's appointment, he retained his post for the duration of the junta's three and a half years.[47]

Expectedly, the Junta de reforma de abusos, as it came to be commonly known, caused tangible strains in the relations between the Vizcayan leadership and the royal administration: in particular the Ministry of Finance which was the junta's sponsor. Sharply conflicting perspectives and interests were patently at play. For Vizcayan traditionalists the junta was little more than a covert attack on the fueros, yet for Madrid's bureaucrats the body was a legitimate effort to halt a fraudulent trade that undermined revenue collection from customs duties. While the recommendations submitted by the junta in April 1819 pointedly omitted the fueros, it was nonetheless clear that some important conclusions clashed head-on with the region's privileges. Thus, when the junta recommended the complete abolition of government tariffs on all Vizcayan manufactures, it was contingent upon other proposals that were wholly unacceptable to Basque conservatives—to wit, the enfranchisement of Bilbao and San Sebastián along with the establishment of customs houses by the sea.[48] Aborted in part by the 1820 revolution, some of these questions lingered unresolved and would remain major problems throughout the next two decades.

However, the junta was only a single part of what one writer called

the "politics of hostility" practiced by Ferdinand VII's administration against the Basque region during the First Restoration.[49] In yet
another controversial measure, the central government in April 1817
expanded the geographical scope and administrative attributes of Bilbao's judgeship of contraband.[50] To wary Vizcayans, the post was so
radically altered that it now amounted to a semi-official customs
house. Adding to the provincial discontent, since 1816 the position's holder had been none other than Marshal Francisco Longa, the
rugged and sometimes ruthless native hero of the War of Independence. His uncompromising pursuit of smuggling, especially after
his authority was increased, was the source of nearly constant tension between his office and the local authorities and merchant community.[51] A host of other governmental policies and rulings adversely
affected Vizcaya's economic life. In addition to the duties on local
manufactures, which made Vizcayan goods less competitive vis-à-
vis foreign imports, even Castilian productions were at times forced
to pay export duties ("rights of extraction") upon entering the Basque
provinces.[52] Still, one of the harshest rulings against the provinces
occurred in the crucial area of foreign and colonial trade when, in
July 1817 in response to a minor infraction, the central government
moved to curb trade abuses and fraud by considerably tightening
controls over trade in the region.[53] Though desirable from the ministry's point of view, the new measures forced Basque merchants to
pay double customs duties on certain imports—once upon entering
the region, and then again upon leaving it. Although the ruling was
continually appealed, it was not rescinded by the central government
until January 1819—and then, according to local opinion, only after
substantial damage had already been inflicted upon Basque commerce.[54] A stern royal order addressed to the Basque diputaciones (on
21 October 1817) vigorously denied that the fueros had been contra-
vened and defended the crown's firm policies, citing the "nation's
general interests," the "system of unity", "order", and the "prerogatives of the sovereign and supreme authority."[55] In sum, the order
stated that the commonweal and royal power should take precedence
over Basque interests.

Equally disturbing to Basques was that during the First Restoration the attitude of many royal administrators toward the region
became increasingly distrustful and hostile. Animosity was greatest among government military and financial officials. To the central
government's dismay, in nearly every instance where help and

contributions were requested—in the form of men for the army, voluntary donations, loans, and other taxes—the Basque diputaciones steadfastly refused, usually basing their resistance on the fueros. Essentially, royal administrators felt that Basques were avoiding basic responsibilities. Pedro de Ceballos, a vocal council of state and critic of the Basques and their liberties, angrily suggested in September 1816 that it was "necessary to change the system . . . to banish even the name of privileges and titles of Exempt Provinces."[56] Of course not all of the central government's representatives shared Ceballos's seemingly hard-line stance. For instance, other bureaucrats who stood by traditional practices believed that Basques would come to the monarchy's aid if the fueros were safeguarded.[57] Certainly not alone, however, Ceballos remained completely unconvinced, arguing that he doubted appeals to the Basques would have the same effectiveness as outright commands.[58] Several examples from the 1814–1820 period abundantly bear out Ceballos's opinions.

In 1818, the Basque provinces and Navarra, acting as a well-coordinated bloc, refused to comply with provisions of the central government's 1817 *quinta*—i.e., the act of drawing lots for service in the army.[59] Their main objection had less to do with the principle of military service than with the method of conscription, a coercive procedure that supposedly violated key provisions of the region's fueros. The Basque and Navarran leaderships' strategy was plain and consistent: by resisting conscription but grudgingly consenting to a cash settlement—little of which was actually paid—they hoped to create the impression and establish the precedent that their contribution to the military had been voluntary and therefore not in violation of the regional freedoms.[60] The state did not fare much better in the areas of private loans (*empréstitos*) and direct taxes.

After the war the central government made continual requests for loans, in part to finance its colonial ventures. Many of the demands were addressed to the Consulados and commercial centers of the peninsula. However, as in other instances, both the Consulado and the Vizcayan Diputación commonly invoked the fueros in strongly resisting these loans. Apparently, the Vizcayan elites were not interested in the reconquest and pacification of the rebellious colonies. Perhaps Vizcayans, who had never possessed a legally enfranchised port for direct overseas trade, in their role as outsiders felt confident enough about their connections, capital, and expertise to attempt to seek an accommodation under the new adverse conditions.[61] But failure to contribute could also bring about punishment, as was the case in November 1816 when, in apparent retaliation, Bilbao was forced to quarter four battalions of royal troops.[62] The most controversial empréstito of the period, known as that of the "Eighteen Million Reales," was ordered in November 1818, and reaffirmed and clarified in no less than eight subsequent royal orders.[63] The Consulado of Bilbao's initial share of 880,000 reales was eventually lowered to 500,000 after repeated protests. In addition, the city's commercial oligarchy secured major concessions from a financially beleaguered royal administration. Thus, in return for the promised sums—again, little of which was rendered—the Consulado and Diputación (in January–February 1820) won removal of the important blockages that had hurt the Vizcayan economy in recent years.[64] As far as direct contributions, the Vizcayan leadership was even more adamant in its resistance and, consequently, here too the central government made little headway. For instance, when Martín Garay presented his now famous system of finance in 1817, an amendment to the plan called for direct taxation of the Basque provinces. However, the Vizcayan Diputación lobbied successfully to block the dangerous innovation through its agent in Madrid, Casimiro de Lóizaga, and the project was rapidly shelved.[65] The only payments made by Vizcaya during these years were in the form of small donations and generally attached to specific conditions. From all appearances, Vizcaya's contributions had fallen dismally short of the central government's expectations.

In conclusion, by strongly asserting centralist prerogatives in a wide-ranging spectrum of policy, the royal administration gradually alienated key sectors of the Vizcayan elite, eroding their confidence and support. Some Vizcayan leaders had sought a return to the pre-1808 relationship between the province and the crown, but the quest proved elusive. Reasons of state and government financial needs repeatedly clashed with Vizcayan traditions, laws, and interests. As the absolutist regime finally collapsed in 1820 before the constitutionalist challenge, it was evident that at least some important Vizcayan interests were not concerned with its survival. To most of Bilbao's generally liberal business community, a national political overhaul probably seemed a necessary measure. The troubling events and tensions of 1814–1820 may possibly have convinced other influential Vizcayans of the need for basic reforms and new policies. Yet even as some welcomed the removal of barriers to greater political participation and economic prosperity, lurking about intimidatingly were the omnipresent fueros, to which most Vizcayans—and in particular the provincial elite's most conservative sectors—were tenaciously attached. In an atmosphere of political uncertainty, Vizcaya was about to enter its second constitutional experience.

II. THE LIBERAL TRIENNIUM AND INSTITUTIONAL CHANGE (1820–1821)

The time has come in which there must disappear, without exceptions, such monstrosities and injustices. Because in the same way that there is but one national representation, one king, and one set of laws, one must also be the rights and obligations of those who until now have thought themselves to be exempted from them.

Consulta *of the Council of State entitled "In order to establish in the Basque Provinces and Navarre the system of finance according to the Constitution," 23 August 1820.*

According to Auguste Regnaudin, the French commercial agent in Bilbao, the reestablishment of the 1812 Constitution was not surprising to Vizcayans.[66] Equally true, the far-reaching political changes of 1820 were initially accepted in the region with a fair measure of skepticism and even resignation. An anonymous commentator in Bilbao wrote: "It would be an error to flatter oneself with the idea that [the Constitution] had been welcomed in Vizcaya with the same enthusiasm as in the rest of the peninsula."[67] Another correspondent, attempting to refute these assertions, tellingly argued that no province had welcomed the constitution "with greater order and exactitude" than Vizcaya—still a far cry from joy and revolutionary fervor.[68]

The main stumbling block to acceptance of the new system of government was the widespread local concern over the eventual fate of the fueros and Vizcayan institutions. Would they be preserved or modified? And if the latter, how much? Would they be abolished altogether? What other significant innovations might ensue? Moreover, from the outset some of these focal questions acquired a sharply polemical and partisan character. One orthodox constitutionalist line led by Lorenzo Antonio de Vedia, a newly appointed provincial governor (*jefe político*),[69] maintained that the fueros, hav-

ing been eroded by the previous years' despotism, were virtually de-
funct by 1820. While it was not worth conserving them, said Vedia in
an important proclamation, it was therefore desirable to replace the
liberties with the liberal charter.[70] More moderate liberalism, though
supportive of the constitution and in favor of some reforms, nonetheless realistically insisted that it was imperative to recognize the
Basque privileges' strength and relevance.[71] Finally, Vizcayan conservatives thought it preferable to keep traditional Vizcayan laws and
institutions intact.[72] While many—perhaps even the majority—remained politically undecided in the early stages of transition, other
Vizcayans were surprisingly quick to take a stance toward the new
system. Generally speaking, those who did (most of the province's
merchants and capitalists, including those with properties in the
countryside), embraced constitutionalism. On the other hand, the
entail holders (mayorazgos), nearly all of the clergy, and many of
the artisan classes and peasantry sided with the traditionalist royalist
current.

Significantly, the outgoing local authorities made a futile last
minute attempt to preserve the province's unique laws and institutions within a constitutional framework. Hoping to gain time and
concessions, a commission of prominent Vizcayans reported to the
hastily convened March 1820 juntas that it was necessary "to secure
. . . the explanations and accommodations . . . compatible with the
general well-being of the monarchy and of the Señorío." To do so, the
commission suggested that the Diputación "be charged with making
the proper recommendations to the government in preparation of the
necessary transactions and measures, without there being in the interim any innovation in the system of the Fueros."[73] In fact, when
it became apparent that traditionalists at the assembly would use
these arguments to delay acceptance of the constitution in Vizcaya,
the representatives of Bilbao, Portugalete, Valmaseda, and the Valley
of Carranza pressed hard for an official recognition (jura) of the 1812
charter.[74] Despite these complications, pressure for a speedy resolution was heavy and the provincial civilian, military, and ecclesiastical authorities pledged loyalty to the constitution in late March—
early May—much to the satisfaction of the fast-growing Vizcayan
liberal party.[75] Not all of the province's towns, however, acted with
the same swiftness and determination, and the new governor soon
complained of complacency in certain parts of Vizcaya.[76] In sum,
through a combination of fiat from without (royal orders dated 9,

16, and 17 March 1820) and prodding and acquiescence from within, the institutionalization of the constitutional regime—a piecemeal process to be sure—was now under way.

Initially, the constitutional government designated Antonio Leonardo de Letona, the former provincial governor of the 1813–1814 period, to head the new administration in the province. However, Letona, a man of "advanced age," made way less than two weeks later for a new younger governor, Lorenzo Antonio de Vedia, a member of a prominent liberal family from Valmaseda in the Encartaciones.[77] In addition to the consolidation of the constitutional system—the authorities and administrative structures—the governor was confronted by important problems requiring considerable and immediate attention: namely, the selection of representatives to the parliament (Cortes) and to the Diputación Provincial (royal decree of 22 March).[78] The electoral process turned up some interesting political surprises. Even though it is difficult to ascertain the individual views and positions of each of the new deputies in the Cortes and the Diputación, by virtue of restrictive suffrage and the "establishment" orientation of many of the electors, the victors were predominantly moderate and conservative. Thus, among the newly elected were mild constitutionalists (Yandiola, Torre, and Zabalburu) as well as status quo traditionalists (Batiz, Lóizaga, et al.).[79] Tellingly, even in Bilbao where constitutionalists managed to sweep most of the new posts during the spring 1820 municipal elections, several prominent conservatives—notably José María de Jusué and Pedro Novia de Salcedo—also slipped through.[80] Liberal-oriented merchants (Lemonauría, Lezama, Leguizamón, Trotiaga, Aguirre, and others) combined with wealthy progressive landowners (such as Mariano de Eguía) to make the municipality—along with the Consulado—the constitutionalist center par excellence in Vizcaya. Bilbao's official liberalism would eventually bring the city into open conflict with other provincial authorities, most particularly the Diputación, the last refuge of organized conservatism in Vizcaya.

To make the constitutional system more palatable to wary Vizcayans in the budding phases of the Trienio, the leadership in the province (especially the governor) engaged in a deliberate campaign to demonstrate that the reestablishment of the 1812 charter amounted to a generalization of the fueros. This resulted in a cluster of ideas that could aptly pass for the politico-ideological *grande équivoque* of that period in Vizcaya.[81] This phenomenon encompassed a wide array of themes and variations. For instance, a memorial of the Diputación Provincial proudly declared that the province's "laws and customs only resemble the freedom which thanks to the Sublime Code will forever be common to the rest of the nation."[82] Another proclamation issued in June 1820 likened the fueros to the national constitution, adding that the people had known how to safeguard the privileges "until the heavens have desired that they become general."[83]

Doubtlessly aimed at assuaging traditionalists, and possibly at coopting them as well, numerous constitutionalist documents publicly (if somewhat artificially) praised the region's liberties, institutions, and customs. One text, for instance, struck the ever-popular theme of the alleged immemorial Vizcayan freedom, claiming that the inhabitants had been "free before as Vizcayans and in possession of a Code" that had served as a standard to others.[84] In another important document, dated 29 December 1820, Juan José María de Yandiola—the former afrancesado and member of General Thouvenot's administration, now the recently appointed intendant in his native region by the government of the Cortes—flattered his fellow Basques in exalted terms. Declared Yandiola: "Your proud neck was never bowed under the ominous yoke of tyranny, nor have you ever dragged the chains of enslavement." The intendant also called Vizcaya a "sacred district" and the "asylum of civic virtues," reserving his warmest praise for the fueros' provisions that safeguarded individual freedom and personal security against arbitrary rule—assuredly attractive assets to the liberal credo. Imbued with optimism, Yandiola euphorically announced a new dawn of prosperity for the Basques: "Your children will enjoy its plenitude. You have been free and poor; they will be free and rich."[85] Unwillingly perhaps, but no less effectively, the grande équivoque helped to keep alive the important question of the region's privileges. In addition, to the extent that considerable attention was focused on this vital issue, the grande équivoque must ultimately be regarded as a victory for Basque and Vizcayan traditionalists. A broad assortment of changes emanating from Madrid in 1820–1821 would increase tensions in the province.

Expectedly, the constitutional system's initial policies clashed with a wide range of entrenched Vizcayan interests and institutions. While some of the central government's decisions admittedly touched only certain groups, social classes, and entities, there was hardly a measure which was not perceived by the local population to affect the entire province. Consequently, in cases of potential danger, Vizcayans—in rare displays of harmony—united to oppose those administration policies deemed particularly misguided and adverse. And so, a series of nettlesome disputes between Vizcaya and the Cortes quickly broke out over the rank of the port of Bilbao, the location of the intendancy in the Basque provinces, and the new territorial division of the peninsula.[86] Despite strong centralist pressures, in every one of these instances Vizcayans stubbornly held their ground and, in fact, were able to limit the damage and successfully extract some concessions from Madrid. To the Cortes government's displeasure, even the seemingly routine reform of the customs administration in the Basque provinces met with unexpected obstacles and problems.

From the start of the second constitutional experience, few Vizcayan oligarchs doubted that major changes would ensue in the province's commercial privileges. Article 354 of the 1812 Constitution was unequivocal, stipulating that "no customs houses" would exist "except in seaports and at the frontiers."[87] So inevitable appeared this fact that in April 1820, Regnaudin spoke of the location of customs houses in Bilbao as a fait accompli.[88] Ample proof that the new government was earnest in its projects was swiftly conveyed to Vizcaya by way of a 29 April 1820 communication of the General Direction of Public Revenue to the provincial governor of Vizcaya requesting information on the establishment of customs offices in the province and on the creation of a backup barrier or system of checkpoints (*contrarregistros*).[89] On the first point, the governor matter-of-factly outlined where the main customs bureaus and their guards (*resguardos*) should be set up. According to Vedia, the chief customs house should be in Bilbao, with secondary offices (*aduanillas*) in the smaller coastal towns. (As noted below, the transfers of the bureaus from the inland sites to the coast would become effective on 1 January 1821.)

The provincial governor also endorsed the creation of contrarregistros in Vizcayan territory. The second proposal proved far stickier and more controversial than the first. In fact, the checkpoints—not meant as temporary measures but as permanent fixtures—immediately became the object of heated debates. Quite simply, to many the contrarregistros amounted to a second line of customs offices and were therefore a superfluous nuisance. Nonetheless, the central government insistently favored the move as a safety mechanism should the primary customs houses fail to perform effectively. What the constitutional administration would not say openly was that the checkpoints were primarily designed to deter smuggling. But the Vizcayan Diputación Provincial, if grudgingly willing to acquiesce to the transfer of the customs houses to the sea, was adamantly opposed to the second line of defense. Nor was it the only body opposed to the contrarregistros. The very constitutional Consulado, alleging that they were an irksome barrier to the city's trade, strongly petitioned for the checkpoints' suppression.[90] Even the governor, who was originally a supporter of the contrarregistros, made an about-face when exposed to severe local pressure, and was in opposition to them by the fall of 1820. The Cortes's clumsy policies on this issue provided ready-made ammunition to Vizcayan traditionalists, enabling them to raise openly, indeed unabashedly, the politically thorny question of the province's trust in the new institutions.[91] Moreover, addressing the possible harm to Vizcayan manufactures as a result of the checkpoints, the Diputación daringly (maybe even tauntingly) compared the former privileges to the new system. Unless the government's policies were reversed, said the Diputación, some would "rightly cry out, 'where are our ancient freedoms and franchises, and where are the benefits of the much-vaunted Constitution?'"[92] Perhaps in response to these pleas and hoping to appease Vizcayans as well, the central government reaffirmed that complete freedom of internal circulation would be maintained and that the checkpoints would be located so as to reconcile the nation's finances with the comfort of the Basques.[93] Essentially, however, despite explicit evidence of generalized Vizcayan opposition to the contrarregistros, as well signs of continued attachment to certain commercial franchises, the Cortes reaffirmed their intention to uphold the second line of controls.

Obviously part of a sensitive agenda of reform, the installation of customs bureaus by the sea held the potential for significant complications. This point was sharply underscored in an 11 October 1820 secret session of the Cortes. At that time the deputies heard a confidential communication from the Ministry of Finance addressing the need to exercise "the utmost care, prudence and delicacy" in establishing "in its totality the constitutional system, stamped paper and the customs offices in the Basque provinces."[94] Less than a month later (8 November 1820) came the much-awaited decision that finally transferred the customs offices to the coast (Portugalete, Plencia, Bermeo, and Lequeitio). However, the main facility turned out to be at Bilbao and not at Portugalete as initially (and mistakenly) decreed.[95] By late November, Vizcayan and bilbaíno merchants in particular were bracing themselves for the change that would take place on 1 January 1821. Intendant Yandiola offered some last-minute reassurances to a population about to undergo a major change in the customs administration for the first time since the Napoleonic Era —not a particularly happy precedent. Yet brimming with optimism, Yandiola predicted prosperous times for the area as a result of the opening of direct trade to America and Asia, an opinion strongly echoed by Regnaudin.[96] In other words, the constitutional government believed that entrepreneurs, attracted by the opening of new business opportunities at a time of painfully stagnant trade, would fully support the impending administrative and political changes. In a broader framework, the removal of the inland customs barrier vividly illustrated constitutionalism's attempts at administrative uniformity and national integration—projects that were, however, staunchly resisted at all times by Basque conservatism.[97]

At year's end, while arrangements for the installation of the customs bureaus were being finalized, Bilbao merchants went on a massive and frantic eleventh-hour buying spree in England, France, and the Baltic. Their patent aim was to stockpile as many goods as possible in anticipation of government tariffs and prohibitions. The merchants' main rush was on products destined for the American colonies (cloths, spirits, and others) and on the so-called colonial goods for the peninsular markets (coffee, sugar, cacao, and spices).[98] As the deadline approached, the pace quickened in December, and the French commercial agent at Bilbao noted the "incredible activity" that reigned in the city. During these days, Bilbao worked feverishly around the clock to unload the numerous ships that cluttered the narrow river port.[99] The scramble to stock up was so intense that Regnaudin reported that the entrepôts at Bordeaux and Nantes had been emptied in order to fill those in the Basque region and Navarra. Meanwhile, the cost of maritime transportation had increased by a staggering 400 percent, and premiums of 15–20 percent were offered by avid speculators on articles thought to fall within the looming duties and bans.

The bold move by Basque and Navarran entrepreneurs simply could not escape the wary eye of the government and the rival commercial centers. Zealous bureaucrats at the Ministry of Finance, as well as the competing commerce of Santander, swiftly accused those regions' merchants of bad faith and conspiracy to defraud the fisc. The charges and countercharges had far-reaching political consequences and led to acrimonious debates in the Cortes between defenders and detractors of the parties and interests involved. In fact, a somewhat embarrassed central government hastened to seek a negotiated solution to the controversy along the following lines: the intendants in the Basque provinces and Navarra would try to reach an agreement with the provinces' respective commercial centers regarding a monetary settlement for all of the merchandise hastily introduced prior to 1 January 1821, and which subsequently entered the Spanish heartlands unimpeded.[100] In the case of Bilbao, after months of considerable wrangling an agreement between the central government and the Consulado was hammered out and concluded on 6 May 1821. In compensation for the imports, Bilbao's merchants agreed to turn over 2.5 million reales to the central government within sixty days.[101] Although this sum was slightly higher than previous assignations, Bilbao's merchant oligarchy was anxious to end the dispute, and acquiesced gladly to the new stipulations.

Throughout the months of debates and negotiations, Bilbao had found an able and committed advocate in Juan Antonio de Yandiola —one of Vizcaya's representatives in parliament, an influential moderate constitutionalist, a future treasurer of the Cortes, and a close relative of Intendant Yandiola in Bilbao.[102] Closely identified with business interests, Juan Antonio de Yandiola skillfully pleaded the cause of the merchant community: "The commerce of Bilbao has acted with the greatest good faith and even with unselfishness and patriotism." He also warned the government against creating discontent "among that part of the nation . . . most interested in the (constitutional) system," as was the mercantile class.[103] These remarks were particularly appropriate with respect to Vizcaya, where the urban merchant bourgeoisie had been the only sector in the province to offer constant (and at times enthusiastic) backing to national constitutionalism from the Trienio's outset. However, it should be emphasized that the actions of Bilbao's capitalist oligarchy were probably motivated as much by material self-interest as by political and ideological conviction. More to the point, the previous years' allegedly disastrous government policies—and the ensuing blockages to trade—had thoroughly convinced local businessmen of the changes needed to liberate economic activity from unwarranted constraints. Strategically, this meant placing Vizcaya on the same ad-

ministrative and institutional footing as the rest of the nation, regardless of the privileges that might have to be relinquished. Of
greater immediate concern, Bilbao merchants also embraced constitutionalism as a way of ending the profound economic crisis which
had afflicted the city since the end of the War of Independence. In
other words, it is precisely in the context of this crisis, and very definitely as a response to it, that the efforts of the Bilbao bourgeoisie
to activate its trade and embrace constitutionalism simultaneously
must be understood. And yet, it would be wrong to construe the merchant elite's actions as purely opportunistic or conjunctural. Rather,
they must be viewed as a natural, indeed logical, continuation of the
perennial search for new markets—a process in which the attrac-
tion of direct Western Hemisphere trade played a central role and
accelerated acceptance of the new regime.

Although the general strategy was certainly sound, a host of adverse circumstances combined to thwart its main objectives. For instance, Bilbao merchants had clearly hoped to make up for the loss
of the port's traditional franchise by directing substantial shipments
to the colonies but, as noted earlier, the colonial struggles greatly
undermined the advantages gained from the installation of the customs bureaus by the sea and from the authorization of American
trade.[104] And so, despite the bustle in Bilbao in late 1820–early 1821,
the normally optimistic French commercial agent—in what would
become a sadly recurring motif—reported that overseas trade was
not large enough to compensate the Basque "working class" for the
advantages derived from the previous freedom of its ports.[105] Other
nettlesome problems intruded as well. For example, Bilbao importers began to realize that the Cortes's protectionist policies would
hinder trade by sharply limiting the range of imports. And yet, without a strong home industry and with stern measures on the books
against illegal imports, the Basque economy would be unable to satisfy its own local demand for manufactures, let alone that of the
national market. There was also the danger of massive numbers of
imports in late 1820, since a glut in the local markets had become
an all-too-real possibility. In sum, the government's protectionism,
while good for national and local manufactures and agricultural production, combined with the temporary saturation of the internal
markets to create a kind of business recession: one that, when accompanied by a worldwide downturn in prices, would begin to hit
hard at commercial enterprises. There were no easy choices for Viz-

cayans. Aided by protectionist legislation, local manufacturers could try to swiftly develop industry to satisfy internal demand, and this would prove a most difficult task. Or, alternatively, they could try to supply the regional and national markets with imports—legal or otherwise. In either case, however, there were sure to be conflicts between manufacturers and the comprador bourgeoisie on the one hand, and the constitutional authorities and the Vizcayan population on the other, since the province's inhabitants now found themselves unable to legally acquire their goods duty free in the former *zone franche* (free zone).[106]

Inevitably, as some clung to the real or imaginary benefits of the provincial economic structures under the fueros, invidious comparisons were made and serious contradictions quickly arose between adherents of the old system and proponents of the new. By early 1821 insidious anticonstitutionalist criticisms were already circulating in the province and, apparently, with a fair measure of success. According to one line of argumentation, Vizcayans had correctly foreseen the loss of certain privileges but had also hoped that other important ones, such as the commercial franchises—reputedly the source of their legendary prosperity—would be preserved by the Cortes, something that obviously had not occurred. Signs of disillusionment were soon evident in Bilbao, particularly among the lower classes who had secured fewer gains under constitutionalism than the emporium's more powerful entrepreneurs. In fact, as protectionism proved unable to overcome the city's commercial crisis and as unemployment there started to affect greater numbers, a noticeable public malaise began to set in by the spring of 1821. Somewhat ominously, a French official in March 1821 observed that "a feeling of dissidence, although generally concealed, has not been ignored by the authorities."[107] The gradual alienation of Bilbao's lower classes would play a significant role in subsequent political developments.

Despite the less than triumphant start of constitutional rule in Vizcaya, from the beginning Bilbao's entrepreneurial classes gave their firm support to the new government. This was perhaps most palpably evident in the organization of the constitutionalist militias formed in June–July 1820.[108] Prominent young merchants, manufacturers, and landowners rushed to enroll in the National Voluntary Militia (*Milicia Nacional Voluntaria*). In fact, its membership reads like a "Who's Who" of the Bilbao bourgeoisie.[109] So great was the zeal and enthusiasm of the members that, significantly, the Milicia

Voluntaria had been hastily and spontaneously constituted prior to the arrival of formal orders from Madrid.[110] A senior citizens' equivalent of the Voluntary Militia was also formed in Bilbao. This was a group called the Holy Company of Elders (*Compañía Sagrada de Ancianos*), usually made up of men fifty years or older. Its main task was the preservation of order in the city during emergencies or when the local militias were out of town.[111] Swelling the ranks of the Holy Company were the older merchants and property owners. While their younger counterparts in the Voluntary Militia were in many instances the firebrands (or *exaltados*) of Vizcayan liberalism, the Elders, while also constitutionalist, embodied the more politically moderate or "responsible" business establishment.

Orders arrived from Madrid in October 1820 for the formation of a Regular Militia that eventually came to be known as the *Milicia Reglamentaria* or *de la ley*.[112] A general registry (by neighborhood) was compiled, and twelve companies, each consisting of seventy to a hundred men, were assembled in Bilbao. Shortly thereafter, the companies were reduced to four, but the total membership remained fairly constant. By December 1820, the Regular Militia outnumbered the voluntary corps by more than ten to one—or, to be more precise, 1,335 to 129.[113] Even though in theory the two bodies were structurally linked, they preserved separate commands. From the very outset, and for reasons not altogether clear, there developed sharp conflicts between the corps along political lines. For one thing, suspicions arose among liberals about the Regular Militia's loyalty to the new system. Interestingly, at least part of its leadership was still royalist. In fact, one of the Regular Militia's leaders was none other than Pedro Novia de Salcedo, a young and prominent political conservative (born in 1790), and a future spokesman of Vizcayan traditionalism and the fueros. So undesirable was Novia de Salcedo to constitutionalists that an unsuccessful attempt to remove him from the municipality of Bilbao had already been made in 1820.[114] His prestige was probably enhanced by this episode, and Novia de Salcedo went on to become commander in chief of Bilbao's Regular Militia.[115]

To some extent, the social composition of the militias accounted for their divergent political orientations. The regular corps were overwhelmingly recruited from the middle and lower echelons of society; thus, the Regular Militia included shopkeepers, artisans, wage laborers, small property holders, and others from the more humble trades and occupations—i.e., many of those traditionally opposed to Bilbao's wealthier classes. Perhaps even more importantly, membership in the Regular Militia was obligatory, and this too could have contributed to the anticonstitutionalist temperament of its men. A coercive enrollment clearly increased the chances of evoking traditionalist—ergo hostile—reactions against the new institutions in a community unaccustomed to conscription-like methods.[116] At first, the political disputes between the Regular and the Voluntary militias were not overly serious, but their differences grew steadily with time.

After several months of constitutional government, as 1821 approached many important questions remained unsettled—foremost among them the problem of taxation, a thorny issue not yet satisfactorily addressed by the Cortes. Several major stumbling blocks made direct taxation of the Basque provinces extremely difficult. First, the central government had no viable established bureaucracy in the region to fully implement constitutionalism's new fiscal policies. Second, there was the crucial and unresolved problem of the Basque provinces' (and Navarra's) internal public debts. These had largely accrued from borrowing for public works projects as well as from the circumstances surrounding the War of Independence. Third, as virtually independent political entities, the Basque provinces had previously maintained separate systems of finance that had traditionally operated beyond the control of Madrid. Fourth, the central government patently lacked reliable statistical bases for taxation. In essence, Vizcayans had skillfully managed to withhold vital data on agriculture, industry, trade, and personal income derived from these economic sectors. Fifth, and perhaps most troublesome, there was a marked unwillingness among a broad cross section of Basque society to part with traditional privileges and exemptions. In tackling each of these problems, the Cortes—and in particular the Ministry of Finance—were thus forced to move cautiously in areas that must have appeared at times to belong to the realm of the unknown. Not surprisingly, governmental activity on these matters reflects considerable difficulties.

Much of the government's thinking on these questions is contained in an important 23 August 1820 *consulta* of the Council of State. The consulta was rendered after an examination of "an infinity of papers and petitions" contained in a voluminous dossier transferred by the Ministry of Finance to the council in order that the latter body formulate recommendations "so that the system of finance according to the Constitution be established in the Basque provinces and Navarra."[117] From the start, the council set a harsh and uncompromising tone for the rest of the consulta, noting that everything boiled down to "a continuous and badly directed struggle between the government and its agents and those provinces, the first wanting to establish, as they should, the general system already in effect throughout the monarchy, while those provinces have attempted to except themselves from it, since (it) was said to be opposed to the fueros and privileges and, above all, to their benefit."[118] The council emphasized at some length the harm that would come to the rest of the nation if the liberties were preserved. Clearly, in its view, the constitution had equalized the rights and obligations of all Spaniards. Hence, all differences and inequalities, including the regional ones, should cease immediately—in the council's words, "those hateful distinctions that created a barrier of separation between the subjects of the same government."[119] Taking direct aim at past practices, the council also criticized military service among the Basques, a system said to disadvantage the "poorer" inland provinces. And echoing the recent conclusions of the Junta de reforma de abusos, the council strongly attacked the customs administration in the Basque region as well as the smuggling carried out under the aegis of the fueros. Pointedly, the council asserted that the Basques had vigorously and selfishly defended their freedoms but, in so doing, had effectively helped to destroy Spanish industry and agriculture, promoted foreign manufactures, and hurt some of the more profitable branches of public revenue—a clear reference to the evasion of payment of customs duties. In effect, the Basque freedoms were detrimental to national economic development, a state of affairs that simply had to change. The conclusion of the consulta was therefore predictable: since the constitution had been sworn and accepted in the Basque provinces, it was necessary to establish the new system of finance there. However, in contrast to the severe tone of the consulta, the council's proposed line of approach was extraordinarily cautious. In other words, instead of a swift (and potentially disruptive) introduction of full-scale taxation in the Basque provinces and Navarra, the council suggested a careful step-by-step procedure in order to gain time and greater acceptance for the constitution.

First, the central government needed a few good officials in the region; men of high moral integrity and competence. Second, intendants should be named as quickly as possible.[120] Third, the appointees should report to their posts immediately and, upon arrival, they and their subordinates should carefully lay the groundwork for changes by working with the new diputaciones, rather than with their former members. Fourth, the Cortes would meanwhile be given sufficient time to determine the Basque provinces' public debts, install the customs bureaus at their new sites, and make the final preparations for the introduction of new taxes. The council felt that nothing else should be done until the Cortes ratified the new national territorial division and produced reliable data and uniform statistical bases. The Cortes did not act upon the Council of State's recommendations until 11 October 1820, and then, significantly, only in secret session. Without legislative action, the dossier was entrusted to one of the congress's finance committees for additional review.[121] With the matter bottled up in committee, the Basque provinces and Navarra were conspicuously absent from the assessments when the Cortes decreed some of the new government's contributions on 6 November 1820.[122] Two days later the Cortes enacted the long-awaited decree establishing the new customs houses and intendancies in the Basque region. The decree's third article, addressing the question of Basque and Navarran taxes, left the matter in the government's hands: "It remains up to the government to propose to the Cortes the time at which the other taxes must be established." Sensibly, the article also ordered that "sufficient information on the four provinces' public debt" be acquired "so as not to levy new taxes upon them until they have been relieved of it."[123] Interestingly, the congress also recommended that the government "keep in mind those who have worked in the said provinces, not only because their number is small, but because knowing the [Basque] language they can communicate with the people there."[124] From 8 November on, matters moved more briskly. On 13 November, the monarch approved the Cortes's 8 November decree. It was then forwarded to the minister of finance, José Canga Argüelles, who transmitted substantive parts of the decree verbatim to the Vizcayan authorities on 15 November.[125] Finally, on 25 November in accordance with earlier decisions, Canga Argüelles requested extensive information on the region's public debt from the intendant of the Basque provinces.[126]

Though political imperatives were undoubtedly at play, the Cortes and the central government could scarcely have followed a more flexible and accommodating fiscal policy toward the Basque provinces and Navarra during the transition period. In fact, much credit must be given to the congress and the administration for their display of skill and patience, even when this meant making concessions. Simply put, the state could not afford to alienate through brusque changes those accustomed to living under the umbrella of the fueros. In light of the coming months' serious developments and, as the opposition to constitutionalism increased in 1821, the government's prudent tax policy and strategy certainly appears warranted in retrospect. Significantly, not until mid-1821 did the state finally act decisively in the Basque provinces and Navarra with respect to three key areas of finance: the establishment of the first direct taxes, the liquidation of those regions' public debts, and the extension to all the monarchy of stamped paper (*papel sellado*)—a dreaded tax previously absent from the regions because of the privileges.

On the surface, the transition to constitutionalism in Vizcaya was effected smoothly and without upheavals, but not far beneath the apparent peace lay hidden the potent seeds of sociopolitical discord. The defense of local interests—be they provincial or regional —by traditionalists, would soon lead to open and major confrontations. If most Vizcayans ostensibly complied with the new system's mandates, probably just as many (if not more) continued to harbor a profound attachment to their fueros that, if never abolished de jure, had been seriously undermined de facto by the government of the Cortes. Sobry, Regnaudin's conservative assistant at the French commercial office in Bilbao, expressed well in March 1821 what may have been many Vizcayans' misgivings when he remarked that the government surely could not return to Vizcayans their liberties ("remnants of their former feudality") since the "Constitution had to destroy them."[127] However, according to Sobry, the government could only prevent Vizcayans from pining for the fueros by ceasing to impress upon them "an equality of misfortune." This, ironically, was what Madrid had done by equating the Basques with the inhabitants of the other provinces. In essence, since the privileges had allowed a higher standard of living for this region than elsewhere in Spain, the equation with a poorer or more disadvantaged province was patently undesirable to Vizcayans and other Basques as well.

The tasks then facing the central government were enormous, for in a short time it was forced to produce concrete benefits. Failure to do so would undermine its credibility and, eventually, its viability. Politically, therefore, constitutional rule faced the classic prob-

lems of a reform-minded government attempting to improve existing conditions rapidly after long periods of structurally determined
immobility. *A fortiori,* for constitutionalism to prove successful in
the Basque provinces, it was essential for it to demonstrate quickly
the advantages of its system over that of the fueros. But caught between the old and the new, many Vizcayans—particularly those of
the rural classes—would continue to cling stubbornly to tradition.
A disquieting (though accurate) assessment of the situation came
from an authoritative source, Lorenzo Antonio de Vedia, the provincial governor, who observed that Vizcaya was "not happy in general
with the new institutions."[128]

III. FROM OPPOSITION TO CIVIL WAR (1821–1823)

The religion of Christ persecuted, the ministers of the
faith ridiculed, the ecclesiastical power attacked in its
functions, some bishops exiled, the monastic orders extinguished, the other orders on the verge of disappearing,
nearly all the public offices occupied by impious and
immoral men, the State's revenues used in seditious
plans, in pieces the army which was to carry peace to the
Americas and make happy those beautiful countries, the
King despoiled of his sovereignty . . . the grandees without any representation, the nobility dejected, the roads
infested by bandits, anarchy throughout the nation.

Anonymous royalist manifesto entitled Grito de un español
verdadero a toda la nación, *appearing in Navarra, December
1821.*

One of the most important consequences of the Trie-
nio's institutional changes was the noticeable shift in the locus of
political power. If formerly largely in the hands of the provincial
ruling elites, power was now increasingly under the direct control
of the central government via the provincial governor who accumulated a significantly greater number of functions than any corregidor
had previously held. In Vizcaya, for example, the provincial governor's attributes were nearly identical to those of Benito San Juan
(1805–1808) at the time of Godoy's institutional reforms. There were
other areas of public life in which Vizcayans could tangibly sense

the loss of autonomy and home rule. Under the constitution there would be no more general assemblies (juntas), ostensibly the vehicle of the much-vaunted Vizcayan representative government.[129] And along with the liquidation of the Diputación General (replaced again by a Provincial, as in 1813–1814), came the abolition of the influential post of consultor.[130] The local administration of justice was also profoundly modified. Vizcaya was divided into four districts (*partidos*). A judge (*juez de primera instancia*) was directly named by the government and placed in each, thereby taking over the judicial functions of both the former corregimiento and the Diputación General.[131] Finally, the highest appellate court of Vizcayans—that of the juez mayor at Valladolid, deemed not "to be compatible with the constitutional regime," was quickly suppressed and matters pending therein were distributed among other branches of the Chancilleria.[132]

As centralization and reform increased in Vizcaya, so did the resistance of entrenched conservative local and provincial oligarchies (and various other interest groups) bent on conserving age-old privileges. The tensions from these conflicts were plainly visible at several institutional levels. Among the earliest and most apparent was the burgeoning dispute between the provincial governor and the Diputación Provincial regarding the latter's powers and attributes. The generally conservative Diputación complained bitterly to the Cortes on 10 February 1821 about the stringent limitations placed on its operations by the enlarged authority of the central government and of the provincial governor in Vizcaya.[133] According to the Diputación, in the provincial governor the new government had attempted "to make a perfect imitation of the French Prefects." Furthermore, the petition argued that there were no corresponding local mechanisms to check the powers of the governor and the intendant. In short, if past provincial governments had found ways of maneuvering around—or working with—the corregidor, the new Diputación Provincial now found itself under the uncomfortable tutelage of the government's representatives in Vizcaya, something deeply resented throughout the Trienio.[134]

Considerable evidence also points to opposition to the provincial governor from some of the province's smaller towns. This resistance grew in 1821–1822 in direct proportion to unpopular government fiscal demands. Much to the provincial governor's dismay, Vizcayan townships (and many citizens as well) often dragged their feet to avoid compliance with the Cortes's tax and military policies.[135] Even the municipality of Bilbao, normally a constitutionalist stronghold, was visibly dissatisfied with the new institutional arrangement. Feeling severely hamstrung by the limited capacities to which it had been reduced, on 19 September 1821 the Bilbao city government petitioned the congress for greater responsibilities.[136]

Led primarily by the clergy, a more determined and well-concerted Basque royalist-legitimist movement—"Altar and Throne!"—began to emerge in early 1821. The alliance of traditionalist forces opposed to constitutional rule encompassed many classes and groups of society: numerous peasants, a handful of prominent landowners, some artisans, retired bureaucrats (including some from the former Diputación), War of Independence veterans, members of the Regular Militia, smugglers and marginal elements and, of course, large numbers of clerics from the regular orders and the secular branch. There were excellent reasons why the opposition to constitutionalism should acquire such a predominantly religious orientation from the beginning.[137] The Vizcayan clergy was among the very first to feel the effects of reform. A series of constitutionalist measures attacked the foundations of the clerical establishment. On 1 October 1820 the monastic orders were suppressed, and the regular ones were reformed.[138] These measures were generally accompanied by the expropriation and disentailment of lands traditionally held under the system of *mortmain*, that anathema of bourgeois reformers. Significantly, by mid-1821 the Cortes had reduced the tithe by one-half.[139] Beyond material considerations, the local priesthood was also forced to confront a rising tide of attacks and denunciations—in some cases from the authorities—that threatened the church's singular spiritual, ideological, and political role in Basque society. In essence, the forced secularization of monks and suppression of convents, the undercutting of the economic base and the campaign of anticlericalism, all combined to thrust the clergy into the militant forefront of the protest, not only in the Basque region but elsewhere as well.[140]

Regnaudin's annual 1821 report criticized the haste with which the government of the Cortes had undertaken the ecclesiastical reform.[141] He observed that the Congress would have better served its own interests had it waited longer before taking these risky actions. From this perspective, through ill-advised clerical policies the government had in effect scandalized and alienated large sectors of the population. In a passage worthy of note, Regnaudin said of this population:

It is fanatical rather than religious, and it confuses, and will still confuse for a long time, religion with the domination and well-being of the clergy. As for the latter, interested as it is in maintaining the people in error, it finds itself naturally placed at the head of all the discontented and, above all, [leading] a large number of partisans, the most enterprising and most vehement of all, believing to defend the cause of God.[142]

Among the earliest and most important priests to rise against the constitutional system in Vizcaya was Domingo de Guezala who, by January 1821, had already taken up arms.[143] The provincial governor remarked suggestively that the cleric from the Lezama had "many connections in the region because having been commander of the Cantabrian Hussars during the French invasion he is influential among the popular folk."[144] Guezala's appearance on the side of the royalist insurrection coincided with a bold campaign aimed at subverting the constitutional system—a movement in which numerous priests and monks participated.

In late January and early February 1821, Bilbao was treated to a flurry of nervous excitement when seditious printed libels appeared at dawn in public places.[145] By mid-March it was clear to the authorities that the clergy was not only leading but also financing a surging opposition that would shortly lead to a full-fledged armed struggle. Clearly in preparation of the revolt, retired military officers and priests already had active correspondence.[146] It was even believed that Franciscan monks hid arms in their convents, a rumor that elicited swift constitutionalist retaliation.[147] Vedia, the provincial governor, was also very concerned about the purported relations between recalcitrant ecclesiastics and the former judge of contraband in Vizcaya, Francisco de Longa, a committed royalist and a political casualty of the new system.[148] In fact, to the dismay of Longa's numerous conservative admirers, the popular veteran was arrested and deported from the province by the constitutional authorities.[149]

On the heels of the important royalist uprising at Salvatierra (in Alava), an episode which produced serious repercussions in Vizcaya, accusations of clerical involvement became more explicit. In late April 1821, for example, Regnaudin observed that the clergy promoted discord and had a large following among the peasants "who receive two francs pay a day," a means of galvanizing opposition during every period, "but particularly today when poverty has reached its peak and when trade, which is entirely paralized, does not offer them any means of livelihood."[150] Descalone, the French police commissioner at Bayonne, while severely criticizing the "lack of skill" of the Spanish ministry in its treatment of the church, added significant information regarding the recent seditious movements: "The insurrections for which these provinces were the theater were not due to an isolated cause but were part of a prior plan, formed and executed after Holy Week by the clergy to oppose the new order of things, while using all of its influence over the peasantry."[151] The clergy's influential opposition manifested itself in other ways as well. For instance, ecclesiastics attempted to undermine public confidence in the new institutions by asserting that the constitution was opposed to Christian doctrine, an effective argument that the authorities were forced to refute at some length and with considerable difficulty.[152] In a related matter, parish priests were required by law to explain the constitution to the citizenry. However, despite persistent objections from the provincial governor, this obligation proved repugnant and was easily avoided.[153] In effect, nearly all of the Vizcayan clergy was squarely aligned with the royalist opposition.[154]

Even in Bilbao, the liberals' stronghold par excellence, the clergy was defiant in its resistance, and numerous priests and monks there actively opposed the constitutional government. Significantly, in August and September 1822, the authorities arrested and deported numerous Bilbao churchmen of suspect political opinions.[155] Some ecclesiastics eluded the constitutionalist persecution and managed to make their way to Bayonne, where they joined scores of clerics from Bilbao, notably Franciscans from the abolished convents.[156] In several instances, the local clergy showed a remarkable ability to work within the system. For example, by playing upon traditionalist sentiments among the urban lower classes, the clergy made important gains in the December 1821 Bilbao municipal elections. This forced the provincial governor to remark disparagingly that some of the newly elected "were neither citizens capable of fulfilling their posts nor individuals attached to the system, because the majority of the electors belonged to the opposition, or call it [the] clerical party."[157] Even one of the two Vizcayan representatives to the 1822–1823 Cortes, a priest from the village of Mañaría, José Apoita Mallagaray, appears to have belonged to what the provincial governor derided as the "servile or ecclesiastical" party.[158]

As the Trienio progressed, large numbers of priests abandoned their curacies to join the royalist guerrillas in the countryside.[159] Understandably, in the cycle of political violence the swelling ecclesiastical opposition led to a growing and vicious anticlericalism on the authorities' part. Among the numerous examples, witness the two powerful broadsides of the new provincial governor, Antonio de Seoane, against the rebellious priesthood:

> At the height of their perversity and depravity, several ministers of a God of peace have become the heads of the insurrection, and daily soil their consecrated hands with the innocent blood of the citizens.[160]

And:

> With a dagger in one hand and the Holy Image of Christ on the other, they desolate, burn, rob, and murder; they render difficult the useful labors of the peasant, obstruct trade, industry, and communications, while invoking the name of a God of peace in the midst of these horrors.[161]

Finally, judging from what little of Bilbao's constitutionalist press is now available, several issues of the newspaper *El Verdadero Patriota* also show a profound anticlerical streak.[162]

To contemporaries, and in particular to the royalist opposition, there were compelling parallels between the Trienio and the Napoleonic Era—e.g., institutional changes, constitutional reforms (be those of Bayonne or of Cádiz), introduction of new taxes and compulsory military service, attacks upon the clergy and, of course, the monarch's alleged captivity at the hands of foreign and/or radical elements. These considerations effectively inspired, shaped, and guided much of the resistance to the constitution. A case in point: the reestablishment of a purportedly usurped royal authority became one of the legitimists' central objectives. Also inviting comparisons, from the moment that the opposition's actions coalesced into open struggle in 1821, the conflict became a scaled-down military replay of the War of Independence. However reminiscent of the past, the Trienio's struggles were also a kind of dress rehearsal for the Carlist Wars. In what would become a recurrent sociopolitical reflex against innovation and reform, during the Trienio traditionalists organized partisan warfare in the countryside and then relied heavily on the rural population as the primary source of opposition. And with good reason too, since increased fiscal pressures, government demands, disentailment of commons and clerical lands, and a decline in the standard of living doubtlessly impelled many peasants—landowners or not—to join the royalist insurrection, not only in the Basque provinces and Navarra but in other regions as well.[163] Hence, in countless ways the royalist opposition was characterized, both strategically and tactically, by its rural foundations. In fact, so deep was this identification that royalist resistance came to be synonymous with the concept of "loyal farmers" (*leales labradores*). Adding important new dimensions to the secular opposition between city and country, from 1821 to 1823 agrarian traditionalists fought tirelessly to contain change—be it political, economic, fiscal, or administrative—especially when it meant greater government intervention and centralization. On behalf of age-old regional institutions and laws, and the preservation of the status quo, the self-styled Defenders of the Faith wielded the trilogy "King, Religion and Fueros" with increasing success.

To counter the mounting royalist resistance, the provincial governor requested additional troops. Vedia's objective was to establish small detachments of about 25 men each at key points in Vizcaya from which to attack the insurgents' strongholds.[164] As soon as the reinforcements arrived, the governor ordered them to pursue all suspected "agitators" in the villages.[165] However, despite the new military personnel, the royalist guerrillas made steady progress, and by the end of 1821, bands of armed insurgents roamed freely at Bilbao's outskirts.[166] Even with abundant signs that a generalized uprising was still under preparation in the region—i.e., only in its incipient stages—in essence, the situation had already begun to be critical for the constitutional authorities. For instance, with self-assured arrogance, the priest Domingo de Guezala issued manifesto-like orders to the towns' mayors demanding recruits to bolster the ranks of those struggling, as he put it, "in defense of the rights of our Catholic Monarch Ferdinand VII and the restoration of the Fueros of Vizcaya."[167]

Compounding constitutionalism's problems, fear of subversion in Bilbao was confirmed with the interception of correspondence between Guezala and Pacho Landa, a royalist captain of the Regular Militia in the city.[168] The sense of danger visibly increased as urban royalists—primarily of lower-class backgrounds, such as artisans, shopkeepers, smugglers, and others—started to defect to the rebels in large numbers.[169] In fact, after significant desertions from Bilbao in the spring of 1822, the situation appeared to become considerably more precarious for the authorities, and there was a tendency to succumb to the fear of encirclement. Alarmingly, an anonymous French correspondent writing from Bilbao asserted that the "Army of the Faith" surrounded the city.[170] To break the stranglehold, the Voluntary Militia of Bilbao and the regular army corps stationed there frequently ventured into the countryside to chase the rebels tirelessly. More often than not, however, the constitutionalists returned empty-handed after failing to engage the insurgents—the latter, continually warned in advance by the rural population.[171] Both politically and strategically, therefore, the linkage between the rural and urban royalist opposition was a profoundly troubling development for constitutionalism in the region.

As Fernando de Zavala, the priest Domingo de Guezala, and other royalist chieftains applied increasing pressure on Bilbao and other urban centers, matters took a turn for the worse for the constitutional system in mid-1822. Always attentive to important events on the other side of the border, the usually well-informed sous-préfet (sub-prefect) of Bayonne wrote in July:

> It is certain, even from the Spanish newspapers, that the insurrection makes great headway in Vizcaya. The insurgents are audacious; in broad daylight they enter the towns of some importance, commandeer arms, provisions, and money, and make recruits. The constitutional columns that are directed against them, composed of regular troops and militias, seem incapable of checking these disorders.[172]

Further complicating the general situation (as had occurred in December 1821), the authorities uncovered a royalist conspiracy in Bilbao in July–August 1822. This time, however, constitutionalism reacted more sharply. In response to the would-be seditious movement, and with the central government's complete backing, the authorities disarmed the Regular Militia of Bilbao, arrested several alleged royalist plotters and their sympathizers, and ordered the creation of the Holy Company of Elders alluded to earlier.[173] Predictably, the spiral of violence and frustration led to severe retaliations and counter-reprisals on both sides. During one such bloody incident in early August, thirteen constitutionalist soldiers were sacrificed at Durango by the royalists.[174] The reaction in Bilbao to the bloodbath at Durango was a series of violent outbursts, during which some of those suspected of being *serviles* (pro-monarchists) were abused, attacked, arrested, and swiftly deported.[175]

In a belated formalization of the civil war, the government in August 1822 decreed a state of war in the fifth military district—i.e., Northern Castile, the Basque provinces and Navarra.[176] And, in early September, the Cortes undertook a major counteroffensive against the insurgents, amassing large numbers of troops in the north. Tellingly, some of the constitutionalist corps were led by War of Independence veterans, themselves experts in guerrilla warfare.[177] Even though it is difficult to thoroughly evaluate the counterinsurgency campaign, it appears that the government forces made significant headway in late 1822 and early 1823. Regular army and militia units pushed the rebels into the mountains and succeeded in stabilizing the situation in the field to some extent.[178] However, despite ambitious attempts to relieve pressure from the beleaguered cities, and notwithstanding modest successes, the constitutionalists were unable to break the back of the insurrection. Inspired by the likelihood of a French intervention and the prestige of commanders Eguía and Quesada, the royalist rebels regrouped and once more threatened Bilbao in early 1823. To withstand an eventual direct attack, by January–February 1823, the city had in fact already undergone extensive fortification work, some of it done by radical French refugees sympathetic to the Cortes's cause.[179] Nor was Bilbao the only objective of the insurgents. From January 1823 on, the Defenders of the Faith demonstrated high levels of combativeness in numerous areas of Vizcaya.[180] On 3 April, only a week before the evacuation of Bilbao by the constitutionalist troops and authorities, royalist forces led by Zavala inflicted a severe defeat near Munguía upon a government column commanded by Colonel Juan Gómez Campillo.[181] However impressive these royalist victories, it is highly unlikely that the rebels could have tilted the military stalemate in their favor without French support. In other words, on the strength of indigenous forces alone, it is extremely improbable that royalism would have toppled constitutionalism in this region or elsewhere in Spain.

With some notable exceptions, the backbone of the Vizcayan royalist opposition was made up of the clergy and the lower social classes. Affected early and deeply by constitutional innovations, the clergy—given its influential role in society—became the logical rallying point of many other disparate elements that were in open conflict with reform. As noted before, numerous opponents of the constitution came from the lower orders of Vizcayan society, most notably artisans and peasants.[182] Moreover, linked to the peasant strata of the struggle were some of the more marginal elements of the rural world, namely, those without a fixed occupation or full-time profession—smugglers, criminals and social outcasts and, of course, the unemployed and the underemployed. For example, in light of the predominantly rural character of the insurrection, the interpenetration of smugglers with royalist forces was inevitable.[183] The contrabandists' knowledge of the terrain and experience in transportation made them valuable allies. In politically motivated attempts to discredit the opposition, though not without some justification, the constitutional authorities continually stressed the presence of criminals (e.g., "highway robbers") and other questionable elements, among the royalists.[184] In fact, the insurgents' leadership often included individuals who were a curious blend of social bandits, adventurers, and soldiers of fortune but, even more importantly, staunch defenders of traditional values and vested interests.[185] Finally, working with, or within, the rebel camp were what might be called the marginals of rural society. Constitutionalism, with a deeply ingrained upper-class contempt for its lower-class enemies, went out of its way to denounce the "rabble of starved, lazy and ill-kept men," who allegedly served the royalist partisans as informers and in other tasks in exchange for "a poor dinner and a jug of wine."[186] In the crisis-ridden societies of the ancien régime, with structural unemployment and underemployment, the human "reserve armies" in the countryside could in essence be maneuvered by the more powerful and conscious classes for the latter's own aims. And during the Trienio, reform's opponents appear to have skillfully used Vizcaya's marginals by playing upon a host of political circumstances and social antagonisms.

Lest it be thought otherwise, there were also important middle- and upper-class elements in the royalist opposition. Though small in numbers, they were nonetheless of immense qualitative significance. For the most part these men were (1) retired and active-duty military officers, and (2) government bureaucrats, as well as (3) prominent landowners. The first group was led by General Francisco de Eguía, an ultraroyalist whose reputation and extensive provincial ties made him a formidable enemy of the constitutional regime. Forced into exile, he became a tireless plotter from Bayonne.[187] The second category, that of the "bureaucratic-administrative" opposition, consisted primarily of important local traditionalists from the previous Diputación and customs administration.[188] Never reconciled to the loss of office and status and wishing to settle old scores, from all appearances this was a resentful and dangerous lot. Finally, the third category included several wealthy property holders such as the ubiquitous Marquis de Valde-espina, an unrelenting royalist activist, and José María de Jusué and Pedro Novia de Salcedo—the latter two considerably more circumspect but no less determined in their anticonstitutionalism.[189]

Both the role and the function of the middle- and upper-class opposition were markedly different from those of lower-class royalism. Except for Fernando de Zavala and one or two others, Vizcayan royalist magnates did not actually fight alongside the legitimist guerrillas. Rather, the activities of the "Eguía–Valde-espina" faction were primarily political, organizational, and financial. In other words, these notables used their status, wealth, political standing, and social connections to further the insurrection.[190] Loss of political power and prestige, as well as material concerns, undoubtedly propelled prominent oligarchs into anticonstitutionalist positions, but more strictly ideological and political motivations should certainly not be ruled out. This was particularly true of Vizcayan *foralistas* (or *fueristas*), diehard legitimists, devoutly religious individuals, and traditionalists deeply concerned by the sudden sweeping changes ushered in by the constitution. For instance, contrary to Rafael Gambra's assertions that the Basque privileges played little or no part in the 1821–1823 civil war, there is strong evidence that exactly the opposite was true.[191] Pointedly, in June 1821 the provincial governor of Vizcaya informed the central government that the local populations showed a "general tendency not to separate [themselves] from their former constitution."[192] This attitude was clearly fertile ground for the machinations of the insurgents' articulate foralistas.

In conclusion, despite the markedly popular backing of local anticonstitutionalism, the Trienio's sociopolitical contradictions cannot be reduced to a simple clash between the upper and lower classes. While it is true that the lower orders generally sided with the royalist opposition, on the other hand, in a peculiar form of intraclass rivalry, sharp cleavages nonetheless existed among the Vizcayan elites. While most of the province's merchant and professional classes (particularly in Bilbao) stubbornly upheld and defended the constitutional system, some landowners (both lay and clerical) op-

posed the legal and structural changes introduced by the new system. Also, the breakup of the traditional system of Vizcayan governance and administration had far-reaching consequences on the local
body politic, inasmuch as the process wrested the political monopoly
away from age-old gentry sectors, allowing new groups (especially
from the newer urban bourgeois elites) to capitalize on the redefi-
nition and redistribution of political power.[193] Most of the class and
group alliances of the Trienio, however, only become fully intelli-
gible when analyzed against (or as a function of) the all-essential
question of reform—be it political, administrative, fiscal, clerical, or
otherwise. Whereas only a limited social sector had an undeniable
stake in reform, most of the population—admittedly for conflicting
reasons—did not.

Large numbers of Vizcayans, including most of the peasantry and
other rural classes, undoubtedly resented the establishment of centralized taxation, compulsory military service, the transfer of the
customs bureaus to the coast, and other unsettling innovations such
as the introduction of stamped paper. As Joaquín del Moral Ruiz's
excellent studies have shown, the Cortes's measures profoundly and
adversely affected the Spanish peasantry.[194] Moreover, as some texts
explicitly suggest, urban master artisans (along with their employees) and shopkeepers were hurt by the central government's trade
measures. Initially, in late 1820–early 1821, some skilled craftsmen
quite probably suffered when the Bilbao commercial bourgeoisie
glutted the local markets with foreign goods. Ironically, such craftsmen, as well as retailers and shopkeepers, may have also been subsequently harmed in the economic slump which, according to some,
resulted from constitutionalism's protectionist 1820–1821 measures.[195] Whatever the actual impact of the Cortes's policies upon
the Vizcayan economy—something open to further study and debate
—there is solid evidence that the constitutional authorities were
worried about the obvious links between economic depression, unemployment, and the royalist opposition. On occasion, in fact, the
constitutionalists attempted to enroll the Vizcayan unemployed in
public works projects in order to diminish the potential menace.[196] If
perhaps indirectly, the constitutional system also touched the province's marginals and the poor, social elements that previously had
found greater protection under the paternalistic church-dominated
system of charity. The Cortes attacked the clergy's material foundations but, in the process, cut much-needed aid from those heavily

dependent on clerical relief and employment. In turn, the ecclesiastical establishment, when faced with the reforms of its sociopolitical antagonists, could easily rally its clientele and simultaneously serve as a key link between lower-class discontent and upper-class aspirations.

As a sponsor of—and an active collaborator in—reform policies, Vizcayan constitutionalism found painfully few political allies in the province during the Trienio. Its isolation was so great, in fact, that the only assistance local constitutionalism could seriously rely on was that of the central government. In this situation, somewhat ironically, Madrid came to be Vizcayan liberalism's only firm supporter. Against an imposing array of royalist political and military forces, and with much-needed government aid, Vizcayan constitutionalism managed to survive until French interventionists (the self-styled Sons of Saint Louis) acted in tandem with Spain's most conservative classes and "restored" Ferdinand VII to the throne in the spring of 1823. The forces of reaction, swiftly triumphant, would immediately turn to undoing the constitutional legacy and abolishing the remnants of the Trienio. Beyond the main objective of restoring the political structures of absolutism, the victors would now attempt a full-scale counterrevolution.

CHAPTER 3

In Search of the Old Order: Conservatism and the Fueros

In effect no innovation is prudent in Vizcaya, and the general echo of integral Fueros without modifications already resounds in its mountains. It is time to restore Vizcaya in the fullness of its rights.

Petition of the Vizcayan Diputación to the Regency, 9 June 1823.

Under the pretense of maintaining the integrity of their entitled Fueros, there has arisen a system of opposition to all of the ideas, and even the most beneficial projects, that His Majesty and his enlightened government adopt for his peoples in order to promote public prosperity.

Legal brief issued by prosecuting attorneys of the Supreme Council of Finance, concerning the exploitation of mines in the Basque provinces, 20 November 1828.

I. SETTING THE TREND: PRELUDE TO A COUNTERREVOLUTION

The aftermath of constitutional rule in Vizcaya was rich in substance and consequence. Following the constitutionalists' hurried evacuation of Bilbao the local royalists, scarcely missing a beat, moved swiftly to fill the political and military vacuum. In just a few weeks, under the watchful eye of first the royalist Provisional Junta of Government (*Junta Provisional de Gobierno*), then that of the Regency (*Regencia*)—the highest national authorities pending the monarch's "liberation"—and with the full cooperation of the French allies, the Vizcayan Diputación, corregimiento, municipality of Bilbao, and Consulado (now rid of constitutionalists) were restored by royalists to their traditional structure.[1] These changes were achieved without major complications or opposition. However, in the Trienio's wake the provincial and regional authorities were confronted with significant problems. Among them were (1) the treatment of the vanquished constitutionalists, (2) the organization of royalist militias and paramilitary corps, (3) the preservation of public order and internal security, (4) the relationship with outside military commanders—French as well as Spanish—and other centers of power, and (5) the reestablishment in its totality of the government of the fueros (*régimen foral*) including the perennially thorny issue of the customs bureaus. How each of these was addressed by the triumphant Vizcayan establishment during these early stages would set the tone and, more importantly, the pattern for the remainder of the so-called Ominous Decade (1823–1833).

First, the constitutionalists' plight after the Cortes's demise in Vizcaya was certainly a dramatic one, suffering consistently as they did from a triple form of repression—politico-legal, economic, and physical. Pointedly, as the authorities were restored, known constitutionalists were summarily purged from office, and still others were officially barred from future participation in public life.[2] And as a result of the important spring 1823 measures, royalists would possess a legal monopoly over Vizcayan political life for the next ten years. Further, the local authorities, often in a clear mood of vindictiveness and retaliation, issued stern ordinances curtailing the constitutionalists' rights and privileges: among them those of assembly, travel and movement, association, speech, possession of firearms (even when used for hunting purposes), and other important freedoms.[3] What made these restrictions even more hateful to constitutionalists is that they were often enacted by the authorities in bad faith—i.e., under the cynical pretext of safeguarding the former's security and well-being when, in fact, their repressive intent was manifestly transparent. The pocketbooks of the defeated would also be directly affected. In what amounted to virtual extortion, constitutionalists—especially the returning ones—were repeatedly fined and subjected to other financial hardships by the authorities.[4] Beyond individuals, clearly group and class animosities were also at stake. In the words of the newly restored municipality of Bilbao, "the wealthy class of Bilbao in its majority [had] been implicated in the false march of the constitutional system."[5] Accordingly, royalist policymakers as a whole showed little sympathy for the economic predicaments of their political antagonists. Finally, physical attacks, harassment, and abuse against known constitutionalists were to become painful realities from 1823 to at least 1825 (and possibly later). In the super-charged atmosphere of a nascent though already potent reaction, royalists repeatedly vented their frustrations upon those who until so recently had been their political masters. To the French allies' chagrin, with the tables turned defenseless constitutionalists found themselves the object of a steady stream of largely spontaneous royalist vendettas and insults. Bloody incidents in Bilbao alone between June and December 1823 left one constitutionalist dead and several seriously injured.[6] In sum, a many-sided *revanchisme* (vendetta) against the vanquished was at work from the restoration's very outset.

Second, to defend the territory against the constitutionalists' return and to ensure internal security, the authorities vigorously organized and promoted royalist military corps and militias: *Guardias de Honor, Batallones de Vizcaya, Armamento General del País*, and *Miqueletes*.[7] These bodies, both urban and rural, underwent several reorganizations in the course of 1823. Through the tireless efforts of conservatives, in time these urban and rural royalist forces would coalesce into the armed wing of the Vizcayan establishment and into a permanent and formidable anticonstitutionalist (antirevolutionary), politico-military organization.[8] However, if these bodies served as an effective bulwark against political change and reform, through the mid-1820s they would be the source of repeated public disorders and excesses, particularly in Bilbao.

Third, following constitutionalism's defeat, the maintenance of order and social peace was a central preoccupation of the municipal and provincial authorities. Interestingly, as noted above, the challenge came not from the left but from the ultraright, especially from the royalist volunteers created and sponsored by the municipality of Bilbao in the early stages of the reaction. Often tacitly condoned by a local retributive officialdom that (quite wrongly) tended to blame the constitutionalist victims for their dramatic fate, royalist excesses in Vizcaya, however, were firmly denounced by the French allies.[9] In the process, because of their perceived role as protectors of known constitutionalists and in view of their general sociopolitical moderation, the French earned the animosity of numerous lower-class Vizcayan royalists. Moreover, friction with the local authorities rose sharply following the issuance of the famous Ordinance of Andújar (August 1823) by the French military high command.[10] In essence, so deeply concerned were the French about the treatment of constitutionalist prisoners by the restored authorities throughout Spain that the allies attempted—successfully in part—to take over certain police, security, and legal responsibilities normally in the hands of the local civilian and military bodies. Refusing to give in to French demands, the Vizcayan authorities instead chose to try to end the frequent disturbances and abuses by issuing numerous charters and ordinances in 1823—ironically, as noted previously, some of the toughest of them against the hapless constitutionalist partisans— for the preservation of order.[11] So tense was the situation in Bilbao at year's end, that the Diputación even threatened to move the seat of government to another site unless the "democratic furor" did not end forthwith. Nor was the Vizcayan clergy's role a conciliatory or peaceful one. There is ample proof that revengeful ecclesiastics promoted discord, openly exhorting local royalists (through sermons and other means) against the Cortes's former adherents and sympathizers.[12] Finally, though apparently not as severe as earlier outbreaks of banditry which occurred after wars and conflicts, notably those of 1793–1795 and 1808–1813, a wave of lawlessness rippled through the Vizcayan countryside after the constitutional experience. The challenge, accompanied by a rise in smuggling, was met by the authorities in part with the formation of rural militias and the reestablishment of the Miqueletes, a traditional type of provincial gendarmerie.[13] Notwithstanding these efforts, some aspects of public order in Vizcaya remained clearly precarious through the mid-1820s.

Four, from the beginning of the 1823 restoration, the Vizcayan authorities' interaction with outside commanders and other political powers was often stormy. As the local ruling classes abruptly and boldly attempted to reclaim age-old prerogatives and authority lost under constitutionalism, conflicts with others invariably arose over a broad spectrum of issues and policy. Some of the disputes— especially those pitting the French command against the Diputación and municipality of Bilbao—acquired acrimonious tones. General Bruny, the head of the allied forces in Bilbao, in particular could not resist lecturing the local authorities regarding their glaring failings and laxity vis-à-vis royalist excesses in that city.[14] Offended and responding in unusually heated language, the Vizcayan establishment vehemently rejected the accusations. Though much of the friction with the allies resulted from basic political and ideological differences, traditional local anti-French and xenophobic sentiments were also patently at work.

Fifth, in the political reaction following the Cortes's overthrow in Vizcaya, royalism and the observance of the fueros (*foralismo*) developed a tighter relationship and overlapped to the point of becoming indistinguishable politico-ideological phenomena. The intense identification of absolutism and "legitimate authority" with the cause of the provincial liberties, a hallmark of the 1823 restoration, was at once reminiscent of the Napoleonic Era and a harbinger of Carlism. Regnaudin correctly remarked early on: "One can easily observe the royalism of Vizcayans, who regard the fall of constitutional power as an opportunity to recapture their privileges in all their intensity."[15] In other words, after the de facto abolition of some of the liberties by the constitutional system—e.g., customs offices and taxation— Vizcayans moved quickly to recover their ancient laws. Moreover, having purportedly been on the verge of losing them altogether, the freedoms had become even more significant to Vizcayans. Consequently, during the 1823–1833 political reaction, the fueros would be tenaciously defended by the region's political classes. In the quest for the return of the legal and institutional structures of the old order, the May 1823 Vizcayan juntas unquestionably played a crucial role.[16] Held in an atmosphere of fierce anticonstitutionalism and militant foralismo, the two-week parley was abundant proof that Vizcaya had regained its political identity and legitimacy. Tackling the important question of the hard-pressed provincial finances and in actions sure to displease merchants, landowners, and the wealthier classes in general, the juntas exacted an interest-free forced loan of 500,000 reales from the Bilbao business community and slapped a 10 percent surcharge on properties.[17] And continuing earlier political exclusions, in a far-reaching move the juntas barred constitutionalists from participation in the assembly and from holding office in the provincial government. Lastly, in keeping with the pronounced pro-fueros feelings of the moment, the May 1823 gathering urged the Diputación to strongly petition the Spanish authorities for the return of the customs offices to their pre-Trienio locations—an objective that, to the local authorities' profound irritation, would not be achieved immediately.[18] Constitutionalism, however, could not officially end until the monarch was released from his "captivity" in the south. When news arrived in October 1823 that Ferdinand VII was free at last, the Vizcayan Diputación, with even more determination than before, turned to the fundamental task of fully reconquering the cherished provincial freedoms.

II. THE IDEOLOGICAL FOUNDATIONS OF VIZCAYAN CONSERVATISM

Vizcayan conservatism did not differ significantly from traditionalist politico-philosophical currents dominant elsewhere in Spain except for one peculiarity: the "immemorial" provincial and regional privileges. Ultimately, of course, the fueros were the distinctive element that helped to define the Basque region's specificity and uniqueness, as well as some of its most striking political, legal, and ideological characteristics.[19] More practically, the liberties served as an effective shield against the central government. It is therefore impossible to find a single significant area of public policy where the royal administration's actions did not openly clash with the privileges or, more precisely, with their use by the Basque ruling elites. This was no different in the 1823–1833 decade, a situation made even more remarkable by the seemingly shared conservatism and numerous points of convergence of the restored authorities in the Basque provinces and in Madrid.

For instance, absolutism was undoubtedly one of the principal politico-ideological tenets of Vizcayan conservatism. Under a panoply of labels and ready-made phrases, such as the "sacred and legitimate rights" or the "fullness of the rights" of the throne and monarch, the Vizcayan political classes enthusiastically cast their lot with absolutist rule following the 1823 restoration.[20] Significantly, absolutist sentiment was also deeply rooted among a broad cross section of the province's masses. After all, adversely affected by the Cortes's reforms, they too had opposed the representative government that was generally favored by upper-class Vizcayan constitutionalists.[21] Hence the early and firm Vizcayan support for Fernandine absolutism—a type of government that, interestingly, was far more absolutist in form than in content. In other words, given the widespread and unsettling changes of the Trienio, the Vizcayan leadership attempted to fully reaffirm traditional royal prerogatives in the ensuing political reaction, and did so with the full backing of the population. As might be readily imagined, this political support was scarcely altruistic. By restoring the status quo ante—i.e., the period before the "infamous" events of 7 March 1820—and by reemphasizing the monarch's purportedly untrammeled powers, the Vizcayan elites hoped to restore relations between the province and the crown to their presumably contractual status. Fundamentally, this meant that from a mere province within a nation-state (as was the case during constitutionalism) Vizcaya was reverting to its conspicuous and highly privileged position of a seigniory within an absolute monarchy, one ruled by a normally sympathetic lord-master. Moreover, since after the Napoleonic Era autocratic rule was thought by many Vizcayans to specifically safeguard the fueros, quite naturally, much of the province's population sided with this form of monarchical government. As Regnaudin repeatedly pointed out, Vizcayans would generally tend to support an absolutist regime as long as the latter was willing to uphold the fueros. With heavy sarcasm, the commercial agent was critical of Vizcayans: "The inhabitants here demand an absolute king and they do not want to pay either with their bodies or with their fortunes!"[22] In conclusion, far from reciprocal in obligations, absolutism appeared to require few sacrifices and personal services from Vizcayans.

As in the rest of Spain, the Vizcayans' embrace of absolutism was accompanied by a staunch defense of religion and the "sacred rights of the altar." In early 1824, for instance, the municipality of Bilbao vigorously demanded the restoration of the Inquisition. According to the petition, probably written by then councilman Pedro Novia de Salcedo, "it is abundantly known that the primary cause of the evils that have afflicted Spain has proceeded from the destruction of religious principles."[23] In this popular view, given the "insidious" work of masonic reformers during the Trienio (and other related evils), it was high time to return the nation to the strictest form of religion—namely that of the Holy Office—using it as a weapon against political, spiritual, and ideological subversion. The climate was right for a religious counterrevolution.

Fresh from recent anticlericalism, fully reinstated in the possession of its prerogatives, and under the authorities' benevolent protection, the Vizcayan clergy's presence was apparent in the early stages of the 1823 restoration.[24] For example, with frenetic exhortations, preachers from the regular orders and members of the secular clergy repeatedly aroused the population against known constitutionalists and reformers. Reporting one of the many incidents, Regnaudin said in March 1824: "I attended several sermons; it is impossible to describe the expressions of vengeance predicated by the ministers of a God of peace."[25] Possibly influenced by the clergy, the local authorities made good use of the pervasive climate of sociopolitical and religious reaction to further a campaign of moral reaction.[26] For example, in October 1825 the Vizcayan Diputación, taking note of the "well-justified complaints of zealous parish priests," launched an attack on reputed obscenity and indecency.[27] "Public morality" and "good customs" also found a ready defense in 1826 with the confiscation by the authorities of an 1827 calendar said to contain illustrations offensive to "public decency."[28] Similarly, after the interception in October 1824 of a shipment of forbidden works sent to Juan Bautista de Landeza, a former constitutionalist *miliciano*, the prosecutor thundered against books that "undoubtedly taught impiety, irreligion, and immorality," and contributed to the decline of the "Holy Religion."[29] Significantly as well, royal authority and religious principles were cozily at work with one another. A July 1824 circular of the Vizcayan Diputación, for instance, warned of punishment against the king's detractors as well as against those who criticized the Catholic Faith and its ministers.[30] In sum, in key ways religion and politics continually interacted in the public arena during the early stages of the 1823–1833 decade.

Not surprisingly, in this atmosphere numerous Vizcayan clerics sympathized with political authoritarianism and, as the 1823–1833 decade progressed, some became openly involved with ultrarightist political movements.[31] A case in point: during Bessières's ill-fated 1825 uprising, although no insurrection seconded his efforts in Vizcaya, his actions found a certain echo in the province. In fact, even if little came of it, there was apparently already talk in Bilbao of a local clerically led junta, thought to be strongly pro-Inquisition and pro–Don Carlos in orientation.[32] There is also evidence that in the 1823 restoration's later stages, sectors of the Vizcayan clergy—notably the Franciscans—joined with legitimists and well-known ultras (*apostólicos*) to advance the Carlist pretender's absolutist cause.[33]

In addition to the realms of the temporal and the divine, Vizcayan conservatism was acutely aware that a struggle between absolutism and the forces of change was being waged simultaneously on many fronts—national and international—and with a rich diversity of actors—declared and undeclared—in a variety of means and methods—open and covert. According to this view, the entire world was the scene of an ongoing, all-out confrontation inexorably pitting legitimate authority and religion against their sworn enemies. In a Manichean political and ideological universe, it was essentially a battle of right and wrong, good and evil. Interestingly, despite important setbacks for the forces of change—1823 in Spain would surely qualify—the cancer of subversion had never been totally extirpated. In what are probably the words of Novia de Salcedo, "the revolution has stopped, it has changed its course but has not been destroyed."[34] Hence the need for eternal vigilance to resist the "revolutionary hydra"—i.e., that "ominous monster" created, financed, and led by the secret sects to promote anarchy and change. Unquestionably sincere in its convictions, Vizcayan conservatism, however, was quick to ascribe any adversity to the "evil" machinations of freemasonry and its political foes.[35] Understandably therefore, Vizcayan conservatism closely followed its constitutionalist opponents' fortunes. News of the latest national occurrences—in particular would-be plots and conspiracies—apparently arrived swiftly in Vizcaya. In turn, these political developments became the object of passionate and important discussions that contributed to the formation of local public opinion.[36]

Vizcayan police files also confirm that the province's royalists and constitutionalists maintained more than a passing interest in international political affairs, including those of the former colonies. A fairly typical mid-1820s entry in a police register reads, "the news concerning the progress of Portuguese royalist arms is well received; constitutionalists expect the English to protect the cause in Portugal."[37] Since each local camp saw itself as the extension of broader international struggles, political alignments in Vizcaya became automatic: royalists sided with legitimists everywhere and the Portuguese *Miguelistas* in particular, while liberals identified with English, French, and other reform-oriented movements such as Don Pedro's cause in Portugal. Consequently, in the mid and late 1820s the Vizcayan political classes kept a close watch upon events in Portugal, where English-backed constitutionalism posed serious challenges both to Portuguese absolutism and to the European conservative bloc.[38]

For these reasons and following the central government's lead as well, Vizcayan conservatism tried hard to isolate local society from foreign politico-ideological contagion. However, resistance to, and distrust of, foreign influences consistently led the provincial authorities and much of the population to ugly xenophobic stances, both explicit and implicit.[39] The French commercial agent's correspondence of the Ominous Decade is replete with complaints of attacks, harassment, and abuse—some of it plainly political—against his fellow countrymen in Vizcaya.[40] Nor was xenophobia (and in particular Francophobia) a monopoly of the ruling classes. In fact, it was a deep-rooted historical sentiment that had been recently compounded by the multiple links of Vizcayan reformers to foreign political practice and thought. Vizcayan xenophobia was not, however, based solely on politico-ideological considerations. Understandably, much of its raison d'être was derived directly from historical, local socioeconomic factors. In essence, following long-standing protectionist policies, during the 1823–1833 decade the Vizcayan authorities consistently defended native artisans and merchants against foreign competitors. For instance, at the May 1824 juntas Bilbao's delegates decried the "excessive" number of foreigners—most probably small merchants, shopkeepers, and artisans—in the Señorío without having fulfilled the basic residency requirements, namely, proof of nobility and "purity of blood."[41] The Diputación was particularly receptive to these accusations. While sincere in its intentions the provincial government, by constantly raising the specter of undesirable outsiders, and by moving to control their numbers (through harassment and other means), catered neatly both to the economic interests of its urban clientele and to the politico-ideological concerns of traditionalists. There is evidence that the difficult-to-satisfy requirements, grounded legally in the fueros, were conveniently revived in the 1820s after decades of nonobservance or, at best, mild enforcement.[42] Complementing the pervasive antiforeigner attitudes, the Vizcayan establishment repeatedly attempted to assert the wholesomeness of the provincial population (especially that of the rural sectors), extolling the virtues of local customs and tradition.

In opposition to cosmopolitanism and foreign influences, Vizcayan restorationist leaders glorified the countryside's inhabitants, creating an attractive peasant motif—that bucolic intent embodied purity, simplicity, fidelity, honesty, and laboriousness.[43] In fact, the ideal of the "pure royalist labourer" (praised by the Carlist sympathizer Henningsen) became central to Vizcayan conservatism in theory and in practice.[44] Basically, this meant that the countryside was regarded as the depository of tradition and the privileges, as well as the bulwark against change and revolution. Given the enormous strength of royalism among the peasantry, the "rural" political line pursued by the Vizcayan ruling elites appears to have been right on the mark. Regnaudin summed it up well early in the restoration: "the discontented are not to be found in the countryside . . . royalists all, guided by the fire of religion and armed in great part, it would not be easy to defeat them."[45] On a more strictly ideological level, Vizcayan conservatism was rooted in appeals to tradition and denunciations of potentially disruptive innovations. The writings of Novia de Salcedo—unquestionably the period's chief Vizcayan political tory, traditionalist ideologue, and the very embodiment of the political reaction—are laden with stinging criticisms of "abstract reason," the Enlightenment, and other manifestations of "modernism."[46] Ironically, for a thinker who more often than not so vehemently rejected foreign philosophical currents, these views clearly formed part of the well-known, early nineteenth-century Romantic revolt against reason. According to this author, established values were quite naturally preferable over purely theoretical and untested reforms, no matter how attractive the latter.[47] More to the point perhaps, against nationalism's philosophical doctrines that purportedly stressed universal equality and human rights, Novia de Salcedo counterposed Vizcaya's and the Basque province's historical uniqueness. In so doing, he was trying to erect a solid, conservative, ideological shield for the region vis-à-vis the era's dangerous onslaught of "leveling" trends.

Of profound concern to the Vizcayan leadership, the Enlightenment had ushered in political and philosophical tendencies that, with negative connotations, came to be commonly known in the province as "universal leveling" (*nivelación universal*).[48] Allegedly propounded by state innovators and reformers, in Novia de Salcedo's view universal leveling was clearly aimed at equalization and uniformity. In other words, Vizcaya was besieged, and its very identity threatened, by "levelers" (*niveladores*) seeking independence and harmony through privilege eradication and the abolition of regional "anomalities." Novia de Salcedo and fellow Basque conservatives knew all too well that it would be virtually impossible to safeguard regional pluralism and diversity in a political system of national integration. In their view, the successful application of leveling policies by a national government was certain to undermine—and possibly even obliterate altogether—local uniqueness, tradition, provincial institutions, and of course the fueros. Hence the pressing need for strong and concerted attacks, such as the incisive ones of Novia de Salcedo, against the ideological underpinnings and political indications of universal leveling. Nor were Vizcayan assaults on nivelación limited to abstract or theoretical arguments. In fact, consistent with activist practices regarding crucial political and legal questions, throughout 1823–1833, the Vizcayan Diputación aggressively challenged universal leveling in numerous petitions to the king and the central government.[49]

Still, the mere denunciation of leveling was apparently insufficient to totally satisfy Vizcayan conservatism's political and ideological purposes. To fully assert Vizcaya's uniqueness (and that of the rest of the Basque provinces as well) it was conceptually imperative for local traditionalism to convincingly prove the complete independence and separation of the province and region from the rest of Spain. In essence, if the territory had been free of the Spanish (or Castilian) yoke, with what right did levelers now attempt to destroy the Basques' "immemorial" rights and the region's very sovereignty? A bold and risky political endeavor, this Vizcayan line of argumentation was certain to meet with displeasure at the highest levels of the central government. This might account for the fact that, although completed in 1829, Novia de Salcedo's extraordinarily daring polemical *Defensa* was not published until 1851. In this no-holds-barred apologia of the Basque provinces, the author expanded anticentralism, regionalism, and particularism into a coherent demonstration of his native land's historical separation and independence from Spain. According to Novia de Salcedo, every major sphere of human activity in that region embodied irrefutable proof of these contentions. Pointedly, a concluding chapter to the second volume was provocatively entitled "Concept of separate and distinct from Castile that the Basque Provinces have enjoyed after their union to the Crown." And Novia de Salcedo, in an iconoclastic vein, was not afraid to pose rhetorically, and answer bluntly, highly sensitive and controversial questions: "What point of contact or similarity do [the Basque provinces] have with the Crown of Castile? Not even the slightest."[50] Elsewhere he insisted that the Basque laws were "completely different from those of Castile," a claim repeatedly made throughout the *Defensa.*[51] But, as in the case of the fueros, where theory and practice were seldom far apart, Novia de Salcedo's profoundly regionalistic and separatist theses, extreme as they might appear at first blush, were nonetheless perfectly in keeping with the traditional "common front" political tactics and strategy of the

Basque diputaciones.[52] Joint conferences in the Basque provinces and well-orchestrated united stances in Madrid formed part of a general policy with which the regional leaderships resisted economic and political assimilation, as well as centralist encroachment. Largely in response to the state's actions and demands, the Basque rulers held eleven conferences between 1824 and 1833—nine consultations alone during the 1827–1833 period, when relations between the region and the central powers had become noticeably strained.[53] Undeniably, Basque resistance to incorporationist currents emanating from Madrid already contained many of Carlism's regional elements. In sum, for the region's conservatives (including many Navarrans), there was a fundamental link between the defense of local interests and the preservation of autocratic legitimism. And this was, of course, in direct opposition to structural, political, and administrative reforms (such as those of the Cortes) that might introduce modifications in the special relationship between the state and the region, in the Basque institutions and modes of government and, most particularly, in their original laws or fueros.

To Novia de Salcedo and most Vizcayan conservatives, the provincial liberties were unquestionably one of the most convincing manifestations of the region's uniqueness.[54] Carrying this argument still further, an undaunted Novia de Salcedo postulated outright: "If attention is given to [the Basque] legislation everything concurs to the same end; to prove [the territory's] independence."[55] Again, this was a powerful way of counterposing regional interests—via the fueros—to Castile's and the state's centralist and homogenizing designs. However, these assertions—and, more importantly, the political praxis of the Basque elites (see the next chapter)—led to constant and significant tension between the region and the central government over an impressive array of issues. Not strangely therefore, the Vizcayan fueros were also engulfed in controversy during the Ominous Decade, resulting in their eventual review by the central government.

III. THE CHALLENGE OF THE FUEROS

In the Vizcayan establishment's view, after the 1823 restoration—far from strictly observing the privileges—the royal administration began to infringe upon them consistently. Even if the alleged encroachment was indirect, half-hearted and ultimately ineffectual, Vizcayan conservatives were alarmed and dismayed by the central government's actions, especially given the province's—and for that matter the entire region's—unswerving loyalty to royalism during the constitutional era. After all, as the crown openly admitted in 1824, had not the Basques sacrificed so much of themselves and rendered such valuable services to restore the monarch's legitimate rights?[56] In the lengthy and often heated disputes of the period, it is essential not to be misled by the apparently shared conservatism of the parties. Considerably more than ideology was at stake. It should now be abundantly clear that Vizcayan traditionalism, though thoroughly orthodox and undoubtedly royalist, defended particular regional interests. Conversely the central administration, politically stodgy as it was, found it necessary to challenge parts of the provincial freedoms in order to begin the task of forging a truly national government. The constant and mutual recriminations, the sharp accusations and countercharges, and in brief the jockeying of the 1823–1833 decade were all eerily prophetic of far larger subsequent clashes pitting the center against the northern region.

Either in a mildly facetious or suspiciously naive vein, Regnaudin remarked in 1826: "I have heard it said that the privileges were a heavy burden to [Vizcaya's] trade; this is perhaps one of the reasons they are so coveted."[57] Though impressionistic, the commercial agent's suggestive observations—indeed the very notion—of the liberties' value are profoundly important. At the heart of the matter were key (and still largely unanswered) questions regarding the socioeconomic cost of the freedoms. For example, were they profitable to the señorío's population as a whole? If not, then which social strata did they benefit and which ones did they not? Or else could it be, as some claimed, that they were in fact a net liability for the province? The debate, which began to crystallize with some intensity in the 1820s and 1830s, was far from academic. Lacking the necessary in-depth cost-benefit analyses to ascertain the freedoms' actual advantage or burden, one must rely instead on common socioeconomic and political opinions and attitudes. Generally, conservatism, representing the majority of Vizcayans—peasants and artisans—loudly proclaimed its beneficence. On the other hand, constitutionalism, speaking in the main for a compact and powerful bourgeois minority—commercial classes, large landholders, and some influential professionals—had already begun to question the fueros' value.[58]

Concretely, according to this line of thought, if extensive exemptions shielded Vizcaya from national fiscal obligations and social responsibilities, then by virtue of the same privileges the province was subjected to unfavorable economic policies by the central government. For instance, when Vizcayan iron and other manufactures were treated as foreign commodities by the ministry, de facto independence was not (as Novia de Salcedo would have argued) to the advantage of the province's industries but indeed to their detriment. Still, given the right and ability to import duty-free nearly every conceivable good and enjoy other protections from centralist taxes and military service, Vizcayans were quite possibly justified in regarding the franchises as essential to their socioeconomic well-being.[59] In many respects the debate over the value of the fueros essentially reflected the rapidly growing conflict between domestic producers and consumers: the former interests increasingly opposed to the liberties, the latter ones continuing their long-held attachment to them. More to the point perhaps, irrespective of the fueros' actual or objective worth—again, a crucial issue upon which there was little agreement—the freedoms were at all times perceived or regarded as advantageous by the majority of Vizcayans. Any weakening of the freedoms or their possible abolition (clearly an even more dire prospect), was therefore bound to have a negative impact upon the fueros' defenders and, in the process, perhaps also alter the local social balance of forces. In any case, such unwelcome eventualities were sure to be greeted with considerable opposition from most of the Vizcayan population. Consequently, the Diputación's unrelenting stewardship of the liberties during the 1823–1833 decade consistently met with the province's nearly unanimous approval.

Equally true, however, the Vizcayan establishment's unyielding posture concerning the freedoms inevitably placed the province and the central government on a collision course over a host of contentious matters. In areas of monetary donations and taxes, trade and commerce, customs bureaus and smuggling, military and police affairs, the status of foreigners in the region, mineral and natural resources, legal proceedings involving the manner in which municipal elections were held, and even in the central government's 1824 amnesty declaration, the royal administration's policies became hopelessly entangled in liberties-related considerations.[60] In effect, aided by the privileges' breadth and strength, Vizcaya was able to resist and obstruct key central government measures. So widespread was the opposition that well-informed and normally sympathetic foreign observers even charged the provincial authorities with an excessive, albeit expansionist, interpretation of the privileges.[61] The Diputación's handling of the privileges would certainly not escape local constitutionalist criticism nor the crown's and the central government's displeasure.[62]

Broad challenges to administration policies, as well as disobedience of royal orders based on the liberties, led to a gradual but visible hardening of the central government's attitude toward the Basque region as the Ominous Decade wore on. For example, in the face of resistance, irritation cumulatively gave way to extreme annoyance and strident censure of the diputaciones' purported abuses committed under the aegis of the privileges. Some measure of the central administration's growing exasperation can be glimpsed in a severe 1829 indictment of the Vizcayan Diputación's actions by attorneys for the Ministry of Finance. In a legal brief they sharply attacked the provincial government's "arbitrariness" and "transgressions" against the state. The scathing statement—which included significant threats and hints of retaliation—made an extraordinarily serious charge which accused the señorío of loosening all bonds of subordination to the monarch. Wrote the ministry's attorneys in a crucial and memorable passage:

> [The Diputación] seems to aspire to becoming independent at least in the matters that have been the object of its unlawful deliberations, exercising a legislative and coactive power only reserved to the Sovereign, and constituting what statesmen call *status in status*, a most criminal absurdity, as it wounds the most sacred of royal authority, undermines the imprescriptible and eminent royal prerogatives of sovereignty; and should it not be repressed with an iron hand, it might become the source of the most nefarious consequences.[63]

To comprehend more fully the royal administration's mounting disenchantment with Basque officialdom and its manipulation of the freedoms, the mid-1820s provide an excellent point of reference.

One of the earliest indications of explicit central government dissatisfaction with the handling of the fueros by the diputaciones occurred in September 1825 when Luis de Salazar, minister of the navy and a native Vizcayan, sharply denounced the formers' "extravagant demands under the pretext of [the] Basque privileges."[64] Given the

Basque provinces'—and most particularly Vizcaya's—opposition to a wide spectrum of policies emanating from Madrid, combined with the intransigent defense of the fueros following the 1823 restoration, Salazar's remarks appear quite justified. A November 1825 communication of the Diputación to Novia de Salcedo, then its chief envoy or commissioner in Madrid, amply illustrates the provincial leadership's recalcitrance with respect to the freedoms. The revealing letter reads in part: "[Novia de Salcedo] is ordered to inform the Council of Ministers that Vizcaya will never consent to even the most minor alteration in its Fueros."[65] On the surface at least, this tough position was at considerable variance with Vizcaya's proclaimed and unswerving loyalty to the monarch, a pledge repeatedly articulated in firm though extremely deferential petitions to Ferdinand VII and his administrators throughout the 1823–1833 decade. Clearly, the obvious chasm between the Diputación's actions and its professed allegiance to the crown understandably deepened the central government's misgivings about the liberties. Worth underscoring, neither the crown nor the royal administration as a whole appear to have harbored a particular animosity against the Basques *qua* Basques or against the Basque provinces. However, increasingly aware that the privileges hampered royal policymaking, the central government during the second half of the 1820s began to warn the Vizcayan Diputación of the limits of its fueros so that it would immediately cease its "equivocal" use of them.[66] Still, despite the royal administration's increasing irritation over the Basques' "misuse" of their franchises, available evidence simply does not sustain the view that the state seriously planned the fueros' abolition nor envisaged any fundamental modifications in the region's institutions during the Ominous Decade. A December 1825 session of the Council of Ministers, in fact, tellingly reveals that Ferdinand VII wanted to preserve the freedoms.[67] Even the normally wary Vizcayan Diputación was reassured by the king's benevolence vis-à-vis the liberties. For instance, in January 1826, a visibly satisfied provincial leadership wrote Novia de Salcedo that Ferdinand VII's recent actions—referral of important Basque petitions to the conservative Council of State and the start of negotiations with the region's representatives—were "proof of the affection that [the king] professes [for] them and of the desire of conserving their Fueros and privileges despite the innovative ideas that some have formed."[68]

Rather than seeking to abrogate the freedoms altogether, it seems

that at most the king and his advisers sought to weaken the fueros'
strength through propaganda, coercion, and administrative measures. Such a strategy, if successful, would bring tangible bonuses to
the central powers. First, inflated Basque claims about their freedoms
would be discredited. Second, the diputaciones' stranglehold over
the privileges might well be loosened. Third, the ensuing Basque
defensiveness would probably redress political relations with the region, tilting them in the royal administration's favor. Fourth, from
a position of greater strength, the crown would be in a far better
position to elicit concessions from the Basque provinces and effectively enforce controversial measures in the region. It is of course
possible that the general review of the Basque fueros (launched by
the crown during the early 1830s), a move accompanied by the publication of Tomás González's mammoth *Colección* (1829–1833)—
a move nearly identical to Godoy's 1805–1808 inspection of the
freedoms and Llorente's *Noticias*—was merely a well-orchestrated
prologue to a more determined subsequent attack against the liberties. But whether this was Madrid's intention remains a matter of
conjecture.[69]

Naturally, a frontal assault on the fueros by the central government would have been an extraordinarily difficult and perilous undertaking. Among the important factors preventing an active anti-
liberties policy were the widespread influence of the Basque party
at court and throughout the royal administration, as well as the
monarchy's political and military weaknesses. The king himself was
acutely aware of the limits of royal power and, by extension, of the
need to pursue a somewhat moderate and flexible conduct toward
the freedoms while maintaining substantial political pressure on
the diputaciones. Ferdinand VII appears to have sensed correctly
that outright force against the region could prove counterproductive and perhaps even reckless. Significantly, when at one point an
exasperated Council of Ministers recommended sending troops to
the Basque provinces to force compliance with important royal measures, the monarch vetoed the potentially foolhardy plan. Without
relieving all pressure, Ferdinand VII opted instead for a conciliatory
two-pronged course based on the submission of written petitions by
the Basques for royal consideration and on face-to-face negotiations
with the provinces' representatives.[70] Even when Basque refusals to
meet the central administration's demands again raised the possibility of military force against the region—notably in 1827 and 1830

—the apparent threats, no matter how serious, were more in the spirit of intimidation than in the nature of an impending confrontation.[71]

Still, from approximately 1826–1827 on—as noted, partly at the central government's own urging, though ironically to its obvious irritation as well—there began to arrive in Madrid a steady stream of remonstrances and petitions from the Basque diputaciones. The nature and composition of these memorials were invariably twofold. First, most of them specifically protested a government action or decision, or complained about a series of related matters that adversely affected the region. Second, nearly all remonstrances contained an explicit request for the general preservation of the regional and provincial liberties which were presumably violated in some manner by the royal administration's policies. A case in point from among many examples: two 1827 royal orders concerning military demands elicited a joint Basque petition for the privileges' safeguard. In the request's words: "It was believed desirable to write His Majesty asking for the conservation, protection, and maintenance in their tranquil enjoyment of their fueros and exemptions."[72] Strong petitions for the freedoms' preservation also arose at the June 1828 and March 1830 conferences of the Basque leaderships.[73] And, significantly, at the September 1828 consultation in Vitoria, though no common petition to the monarch was apparently drafted, the conferences' minutes clearly show the growing apprehension among Basque conservatives that the franchises would indeed suffer if centralist measures were successfully enforced. In fact, as the latter gathering indicates, even in a period of apparent political relaxation and with Vizcaya at the helm, increasing militancy was at work on the Basque side. In a move sure to displease the central powers, the conference expressed the desire "that all the Fueros, franchises, liberties, good uses, and customs of the sister provinces be safeguarded in their entirety."[74] A similar climate of distrust and concern of state innovations was also evident at the Basque diputaciones' January 1829 conferences in Mondragón. There, in a remarkable document, after petitioning Ferdinand VII about infringements on the liberties by recent centralist measures, the delegates even went so far as to detail a series of hypothetical royal administration actions "that should they be realized, would form the basis of new remonstrances."[75] By identifying a host of undesirable eventualities, preemptively as it were, the diputaciones were openly laying the legal and political foundations against forthcoming centralist attacks. Not unexpectedly, in response to Basque recalcitrance, countervailing tendencies were noticeably at work throughout the royal administration.

In late 1827, with the king in Barcelona in the wake of the *Agraviado* uprising, a special Basque delegation presented him with a set of objections to state policies toward the region in the areas of industrial production (primarily iron and steel), donations, taxes, and the military.[76] On 10 January 1828 Ferdinand VII, through the Minister of Justice, forwarded the petitions to the Council of Ministers, where they were reviewed on 15 January. In comments that could well help to explain the circumstances under which Tomás González was about to undertake an important investigative task for the central government, the Council of Ministers suggestively observed that there were numerous documents in royal archives—particularly at Simancas—relative to the fueros that should be known to administrators. The remarks would certainly seem to indicate that the council wanted a search for, and collection of, this important data for use among royal bureaucrats and policymakers. However, during the same session the Council of Ministers, perhaps flinching a bit, recommended that the matter—in its words, "one of the most important and fundamental of the monarchy"—be transferred to the Council of State, a suggestion that met with the king's wholehearted approval as shown by the personal annotation on the margin of the minutes.[77] At face value at least, the process would have theoretically resulted in the unearthing of vast quantities of Basque-related documentation enabling the crown to evaluate the petitions' legitimacy and solid foundation. Nevertheless, such an administrative review was bound to profoundly unsettle the ever-wary Basques, especially if they construed it as the first stage in the fueros' piecemeal abolition. Developments in Madrid during the following months undoubtedly confirmed some of the Basques' fears about the central government's intentions.

In keeping with Ferdinand VII's decision, orders went out in early 1828 to key branches of the royal administration requesting documents regarding the Basque provinces. Revealing the broad scope of the enterprise, one order demanded compliance in these terms: "The King, Our Lord, has deemed it appropriate to order that your excellency deign remit me an index of all the dossiers that might be in the archive of the ministry of your charge concerning the fueros, agreements, exemptions, privileges of the Basque provinces . . . and their reclamations."[78] And yet, despite the seeming urgency of these matters, with characteristic bureaucratic slowness, the bulk of the documentation for review in the Council of State did not arrive at its destination until May 1829.[79] In the interval, as a parallel and probably not unrelated venture to the projected proceedings in the Council of State, in October 1828 the monarch commissioned Tomás González to undertake the collection of extensive documentation—eventually, most of it Basque-related—for an ambitious though at the outset still nebulous project.[80] Late 1828 deliberations of the Council of Ministers, however, leave no doubt that González's enterprise was a direct response to the Basques' continuing fueros-based resistance to the central government.[81] It would soon become equally evident that González was actually engaged in a highly partisan academic and political undertaking nearly identical to Llorente's. With firm royal backing, unlimited access to important sources and the ready cooperation of fellow colleagues, the Simancas archivist rose to the task and worked feverishly on his assignment. In fact, in May 1829—not quite eight months after receiving the formal commission and, interestingly, the day after considerable documentation regarding the Basque region finally arrived at the Council of State—Gonzalez obtained royal approval for the publication of the *Colección*.[82] As with Llorente's *Noticias*, González's multivolume opus provided the administration with solid legal and historical precedents—i.e., potent political ammunition—purportedly demonstrating the superiority of royal prerogative and central authority over Basque claims and freedoms. Tellingly, most of the data chosen by González were drawn from the medieval period and, in particular, from examples of royal concessions of grants and privileges to the Basques. The main conclusion to be drawn from all this was inescapable and, of course, quite disturbing to the Basques; namely, that what the crown could give it could also take back. Closely echoing one of González's main theses, an anonymous staff member of the Supreme Council of Finance tantalized the monarch in 1829 with the following observations:

> The Council, Lord, has made repeated recommendations to Your Majesty in which it believes to have demonstrated that your sovereign authority is responsible for [whether] the Fueros granted by your august fathers to the Basque Provinces, [and which] are wrongly entitled pacts, agreements or treaties by their inhabi-

tants, subsist, are modified, [or] are even annulled if this were
useful to the well-being of the kingdom.[83]

Notwithstanding its far-reaching implications, the statement (indeed a rare one of its kind) should not be interpreted as a ringing
call for the fueros' abolition. Rather, it should be seen as part of the
central government's efforts to establish the theoretical and political bases of royal supremacy over the Basques, a crucial enterprise
to which González made a profound contribution. Still, the publication of the *Colección* proceeded with breakneck speed, and by
August 1830 five volumes were already in print. They were immediately made available to the Council of State to aid in its review of
the Basque dossiers.[84] The two ventures had finally officially crossed.
Fundamentally, as a quarter of a century earlier, historical scholar-
ship had been placed at the service of royal politics. As for the *Colección*'s counterpart, Novia de Salcedo's *Defensa* was also completed
around May 1829. However, the strained relations between the royal
administration and the Basque provinces, as well as the generally uncertain political circumstances, clearly made its publication risky,
postponing the work for over two decades.[85]

Along with these developments, continued Basque resistance to
several royal orders regarding military matters contributed in no
small way to the growing rift between the central powers and those
provinces' ruling elites.[86] Government impatience however, though
very much on the surface in the late 1820s, had not led to an outright
showdown with the Basques. With good reason too, since the central government had to treat the provinces cautiously given the region's general strategic importance and, more particularly, its tempting proximity for Spanish liberal revolutionary exiles operating in
France just beyond the border.[87] But ironically, by the same token, the
Basque provinces required considerable military attention from the
central government. Not surprisingly therefore, the Council of Ministers again reexamined the military dossiers of the region in March
1830. Both the tone and the substance of the discussions strongly suggest a mounting disenchantment with the administration's moderate
policies toward the diputaciones, especially in light of the latter's
lack of active cooperation and seemingly endless obstructionism.
Yet despite the government's avowed intention of strengthening its
military presence in the northern region, the ministers disappointingly learned that neither the army's budget nor the size of the army

itself could sustain such a measure. Hence, although the council had urged the monarch that "the greatest imaginable effort be made to supply payment" for such an eventual additional force, in light of the monetary and logistical difficulties, the members backed off from an apparently firm determination.[88] Settling for less and to force Basque compliance with important royal decisions, the Council instead endorsed a political line of pressure aimed directly at the diputaciones and the fueros, and one in which González's *Colección* would play a pivotal role. Unrealistically perhaps, to extract concessions the Council hoped to keep the foralista-controlled Basque governments on the defensive. In June 1830 with all methods of persuasion seemingly exhausted, a palpably frustrated Council of Ministers unanimously approved the speedy transfer of Basque materials over to the Council of State to join the others in its possession since May 1829.[89] Following a long two-month interval, Ferdinand VII endorsed the Council of Ministers' recommendations and ordered all the relevant materials turned over.[90] It was a critical political juncture: the shock waves of the French July Revolution were soon to be felt on Spanish soil.

Though surely alarming to the Basque authorities, the revolutionary upheavals in the neighboring country, unexpectedly perhaps, were not without significant benefits for the region. Fear of a spillover effect into the peninsula prompted requests for more troops from royal military commanders in Guipúzcoa and Navarra. This, in turn, persuaded the central government to tone down its actions toward the Basque provinces. Additionally, and more importantly still, the Council of Ministers, in attempting to enroll all available Basque aid, explicitly reassured the diputaciones that any measures undertaken by the central government to forestall crises in the area would be with their participation and in "accordance with their fueros and privileges."[91] In light of the delicate political circumstances, quite understandably, the central powers did not wish to antagonize the usually restless Basque officialdom.[92] Even if this shift was certainly a retreat from recent tougher stances, one simply cannot agree with John Francis Bacon's emphatic assertion that "*it was the Revolution of July which saved the Basque Fueros.*"[93] The same applies to Antonio Pirala's belief that the liberties had never been as threatened as they were in 1829–1830, although this, it must be underscored in the author's defense, is a somewhat ambiguous formulation that in no way suggests that Pirala felt that the fueros' abolition was imminent.[94] More to the point: Bacon's and Pirala's shallow interpretations suffer from considerable evidential and logical shortcomings. To start with, as has been stressed, from everything that is known it is far from certain that the central government intended to abrogate or even sharply curtail the privileges in 1829–1830. More likely, Madrid merely sought to pressure the Basques so as to enforce key—and, from its point of view, undoubtedly long overdue—centralist policies in the region. To be sure, this had been done with an ostensibly formidable array of military, political, and ideological tools: imposing weaponry, physical or otherwise, that probably misled Bacon and Pirala into assuming that the freedoms' end was near. In sum, the best available evidence does not sustain the view that the fueros were in extreme danger or on the verge of extinction around 1830. Paradoxically, as additional proof that the Basque privileges had not been under the threat of imminent demise, once the 1830 scare was over the central government simply returned to its previous order of business, namely, to the examination of the voluminous dossiers in the Council of State.

Whether an active review continued in this council in 1831 is unclear, but by January 1832 the body was again busy at work considering the Basque provinces' petitions concerning their liberties and other grievances.[95] With this second review, ministerial rhetoric again acquired a sharp anti-Basque tone in some branches of the royal administration. For instance, relating Vizcayan opposition to the stationing of royal troops in its territory, the Council of Ministers observed in a January 1832 recommendation to the ruler that "it must be understood once and for all that in His Majesty resides in any period the right and the power to send to that province the forces that he judges necessary . . . without this being in any way contrary to the fueros it enjoys."[96] Matters were more relaxed in the normally more sympathetic Council of State. And, if haphazardly, the review nonetheless managed to crawl ahead slowly. Parts of the general Basque dossier were examined by the body in February 1832.[97] Inexplicably, however, the council apparently again adjourned the review sine die in early March of the same year. Indications that the matter had not been totally dropped do not appear until nearly a year later.[98]

With the arrival of new military-related materials, the Council of State resumed its inspection of the general Basque dossier in January 1833.[99] Judging from the new regularity and wide attention now devoted to the matter, it is clear that the state wished to proceed with greater determination. Moving swiftly, the council reviewed Basque petitions and other documents at consecutive meetings on 4, 11, 18, and 25 February; and on 4 and 11 March, when the examination was abruptly terminated.[100] While the brief review lasted, relying heavily on González's *Colección*, the council tackled the crucial issue of military substitution in the northern region.[101] So urgent was this matter that the council agreed on 4 March to notify all of its members of an important session to be held on the 11th of that month. In a surprising development, the summons was overruled only four days later by the Council of Ministers. According to this body, it was not "prudent or politic to discuss this question under the circumstances," a view endorsed by Ferdinand VII.[102] Consequently, when the Council of State convened on the eleventh, it was officially notified of the monarch's 8 March order halting the review forthwith.[103] Undoubtedly, even if the controversial nature of the Basque dossiers was an important consideration in the decision, the cancellation was primarily dictated by ominous political stirrings: among the most significant were power struggles within the state apparatus that an old and sick ruler was unable to check, and increasing Carlist sympathies. It is important to recall that the royal decree for the infante Carlos's departure for Portugal was dated 13 March, effectively putting an end for the time being to a long and heated succession struggle.[104] Of course, Don Carlos had long been a favorite of Basque *apostólicos* and defenders of the privileges. If his leave was certain to displease traditionalists in general, the suspension of the dossiers' examination would hopefully placate, if only temporarily, the heavily Carlist-oriented diputaciones.

Although the state by now had shelved its review of the fueros, and to some their projected abolition—a view this author does not share—the previous decade's episodes had created a legacy of profound distrust of, and opposition to, the central government among the Basque ruling elites. Moreover, Madrid's attacks against the region's laws and institutions, apart from invariably producing strong reactions to centralist policies, also had important repercussions on local politics. For instance, the Vizcayan Diputación and the notorious fueristas that were in control during the 1823–1833 period, responded to the challenge of the liberties with a two-pronged assault against state policies and local reforms.[105] On the first front, in addition to factors already discussed, during 1828–1829 a stubborn

defense of the freedoms even led to incidents of armed Vizcayan resistance against royal measures. The chief acts of insubordination involved the Diputación's armed protection of a handful of merchants
while they unloaded goods that were prohibited by the customs administration.[106] The provincial authorities' actions so incensed the
state that orders were issued for a royal commissioner to visit Vizcaya and conduct a criminal investigation of those accused of dis-
obeying the central government. However, here too Vizcaya profited from unforeseen political circumstances, and the mission was
aborted. In remarks that cast considerable light upon the effects of
the July Revolution in the region, P. P. de Uhagon (a key liberal critic
of the Diputación) noted that the "Parisian upheavals of 1830, and
the simultaneous invasion from France of a Spanish faction [Mina's]
with the object of restoring the constitutional system, gave rise to a
government suspension of the royal commission conferred upon . . .
Mr. Cabanilles [Cavanilles]."[107] If the cancellation was beneficial to
Vizcaya, it is nevertheless important to underscore that Cavanilles's
mission was not meant to abolish the fueros and that, consequently,
here too it is grossly incorrect to believe (as did Bacon) that the summer uprising in France directly or indirectly rescued the privileges
from impending doom. On the second front, the fueros' partisans
skillfully utilized the critical 1828–1830 and 1832–1833 junctures
to criticize and stifle reformism at home.[108]

Extolling its patriotic efforts on behalf of the privileges, the Vizcayan Diputación, in a shrewd and self-serving policy, consistently
attempted to keep the economically powerful (though socially isolated), domestic liberal-reformist forces on the defensive via the use
of the provincial freedoms. In a stinging and enlightening critique of
the fuerista opposition to local and national reform, P. P. de Uhagon
exposed some of the more salient techniques wielded by Basque conservatives to discredit their sociopolitical opposition:

> It also followed logically that the party that hoisted the banner
> of the fueros should acquire a claim to public confidence and be
> given a privileged role in the province's government, with the ab-
> solute separation of those arbitrarily censured as traitorous and
> constitutionalists, and to whom were attributed an identity of
> opinions with the ministry.[109]

In other words, although the 1828 royal visit to the Basque provinces
and Navarra (as will be noted below) had begun to reconcile local

factions—at odds over an impressive gamut of issues including the franchises—their differences remained irreconcilable. Vizcayan reformers, whose objectives (it is true) sometimes uncomfortably coincided with the projects of Madrid innovators, pressed for political, economic, and administrative changes. At opposite poles, the party of the fueros, a broad coalition of convergent interests, doggedly upheld tradition and the old order.

Better organized after 1830, Vizcayan conservatism, already presaging the rise of Carlism, tightened its grip on the privileges. Simultaneously erecting itself as the bulwark to revolution during Mina's disastrous 1830 venture into Navarra, the Diputación accused the invaders of being "the enemies of the Lord and of their ancient and cherished Fueros."[110] Unrelenting, the Vizcayan ruling elite in October 1831 urged joint action with the sister provinces to preserve the liberties.[111] And in March 1832, the Diputación tried to snap the provincial civilian militias out of their purported lethargy by pointedly appealing to them to heed "the call of the Fueros and of the land."[112] Finally, as political events raced toward the October 1833 denouement, if one is to believe P. P. de Uhagon's liberal account, the foralistas' tone became even more strident and perhaps desperate. Consider these extraordinarily suggestive assertions:

> [They] slandered the present governing Queen with the most sinister suggestions, calling her the enemy of her august and beloved husband, and consequently of our Fueros, divulging that their conservation could not last while the peninsula had a government founded on the principles of equity and justice that they labeled liberal, impious, and anti-monarchical.[113]

Pro-Carlist sympathies among Basque officialdom were in all likelihood part of a political exchange solution to support the absolutist infante in the hope that he, in turn, would protect the endangered privileges on a quid pro quo basis. Wrote P. P. de Uhagon in another spirited passage:

> The apostles of despotism and sedition disseminated and propagated constantly the most eminent commendations in praise of their hero Don Carlos, presenting him as the firmest support and foundation of that which they called [their] paternal laws, and consequently of their privileged domain which was what they entitled the Fueros of Vizcaya.[114]

Clearly, this and other evidence strongly suggests that the regional liberties played a crucial role in the gestation of Basque Carlism in the late 1820s and early 1830s. Moreover, if further proof were necessary it would be easy to show that once the conflict erupted in October 1833, those who had been the most committed defenders of the fueros were also the leaders and mainstay of Carlism. Consistently as well, in the opposing political camp there was clearly a tacit alliance between Vizcayan liberalism and centralism as local reformers and the royal administration sought—even if most probably for contradictory reasons—to protect vested interests and, in the process, curtail the power of the Diputación and its use of the liberties.

The 1823–1833 decade had come to an end in much the same way it had begun—with an unyielding defense of the fueros by the provincial elites. Vizcayan conservatism—deeply religious and theocratically inclined, xenophobic, absolutist, anticonstitutionalist, and antireformist—was profoundly aware that no complete restoration of the old political and institutional order was possible without the privileges. Therefore, after the Cortes's overthrow in 1823, and at considerable political risk and socioeconomic cost to the region (see the concluding remarks to chapter 4), the rightist provincial establishment struggled with stubborn determination for the liberties' integral preservation. For its part, to advance important policies and initiatives in the region, the central government countered—inconsistently and ineffectively perhaps—with political pressure against the use of the freedoms by the Basque diputaciones. In fact, at the end of the Ominous Decade it was plain that the challenge of the fueros had been fought to a stalemate. The outcome, however, if seemingly beneficial to Vizcaya (and the sister provinces as well), had not been achieved without far-reaching consequences for the region. Significantly, its recalcitrance engendered distrust and ill will toward the Basques among central government administrators, solidifying the latter's views of the fueros. And so, in more than one way the previous decade's developments regarding the franchises had convinced royal policymakers of the need for basic changes in the Basque region's status. But the same events had also paved the way for Basque Carlism and, in the process, laid many of the political and ideological foundations for the vicious fratricidal struggle that would break out in October 1833.

CHAPTER 4

The State and Vizcaya During the Ominous Decade

Lord, it is beyond doubt that Spanish levelers work incessantly to destroy the Basque Fueros so as to partially attack afterwards the privileged classes, including that of the clergy, and leave the throne defenseless of its best guardians in the acute crises of the monarchy. With this Machiavellian objective they threaten to destroy Basque industry while, simultaneously, and through various forms and indirect means, they attempt to subject the Exempt Provinces to permanent taxation.

Petition of the Vizcayan Diputación to the king, 31 August 1827.

In addition to the omnipresent and nettlesome fueros, major problems contributed significantly throughout the 1823–1833 decade to the troubled and often adversary relations between the state and Vizcaya. At least four fundamental areas of conflict stand out: (1) central government demands for monetary contributions or donations; (2) royal administration requests for troops for the national armed forces (or, in their place, a monetary equivalent); (3) state policies toward Vizcayan manufactures, notably iron, a problem compounded by shifting overseas relationships and economic crisis; and (4) a cluster of interrelated issues affecting the territory's trade and commerce (licit or otherwise), both with the extrapeninsular world and with the other Spanish provinces. In analyzing the main points of contention, it is well-advised to keep in mind some of Vizcaya's special characteristics: (1) liberties that meant the absence of direct taxation and military conscription, and that provided substantial commercial privileges to the province; (2) an enclave-type economy with substantial overseas interests and, simultaneously, excellent proximity to developed European nations; (3) a traditional propensity for engaging in the illegal distribution of foreign goods into the inland Spanish provinces (smuggling), an activity facilitated by the location and organization of the customs bureaus; and (4) the potential for domestic economic growth and development based on mining and metallurgy. In essence, state needs and Vizcaya's political and socioeconomic peculiarities determined to a remarkable extent the tenor and status of relations between the central powers and the province—indeed the entire Basque region—during the Ominous Decade.

I. CONTRIBUTIONS

Fresh from the tribulations of the Trienio, on 16 February 1824 Ferdinand VII demanded a contribution (*donativo*) from the Basque provinces and Navarra to alleviate "the deplorable state of . . . Royal Finance."[1] According to the royal decree issued the Basques:

Article 1. The Basque Provinces will be asked for a temporary donation of three million reales each year.

Article 2. This donation will last from three to four years.

Article 3. The Diputaciones of the provinces will be in charge of allotting, collecting and delivering the donation.

Article 4. These operations will be carried out in accordance with prior apportionments, or according to the custom there might be for this in the region.

Article 5. Being unjust to burden one province as much as another, in light of their inequalities in population and wealth, the Diputaciones will come to an agreement on the amount that each is to provide.

Notwithstanding the seemingly favorable stipulations and large autonomy granted by the ruler for raising the funds, the request met with firm regional resistance from the start. In fact, clear indications of trouble already emerged at the March 1824 conference of the Basque provinces in Bilbao. There, the diputaciones adjourned the consultation without agreement on the chief subject prompting the convocation, deciding instead to refer the matter to the respective provincial juntas for more substantial consideration.[2]

It might appear that the Basques had no valid moral or political grounds—and certainly no legal ones given the voluntary nature of the donation—for refusing the royal demand now that an absolutist regime was safely installed in Madrid. However, the requested sum was sizable, and matters were soon complicated by parallel and still unresolved considerations. Predictably therefore, at the provincial assemblies the response to royal demands (now compounded by newly arrived military orders) was generally cool. And so, when the tripartite conferences reconvened on June 1824 in Bilbao, the delegates—probably acting upon a suggestion boldly advanced at the May 1824 Vizcayan juntas—offered the king a markedly lower contribution (1 million reales for a seven-year period), with strings attached: namely, in return for quid pro quo concessions from the central government on economic, military, and police matters.[3] In other words, in what would become a familiar and effective defense tactic and one that would apply to other contentious matters as well, from the very outset the donation issue was cleverly linked by the Basque leaderships to other unresolved problems. In the following years the Vizcayan Diputación continually made reference to the joint 12 June 1824 petition to Ferdinand VII as the legitimate source of its demands, a position from which it never wavered. This broad strategy proved vastly successful in at least two ways. First, in an immediate development, the central government quickly yielded on police matters, leaving their control and management to the Diputación. Second, and more importantly still, when the royal administration refused to budge on issues with which the donation had become inexorably intertwined, the defiant Vizcayan establishment was able to withhold virtually all payments.

Following the June 1824 Basque counterproposal, the donation question remained dormant until the fall of 1825. At that time representatives from each of the provinces were hastily summoned to Madrid to confer with royal administrators on contributions and other matters.[4] In October 1825, the minister of finance (for quite unknown reasons) believed that there would be no great difficulties in securing Basque payment of the donation or, at the very least, a promise that it would be delivered. However, Ballesteros's optimism, if pleasing to colleagues at the Council of Ministers, turned out to be grossly premature and unfounded.[5] To the administration's dissatisfaction, by mid-December it was evident that the ministry had not made any headway in what must have been extremely tough bargaining. Visibly frustrated, Ballesteros explained that "under the pretext of their Fueros he had not been able until then to secure even the smallest amount."[6] Moreover, in splits highly advantageous to the Basque cause, the increasingly thorny donation question quickly revealed sharp differences of approach and purpose among key branches of the central government.

As some have noted, but only Josep Fontana has conclusively demonstrated, during much of this period the conservative Council of State was continually at odds with the moderate Council of Ministers.[7] The former body, now in charge of an important segment of the donation dossier (as noted previously, a circumstance openly applauded by the Vizcayan Diputación), was unquestionably more sympathetic to Basque grievances. Basically, the Council of State wished to pursue an understanding—albeit "soft"—political line toward the Basque provinces, stressing the need "to excite their zeal and loyalty."[8] Ballesteros, on the other hand, was considerably less tolerant and charitable. For instance, his 1826 ministerial report, written in the wake of the failed negotiations with the Basques, severely chastised the provincial elites for refusing to satisfy the royal administration's demands. In what would become a sadly recurrent refrain, Ballesteros's *Memoria* bitterly observed that the donation "did not find in these [provinces] the reception, place and observance that were to be expected."[9] And calling "troublesome" the region's "most ample rights," the minister chastised the "abuses committed under the shadow" of the privileges—freedoms that caused "irreparable harm to the tax-paying provinces."[10] Buttressing his case with moral and political arguments of centralist prerogative, Ballesteros concluded that the Basques should provide "the donation in the terms they were asked." The minister of finance would never waver from this conviction: a fact that, together with other unpopular centralist economic policies toward the region, would earn his ministry the harshest Basque censure and discourteous language, bordering at times on insults.[11] Worse yet, notwithstanding Ballesteros's strong denunciations, Madrid patently lacked both a coherent plan and the resolve to deal with the donation issue. In sum, an indecisive central government had succeeded in letting the Basques off the hook. And so, to the ministry's enormous displeasure, the Basques' stubborn opposition to what had become a question of *forced* taxation would continue until the end of Ferdinand's VII's reign.

The Vizcayan Diputación, undoubtedly the most recalcitrant of the Basque governments, continually balked on the donation question as long as it failed to obtain favorable resolutions from the central administration on other long-standing areas of interest. Essentially, Vizcaya simply reaffirmed earlier offers and terms. For instance, in June 1826 the provincial leadership pledged to share in the 7 million reales proposed two years earlier, but only under three very specific conditions: (1) the removal of surcharges on Vizcayan products (mostly iron) upon entry into the Contributing Provinces, (2) the protection of Vizcayan trade, and (3) the strict observance by the central government "of their respectable and ancient Fueros and franchises."[12] Expectedly, these stipulations were completely unsatisfactory to royal administrators. Not surprisingly therefore, the years 1826–1827 would witness a growing exasperation in Madrid with the Vizcayan—and more generally, the Basque—obstructionist methods to avoid the contribution. A case in point: citing the "indisputable right of the crown that all the regions and provinces contribute proportionately to its expenses," the Archbishop of Toledo, a prominent member of the normally conciliatory Council of State, voiced strong dissatisfaction in May 1826 with Basque resistance to donation.[13]

In general, the central government's tone became significantly more strident in mid-1827. Suddenly, in fact, there were threats of military intervention in the Basque region to force payment of long overdue contributions.[14] As was the norm, no troops were sent—possibly on account of a royal veto—but the crown issued another order dated 30 June 1827, severely criticizing the excuses and delays by which the Basques attempted to extricate themselves from their "rightful obligations."[15] Unfortunately for the central government, the order's timing and tone were extremely ill-conceived. Arriving during the July 1827 juntas (at the height of foralista sentiment, and just as the assembly prepared to vote on an important general military plan for the province), the royal order, designed to pressure Vizcaya, instead backfired on Madrid.[16] Bolstered by the profound pro-fueros political orientation of the recent gathering, the incoming Vizcayan Diputación again defiantly challenged the royal administration. A particularly tough August 1827 petition to the king protested the attempts to subject the Basques "to a forced donation without the redress that justice demands that their industry be freed from the surcharges that it suffers." More strongly still, in language not customarily heard in Madrid, the provincial establishment demanded "that once and for all the solemn declaration be made that they are free and exempt from any type of subsidy or forced donation, and of every substitution for the army, be it in men or in its monetary equivalent."[17] Unexpected events soon reinforced the hard-line Vizcayan positions.

In October 1827, to the obvious satisfaction of the central government, Basque civilian militias easily crushed an ultrarightist regional uprising led by Lausagarreta. But far mightier political storms were at hand: notably, the rebellion of the equally right-wing Agraviados in Catalonia—a troublesome revolt that, as is well known, seriously threatened royal authority and political stability. So widespread was the Agraviado sociopolitical movement that Madrid was forced to dispatch large numbers of troops to the region to quell the peasant, artisan, and clerical insurgency.[18] The ever-alert Basque diputaciones correctly sensed that the national political conjuncture was clearly in their favor. Consequently, when the Basque provinces convened joint conferences in November 1827, the delegates skillfully presented the monarch with a self-serving recitation of their exploits against Lausagarreta's band, while in turn offering a donation of 3 million reales.[19] But, as usual, the sum was not volunteered without preconditions. Pointedly, the conferees "agreed to remind His Majesty of the pending reclamations . . . especially those expressed . . . on 12 June 1824." Both the monetary offer and the list of grievances were eventually turned over to Ferdinand VII in Barcelona (during his December 1827 stay) in the aftermath of the Agraviado episode.[20] There was nothing significantly new in the Basque petitions, which to royal administrators were little more than variations on unacceptable and already-rejected offers. Thus, the deadlock continued, and with it an uncomfortable political malaise on both sides. As Basques jointly discussed their plans for 1828–1829, Tomás González would be busily at work gathering information for the massive *Colección*.

There are other excellent indications that the ministry was losing patience with the diputaciones' obstinate resistance to taxation which they based on the liberties. Expressing annoyance, José López Juana Pinilla, head of the General Direction of Revenue, reported in

October 1829 that since the donation had been decreed only "the petty and insignificant sum of 900,000 reales" had been collected, thereby leaving Navarra and the Basque provinces some 36 million reales in arrears.[21] Ballesteros's 1829 *Memoria* wholeheartedly concurred with López Juana Pinilla's remarks but, going well beyond what was customary, this time the minister's report contained important threats against the Basques. The extraordinary passage merits close attention:

> It seems to me that the time has come for the Basques to realize that in order to enjoy the benefits it is necessary to contribute with sacrifices, and that their resistance to do so with those required for the conservation of the state could result, among other things, in Your Majesty's closing of the doors to their entrance and promotion in all careers (for them so generously open), as long as they withhold their persons and properties from the fulfillment of the tasks which in every region and period are inherent in the order of political societies, whatever may be their laws and particular privileges.[22]

Despite the seemingly renewed determination on the royal administrator's part, no effective actions were taken to induce payment of the Basque donation, a course that became increasingly risky (perhaps even unthinkable) following the political ramifications of the 1830 July Revolution. As for the careers of Basque officials in government who were singled out for possible retribution by Ballesteros, there is absolutely no indication that the threats were ever carried out.

But the issue of donation, though apparently shelved, could not be totally forgotten by an administration in dire financial straits, and whose loss of overseas revenue now forced it to try to tap hitherto inaccessible resources. In a move that foretold of economic reforms, the crown in early 1831 created a special *Junta de Jefes de Hacienda*, composed of department heads from the Ministry of Finance.[23] The body's chief objective was to suggest measures to redress the state's profound financial problems. Among the junta's first set of recommendations (submitted in February 1831) was one that called for payment of the sums owed by Navarra and the Basque provinces.[24] However, on 28 March in the first of two ministerial reports presented in 1831, Ballesteros was pessimistic about securing the unpaid Basque monies. Explained a grim and resigned minister of finance:

Its realization can now be attempted but with the same fruitless consequence, due not only to the constant resistance but also to the extraordinary expenses which those provinces next to France have made and must make to prevent the entrance of the revolutionaries through that border.[25]

The second *Memoria*, presented on 24 September 1831, while painting a decidedly gloomy picture of the economic situation, harshly rebuked the Basques and Navarrans for their continual refusals and delays.[26] And yet, in contrast to the scathing broadside, the conclusion to these assertions was sober and realistic. Said Ballesteros in a masterful understatement: "The collection of the debt in the exempt region has always offered, and is probable will continue to offer no small difficulties."[27] Not oblivious to these problems, Ferdinand VII signaled caution and in April 1832 proposed a conciliatory approach toward the Basques on the donation issue.[28] Though little is known about the details of the contribution during the final stages of the Ominous Decade, it is evident that then too the northern region failed to meet its monetary "obligations" to the state.

Remarkable in all this was the surprising inability of the central government to enforce its 1824 donation orders and collect only token amounts from the Basques. The record shows a great deal of loudly voiced official displeasure, but little concrete action to force compliance. Not to be overlooked, an opportunistic Vizcayan leadership made excellent use of the favorable circumstances arising from the 1827 and 1830 political conjunctures when the state was much less willing to press its demands than might otherwise be the case. In point of fact, however, throughout the 1823–1833 decade there was a deep reluctance on Madrid's part to use physical coercion against the steadfast regional opposition to taxes. Therefore, when the central powers' insistent attempts at persuasion failed, a stalemate ensued. However seemingly favorable to Basque interests, in a larger sense, the deadlock was possibly quite detrimental to them. Essentially, the region may well have been harmed economically when the state, in retaliation, refused to relax trade restrictions, lower the surcharges on iron, and alter its military policies. On the other hand, both politically and financially, the 1824 Basque donation proved a monumental and humiliating failure for the royal administration.

II. MILITARY SERVICE

In many striking respects the question of Basque military service closely paralleled the donation issue. The starting point of this dispute was a 30 April 1824 royal order for the reorganization and substitution (*reemplazo*) of the existing army.[29] Among others, the order stipulated a national draft of 36,000 men to replace and revamp part of the standing army. Vizcaya's share of the total was 387 men. The Diputación was quick to point out that inclusion within a quinta (in itself a form of military conscription) amounted to a clear violation of the regional fueros. Consequently, when the Vizcayan juntas met in May 1824, the matter of military service was left pending until it could be discussed with the sister provinces.[30] And then, predictably, at the June 1824 tripartite conferences —claiming that "they were exempted from military substitution because of their Fueros," and warning that "their spirits become full of terrible omens when an effort is made to force them into military substitution"—the Basque leaderships vigorously protested the central government's recent measures.[31] Significantly, as in the donation question, the Basque elites from the outset gave unequivocal signs of preparing for a hard (and possibly long) struggle. However, after the oft-cited 12 June 1824 remonstrance to the monarch, the issue of Basque military service lay strangely dormant for over two years. In short, there is scarcely any evidence that the state pressed its demands for men (or a monetary equivalent) during 1825–1826.[32]

The central government's new 1827 quinta, with the previous one apparently still unresolved in the Basque provinces, again included the region in its calculations.[33] When the Basque diputaciones refused to carry out the provisions of the 8 February 1827 royal order for substitution in the national army, the state countered with a 21 May 1827 order redemanding compliance. Yet, in a manner reminiscent of the precedent-setting 1818 agreement between the state and the northern region, the hard-pressed royal administration was willing to make some seeming concessions to the Basque and Navarran establishments. Explained the most recent order: "Only as a result of His Majesty's special condescendence it will be permitted to commute the said service for a monetary equivalent destined [to pay for] the clothes and equipment of the new army."[34] Fundamentally, far more was at stake than a few hundred recruits—259 from Vizcaya by the most recent request. Important principles were involved: for the Basques, the regional freedoms; for the central government, royal prerogative and the power to command. Such weighty matters naturally called for new consultations among the Basques. Fresh protests and counterattacks were imminent.

In June 1827 the Basque conferees at Vitoria agreed to petition Ferdinand VII for the "conservation, protection and support . . . of their Fueros," while reminding him of the pending reclamations.[35] Stiff resistance to the state's military plans likewise surfaced at the Vizcayan general assembly held in July 1827. A special committee entrusted by the juntas to report on Vizcayan military service routinely endorsed all previous opposition and recommended that it continue.[36] In other words, if the ministry's impatience had noticeably grown during the summer, so had Vizcayan determination to resist even the slightest infringement upon its legal exemptions. In defense of its actions, the Diputación continually emphasized the province's military readiness, drawing heavily from carefully constructed traditionalist warrior myths.[37] More basically still, as had now become customary, the Vizcayan leadership stressed that military substitution was "an ordinary tax" and therefore contrary to the liberties.[38] Finally, so as to underline the rightfulness of its cause, the Diputación noted that the issue of Basque military service was in an identical state to what it had been three years earlier and repeated its request to be free of all reemplazo obligations.[39] Despite Basque foot-dragging, a hard-pressed royal administration kept the military issue alive throughout the fall of 1827.[40] Still, the regional leadership did not budge, and following the joint conferences in San Sebastián (November 1827), new Basque petitions were delivered to the ruler in Barcelona.[41] After the remonstrances were referred to the Council of State—a move sure to somewhat assuage the Basques—the controversy over military substitution lay dormant throughout 1828 and much of 1829 until the central government revived the matter with apparently renewed determination to force compliance with the previous orders.[42]

Possibly on account of the Council of State's inadequate treatment, Ferdinand VII turned the issue over to the Ministry of War on 28 August 1828 for further consultation. Significantly, it took the Supreme Council only two weeks to issue a lengthy and important *consulta* (on 12 September 1829), asserting that—the points of contention having been overruled by the monarch since 1818 in several orders—"the said provinces should contribute in the successive drafts with the numbers assigned to them."[43] Next, the king referred the consulta to the Council of Ministers where, with minor qualifications and modifications, it was approved in the main. Despite concessions to make the military draft more palatable to the Basque and Navarran diputaciones, the reaffirmation of prior orders, coupled with the certain inclusion in future quintas, were more than sufficient to put the region's elites on the alert once again.[44] In fact, their worst fears were undoubtedly confirmed when a 13 January 1830 royal order again made the Basque provinces and Navarra eligible for military substitution in the new draft.[45] In response, the diputaciones feverishly began to prepare joint forums. Almost simultaneously, an extraordinary Vizcayan general assembly was hastily convened to deal with the latest centralist measures.[46] The special committee that reported at the February 1830 juntas on the subject of military service, not deviating from the classic Vizcayan position, proposed new joint Basque petitions for the privileges' conservation.[47] With rumors flying about of an impending regional federation to repel centralist attacks against the fueros, and in an atmosphere of heightened tensions, Basque delegates met in Bilbao (11–13 March 1830) solely for the purpose of conferring on the recent 13 January order.[48] On the closing day of the parley, the Basque diputaciones drafted a long petition to the sovereign urging him once more not to include them in the reemplazo and stressing the need for the strict observance of the freedoms. Even though the remonstrance broke little new ground, in crucial remarks the Basque leadership correctly warned that the continuing violation of their exemptions through compulsory military service would necessarily lead to assaults against other branches of their special administrations.[49]

Not quite three weeks later, the Council of Ministers examined the most recent Basque petition along with the entire military dossier of that region and of Navarra.[50] The body did not wish to give in to Basque and Navarran demands, but the council's minutes leave little doubt that internal and external political developments had already begun to affect the royal administration, forcing it to adopt more cautious policies toward those territories. Tellingly, the council sought to increase the state's military presence next to the French border while at the same time proceeding carefully on the perenially delicate Basque military issues.[51] The council's general approach might best be described as follows. By maintaining a low profile and acting confidentially, the ministers hoped to keep the Basques off balance. In this manner the royal administration might be able to preserve a much-needed political initiative against the "agitators" who controlled the diputaciones. Meanwhile, whatever time was gained would enable Tomás González to complete the *Colección*, a work permitting the state to set forth a categorical legal exposition on the fueros' limits.[52] Despite the council's neatly laid plans to sidestep the reemplazo question while still obtaining some favorable results, the Basque military issue simply would not disappear. In late May 1830, the minister of war reviewed essentially the same materials before the Council of Ministers and strongly reaffirmed the positions of his department. After a detailed account of the dilatory tactics of the regional elites and not finding anything new in the latest Basque petition, Zambrano concluded that the diputaciones be made to comply fully with all of the stipulations of the 13 January 1830 royal order.[53] Obviously persuaded by these arguments, the full council ratified the minister of war's recommendations. As on previous occasions (with this and other matters), it now appeared that the state was about to launch a renewed and more determined effort relating to Basque military service.

As things stood in mid-1830 the struggle promised to be fierce, although some highly placed and usually well-informed observers doubted that Madrid would use force against the recalcitrant Basques. Nor did they feel that an attack would succeed. "At the very least the moment would be badly chosen," remarked the French ambassador to Spain in early June.[54] Almost simultaneously, the Ministry of War informed the Council of Ministers of the widespread difficulties in properly maintaining the troops stationed in the north—corps sent there in part to pressure Basques on military questions and on the transfer of the customs offices.[55] Notwithstanding the war department's urgent request for a speedy resolution, the Council of Ministers failed to come up with a satisfactory response, skirted the issue yet again, and (with the ruler's consent or acquiescence?) deferred the dossier once more to the Council of State.[56]

It was, however, the July Revolution that most tangibly altered the central government's military policies toward the Basques. New concerns and changing tactics were evident when the Council of Ministers met in August 1830 to coordinate defense measures in the northern sectors. In an obvious attempt to secure voluntary help, the council now struck a conciliatory tone vis-à-vis the Basque diputaciones. Accordingly, a royal order was directed to the provincial authorities requesting the immediate dispatch to Madrid of amply empowered commissioners in order to discuss the best means of national defense in conformity with the fueros.[57] However, things did not go smoothly. When the Basque representatives were introduced in the council on 11 September and asked about the extent of their mandate, it turned out that only the Alavese and Guipuzcoans had been granted wide-ranging powers. The Vizcayan delegation was poorly prepared for the deliberations because, among other reasons, the provincial juntas had not yet convened and therefore no important commitments could be made.[58] Despite the urgent, indeed crisislike atmosphere that existed when the juntas finally assembled, they unequivocally reasserted Vizcayan opposition to compulsory military service and duty outside the province.[59] Meanwhile, to make matters worse, the discussions in Madrid proved unsatisfactory, and the Council of Ministers angrily rejected a Basque offer of help that fell considerably below expectations. Instead, the body authorized the minister of war "to meet anew with the [Basque] commissioners to urge them to raise at least 1,000 men or supply the sum that is deemed necessary for the maintenance of an equal number of troops."[60] Quickly convened at joint conferences, the provincial elites opted for a temporary monthly subsidy of 100,000 reales as long as the extraordinary circumstances persisted.[61]

Once the revolutionary efforts were crushed in the north and the borders were stabilized, the Basque leaderships probably felt that there was little justification for additional military contributions to the state. Interestingly, there is no evidence that the sums pledged in October 1830 were ever rendered. And when the Vizcayan Juntas assembled in July 1831, no reference was made of the promised monetary service. Even the usually controversial problem of military substitution only obtained a perfunctory and businesslike mention. The absence of debates on these issues shows the extent to which both had been shoved into the background by recent events. Moreover, with the Basque military question effectively bottled up in the Council of State until early 1833, the diputaciones had little to fear in the interval.[62] And when the dossier was revived briefly at the time, it was only a passing concern of no consequence. In conclusion, as in the case of the donation, the victor in the reemplazo/quinta controversy and in military issues in general, was the Basque leadership, whose tenacious resistance had succeeded in holding the state at bay throughout the 1823–1833 decade.[63]

III. BASQUE MANUFACTURES

The third important point of contention between the central government and Vizcaya was quite an old and a familiar one: a knotty host of issues concerning Basque manufactures, in particular iron. As noted earlier, for some time foreign competition and national surcharges had plagued Vizcaya, by far the region's largest iron producer. Hence, to protect and promote local manufactures, successive Vizcayan leaderships had continually sought a total ban on foreign iron imports and the abolition of the tariffs that the royal administration had slapped on the province's domestic products upon entering the so-called contributing provinces since the late 1770s.[64] However, the governmental system of tariffs (a strong hindrance to local economic development) was in place in large part because of the region's commercial exemptions—franchises that, according to royal administrators, flagrantly facilitated Basque smuggling. Still, eager to improve a critical sector of a deeply troubled economy that was now reeling from the double impact of foreign iron and the loss of key colonial markets, the Basque elites in recent years had continued to oppose strenuously the duties on locally manufactured goods. Whatever the reasons—and there were many legitimate ones—their unflagging insistence on the proscription of foreign iron goods and the duty-free entry of Basque ones into the Spanish tax-paying provinces, pitted the northern region squarely against centralist policies. Finally, although in many respects these issues predictably followed the general trajectory of Basque donation and military service for much of the 1823–1833 decade, there was a major and far-reaching difference involved. Whereas the state was the chief initiator and prime mover of the previously examined questions, in the case of Basque manufactures it was exactly the other way around—that is, with the exempt provinces requesting concessions and relief, and the central government (especially the Ministry of Finance) reacting to the demands.

The now familiar 12 June 1824 Basque petition to Ferdinand VII devoted considerable attention to the problems besetting local iron.

Lashing out forcefully against the bureaucratic levelers, allegedly bent on national uniformity, the diputaciones underscored the harmful effects of insufficient protection against foreign imports, as well as the loss of colonial outlets which, until the Spanish-American revolutions, had been an essential market for Basque manufactures. The leaderships then warned (for the second time in the remonstrance) of the socioeconomic devastation to the region should the ministry continue its policies:

> If the introduction of the said iron manufactured abroad is not completely prohibited and Basque iron is not considered a national production and consequently free of all importation duties, all of the handsome factories that still exist will be destroyed very shortly, filling the greatest part of the population with affliction and misery, and depriving Spain at the same time of essential and necessary hardware products.[65]

Expectedly therefore, in a recurrent theme of the Ominous Decade, the important document requested a total ban on foreign iron along with the tax-free entrance of Basque production into the tax-paying Spanish provinces.

The pressure to secure these objectives came from various local groups with vested interests in iron—manufacturers, mine operators, master artisans, charcoal makers, some merchants and transporters, public officials, and others—who continually asked the diputaciones for decisive action. However, the Basque political classes were not equal to the difficult tasks demanded of them by their constituencies. In spite of continual protests and extensive lobbying efforts, the regional elites were unable to persuade key government aides to alter long-standing views on Basque iron and related commercial matters, opinions lately reinforced by the influential report of the Junta de Reforma de Abusos (1819). In essence, the ministry was deeply troubled by Basque smuggling and, in answer to the financial harm of this practice, duties and other restrictions had been placed on the region's manufactures lest foreigners take advantage of the Basque area's commercial franchises to introduce iron imports into Castile (and elsewhere as well) as if they were wholly domestic products. In other words, in addition to the normal surcharge on foreign iron, it was also government policy to tax *all* Basque iron—indeed penalize it—in the event that it should be of foreign origin. That the central administration's fears were justified was interestingly demonstrated, for example, by complaints of Vizcayan iron producers (and closely linked socioeconomic sectors) that such subterfuges sometimes occurred in order to defraud the fisc.[66] Given this situation, the state was extremely unlikely to regard sympathetically Basque pleas for help. If anything, Madrid's positions hardened somewhat during the 1823–1833 decade.

In the mid-1820s the central government stiffened enforcement of policies designed to curb the possible fraudulent introduction of foreign iron via the Basque provinces. Unavoidably, the exempt provinces' iron manufactures were affected by the new controls. For instance, in an important decision the Ministry of Finance ruled in October 1825 that Basque ironware shipped anywhere in the peninsula without certificates (*guías*) issued by the judgeships of contraband (at Bilbao and San Sebastián), clearly indicating its domestic origin, would be assessed the full duties normally tacked on foreign iron.[67] The measure's main object was the elimination of the liberal issuance of export licenses by Basque local authorities regardless of governmental restrictions—a popular (if questionable) procedure in the region. Under the shadow of the freedoms, this practice took place primarily in relatively remote ports with busy coasting trade, where there was little or no state supervision and, consequently, few checks on fraudulent reexport activities. The new curbs were far more than a bothersome intrusion into local domain; they represented a serious economic and political challenge. The Vizcayan Diputación therefore took advantage of Novia de Salcedo's mission at court to activate its opposition to the recent "obstacles" placed upon its industry.[68] The Council of State in fact examined this and other petitions in March 1826, but took no conclusive action on any of them, deciding instead, in an ominous development, to refer them to the Ministry of Finance, the Basques' traditional antagonist.[69]

Illustrative of the problems involved, not long thereafter some confusion occurred when—in a careless bureaucratic slip—royal officials in Asturias and other areas mistakenly started to treat and tax Basque iron as a foreign commodity.[70] Friction between the northern region and the central government was only eased when the general direction of revenue, redressing what was officially labeled a misunderstanding, declared that no Basque manufactures should be considered foreign—a welcome clarification that in Vizcaya, and possibly elsewhere in the area, did much to calm angry spirits.[71] The ministry was far less accommodating on other issues of importance to Vizcayans. For example, on the fundamental question of duties levied on the province's iron upon entering the tax-paying regions, the royal administration did not change its policies in the slightest. Subsequent and repeated Vizcayan, indeed Basque, demands for the duty-free entry of local iron into all Spanish territories clearly attest to the state's steadfastness on the matter. And this occurred, significantly, despite the dramatic and rapidly deteriorating state of Basque iron.

A candid and critical assessment of the problems confronting the region's iron is found in the lucid report (*Memoria*) submitted to the 1827 Vizcayan Juntas by the outgoing diputación of Novia de Salcedo and Valde-espina.[72] The document identified several important causes (among them unfavorable centralist policies) responsible for the crisis of Vizcayan iron manufactures:

> The nefarious state of the Americas closes for now the entrance of our iron while opening the way to foreign production; and an unfortunate theory of general uniformity that [has] caused so much damage until now, also steals from us the advantage over foreign iron in the limited peninsular production.[73]

After focusing more fully on foreign competition and scoring the gross inadequacies of governmental protection, going further still, the Diputación charged the central administration with direct and indirect discrimination against Vizcaya. Throughout, the language was inarguably blunt and challenging; the conclusions no less stunning. In a final barb at Madrid the *Memoria* asserted:

> If Vizcaya wants to save [its iron industry], if it desires to prevent this sector, which could be the solid foundation of its prosperity, from slipping away, it must not waste time. This harmful situation demands a swift and efficient solution, *but Vizcaya must only rely on itself. Any remedy that depends on other hands is surely inaccessible [and] imaginary.*[74]

Notwithstanding the sharp criticism of the central government, and the political classes' newly proclaimed self-reliance, it was impossible for Vizcaya to go it alone.

Vizcayan entrepreneurs were well aware that even with steep surcharges tacked on to it, foreign iron was still only slightly more expensive than most local iron manufactures.[75] In other words, competitive imports threatened to swamp the peninsular and colonial outlets of the increasingly obsolete local iron manufactures. Hence, barring major improvements in Basque production methods in the foreseeable future, it was evident that the region's iron sorely needed the ministry's economic and political support. Accordingly, the incoming Vizcayan Diputación, seemingly disregarding the strong recommendations and spirit of Novia de Salcedo's and Valde-espina's *Memoria*, on 31 August 1827 renewed earlier efforts to secure the oft-cited dual key objectives of a total ban on foreign iron and the complete opening of all Spanish markets to local iron in a tariff-free capacity.[76] When no resolution to these petitions occurred, the Vizcayan leadership insisted anew in the remonstrances presented to Ferdinand VII during his winter stay in Barcelona.[77] Still, the royal administration would not act on the Basque requests. However, in a separate development, after the February 1828 enfranchisement of Bilbao and San Sebastián by the central government for direct overseas trade, there was some hope that the measure might reactivate Basque industry. Unfortunately, as matters became mired in controversies over the fueros, the results of the ports' new status proved exceedingly disappointing.[78] The Vizcayan political classes were later optimistic that the June 1828 royal visit to the region might yield some tangible benefits to the provinces' beleaguered manufacture and trade but (as had become painfully common) an unswayed sovereign, probably influenced by the Ministry of Finance's views, stuck resolutely to traditional tariff policies.[79] There was little left for the Basque diputaciones to do except to petition for relief again and again, hoping in the meantime for an eventual relaxation of the central government's attitudes.

Madrid's continued refusal to meet Basque demands naturally resulted in new efforts on behalf of the region's iron manufactures and other productions.[80] By September 1829 several Basque petitions—new and old—on these and other questions were before the Council of State. Nevertheless, while the body waited for further unspecified materials, the Basque dossiers' review was postponed.[81] It is important to note that as opposed to the donation and military service disputes, where delays favored the Basque provinces, in this instance governmental inactivity and foot-dragging proved increasingly detrimental to the northern region's interests with each passing day. Unwilling to tolerate this situation for long, in yet another joint petition to the king (13 March 1830), the diputaciones protested the existent duties on Basque commodities that, for all intents, objectively transformed them into foreign products.[82] Possibly as a sign of goodwill, the Vizcayan authorities were meanwhile attempting to end some of the deceptive practices (alluded to earlier) by which imported ironwares were made to pass for domestic ones.[83] Nevertheless, the central government remained unswayed and, in view of the intransigence, some weariness (bordering on deep dejection) had begun to noticeably affect the Basque side.

Apparently, the last Basque bid of the 1823–1833 decade concerning iron manufactures came out of the December 1830 conference of the diputaciones. With now familiar themes, the Tolosa parley appealed dramatically to Ferdinand VII to "extend his protective hand over this sector" and "permit the free introduction and circulation of Basque [iron] in the contributing provinces [as if it were] a national product."[84] In spite of the petition's urgent and rueful tone, the ministry failed to act expeditiously on the request. Visibly disappointed, the July 1831 Vizcayan Juntas reported that the Basques' "energetic exposition" of December 1830 was still unresolved.[85] Nor did these crucial matters receive much attention in the following two years. In fact, the next indication that the remonstrances on iron (and other manufactures) were still under government consideration dates from early 1833 when, as noted previously, a review of the fueros and other contentious issues was taking place in the Council of State.[86]

In sum, the state's unwillingness to modify longtime policies toward Basque iron manufactures was part of a consistent strategy designed to simultaneously protect against fraudulent traffic and to pressure the diputaciones into compliance with the monarchy's general laws. The fundamental lessons were clear: It was unrealistic for the diputaciones to think that they could preserve their privileges intact and still obtain from the ministry the same treatment as other Spaniards in industrial and commercial policy. The central government firmly believed that the only effective way to begin to redress the state of Basque manufactures and clear up persistent doubts over the origin of certain ironwares was through the establishment of customs houses by the sea, a move that was an anathema to the region's political classes. In essence, by holding staunchly to these positions the state probably meant to show the Basque provinces that major changes would have to ensue in their privileged local administrations and economic institutions if their products were ever to arrive in Castile untaxed. In conclusion, if Madrid's efforts failed to achieve their goals in the donation and military service spheres, this was not the case in the area of Basque iron production. To the profound displeasure of the regional elites, as the Ominous Decade came to an end the status of Basque manufactures (and the issue of their introduction in Castile) was exactly what it had been ten years earlier.

IV. SMUGGLING, TRADE, AND CUSTOMS BUREAUS

The fourth area of contention between the state and the Basque leaderships was a series of intricately related problems regarding smuggling, trade, and the eternally troublesome issue of customs bureaus. Each one of these matters generated tension—and at times outright hostility—among the parties. Even though these issues are intimately connected, they will be analyzed separately here for greater clarity—hopefully, without losing sight of their multiple points of convergence.

A) *Smuggling*. The previous years' disaccord brought on by this problem remained great during the 1823–1833 decade. For instance, the conflict between the Vizcayan Diputación and the central government—notably the Ministry of Finance—raged on two fronts, one practical, the other theoretical. The first involved primarily the judgeship of contraband in Bilbao and the alleged smuggling abuses committed in the province. The second, perhaps more abstract but no less important, was part of a larger, ongoing debate concerning the purported harm that illicit Basque trade would do to the Spanish collectivity as a consequence of the fueros. Basically, although smuggling was a pervasive local reality that could not be denied or, for that matter, ignored, the Vizcayan political classes had never fully resigned themselves to the institutional fait accompli of the judgeship of contraband. Not surprisingly therefore, the Diputación continually engaged in attempts to limit its functions and scope. Already in early 1824 there were sharp exchanges between the provincial leadership and the judge of contraband when the former wrongly insisted that the latter's responsibilities were strictly circumscribed to the Bilbao city limits.[87] The Diputación's tough stance was in manifest contravention of two 1817–1818 royal orders explicitly extending the judge's jurisdiction to include all of Vizcaya.[88] In short, the provincial leadership's refusal to accept the judge's full powers and attributes naturally led to a running dispute between the two parties throughout most of the decade.

Disapprovingly, Regnaudin reported in February 1824 the judge's repeated seizures and other purportedly arbitrary acts.[89] Then, a string of incidents (some of them apparently serious) pitting the Diputación against the judge and his staff (*celadores* and *dependientes*) occurred in 1824, 1825, 1826, 1827, and 1829.[90] Vizcayan animosity toward the judge was also vividly expressed in April 1825 with the appearance in Bilbao of an insulting anonymous libel against him, an action usually reserved for more patently political protests.[91] The renewed Vizcayan opposition to the judgeship of contraband, it should be noted, coincided with a host of recent governmental measures to curb smuggling in the region.

Much to the dissatisfaction of the Basque diputaciones, no fewer than three important royal orders dealing with major aspects of smuggling in the region were issued on 25 February 1824.[92] To combat the illicit or fraudulent trade (*contrabando* or *comercio de mala fé*), the central government was instituting new tough checks and controls. For example, one of the orders contained these stringent provisions:

> That the foreign and colonial goods arriving by land or by sea from the Exempt Provinces and Navarre into the Contributing [ones], bring precisely expedited safe-conducts destined for the main customs offices or for the first [point of] entry of the respective line and, in addition, [carry] certificates as to their origin from the Judge of Contraband of Bilbao and the Subdelegates of Guipúzcoa and Navarra, without which requirement[s] the goods will be seized.[93]

Laying the groundwork for a possible fight, at the Vizcayan juntas of May 1824 the Diputación counseled vigilance and readiness should the recent centralist measures infringe upon the liberties in matters of trade and commerce.[94] Another governmental action that undoubtedly incensed the Basque leaderships—even though it was probably never fully enforced in the region—was an experimental February 1825 charter for the pursuit of smugglers by regular troops, a measure from which the Basque provinces were not exempt despite compromise gestures to conciliate the new *Reglamento Provisional* with the area's privileges.[95] But if the Basques were able to largely dodge this ordinance, other bothersome measures emanating from Madrid were in the offing.

In late 1825, in a two-pronged assault on smuggling, the state moved to strengthen its hand in the region by (1) requiring Basque iron to carry certified licences from the judge of contraband at San Sebastián, and by (2) reaffirming the territorial extension and attributes of the judge of contraband at Bilbao.[96] Predictably, the Vizcayan response was immediate and extraordinarily angry. In November 1825 the Diputación severely criticized the "levelers who efficaciously undermined the foundations of the throne," and made the extravagant demand of having all matters on the question returned to their April 1808 status.[97] Ballesteros's February 1826 ministerial report addressed some of these issues directly. Acknowledging the gravity of the smuggling, and pointedly not only that of the north, the minister observed that the "contraband of the Basque Provinces combined with that of Gibraltar and Lisbon [was] sufficient to wreck [the national] commerce."[98] Ballesteros was therefore unsympathetic to protests against the recent antismuggling decrees, particularly when the latter were intended to stifle illicit trade while raising royal revenues. Yet, in a glaring inconsistency, the central government in March 1826, upon prodding by the conservative Council of State, allowed the Basque provinces to import freely during a year's term any military matériel for their royalist militias—an untimely and possibly costly decision according to Estanislao de Kotska Bayo, one of Ferdinand VII's chief critics, who asserted that the action had opened yet another door to smuggling.[99]

After a nearly three-year lull in the controversy over smuggling, and largely as a result of important central administration measures and local events, conflict between the Basques and the state broke out anew in 1828–1830. Following indications of ministerial displeasure over serious smuggling incidents in Vizcaya in 1828, the January 1829 conference of the diputaciones was already prepared for future petitions should Madrid try to increase the judgeship of contraband's powers and personnel in response to alleged wrongdoings.[100] The most immediate centralist challenge of the Basques' autonomy and freedoms, however, arose in another manner: namely, by way of the March 1829 creation of the Corps of Coast and Border Carabineers, a body whose main task was the pursuit of contraband.[101] The Vizcayan Diputación quickly attacked the Carabineers, in particular the planned establishment of watchtowers on Vizcayan territory and the authority given to coast guards to search vessels arriving in the province—measures that, according to the local authorities, were in flagrant contravention of the fueros.[102] To make matters worse, the Diputación soon became incensed over the violations of the province's territorial integrity by Santander detachments of the Carabineers that engaged in "hot pursuit" of smugglers into Vizcaya. Notwithstanding a 14 January 1830 royal order attempting to quell all Vizcayan opposition, the disputes between the province and the Carabineers continued at least until mid-1831 and possibly later.[103]

Of much greater gravity was a series of events surrounding the Vizcayan Diputación's armed guard for the unloading of forbidden merchandise at Bilbao—occurrences with far-reaching legal and political ramifications, among them the drawing up of criminal charges by the judge of contraband in that city and the special commissioning of José de Cavanilles in late 1829–early 1830.[104] Even if the mission was eventually aborted (under circumstances discussed below but that remain to be fully elucidated) before the fact, Vizcayan officialdom could only view this development with considerable alarm. Commissioner Cavanilles, endowed with broad powers, was entrusted with the task of bringing charges against the suspected violators of national laws during the Bilbao incidents. It was an assignment sure to clash with the local elites and the provincial freedoms. The confidential instructions given to the royal commissioner contained suggestive observations on Vizcayan smuggling that cast considerable light on the central government's views of the question. Articles 10 and 11, for instance, assailed the abuses—and of course the harm—committed under the aegis of the liberties:

> 10. That their Fueros and privileges were granted because of the sterility of the terrain and the small population, even though, as it is well known, different considerations intervene today, and it is unfair that with such motives, for which there is no longer justification, damages are occasioned to the rest of the kingdom.

> 11. That the Señorío has been considered at all times a part of the royal crown, and that it is not fair that its inhabitants, far from serving the state that honors and rewards them, become its enemies, as they do by facilitating the smuggling that ruins the monarchy.[105]

Interestingly, the royal administration's general thinking on these issues coincided to a large extent with that of at least part of the Vizcayan entrepreneurial sectors—represented by liberal-leaning merchants such as P. P. de Uhagon—which felt that the Diputación's approach to smuggling was detrimental to the province's economic interests, in particular when the authorities inappropriately provided the muscle to protect the questionable trade.[106]

Visibly on the defensive, the Diputación responded to the rapidly escalating accusations with repeated appeals to the sovereign and a broad public relations operation to demonstrate that the local authorities could (and did) effectively combat smuggling without governmental intervention. As part of the overall strategy, the Vizcayan leadership also unswervingly defended past centralist rulings favorable to the province's positions and privileges, especially the landmark 1727 Patiño Convention (and subsequent amendments), which the local political elites had always interpreted in the most self-serving and advantageous manner.[107] Key aspects of the Vizcayan counterattack are found in the voluminous 7 December 1829 petition of the Diputación to Ferdinand VII.[108] This feisty document contained sober, albeit realistic, appraisals of the contraband trade in the province and region: "Your loyal Vizcaya will not say that no smuggling is done [here]. To deny its existence absolutely would clash with the principles of reason, since as long as man finds an advantage in fraudulent trade or transport, he will always engage in it." However, the remonstrance also tried to guard against drawing mistaken conclusions from the latter observations. Smuggling, it said, "is not carried out with musket shots, as some pretend, or with the breadth exaggerated by the opponents of the Basque Fueros." The Diputación also scoffed at the opinion of some that the majority of smuggled goods in Spain "could not have been introduced but through the Basque Provinces," and sarcastically added, "as if they were the only [vulnerable] part of the nation and all of the rest was perfectly secure." Finally, the petition insisted on a pet argument of the influential Novia de Salcedo, namely, that unfettered trade was always preferable to government intervention and regimentation. In other words, smuggling would inevitably arise when administrative and/or legal obstacles interfered with normal commerce. Yet, in spite of the vehement protests and the carefully crafted rationalizations of the Vizcayan political classes, much of the central administration, in particular the Ministry of Finance, remained skeptical. For many in the state apparatus, Basque "free trade" was tantamount to a licence to engage in smuggling. Moreover, as long as the region continued to circumvent royal orders on this matter and customs bureaus were not moved toward the coast, contraband would flourish as it had always done in the past. In essence, Basque smuggling—a daring, rough, and lucrative endeavor—was one of most lasting legacies of the ancien régime in the area.

B) *Commerce.* In the age-old confusion between legal and illegal trade, the central government almost invariably took actions that interfered with Vizcayan trade as a whole. It is in the framework of this general context that we must examine the Vizcayan Diputación's insistence on preserving intact the province's commercial franchises in opposition to the trade barriers erected by the ministry to curb smuggling and control other long-standing abuses in the region. In other words, although there were striking points of convergence between the views of the local ruling oligarchy and laissez-faire liberalism, it would be wrong to be misled by their apparent similarities and simply equate the two. Rather than defending free trade per se, in an important difference the Diputación primarily wished to preserve certain provincial privileges, among them economic ones. After all, rather selectively, the Vizcayan political classes' opinions and reflexes tended to be thoroughly protectionist when local manufactures were at stake. Significantly as well, local merchants with somewhat shady—if perhaps legal—business practices, came under criticism from diputaciones who were anxious not to antagonize the ministry and thus incur troublesome attacks against the fueros and the region's economic interests.[109] A sea of ambiguities and subtleties would provide a complex setting for the skirmishes of the 1823–1833 decade.

In the face of repeated allegations of Basque misconduct in trade, the Ministry of Finance began to impose tighter economic controls in 1824–1825. For instance, in an important July 1825 ruling, the central government ordered that the "general measures regarding the prohibition of goods of illicit trade, and national industry and agriculture" would now be in effect in the Basque provinces.[110] Basically, by extending national laws to the region, the ministry was trying to close loopholes and subterfuges through which the so-called merchants of bad faith (Basque or otherwise) skillfully used the duty-free zone for personal gain and in violation of state interests. Such sweeping steps, however, even if rational and well intentioned from a policy standpoint, were bound to conflict with broad local commercial exemptions. Expectedly, the 1824–1825 governmental restrictions resulted in a stream of Basque protests that were prompted in part, it should be noted, by the state's direct urging.[111] While gaining time for further decision making, royal administrators obviously wished to examine carefully the bases for the Basque claims. The central government's initial reaction was extraordinarily negative. Particularly unacceptable to the Ministry of Finance, for example, was the Basque tactic of tying the donation question to commercial issues. As previously noted, at stake was the clever ploy to obtain huge trade concessions from Madrid in partial satisfaction of the donation sums due. In his 1826 ministerial report, Ballesteros forcefully rejected the most recent Basque proposals, noting that for the monarch to receive the 7 million reales offered he would have to grant the region in return more than 40 million in benefits.[112]

In a related matter, the 1826 *Memoria* also alluded to a recent Vizcayan petition concerning colonial trade pending before the Commission on Tariffs (*Junta de Aranceles*). To the central government's displeasure, this had been (and still was) an area of frequent controversy due to Vizcayan insistence on importing directly a wide range of colonial goods in apparent disregard of the 1727 Patiño Convention that required the Basque provinces to import such commodities via the legally enfranchised ports (*puertos habilitados*) and only after having paid the proper duties on them. If smuggling was an excellent (and perhaps the best) way of dodging the controls, it was not the only one. The Basques traditionally had also profited legally both from the intricacies of the situation and from the lack of clear-cut governmental directives on certain questions, a combination that allowed them to skirt compliance by the intelligent manipulation of the gray areas of economic regulation. As Ballesteros reluctantly conceded, the latter considerations worked on the Basques' behalf.[113] In views that threatened the muddled status quo and doubtlessly alarmed the Basque leaderships, according to the finance chief basic clarifications and modifications were in order: "To prevent impediments and reclamations in the future, determining once and for all the extension that the Fuero[s] must have, and establishing clear and definitive rules that combine the mutual interests of Royal Finance and the Basque Provinces, the 1727 agreement [should] be rectified . . . taking into consideration the change in circumstances since the last century."[114] In spite of the minister's ominous remarks, with the Basque petitions safely tucked away in the Council of State for additional review since early 1826 and in view of the stalemate on

other connected matters—e.g., taxation, military service, and manufactures—little or nothing was done during the mid-1820s to alter
existent commercial laws and relationships.

However, after a substantial delay, when the state finally took decisive action the course chosen was surprisingly bold. On 21 February 1828 the central government legally enfranchised Bilbao and San
Sebastián for colonial trade, a seemingly unexpected move that probably caught many Basques off guard.[115] Bilbao merchants of course
reacted favorably but, as the Vizcayan police candidly admitted, the
news of the *habilitación* was "equally welcome in the rest of the
region . . . on account of the impulse that its depressed commerce
will undoubtedly take with this measure and the advantages that
will accrue to its manufacturing industry and to the relations that
its inhabitants conduct with those of the Spanish possessions in the
Americas."[116] Strangely, the police communiqué did not take note of
the opinions of the pro-fueros stalwarts who controlled the Diputación. And they, in defense of the liberties, dreaded the institutional
changes being thrust by Madrid upon the Basque provinces.[117] Consequently, the ports' enfranchisement, eagerly awaited by powerful
Basque entrepreneurs long desirous of ending restrictions and of ex-
panding overseas trade, swiftly ran into well-organized traditionalist
opposition, and the project was in deep trouble from the outset. One
of the main sticking points was clearly the eventuality of customs
bureaus by the sea and border. Certainly not a coincidence to the
Basque leaderships, the 1828 Cortes of Navarra were being actively
courted or pressured by the central government in the hope that the
kingdom would accede to the transfer of the inland offices to the
French frontier.[118] The Consulado of Bilbao, ostensibly predisposed
to the enfranchisement, was immediately put on the defensive by
Vizcayan conservatives who, as watchdogs of the privileges, firmly
opposed a change in the bureaus' sites. Pointedly claiming that its
members were "Vizcayans before being merchants," the Consulado
faced the delicate (and perhaps impossible) task of advancing the enfranchisement of Bilbao while convincing skeptics that in principle
no alterations to the fueros would ensue as a result.[119]

Even during the mid-1828 royal visit to the Basque provinces,
the habilitación issue, subject of significant local controversy, went
unresolved. The September 1828 tripartite Basque conferences, convened to forestall unfavorable hypothetical actions by the royal administration, dealt a serious blow to the enfranchisement decision.

Even though representatives of the Consulado of Bilbao attended the parley—among them P. P. de Uhagon, an outspoken constitutionalist who supported the central government's plans—the enfranchisement's hitherto uneffected changes (as the February 1828 enabling measures specified) were soundly rebuffed by delegates anxious to prevent them before they occurred.[120] The January 1829 Basque conferences at Mondragón—in which, interestingly, the commercial interests were apparently not represented—also stressed a prophylactic approach to highly suspect government plans in the area of trade, attempting to preempt them before they occurred. Furthermore, in a counterproposal the conferees petitioned Ferdinand VII for free and direct access to the American Colonies for import and export purposes—an unrealistic request in light of unflinching Basque resistance to the establishment of customs bureaus by the sea and border or, at the very least, acceptance of a substantial increase in the judgeships of contraband's powers and responsibilities.[121] The resistance and obstructionist tactics not only exacerbated tensions between the Basque leaderships and the central government, they also strengthened the Ministry of Finance's resolve in trade policies and scuttled for the time being any enfranchisement of Bilbao and San Sebastián. In sum, given the commercial crisis that beset the regional economy, the failure to achieve the habilitación in 1828 was in all likelihood a hard blow to the Basque merchant and manufacturing sectors that, as before, were forced to continue business under severe centralist constraints and blockages.

Meanwhile, after 1828 a bitter polemic raged over the Vizcayan Diputación's armed protection for the unloading of forbidden merchandise in Bilbao.[122] In answer to royal disapproval and censure, however, the mid-1829 Vizcayan Juntas adopted a sharp fighting stance and, in an exceptional move, decided to remain convened indefinitely to act on additional disturbing eventualities. Moreover, in August the Diputación designated new delegates for a mission at court to assure that colonial goods be allowed freely in the province.[123] The commissioners faced the thankless task of swaying a traditionally unsympathetic Ministry of Finance amidst the tensions generated by recent incidents and charges leveled by the royal administration at the provincial leadership. The central government was busy as well and, as part of the general response to Basque petitions, the Supreme Council of Finance (during the summer of 1829) had given detailed consideration to an important dossier on Vizcayan trade and other questions.[124]

Predictably, the Supreme Council's two important consultas submitted to the monarch on 19 August and 25 September 1829 were highly unfavorable to Vizcayan positions and interests, probably more so than the province's lobby in Madrid had expected.[125] But, as was customary for most important business, before Ferdinand VII reached a final decision on the matter, he referred the dossier to the Council of Ministers for further consultation. Without significant changes, on 7 November 1829 this body endorsed the tough recommendations of the Supreme Council of Finance, which essentially called for the central government (1) to appoint a royal commissioner to proceed to Bilbao—assuming the royal, local, and financial jurisdictions there—to enforce several royal orders on trade and contraband, and bring criminal charges against all those directly (or indirectly) responsible for the laws' non-observance, and (2) to inform the Vizcayan Diputación in no uncertain terms of royal displeasure caused by the former's conduct, procedures, and cooperation with the transgressors of governmental orders. The Council of Ministers, apparently on its own, then suggested that José de Cavanilles, a high-ranking member of the Council of Castile, be designated for the mission.[126] It was painfully obvious to Vizcayan officialdom that its remonstrances, missions, and other efforts had not yielded favorable results.[127] Far worse, the provincial leadership's intransigence had provoked a centralist backlash of serious dimensions. The Vizcayan commissioners at court were therefore instructed to redouble efforts in defense of the reputedly endangered fueros, although seemingly to no avail since the Council of Ministers was pressing ahead in late November 1829 for Cavanilles's visit.[128]

P. P. de Uhagon, the Diputación's frequent critic, vividly described the menacing situation:

> Around 1830 governmental preparations were acquiring a more imposing character: A Royal Commissioner was being announced, who was to be accompanied by troops and appointed by His Majesty to punish the excesses committed against the Judgeship of Contraband; and everything presaged that an exemplary discipline was going to be meted out on the offenders, while a solution was given simultaneously to other questions that maintained a reciprocal state of distrust between the government and the [Basque] Provinces.[129]

Foreboding trouble for the fueros, though not abolition, were the ominous fifteen-point verbal instructions and four royal orders entrusted Commissioner Cavanilles.[130] A case in point: In the 17 August 1829 petition in which the Vizcayan authorities defended their commercial policies and conduct, Cavanilles was specifically instructed as follows:

> Inasmuch as the Diputación . . . has attempted to justify its actions with the pretext of the Fueros, being necessary to uproot the evils that are produced by their malicious interpretation, or by the malice produced under their shadow, and desirous His Majesty that those inhabitants remove themselves from all error, it is His Royal will that once the cases are sentenced, and establishing a separate dossier with the testimonies of that which they allege is their understanding of their Fueros, the [task] be undertaken to settle several points concerning the [liberties].[131]

As the visit became imminent, in a well-documented 7 December 1829 petition to the ruler, the provincial leadership made another concerted attempt for the Vizcayan commercial franchises' total preservation.[132] In this remarkable document, the Diputación went to elaborate pains to link Vizcayan prosperity to the spawning of economic structures and policies independent of, and in contradiction to, those of the central government and not, as critics insisted, to a thriving contraband trade. Dangerous double-edged arguments perhaps; but vigorously proclaiming their innocence, the political classes again requested that Vizcayans be permitted to import colonial goods freely and directly.[133]

While the Diputación did not secure a favorable decision on its commercial demands, it received a much-welcomed respite when Cavanilles's mission failed to materialize.[134] Fundamentally, in 1830 new realities and dangers dictated a change in the central government's political course. Away from confrontation and with an eye toward greater cooperation between the center and the periphery, a July 1830 royal order commanded the Basque provinces to dispatch commissioners to court to discuss the means of promoting the region's trade and agriculture without modification of the privileges.[135] However, following the French July Revolution, the Spanish administration's bearing soon veered again, this time in the direction of greater military preparedness in the north to meet possible threats. Hence, in August the central government ordered the diputaciones to name new representatives to confer specifically with administration officials on defense-related matters.[136] In this fluid situation, the sudden shift from economic to military affairs worked against the former negotiations. So much so, in fact, that when the issue resurfaced in December 1830, a solution to the general Basque commercial problem was patently wanting.

Citing "the favorable occasion arising from His Majesty's gratitude due to the spontaneous services offered by the sister provinces during the last revolutionary attempts at the border," the Basque diputaciones convened joint conferences in December 1830.[137] The regional leaderships' aspirations were succinctly summarized in "a representation for his Majesty . . . demanding two things: Free trade with the colonies and the free importation and circulation in the rest of the kingdom of the iron manufactured in these provinces."[138] The important petition went on to complain bitterly about the governmental trade-barrier policies that Basques had repeatedly (if unsuccessfully) tried to remove. The conferees denounced as well the foreigners' direct access to the colonies while Basque entrepreneurs were forced to contend with numerous "obstacles." Ironically, claimed the remonstrance, it was far easier for a French businessman to introduce colonial merchandise into Spain through Bordeaux and Bayonne, than for a native merchant to exercise legal trade through San Sebastián and Bilbao. Conspicuously missing from this account, however, was the intermediary role of the Basque provinces in the trade between foreign nations and the rest of the peninsula—a commerce that often took the form of smuggling. In the diputaciones' opinion, the solution to these weighty problems was simple, if also manifestly advantageous to regional economic interests: "Every [difficulty] disappears when the Basques are permitted to trade freely with America, as much as when exporting from their ports, [as] when importing from those ports, with payment of tariff duties in [the] royal customs offices upon entering the colonies; as when importing from those parts, with payments being made in the [customs bureaus] of Cantabria, on their way to the interior barriers of the kingdom."[139] In other words—and this was the key—without changes in the regional commercial franchises and in the customs offices administration. Predictably, as in the case of the major 1829 petitions on trade and smuggling, the most recent request yielded absolutely no results. No doubt disappointed, the July 1831 Vizcayan Juntas learned that the commercial dossier was still under ministerial review.[140] Lucid Vizcayan minds must surely have known that as long as the Diputación (and the sister provinces) insisted on free trade without structural and legal changes in the customs administration or (more specifically) in the privileges, the central government's response would be unqualifiedly negative.

No new developments occurred in the commercial sphere until the November 1832 enfranchisement of San Sebastián for colonial trade.[141] The reasons why the royal administration chose the Guipúzcoan port while excluding Bilbao are largely unknown, although it is possible that the measure was a calculated slight meant to show disapproval with the Vizcayan political classes' recalcitrance on trade matters. After an uneasy period of observation, motivated in great part by the momentous national political developments of late 1832–early 1833, the diputaciones finally objected to San Sebastián's enfranchisement at the conferences held in Vitoria in March 1833.[142] And so, despite the fact that local commercial and manufacturing interests favored the port's enfranchisement, the conferees, including the Guipuzcoan ones, criticized the blatant favoritism of the habilitación, calling it a "true monopoly." Instead, in a familiar refrain, the representatives pleaded for Basque free-trade with the colonies without transfer of the customs offices to the sea and borders— i.e., with tariff duties levied and collected where they had always been before. Unfortunately for the Basques, the increasingly uncertain and unstable national political situation made any adjustments unlikely. Essentially then, as Ferdinand VII's reign neared its end, Basque trade was in no better shape than a decade earlier. However, emerging from the tribulations of recent years was the growing realization among certain sectors of the Basque provinces and the central government that only basic political, administrative, and economic reforms could effectively settle many of these issues.

C) *Customs Bureaus.* In the early stages of the 1823 restoration (following a brief period of uncertainty) the Vizcayan ruling elite secured the rollback of the customs offices to their inland sites.[143] There are intriguing indications, nevertheless, that during the first years of the return of absolute rule the central government, dissatisfied with the return of the status quo, may have entertained the idea of changes in the Basque and Navarran customs administrations.[144] But if any plans were in the offing, there is little evidence that a determined effort was ever undertaken. In spite of this, as has been repeatedly noted, the state could and did manipulate existing customs policies and regulations at will to attack or punish the Basque provinces. However, after a three- to four-year period of calm in the customs bureaus situation, controversy flared anew in 1828 through a series of interrelated government policies and events: the opening of Bilbao and San Sebastián to colonial trade, the incidents in Bilbao over the unloading of forbidden imports, and the complicated political maneuverings at the Navarran Cortes.

The unequivocal Basque resistance to the 1828 habilitación, Regnaudin reported, was based in part on the regional leaderships' fear of a large supervisory royal bureaucracy in the provinces, which they regarded as tantamount to the establishment of customs houses in the designated ports.[145] When the diputaciones resisted the enfranchisement, and as the matter went unresolved during and after the mid-1828 royal visit to the provinces, the Basques were saddled with the continuing disadvantage of not being able to unload colonial goods legally at their ports. Naturally, they therefore often resorted to questionable means to achieve some of these vital economic objectives. As noted previously, both the immediate consequences and the political ramifications of these actions, in particular those of the Vizcayan Diputación, proved disturbingly significant for all parties: for the diputaciones, they meant endemic conflict with the personnel of the Cantabrian aduanas, the judges of contraband, and other royal officials; for the central government, they typified smuggling, abuse, and the persistent violation of royal measures.[146] It was in the midst of the crucial 1828 conjuncture (and quite possibly in an attempt to undermine Basque solidarity on the customs bureaus question) that the royal administration, in a major policy move, undertook an effort at the Navarran Cortes to secure the transfer of the offices away from their traditional locations and toward the sea and borders.[147]

Following a prolonged and difficult political process, the central government eventually withdrew the disputed project in March 1829, but not before creating fertile conditions for distrust and mutual recrimination between itself and the Basque provinces and Navarra.[148] Vizcaya in particular was instrumental in helping to scuttle Madrid's designs. For instance, although the province was not even included at the time in the government's plans, the ever vigilant Diputación rushed to Guipúzcoa's aid when the neighbor was threatened with territorial dismemberment in 1828–1829 to provide Navarra with a port for the latter's use—presumably for customs purposes. As Regnaudin and other Frenchmen reported, the proposed transfer of the customs houses seriously ruffled public opinion in

Vizcaya. Significantly, observed the commercial agent at Bilbao in January 1829 of the intended changes in the Navarran aduanas: "In Vizcaya the opposition is general, real and strongly felt; the passions light up and become tumultuous. This province understands that the determination adopted by the government is a certain and immediate step to the loss of its privileges, and more than ever Vizcaya wants their total fullness."[149] Simultaneously, the Basque diputaciones kept a close watch on events in Navarra, and when it seemed that the royal administration would overcome that kingdom's reticence, the regional leaderships urgently assembled conferences to express their universal opposition.[150] The petition drafted at the January 1829 Mondragón meeting was delivered to the crown by a delegation of Basque notables especially mandated for the occasion. In addition, they lobbied hard through March 1829, and with apparent success since the state *postponed* (not abandoned) the projected transfer.[151] When news of the 5 March royal order shelving the matter reached Vizcaya, amid the popular celebration the Diputación seized the occasion to issue a self-serving circular extolling its efforts—a reliable political method by which the ruling oligarchy erected itself as the main defender of the fueros to ingratiate itself with the population.[152]

The 1828–1829 failure of the aduanas' transfer led to a governmental reevaluation of the issue during the next three years. Much of the examination occurred in the Ministry of Finance, a strong proponent of the shift and, historically, one the Basques' chief antagonists in the central administration. The initial salvo in a budding polemic was fired by Ballesteros in December 1829. The minister left no doubt as to his preferences: "I shall be obliged to insist that the indicated transfer of the customs offices [should] be carried out, and for similar reasons of justice, necessity and harmony, they should be located also at the border and coasts of the Exempt Provinces."[153] Ballesteros believed that these measures would promote Basque manufactures, curb the northern area's harmful fraudulent trade, and end the regional rivalries that had afflicted the monarchy.

Notwithstanding the head of finance's forceful exposition, a plethora of important 1830 events and circumstances pushed the customs bureau issue into the background. So much so, in fact, that the question did not resurface until March 1831 (some sixteen months later) when Ballesteros once again argued for the transfer in the first of two ministerial reports submitted that year.[154] The controversial proposal, along with other suggested reforms, was reviewed and approved by the Council of Ministers. The recommendations—fourteen in all—were then turned over to the king for final resolution. When Ferdinand VII ruled on them in May 1831, he approved only five of the measures which, as Fontana has correctly shown, were clearly the most minor.[155] The transfer of the customs bureaus to "the Pyrenees and the ports of the Cantabrian Sea" (proposal 12, one of the major reforms), was rejected by the monarch with this significant explanation:

> This measure has not merited His Majesty's approval, being his sovereign will that in the proceedings nothing be done on this particular because it is not timely given the present circumstances, but making it a point to explore through higher authorities the opinion and disposition of those inhabitants toward accepting this [measure].[156]

Even though it is difficult, perhaps impossible, to believe that the seasoned king did not know the Basques' feelings toward the question of customs bureaus, the veto nonetheless illustrated a key policy split at the highest levels of government. In essence, a conservative ruler, who was attentive to the political imperatives of the moment and perhaps mindful of the Basque privileges, was pitted against a Ministry of Finance whose overriding concerns—particularly in light of the state's fiscal plight, prevalent commercial crisis, and widespread smuggling in the north—impelled it irresistibly in the direction of reform.

As might be readily expected, Ballesteros's objectives were strongly seconded by so-called *Junta de Jefes de Hacienda*.[157] Closely echoing the minister's views, the junta's September 1831 report to Ferdinand VII totally endorsed the proposed transfer of the customs bureaus.[158] In turn, the junta's conclusions provided Ballesteros with an ideal platform to affirm his views. Asserted the minister in the second ministerial report of the year: "Thus the customs offices stay at the Ebro, and remains unchanged the monstrosity of the existence of four exempt provinces for the introduction and consumption of forbidden or lawful goods . . . with grave harm to royal finance."[159] In spite of the *Memoria*'s almost desperate tone, the sovereign staunchly continued to resist the Ministry of Finance's recommendations. In April 1832, for instance, the Council of Ministers noted that the monarch wanted certain contentious matters between the Basque provinces and the crown (among them the transfer of the customs offices) settled "through friendly negotiations of good faith and without harming in any manner whatsoever fueros and rights that those provinces might have."[160] Behind Ferdinand VII's conciliatory approach there surely lurked a kind of a veto by default (no matter how unconscious) for it is unthinkable that he could have honestly felt that amicable bargaining could clear the way for the customs bureaus' shift after more than a century of unyielding Basque resistance.[161] Tellingly in fact, as noted before, the November 1832 enfranchisement of San Sebastián was opposed by regional leaderships afraid of reforms in the Basque provinces' customs administration.[162] Thus, in the twilight of Ferdinand VII's rule, there still had been no change on this question. If reluctantly willing to incur unfavorable centralist policies on trade matters, Basque conservatives had distinctly succeeded in holding the state at bay. Significantly, the customs bureaus' deadlock would not be broken before 1840–1841—i.e., in the immediate aftermath of the First Carlist War.[163]

In conclusion, simply to view relations between the state and Vizcaya during the Ominous Decade in terms of winners and losers would be unfortunate and nearsighted. While it is true that on specific issues the tug-of-war resulted in tangible advantages for one side (Vizcaya gaining an edge on contributions and military service, the state on manufactures and commerce), such a reductionist perspective could not even begin to adequately convey and explain the importance of the parties' conflictive interaction during the 1823–1833 period. More to the point, beyond the immediate outcome of the disputes between the royal administration and Vizcaya (and the other Basque provinces as well), contemporary events clearly reinforced and fostered distrust and animosity among the feuding parties. The strained atmosphere triggered a profound political reexamination of the issues both in the center and in the northern provinces. In the face of sustained resistance, for example, royal officials were confronted by the fundamental need to modify their outlook and policies toward the fractious Basques. For the provincial leaderships, however, it had become evident that the era's governmental leveling trends—in particular those emanating from the Ministry of Finance—while couched in the political terminology and ideology of the common national good, would gravely undermine the fueros and the uniquely peculiar local institutions and modes of government. In essence, Basque anticentralism would continue to clash openly with the growing push for uniformity and reform among Madrid's would-be nation builders. As the chasm widened, it would become obvious to many that the national government and the Basque leaderships, especially the Vizcayan Diputación which was by far the most intransigent regional authority, were on an inexorable collision course. Inescapably therefore, the troubled relations between the central government and the regional political classes must be considered one of the central ingredients in the long-range incubation of the conflict that erupted in October 1833. Another essential component was the counterrevolution implacably fashioned in the region by the Basque political classes during the 1823–1833 decade. In Vizcaya the rightward political process would perhaps be most manifest in the creation of the local police and the paramilitary *Brigadas de Paisanos Armados*, the subject of the next chapter.

CHAPTER 5

Instruments of Counterrevolution: The Police and the Brigadas de Paisanos Armados

The police regulations and the law of passports were introduced into the [Basque] Provinces in defiance of the Fueros, the Carlist party only claiming the management; and unsparingly they used this new arm against their political antagonists.

John Francis Bacon, Six Years in Biscay.

The great object of the establishment of these corps is to combat and exterminate the revolution and the conspiracies against religion and the state.

From article 52 of the charter of the Vizcayan Brigadas de Paisanos Armados, 21 September 1827.

During the 1823–1833 decade the Vizcayan ruling classes organized and developed two formidable bodies of repression and counterrevolution in the police and militias known as the Paisanos Armados, the latter sometimes referred to by the formal title of *Armamento General del País.* Numerous factors contributed to their establishment, not the least of which were the Diputación's fear of constitutionalism's return, the need to contain the spread of revolution and/or reform, the preservation of public order, the growing threat of centralism, and concern over the possible loss of the fueros. Given their common counterrevolutionary political and military objectives, not surprisingly, both organizations—one of them primarily civilian, the other paramilitary—often overlapped in functions and attributes. Exclusively in the hands of an intransigent royalist party, the police and the Paisanos in the process became essential supports (veritable power bases, really) of the period's Vizcayan leaderships. In the creation of both bodies, the central government inexplicably relinquished early on important prerogatives to Vizcaya (and the other Basque diputaciones) that Madrid would unsuccessfully attempt to recuperate later. Meanwhile, expectedly, the clear beneficiaries of the state's weakness and lack of determination were the leading conservative provincial political interests and politicians who intelligently wielded the repressive tools to consistently further an unrelenting rightist strategy. In addition to tracing the gestation and growth of the organizations in question, this narrative examines some of their most salient links to Carlism.

I. THE VIZCAYAN POLICE

An 8 January 1824 royal order established the General Superintendency of the Police of the Kingdom. Nevertheless, almost from the outset, the project to set up a national and centralized police met with firm protests from the Basque diputaciones, which objected on the fundamental ground that the new system substantially infringed upon the region's privileges.[1] More specifically, the diputaciones, in particular the outspoken Vizcayan government, based their resistance on the alleged illegality of the creation of new authorities and institutions without the explicit approval of the provincial general assemblies or other representative bodies.[2] Behind the plausible legal arguments, however, lay the thinly veiled desire of complete local control over the police.[3] After some initial maneuvering, the Basque provinces were unequivocally ordered by the monarch on 8 April 1824 to put into effect the national police plan "as it has been communicated to them." But significantly, in the same breath the royal resolution also made concessions to the Basques through this important qualifier and loophole: *"or tempering [the plan] however possible to conform with the Fueros of the said provinces."*[4] Just as the diputaciones were probably savoring the

victory, in a bizarre about-face, the central government annulled the
8 April measure, leaving the question in limbo. For lack of a better
explanation, Madrid may possibly have had second thoughts about
surrendering so much police authority to the Basques. Nonetheless,
after several months of remonstrances from the provinces, the royal
administration finally relented: a 14 August 1824 royal order left the
diputaciones in total charge of their respective police.[5] The clean
Basque triumph would be deeply regretted by government officials
in the future, especially during moments of regional opposition to
centralist policies. In essence, after August 1824 and for the rest of
Ferdinand VII's reign, for all intents and purposes the diputaciones
and the provincial police forces would be synonymous.

Whatever uncertainties may have existed, notably those engendered by Madrid's vacillation, the Vizcayan government had wasted
little time in organizing the provincial police. The Diputación's
eagerness is amply demonstrated by the fact that by 8 May 1824 the
territory already possessed a comprehensive police charter.[6] This *reglamento* (charter) was complemented in short order by a series of
ad hoc measures enacted in June–July 1824.[7] The new ordinances
covered a broad range of public life such as personal movement and
travel, association, assembly, arms bearing, and numerous other activities.[8] For instance, to control the population more effectively, the
issuance of passports and letters of safe-conduct was tightly regu-
lated, strict curfews were put into effect, and provisions were made
for the close surveillance of restaurants, coffeehouses, and other public establishments. Policemen were given right-of-entry privileges to
search suspicious meetings in private houses. The use of informants
was promoted, and the rights to hunt and bear arms were denied
the constitutionalists—permits and licenses being awarded almost
exclusively to those of acceptable, albeit royalist, political opinions.

Since the local authorities and the corregidor had been traditionally in charge of police operations with similar prerogatives, it is
of course possible to conclude that the 1824 establishment of the
police in Vizcaya did not represent a substantive departure from the
past. This, however, would be a grave mistake. Crucial differences
between the old and new systems clearly reveal the profoundly innovative nature of the new organization. First, the old police method
had been mainly concerned with problems of public order, criminal behavior, and religious orthodoxy. In addition to responsibility
over most of these questions, the functions of the new body were

heavily political in character. Second, whereas the previous police had usually operated unsystematically, concentrating on specific existent problems, the new organization, rigorously chartered and centralized, in addition to its other duties was devised as a prophylactic tool: i.e., to forestall turmoil and disorders, be they politically motivated or not. A case in point was the striking breakthrough of the creation of permanent police officials in the cities and other populated areas. Known as *celadores de barrio*, these functionaries served primarily as watchmen and informers. A related development also broke with former practice: some of the larger urban concentrations such as Bilbao were carefully subdivided into permanent districts to facilitate policing.[9] Third, by coordinating its activities more closely with the local authorities through questionnaires and circulars, the Vizcayan police were able to gain a greater degree of effectiveness and influence in remote areas than had ever previously been the case. Fourth, the new police force was heavily weighed in the Diputación's favor. In other words, having been forced until then to share law enforcement duties equally with the corregidor and, to a certain extent as well, with other local authorities in the townships and villages, the 1824 installation of the police tipped the previous balance, tilting it instead toward the Diputación—without doubt a major political achievement for the provincial ruling elites. Fundamentally, important police prerogatives—many of them previously informal, scattered, and divided—became clearly defined and codified in the hands of the Vizcayan government, greatly enhancing its political strength in the process. The chief losers were unquestionably the central government and its representation in the province. Vizcayan officialdom immediately started to make use of its newly increased police powers.

Among the principal goals of the new Vizcayan police were tighter control of the population in general and of the constitutionalists in particular. In keeping with this, the 8 May 1824 charter called for the formation of a new general census, a task not undertaken until August 1825.[10] The completed parts of this project reveal a surprisingly high level of police penetration into the lives of the province's citizens.[11] The political counterpart to the census was a series of indexes undertaken in 1825 at the national police's direction which detailed all known or suspected constitutionalists and subversives in Vizcaya —or, in the Diputación's words, "all of the persons which the security of the state requires be spied upon most particularly."[12] These so-called Inverse Indexes (*Indices Inversos*)—known thusly because of the lists' "rigorous alphabetical order," that is, with the last names first—included all individuals (male and female) known or suspected of the following political opinions and activities: (1) a sympathizer with, or attached (*adicto*) to, the constitutional system; (2) a national volunteer in the cavalry or infantry corps; (3) a member of a "sacred battalion or company"—i.e., the groups of elder constitutionalists (such as the one in Bilbao) organized to preserve the peace in the cities; (4) a freemason; (5) a *comunero*—a member of a secret, radical sect; (6) an extreme or moderate liberal; (7) a buyer of "national properties"—i.e., clerical possessions nationalized and sold during the Trienio; and finally, (8) a "secularized" monk, or one who abandoned a regular order voluntarily since some were forced out of religious institutions by the government of the Cortes.[13] In addition to information for the Indexes, townships were instructed by the Vizcayan police to include in their reports "anything else that might contribute to giving an exact idea of the [individual's] true opinions manifested during the constitutional reign."[14] Furthermore, municipal authorities were ordered to keep duplicates of these lists for their own use, an excellent additional indication of the Diputación's zeal and determination to keep constitutionalism in check. These Indexes, veritable political and ideological files, were consistently used to control, harass, and blackball the Vizcayan liberal opposition until April 1833 when, after important changes in Madrid following the 1832 amnesty, the central administration recalled the lists—in all likelihood for their destruction.[15]

The Vizcayan police also exercised considerable control, some of it clearly political, through the issuance of safe-conducts or personal identity cards (*cartas de seguridad*) and passports. Grosso modo, the first were used primarily inside the province, the second while traveling abroad.[16] According to the 14 January 1825 police ordinance establishing the guidelines for both types of documents, the cartas were made mandatory (renewable on a yearly basis) for most males over the age of sixteen, as well as for widows and unmarried women not living at home.[17] And outsiders (*forasteros*) staying in the province more than a week, even if in possession of valid documentation, had to take out a Vizcayan carta. The identity cards enabled Vizcayans to travel in the province and adjoining territories (within a limited radius) without passports. By law, violations of these regulations could result in fines and sanctions. For example, anyone found without proper documents twenty miles or more from the place of residence automatically became a suspect (*será tenido por sospechoso*) and was therefore subject to arrest.

Equal, and perhaps greater, control was exercised by the provincial leadership in the issuance of passports. For instance, in September 1824 the Vizcayan police moved to curtail abuses in passport-related matters at the local level. Numerous municipal authorities were in the habit of liberally issuing passports (as in the case of export licenses for manufactures) without notifying the Diputación or the police. Consequently, steps were taken to correct these irregularities. Among others, the Diputación ruled that all passports be issued on printed police paper (presumably distributed by the central office in Bilbao), that the documents be more thorough and uniform, and that all passports for travel abroad be expressly approved by the Diputación should the traveler leave from a Vizcayan port.[18] Shortly thereafter, in January 1825, passport regulations were made even more stringent, particularly for known or suspected constitutionalists. For example, a ruling of the Vizcayan police stipulated that "no passport be given to those noted for their constitutional leanings, especially if they have belonged to the national volunteer [militias], unless the police official[s] know that the individual . . . has good reasons for undertaking the intended trip and someone who can vouch on his behalf."[19] Moreover, those arousing suspicions were often forced to observe a fixed itinerary (*ruta fija*), a procedure that enabled the authorities to follow the travelers' steps more easily. Finally, only the Diputación could issue passports for travel to Madrid and the royal resorts.[20]

Still other police ordinances and ad hoc decisions restricted the constitutionalists' freedom of movement in equally annoying ways. In addition to banning the reformers' meetings "in country houses, farmhouses, nor any of their type under the pretext of dinners, lunches, nor any other," the Vizcayan police prohibited their travel to certain towns such as Portugalete, Plencia, Guecho, and Santurce "with only a safe-conduct and without special license from the Diputación."[21] Scattered evidence from police records indicates that these ordinances were far from pro forma. Wealthy constitutionalists with interests in the countryside in particular appear to have been affected by these forms of harassment. Tellingly, when Guillermo de Uhagon—a Bilbao merchant, landholder, and patriarch of the prominent family—requested permission in February 1825 to visit his properties in Portugalete, the petition was first rejected by the Diputación and then was not granted until seven months later.[22] Constitutionalists, in fact, commonly sought police permits both to attend baths and to travel to possessions near Bilbao.[23] Nor was travel to Madrid (even when on business) a routine affair for the followers of the Cortes, as Ceferino Salazar, a former officer in Bilbao's volunteer militia, discovered in 1827.[24]

Foreign travel was no less controlled and monitored by the Vizcayan police. Acting in the manner befitting a sovereign government, the Diputación collaborated directly with foreign governments, in particular the French, informing them of the projected trips and whereabouts of local constitutionalists. Interestingly, in July 1824 the Vizcayan police alerted the French authorities that a four-month passport for Paris had been issued to P. P. de Uhagon. According to the body, Uhagon was "very suspicious," "of many connections," "fairly affluent," "one of the first voluntary militiamen" in Bilbao and one who had demonstrated "extremism with excessive boldness" during the previous period.[25] Predictably, these independent and highly questionable actions of the Vizcayan police caused diplomatic strains between the French and Spanish governments.[26] Nevertheless, as late as August 1827 and possibly later, the local police dispatches to Madrid ordinarily reported the foreign travels of constitutionalists and voluntary militiamen.[27] These stern policies, however, apparently gave way to greater moderation in the later stages of the Ominous Decade. Essentially, this meant a greater willingness on the part of the Diputación to treat Bilbao's constitutionalist-leaning merchant and business community more tolerantly in matters involving foreign travel. Economic considerations, namely a shaky economy, undoubtedly influenced the Vizcayan government's behavior. Requesting instructions from Madrid in 1831 on how to handle the matter, observed a seemingly bewildered Vizcayan police about local entrepreneurs: "If they are barred from traveling when their affairs require a personal appearance, trade will be damaged and obstructed."[28] In sum, when it came to travel abroad in the waning stages of Ferdinand VII's reign, the Vizcayan authorities, mindful of important economic concerns, appear to have leaned reluctantly toward accommodating the powerful business community.[29]

Early on, the provincial police enacted numerous ordinances to monitor social activities in public buildings and businesses. These measures extended to lodging houses and hostels, eating places, markets, coffeehouses, recreation sites, and possibly even brothels.[30] Boarding places, for example, were required to notify the police within twelve hours of a traveler's arrival and to provide comprehensive information about the new guest.[31] Worthy of note is the fact that taverns, restaurants, billiard rooms, and similar establishments, in addition to being closely watched, were subject to curfews and their owners held liable for their patrons' disorders. Increased police surveillance after 1824 possibly forced constitutionalists and right-wing royalists to associate and operate more cautiously. Clandestine meetings were favorite methods of getting around ordinances restricting the right of assembly. Not surprisingly, therefore, suspicious gatherings were quickly investigated by the police and banned if the circumstances required it. To carry out their tasks more effectively, police officials were empowered to enter any house or establishment suspected of harboring illegal assemblies.[32] One such entry by the Vizcayan police may well illustrate how political meetings were held covertly. In January 1827 a *celador* (agent) in Bilbao entered a house only to find a large group of known constitutionalists, and the host, Juan de Elorriaga, was fined for conducting the gathering without the proper permit or knowledge of the authorities.[33] Likewise, the meetings of royalist volunteers (*voluntarios realistas*) and members of the Honor Guard (*Guardia de Honor*), though tolerated by the authorities in Bilbao, were tightly controlled by a vigilant police organization that kept close watch on the size of the membership, days of assembly, and other pertinent habits.[34] Going further still, the Vizcayan police, in an adventuresome move, experimented for some time in 1824–1825 with an undercover agent (*celador secreto*). The police spy, Elias Storm, kept both the constitutionalists and the right-wing elements under constant surveillance, monitoring in particular the parties' frequent meetings.[35] And yet, as abundant official materials make clear, the brunt of police activity was aimed at constitutionalists, especially those suspected of subversion. Following the 1830 July Revolution, for instance, the specter of revolution in the region brought about renewed police interest in the liberals' suspicious gatherings in the Concejo de Sopuerta.[36]

In the repression against constitutionalists, the Vizcayan police appear to have successfully institutionalized the act of informing, a practice eagerly fostered both among the population at large and local authorities. With the foolproof guarantees of confidentiality and the enticement of monetary rewards, citizens were urged to inform on violators of police ordinances.[37] Moreover, as in 1828, town-ships and villages were asked by the Vizcayan police to report "those who spread alarming or subversive rumors, conduct suspicious cor-respondences, hold secret meetings, or attempt with suggestions to alter the spirits and incline them toward insubordinate ideas . . . and everything else which might contribute to . . . an exact idea of the[ir] true political orientation." Another circular dated July 1832—one suggestively labeled "very confidential"—was even more blunt and succinct: "All of the authorities . . . will incessantly watch over the political conduct of the inhabitants . . . and especially of those whose political status or previous conduct may give sufficient motives of suspicion."[38]

Continuing a policy begun in the earliest stages of the 1823 Res-toration, the local police carefully limited the use of firearms and gunpowder to the royalists and defenders of the political status quo.[39] Those able to bear arms in public (or keep them at home), more-over, could only do so with police permits and after registering the weapons. Exempt from these regulations were the royalist mili-tias, most notably the Paisanos Armados.[40] Control was so strong that former constitutionalists and members of the volunteer militias were required to file affidavits detailing what had happened to their weapons, and those still holding them—even if in the rare posses-sion of a permit—were expected to turn in their arms to the police.[41] Significantly, whereas members of the Brigadas received free hunt-ing licenses with their safe-conducts, constitutionalists were denied the same privilege.[42] Expectedly, the royalist monopoly in arms bear-ing was deeply resented by Vizcayan reformers. As if speaking on their behalf, in a classic statement replete with connotations of class conflict, John Francis Bacon colorfully (if perhaps exaggeratedly) de-scribed the constitutionalists' loss of privilege and wounded pride: "No person whose opinions were other than Carlist, was allowed to shoot or have a gun in his possession, under penalty of fine and im-prisonment. This was hard enough, considering that three-fourths of the land in Biscay belonged to the anti-Carlists. Thus, the arti-sans and peasantry used to divert themselves in sporting over the estates of the Uhagons, Aldecoas, Allende, Salazar, and others, their owners not daring to pull a trigger, nor even complain."[43] The bear-ing of arms exclusively by royalists, in fact, remained in effect until April 1833 when, at the central government's direction, the Dipu-tación was forced into substantial concessions. Visibly against its will, the provincial government declared that all Vizcayans had the right to use hunting weapons, but that offensive—i.e., war-making —arms such as rifles would remain in the sole possession of the Paisanos, the paramilitary corps still under the Diputación's direct supervision.[44]

Fundamentally then, after a shaky and uncertain start which included protests from some local quarters, the Vizcayan police steadily grew in effectiveness and influence throughout the 1824– 1833 period.[45] In October 1830 Regnaudin, not normally sympathetic to the rightist Vizcayan authorities, praised it as a "good interior police."[46] Its small, permanent, administrative staff (three to four officials at most) operated successfully with the diputaciones of the decade to give the police an importance far greater than the number of personnel might indicate.[47] Miguel de Artiñano, the police secretary, senior official, chief architect, and erstwhile archivist of the Diputación in the mid-1820s, eventually became a staunch Carlist. And the first police officer, Antonio de Gurbista, included among his memberships a stint in Bilbao's rightist Guardia de Honor during the heated, early days of the 1823 Restoration. Both unquestionably contributed to the Vizcayan police's extreme conservatism. Through its unyielding methods and ideological orientation—insistence upon the preservation of public order and the political status quo—the tandem Diputación-police force was able to exercise considerable control over a sympathetic and overwhelmingly traditionalist constituency. However, to constitutionalists and their political allies, predictably, police actions and regulations were intolerable. The repeated liberal complaints, in fact, eloquently attest to the Vizcayan police's effectiveness. Speculated the prominent local progressive reformer Victor Luis de Gaminde in 1837: "In which point of Spain was the liberal as vexed as in Bilbao?" Bacon, one of Vizcayan constitutionalism's chief foreign allies, was equally if not more critical. And years later, Antonio Pirala, the noted historian of the Carlist Wars, wrote that the Vizcayan "Diputación served as an intendant, as a subdelegate of police (and with malevolence) against the liberals."[48]

Strong opposition to the Vizcayan police also came from a perhaps unexpected quarter, namely, the central government. Why this was the case is easy to discern. During the last years of Ferdinand VII's reign there are pointed indications—disagreements over organization and methods, distrust, and tension among the parties—that the Basque police forces were probably serving the fuerista interests of the Basque diputaciones far better than those of the state. Of course at the heart of the conflict, particularly from the mid-1820s on, were key questions concerning the provincial polices' status: to wit, who had ultimate control over them. These matters became sufficiently serious to warrant an 1827 governmental review of the Basque police organizations' autonomy and independence from Madrid.[49] Yet, as in 1824, the national administration backed off from a centralist takeover, leaving the polices completely in the Basque diputaciones' hands. Not coincidentally, the latter decision was communicated to the regional governments in October 1827 (from Tarragona), in the midst of the dangerous Agraviado challenge to Ferdinand VII—an excellent indication of the way Basques often benefited from political circumstances and centralist weaknesses.[50]

Notwithstanding the important concessions, mounting troubles and disorders—some of them police-related—in the Basque provinces during the late 1820s continued to nag the central government, forcing it to take action once more. This time the royal administration commissioned Manuel Leonardo Vizmanos, a prosecutor of the Council of Navarra and a trusted bureaucrat with a reputation for rigor and thoroughness, to tour the area, and gather all of the judicial proceedings regarding the latest occurrences, then propose appropriate actions.[51] After suggesting that all royalist militias in the Basque region be brought under direct governmental control, Vizmanos tellingly recommended "the necessity of putting the police in those provinces on the same footing as it is in the rest of the kingdom."[52] Clearly, this meant trying to take the provincial police out of the diputaciones' dominance. Predictably, in 1830 and again in 1832 the central government and the Basque leaderships clashed over the status of the police in the region. Profoundly worried about the influence of the local polices, the royal administration apparently succeeded in wresting much of the police organization from the Guipúzcoan Diputación in 1832.[53] Disappointingly for Madrid, however, Alava and Vizcaya were able to preserve a total hold of their police apparatuses until the end of Ferdinand VII's reign.

II. THE PAISANOS ARMADOS

Despite their similarities and parallels (which included the shared role as counterrevolutionary bodies, conflicts between the Basque leaderships and the central government over their control, links to Carlism and other common points of reference), the police and the Brigadas followed markedly different paths to achieve complete institutionalization. Basically, it would take much longer —about three years—for the Diputación to fully articulate and organize the provincial militias. Nor would the road be a smooth one. Numerous factors contributed to the troubled process: most notably, the important local rivalries over jurisdiction and direction; the differences (some of them political) between the militias' rank and file and the leaderships; the volatile sociopolitical atmosphere of the mid-1820s (especially in Bilbao) that facilitated public disorders stemming from long-standing feuds; the royalist corps' aggressiveness and patent lack of discipline; the sheer numbers (in the thousands) involved; the expense; and, of course, the significant logistics, equipment, and training difficulties. Each of these influenced (in many cases retarding, still in others facilitating) the Diputación's plans for the Vizcayan militias. Fortunately for the provincial government, however, the central administration's policies toward the regional military organizations were a puzzling mixture of fear, ineptitude and, worse yet, inaction. Thus, in the long run the diputaciones were able to overcome local obstacles, capitalize effectively on Madrid's indecision and lack of forcefulness, and gain an unchallenged dominance of the militias. The Vizcayan example amply illustrates these processes.

The institutional origins, indeed the very legitimacy, of the Brigadas are rooted in the early moments of the 1823 Restoration, namely, in the measures enacted by the provincial authorities during April and May to promote social order through the organization of new militias.[54] So it appeared to those attending the May 1824 Vizcayan general assembly. More specifically: An ad hoc commission of the juntas called upon to review the February 1824 royal charter for the kingdom's royalist volunteers—transmitted to the Diputación by the Captain General of Guipúzcoa, the region's ranking military officer—pointedly recommended rejection of the national code and suggested instead the preservation of the local twenty-man system in effect since April–May of the previous year.[55] Furthermore, May 1824 is a significant date since it was apparently the first time that the nomenclature "Paisanos Armados" was applied to a sector of the Vizcayan royalist militias (the other being Bilbao's Guardia de Honor, a body eventually integrated into the first although preserving its original name).[56] Nonetheless, as if to show that the province was not negligent in its duties and feeling some pressure to act, on May 25 the parley enacted new guidelines which added little in fact to the regulations already governing the local militias for about a year. But several important national events and local developments in late summer and early fall 1824 created widespread interest in the formation of a comprehensive charter for Vizcayan armed royalists. This became an all too familiar pattern in the following years. In other words, in a kind of knee-jerk response, specific occurrences—many of them political though often unrelated to local life—pushed the authorities to take action vis-à-vis the local volunteers' organization. Significantly, important lines were blurred in the process, and through the efforts of a conservative Diputación the bodies, initially conceived primarily as a modest rural police, expanded their functions and responsibilities to become more ambitious paramilitary forces with a marked political emphasis on the struggle against revolution and reform.[57] In short, as with the police, peace keeping and political control were closely related in the militias—certainly not an unintentional linkage as far as the Diputación was concerned.

Important national events and local conflicts contributed to the necessity of chartering the Vizcayan militias. In August 1824, as a result of purported liberal activities in southern Spain, the Diputación reactivated the "companies of Paisanos Armados" in accordance with the measures decreed by the May 1824 General Juntas. A fifteen-article ordinance placed the Paisanos under the direct dependence and control of the Vizcayan municipalities.[58] (This would become an apparent point of contention in the following years as the provincial government usurped these responsibilities from the townships and increasingly monopolized all of the Paisanos' effective powers.) Other challenges struck much closer to home, among them the steady return to Vizcaya of former constitutionalist militiamen. The ineptitude of the local authorities in dealing with them and the continual insubordination of the royalist corps at Bilbao resulted in repeated public disturbances during the first part of 1824. The incidents, largely promoted by the municipality's Guardia de Honor, pitted the royalist volunteers against the constitutionalists and their purported French protectors.[59] In a masterful understatement, the commander of French military forces in Spain remarked in April 1824 that the situation in Bilbao "was far from reassuring," a state of affairs that he attributed in part to the royalists' refusal to disarm.[60] At this time the Guardia was between 1,000 and 1,200 men strong in Bilbao alone. A mean-spirited city council used it as its private instrument to "protect public order" although the militia's excesses against the vanquished political faction were already notorious and had begun to alarm the Diputación and others. In mid-1824 the provincial government attempted to end the unrest, albeit unsuccessfully, through fresh measures and recommendations: expulsion from the Guardia of known troublemakers, greater discipline in the corps, and a ban on the use of arms except when on duty. But the municipality fought back to preserve the prerogatives of its forces, and a sharp struggle with the Diputación ensued.[61] The disobedience of the units, however, became so pronounced that even the city council, along with Pedro Novia de Salcedo, commander in chief of the Guardia, requested (with mostly unknown results) the purge of its most undisciplined elements. Given the urban militia's intransigent disposition, a confrontation with the authorities was all but inevitable.

As a prelude to wider disturbances, some of the Guardia's officers severely criticized the local ruling elites' seeming indifference. In an ultraroyalist, manifestolike document dated 24 September 1824, the corps' leaders observed that "in a town such as Bilbao . . . in which so many have distinguished themselves by their opinion in favor of the extinguished system, it seems incredible that everybody may have remained in such a profound apathy."[62] A reservoir of royalist resentment finally exploded on 29 September, triggering a riot that resulted in the ouster of the Marquis de Villarías, one of the general deputies. The Marquis, already under a cloud of suspicion since the May 1823 juntas for alleged constitutionalist leanings, was an obvious target for royalists, along with Casimiro de Lóizaga, the consultor of the Diputación, a political moderate and former Vizcayan representative to the Cortes.[63]

The 29 September disorder began in the course of a popular celebration (to coincide with the anniversary of the king's liberation?) when a group of Miqueletes, deployed by the Diputación to preserve order during the event, attempted to disarm several militiamen and royalist veterans from the Trienio.[64] Affronted, a considerable number of the latter laid vociferous siege to the seat of the Diputación to protest the government's peace-keeping measures and to demand Villarías's resignation. In fact, the angry mob made repeated threats against the Marquis' life—an extraordinarily unusual occurrence in local political life given the respect bordering on veneration

traditionally accorded the highest provincial authorities.[65] Whether
because of fear or for other reasons, Villarías left Bilbao shortly thereafter and retired to his house at Somorrostro. In a letter written soon
after his arrival, while noting the Vizcayan government's "impotent
state," the Marquis expressed his intention not to return to his post
until the Diputación was moved to another town.[66] The government
remained in Bilbao and, more significantly, the general deputy apparently never regained the office relinquished under rightist pressure.

Understandably, the Villarías affair, a contemporary local *cause
célèbre,* sparked renewed interest in the formation of a new charter
for Bilbao's militias. Possibly at the city council's behest, an ad hoc
committee of notables—including former leaders of the Diputación
(*padres de provincia*), clergy, and members of the militia—convened
on 8 October to draft new regulations for the *Guardia de Honor o Paisanos Armados.*[67] León de Jáuregui, one of Villarías's associates and
likely the one in line to succeed him, reported that no one doubted
that "all of the disorders, which unfortunately have been so frequent
until today, will be prevented" if the charter's provisions were "punc-
tually observed."[68] In addition, hoping to improve matters, the municipal authorities carried out reforms (how extensive it is not clear)
in the militias' chain of command.[69] The Diputación also moved
to prevent further outbreaks of violence with a harsh police ordinance dated 12 October, yet the provincial government was visibly
unwilling to start judicial proceedings against the disturbances' in-
stigators. Consequently, despite Villarías's insistence that charges
be pressed to clear the authorities' good name and reputation, a
wounded Diputación sidetracked the politically sensitive issue, perhaps hoping it would eventually fade. In the meantime, still no charter existed to regulate all the Vizcayan militias, and the authorities'
reluctance to bring to justice the disorders' perpetrators probably encouraged the growth of right-wing activism, an important political
force responsible for much of the mid-1820s turbulence.[70] These circumstances forced the July 1825 Vizcayan general assembly to take
yet another look at the militias. Called upon to review the previous charters and make recommendations "on the military forces of
the towns of the señorío," an ad hoc commission balked at tackling
the larger problems head-on. Rather than the necessary sweeping
reorganization, the commission suggested "greater care in the subordination and instruction of the Paisanos Armados, using mild and
prudent correctives, and maintaining in each town an [armed com-

pany] of twenty men, equipped with bayonet[s] and ammunition."[71] In a flagrant demonstration of confidence and lassitude, the juntas totally accepted the recommendations, in effect preserving the status quo. Matters would be quite different, however, under the forceful leadership of Novia de Salcedo and the Marquis de Valde-espina at the head of the Diputación (1825–1827). The most tangible impulse toward change was generated not in Vizcaya but in Madrid.

Somewhat ironically, given the internal discord, Basque actions regarding the royalist volunteers, nevertheless, had begun to create widespread apprehension among central government officials. The administration's concern may well have been partly related to the imminent French departure from Bilbao, effective 1 January 1825.[72] Already in October 1824, the Vizcayan police had sent to central headquarters (probably at the latter's urging) a report on the number of royalist volunteers in the province.[73] Moreover, the ministry's worries increased during 1825, most noticeably as a result of the June–July 1825 disturbances in Bilbao—ostensibly triggered by elections in the Consulado—and because of the numerous difficulties which the central government encountered in connection with the Guipúzcoan and Alavese royalist militias.[74] Governmental attention to these questions is reflected in the Council of Ministers' extensive deliberations.[75]

On 29 June 1825, the council agreed that the corregidor of Bilbao be asked to "inform confidentially" on the state of Vizcaya, and "declare the strength of the royalist corps . . . what forces they have and where they are located, if they have increased or not, and in virtue of what orders."[76] By 10 July the corregidor had received an official report from the Diputación on the state of the Vizcayan militias. According to the document, the Paisanos in the province already numbered 12,680 men grouped into 634 companies of 20 men each although, as the corregidor pointed out, the majority were poorly armed.[77] This was hardly surprising since traditionally the Paisanos' equipment had been inadequate. For instance, the Vizcayan police had reported in November 1824 that the local royalist corps only had 2,696 rifles and 2,090 bayonets.[78] In other words, only about 15–20 percent of the militias were adequately armed. One of the comprehensive and incisive analyses of the political situation in the Basque provinces, and of the challenge to the central government posed by the regional military forces, was provided in September 1825 by Luis de Salazar, the minister of the navy. He observed that without the proper governmental authorization the diputaciones were raising, organizing, arming, instructing, and disciplining the royalist militias.[79] By so doing "with absolute and total independence from the authority of the government," according to the angry minister, the provinces were forging "a kind of feudalism and popular confederation, the most antimonarchic imaginable"—an extraordinarily serious accusation. Consequently, Salazar urged administration colleagues to be vigilant of subversion and to "be prepared ahead of time to undo in every way the possibility of such occurrences." Then, in a key passage that deserves quoting at length because of its far-reaching implications, the minister ominously and prophetically warned: "Because even though we may not believe, as it should not be imagined possible, that the moment will arrive when [Basque] arms will be used in opposition to the sovereign mandates of His Majesty, it is beyond doubt, however, that certain peoples under the government of a federative system, and with the support of such a respectable force, will be capable through threats alone of imposing respect upon the government, and [thereby] give substance to even their most extravagant demands under the pretext of the Basque Fueros."[80] But Salazar was still not through. To underline his concern, the minister observed disquietly that the Basque provinces were capable of forming an army of close to 30,000 men "to defend in their own and rugged terrain the *precious fueros* they enjoy with the patriotic enthusiasm they attempt to instill among these troops. But to whom will the intention be attributed [of] reducing the said Fueros? Consequently, against whom is prepared the resistance of this privileged militia? . . . The answer is no less troublesome."[81] These remarks were consistent with Salazar's previous stances in the council. Earlier that year, in fact, he had recommended dispatching troops to the Basque provinces "with the purpose of forcing compliance and obedience to the measures which the government has taken," a suggestion strongly endorsed at various times by fellow council members, notably those of finance and war but, more importantly, vetoed by a conciliatory Ferdinand VII in September of the same year.[82] Although the monarch's prudent course was doubtless conditioned by short-term pragmatism, in the long run, the central administration would come to regret its weakness at this crucial juncture. The Basque political leaderships (in particular the Vizcayan one) wasted little time exploiting Madrid's passivity.

Working hard to overcome the local squabbles that had plagued the militias, a revivified and considerably more conservative Vizcayan Diputación—with Novia de Salcedo and Valde-espina at the helm—spent most of 1826 securing arms and equipment, reinforcing coastal defenses, and making detailed inquiries into the overall state of the province's royalist corps.[83] Simultaneously, as part of its general military strategy, the Diputación fought and won an important victory on 1 May 1826 when the central government formally recognized total Vizcayan control over the province's royalist forces.[84] As if to underscore this essential point, when the royal administration approved the new June 1826 charter of the kingdom's royalist volunteers, a thirty-two-article addendum (*adición*) to the code clearly specified the Basque diputaciones' newly legitimized dominance of the militias.[85] Freed from uncertainties and constraints, the decisions enabled the Vizcayan government to pursue a more independent and aggressive course. At an increasingly rapid pace, armament was eagerly sought at Santoña, at the royal arms factory of Plasencia, at Pamplona, and elsewhere.[86] Also, as a result of a kind of invasion psychosis and siege mentality that would characterize much of the decade, the Diputación continually stressed the need for coastal readiness.[87] Likewise, foreign developments and the dangers of "revolutionary contagion" were purposefully wielded politically by the Vizcayan leadership to maintain high degrees of tension and vigilance among the militias.[88]

By early 1827, a visibly confident Diputación had decided to systematize the Paisanos' organization and place the corps on a permanent footing. Exactly how these decisions were reached—e.g., what prompted them most directly, the role played by past events and other considerations—is complex and intriguing. At least part of the answer lies in the revealing preamble to the Diputación's 29 January 1827 interim charter for the Paisanos. According to the provincial government's official explanation: "The more extensive armament of the coastal towns [and] the establishment of watchtowers was more than sufficient to prevent the excursion of bandits, but the concurrence of so many factors induced [it] to convince itself that the time was near when *only the organized use of arms could pacify the Vizcayan territory*." And added the Vizcayan leadership: "Unfortunately, the time so expected has finally arrived: the revolution is very close to Spain . . . [and] the Diputación which, with these fears in mind, has made every effort to secure and equip itself with the largest numbers of arms, repairing and preparing the coastal batteries, *believes that the time has come when the Señorío can no longer be considered to be in a state of peace* and that it is consequently necessary and indispensable to adopt the form of twenty-men parties to which the region is accustomed in circumstances of such [a] nature."[89]

The January 1827 code, explicitly a temporary measure, seemingly contained little new in comparison to earlier ordinances. A close examination of the document, however, discloses significant differences of organization, scope, and intent.[90] In addition to spelling out the Paisanos' duties in greater detail, the new regulations restructured the chains of command to improve the militias' operational effectiveness. Moreover, the January 1827 charter makes it clear that the Diputación had begun to divide the province into well-defined military districts, a major innovation from previous measures.[91] Also, when the code was submitted to the inspector general of Royalist Volunteers for approval, the Vizcayan government vigorously defended its policies, citing the province's peculiar geography, terrain, and habitat—factors which, in its view, combined to make a special military organization imperative.[92] In the meantime, the responses to the inquiries circulated by the Diputación in December 1826 revealed not only the continuing material inadequacies of the Paisanos, but also that their numbers had declined and were not nearly as great as earlier estimates had optimistically suggested. A "general state of the organized force in the Señorío," dated March 1827, cast a disappointing total of only 9,230 men, or 27 percent less than the mid-1825 figures. If the numbers had dropped there was some comfort in the fact that of these, 5,478 were now well armed (roughly 60 percent), 3,540 poorly equipped, and 212 of indeterminate status.[93] This ratio was a sizeable three- to fourfold improvement over mid-1825. (Incidentally, the March 1827 ratio would remain strikingly constant in the future, notably, even when the Vizcayan militias increased by as much as one-third over the 9,230 figure.) In sum, even though the 1826 efforts had paid off, the Paisanos clearly needed additional arms. Therefore, during the first part of 1827, the Diputación continued to reach out in every direction to secure weapons and equipment. Several reasons, old and new, accounted for the Vizcayan military buildup.

First, the provincial government wished to present itself before the royal administration as having well-armed militias to prevent centralist criticisms of unpreparedness. Second, in a collateral issue, the Diputación wished to prevent the stationing of royal troops in Vizcaya under the pretext of the provincial authorities' inability to cope with invasions and to preserve internal order. Third, the Vizcayan leadership's efforts coincided with the central government's attempts to disarm the Guipúzcoan royalist forces, the source of considerable friction between Guipúzcoa and Madrid from February until June 1827.[94] If the events next door were indicative of the administration's intentions, surely Vizcaya needed to prepare swiftly to meet unpleasant eventualities. Quite simply, the more Paisanos were armed, the more difficult it would be to disarm them.[95] Fourth, the Diputación may well have wished to bolster the militias' strength as part of the ongoing political struggle against constitutionalism. The speedup of 1827 was particularly noticeable to French officials at Bayonne who found themselves forced to contend with an active illegal arms trade across the borders.[96] Indicative of the Vizcayan political classes' dogged determination, the Diputación even appealed directly to the ecclesiastical sectors, seeking to enroll their assistance in promoting the Paisanos' growth. Using its "notorious discretion," the clergy was urged "[to] contribute to impel the organization of the armament" by "clearing away . . . misunderstanding and . . . apathy."[97]

Unexpected, and in fact unintended, help also came from an unlikely quarter—the central government. The administration's vacillating and inconsistent policies toward the Basque militias doubtlessly encouraged the diputaciones' resistance and accelerated their military projects. For example, in yet another menacing about-face, the royal administration on 11 April 1827 temporarily suspended the May–June concessions and succeeded (at least theoretically) in equalizing the Basque militias with those of the rest of the kingdom. The important reversal was probably a response to the January 1827 interim guidelines for the Paisanos issued by the Vizcayan Diputación, as well as the result of widespread problems in Guipúzcoa over the status of that province's royalist forces. As in the past, however, the central government's firmness was extremely short-lived. On 7 June 1827, for reasons that remain unclear, a royal resolution suspended the 11 April measures, effectively leaving the Basque diputaciones once again in full control of the militias.[98] Madrid's vacillation had set the stage for the great Vizcayan offensive of July–September 1827.

By July 1827, the Diputación's tireless efforts had yielded substantial results. Total enrollment in the Vizcayan militias had reached

12,077, an increase of almost 31 percent over March 1827 figures. Of these, 7,287 were judged to be well armed and 4,790 were not.[99] Despite the increase of the poorly equipped, on balance, the authorities' zeal had unquestionably built up overall royalist military strength in the province. To continue and consolidate these gains, a comprehensive set of regulations encompassing all of the Vizcayan militias would have to be drawn up. Important steps in this direction were taken at the July 1827 Vizcayan Juntas, an assembly held under the sign of militant foralismo.[100] Probably reflecting a growing consensus among the provincial leadership, on 17 July a large ad hoc commission dealing with the Señorío's military forces (*comisión del punto de armamento*) reported to the gathering: "It becomes necessary to expand and widen the charter even more, and this operation . . . cannot be carried out in a brief moment. The commission therefore believes that the enlargement and extension of the charter must be especially entrusted to the Diputación . . . authorizing it competently so that, aided by a Permanent Commission . . . and keeping in mind previous charters of the region and even the general ones of the nation inasmuch as they do not contradict our Fueros . . . , they can realize such a useful task."[101] As one of the ad hoc body's eleven recommendations, four individuals were specifically designated for membership in the Permanent Commission that would draft the new code: the two outgoing general deputies, Novia de Salcedo and Valde-espina, along with Juan Martín de Ibargoitia and José Ramón de Rotaeche. Significantly, all four became top-echelon leaders in the Paisanos Armados, together with five other members of the July 1827 comisión del punto de armamento.[102] Among the most committed advocates of intransigent royalism and the provincial liberties, these nine formed the core leadership of what liberal opponents labeled the "armed party" in Vizcaya. And, as might be expected, the links between the upper commands of the Paisanos and the Diputación remained extremely close at all times.

The newly created Permanent Commission (for Vizcayan Armament)—Valde-espina, Novia de Salcedo, Rotaeche, and Ibargoitia—wasted little time in getting down to work. On 21 September 1827, merely two months after receiving its mandate, the body presented the Diputación with the first general charter for the territory's Brigadas de Paisanos Armados.[103] Immediately accepted by the provincial government, the extensive code was divided into seven parts or chapters and comprised a total of ninety articles. This landmark document merits detailed attention. Chapter 1 (articles 1–37), by far the longest, dealt at length with geography and organization: territorial divisions, strength of units, hierarchy and rank, chains of command, relations between the echelons, nominations, authority, and collateral matters. One significant innovation—more precisely, an important elaboration upon the 29 January 1827 interim charter —divided the province into six major and clearly delineated territorial units known as *secciones o Brigadas*. For example, Bilbao (its Guardia de Honor apparently at last incorporated into the Paisanos' general structure) and several adjacent townships (Abando, Alonsotegui, Begoña, and Deusto) composed the First Section or Brigade.[104] Each section had a military chief known as a *Jefe de sección o Brigada*. In turn, every section was subdivided into three districts— eighteen in all for the province—of battalion-size strength, each led by a commander. Hence, in all, section leaders were responsible for three battalions, or roughly between 1,800 and 2,500 men. Several key articles—e.g., numbers 7, 25, 33, and 36—left little doubt that the Diputación intended to exercise firm control over the Paisanos.

Chapter 2 (articles 38–50), defined the corps' military training. Section chiefs, district commanders, company captains, and other officers were made responsible for their subordinates' instruction. Ambitiously perhaps, the charter stated that the training accorded the Paisanos, if proportionate to their occupations and duties, would be that of regular army personnel. Holidays were singled out as prime times for military training, though the militias were also encouraged to practice on nonfestive occasions after notifying the proper authorities. As part of their instruction, militias were to receive sound indoctrination from their officers regarding the "most salutary and useful maxims and examples of cleanliness, discipline, love of Sovereign, and respect and obedience toward the civil authorities" (article 49).

Chapter 3, entitled "Ordinary Service" (articles 51–64), outlined the Paisanos' normal responsibilities. Consummating a shift of emphasis begun earlier, the new regulations advanced an explicitly counterrevolutionary raison d'être for the militias. Article 52 left no doubt: "The great object of the establishment of these corps is to combat and exterminate the revolution and the conspiracies against religion and the state. The absolute tranquillity of the town where they live and its complete security against the disturbances or attempts of the enemies of the Altar and Throne, offspring of political revolutions, and against the other enemies that can disturb [the peace] is their principal and special charge and trust that they must preserve at every cost." This political responsibility was limited by the code to service in the "interior of each town." It should be underscored, however, that the militias' duties in standard police operations were not abolished by the new charter. For instance, the Paisanos were expected to engage in patrols should the local authorities deem it necessary and, when on duty, check travelers' passports, keep watch over lodging houses, eating places, and other establishments. Moreover, the corps were to aid the municipal authorities in the event of fires, alarms and commotions, conspiracies (*conspiración*), and were supposed to come to the assistance of their neighbors in case of theft, attack plots, or intrigue (*asechanza*). Finally, the Paisanos were expected to pursue and arrest wrongdoers and deserters. Yet, all of these activities were given secondary importance in the charter.

Chapter 4 specified the Paisanos' "extraordinary service" (articles 65–69). The militias' responsibilities under this heading fell largely into duty *outside* their native districts and bases (*fuera del término de la jurisdicción del pueblo*). The Paisanos' heightened political role was vividly reiterated in article 65: "The revolutionaries and the conspirators against the state will be considered by these corps to be in the front line of the wrongdoers or public criminals." Again, and not by accident, the Diputación was able to equate political activism with criminal behavior, an important device with which to clamp down on the political opposition—be it from the right or left. Discipline and subordination in the corps were the subjects of chapter 5 (articles 70–81). The charter dealt sternly with these questions; witness the following: "Subordination consists of obeying without objection or delay in every command concerning service." Another article was also specific on these points: "When the militias assemble to take up arms to perform the duties which are proper to them, at this point begins *the absolute right of command, and among those who are to obey as military men an absolute and most punctual obedience without the slightest delay.*"[105] Those Paisanos punished for infractions of the code could appeal the sentences handed down by superiors, but could do so only through complicated procedures up the chain of command, a process that probably discouraged grievances and made redress difficult to militiamen. There was little of note that was new in the very brief chapter 6 on artillery (articles 82–83). Following the January 1827 interim guidelines, the new charter formally established artillery companies along the coast. Finally, chapter 7, misleadingly entitled "General Measures" (articles 84–90), dealt almost exclusively with the functions and responsibilities of the district commander: e.g., among others, his role as a conduit between the section chiefs and his subordinates, his obligations in the maintenance of the equipment and in the inspection and training of the corps. In conclusion, these regulations, with minor adjustments, essentially governed the Vizcayan militias until the outbreak of the First Carlist War.

After the adoption of the charter, the Diputación continued to arm and organize the Brigadas, doing so even in the face of noticeable adversity. To the chagrin of the provincial authorities, there was lassitude, lack of enthusiasm, and subtle resistance among Vizcayans toward the militias. In effect, these attitudes seemed to suggest an absence of popular support and commitment to the Brigadas. After all, we should not forget that the Paisanos were paramilitary bodies and not full-time military corps. Militiamen for the most part were peasants and artisans whose time away from primary tasks could easily harm their livelihood. As such, the continual exercises and training—veritable hardships—did not sit well with some of the militias. These difficulties were compounded by the Paisanos' poor training and a lack of qualified military instructors.[106] The Diputación tried to overcome these shortcomings with its customary determination and with creative forms of political and ideological pressure. A 31 March 1832 manifesto of the Vizcayan leadership to the Paisanos spoke characteristically of "the imperious necessity of not slackening in precautionary measures, and of always living alertly and prepared to preserve the country from the contagious germ of innovation and disorder which, propagated by its satellites throughout the globe, has spilled torrents of blood and disarranged the political machinery of the nations."[107] Aided by these emotional arguments and, more importantly, by dint of extraordinarily hard work despite some ups and downs, the provincial government was able to maintain the Brigadas at high levels of manpower in the second half of the Ominous Decade. Two reasonably reliable estimates, for instance, place the Paisanos' total strength at 13,362 in August 1833 and at 14,276 at the time of the war's outbreak in October 1833—figures that represent a clear advance over the 12,077 enrolled in the corps in July 1827.[108] According to Bacon, this number was "nearly one-half of those able to bear arms."[109]

Significantly, a few weeks before the start of the war, of the six section chiefs, five had been general deputies during the past decade, and two other top-level officers had held high public offices in the Diputación and the Bilbao city council. It is almost as if *some* of the notables who by 1832–1833 had begun to lose their institutional stranglehold on the province for one reason or another, had decided to retrench in the Brigadas to preserve their considerable political influence through these corps. This is hardly surprising given that at least after 1826–1827 the militias' organization was part of a conscious general counterrevolutionary strategy. An excellent case in point: The Marquis de Valde-espina, out of office and already under suspicion in Madrid since 1830 for supposed ultraroyalist leanings, observed in June 1832: "The number of reformers grows, they occupy important posts, and they are free of our surveillance. *Only arms will be able to contain their projects* . . . [since] apathy is unfortunately becoming generalized, and it is not easy to reestablish the public spirit with words and admonitions."[110] Not quite five months later, Regnaudin reported a sudden upsurge in Vizcayan military preparations.[111] If as Valde-espina and others suggested, public attitude toward the Brigadas was far from enthusiastic and had begun to flag in 1831–1832, the new conservative Diputación headed by Pedro Antonio de Ventades and José Ramón de Rotaeche (both of them Brigade section chiefs) chose to reinvigorate the province's military preparedness. Essentially, then, in a recurrent and impressive display of voluntarism, the Paisanos, conceived and organized from above, were maintained at all costs—even under extremely unfavorable conditions such as those of 1832–1833 described below—by those who had created them. Nevertheless, fortuitous political circumstances also came to the rescue of the Diputación's military projects. Lausagarreta's royalist 1827 mini-uprising in Guipúzcoa (near Vizcaya) and Mina's liberal 1830 invasion of Navarra provided the provincial leadership and the Brigadas with ideal opportunities for testing the militias' loyalty and for enacting military "dress rehearsals" in wait of future eventualities. Furthermore, through self-serving and inflated accounts of its services during the seemingly dangerous episodes, the Diputación skillfully kept tensions high, galvanized public opinion against troublemakers (political or otherwise) and, in the process, reaped an unexpected propaganda bonanza.[112] The Paisanos' successes, however, naturally stirred up misgivings in Madrid and animosity among local reformers.

Control over the Basque militias continued to be a hot point of contention between the diputaciones and the central government during the late 1820s and early 1830s. In October 1829, Commissioner Vizmanos had directly proposed shifting the corps' "immediate command[s]" from the diputaciones to the captain general of Guipúzcoa, a move that would have assured centralist dominance of the volunteers.[113] But as in previous situations involving both the police and the Paisanos, Vizmanos's recommendations were not heeded by the royal administration. And this, despite similar May 1830 advice from the normally pro-Basque Council of State to the monarch that would have seriously curbed the Basque militias' autonomy.[114] By mid-1830, following the scare of the July Revolution in France and its sequels, there was understandably much less willingness in Madrid to alter the Basque militias' status even if, for precisely the same reasons, the recent events had provided the administration with a powerful strategic rationale for strengthening its presence in the north, while simultaneously improving the region's preparedness through unified military commands. Fundamentally, if Ferdinand VII's government squandered this timely occasion to bring the militias into line, Mina's romantic revolutionary attempt of 1830, meanwhile, opened up yet another favorable political conjuncture for the Vizcayan Diputación's military and ideological campaigns.[115] The militias, however, were not without unfavorable domestic consequences. More specifically, the Paisanos' counterrevolutionary role and their overwhelmingly lower-class origins brought them into open and frequent conflict (individually and collectively) with local reformers and liberals.[116]

What limited evidence there is at the individual or personal level strongly suggests mutual and widespread hostility between the Vizcayan Paisanos and the constitutionalists. For example, in December 1826, José de Lezama, a well-known constitutionalist from Orduña, was accused of insulting members of the Bilbao royalist militias.[117] Another case, heavy with overtones of class conflict, occurred in 1827 when Gregorio Calderón, a prominent liberal and former member of the Voluntary Militia, reputedly insulted a young royalist artisan named Eizaguirre in Bilbao.[118] Tellingly, during the incident Eizaguirre, a nail maker, is said to have told Calderón to give him two pesetas because the "blacks"—i.e., the constitutionalists—had "taken money away from [his] mother." To which an irate Calderón replied, *"provinciano de mierda,"* thereby triggering a physical attack upon the former by Eizaguirre.[119] At his trial the artisan attempted to acquit himself with the reckless political defense "that it was of no consequence if a black died because at no time should any[one of them] insult or challenge a royalist."[120] Notwithstanding these bold expressions, Eizaguirre was convicted of assault and soundly reprimanded by the prosecutor. Another near incident involving the militias and the constitutionalists took place in October 1830 (coinciding with heightened tension because of Mina's invasion?) when a unit of royalist volunteers exercising in Gordejuela was unsuccessfully urged by one or two of its members to take away arms purportedly kept by a "black" and then attack him with bayonets.[121] These episodes, in conjunction with the written testimonies of important local reformers, reveal a profound reciprocal antipathy between Vizcayan liberalism and the Paisanos.[122] Nor could it be otherwise given the way the volunteers were used and abused— if P. P. de Uhagon's account is to be believed—by the corps' chiefs "to direct the deliberations in all of the province's townships and in its General Juntas," thereby clashing with liberalism's interests and aspirations.[123]

Led at once by Vizcayan reformers and central government representatives, each with particular grievances and axes to grind, a serious challenge to the Paisanos began to crystallize in 1832–1833. Local opponents of the royalist militias saw the possibility of dismantling an organization long considered (no doubt correctly) a cornerstone of political reaction and an instrument of repression. However, instead of attacking the corps directly, Vizcayan liberalism sought to undermine the Paisanos through the attractive subterfuges of economic savings and administrative reform—therefore ensuring local or municipal dominance of the militias. According to P. P. de Uhagon, a promising attempt to return the Paisanos to the townships' control had begun at the 1829 Vizcayan Juntas: a brave effort whose results, nonetheless, were overturned in 1830–1831 in reaction to Cavanilles's planned visit and Mina's revolutionary incursion in Navarra.[124] However, now greatly strengthened politically by the October 1832 amnesty which had given them a freer hand and wider participation in public affairs, local reformers boldly stepped up criticism of the Brigadas in 1833.

Significantly, in May 1833 when the town of Begoña (near Bilbao) hotly debated a tax linked to the Paisanos' equipment, several participants openly voiced opposition to the township's policies vis-à-vis the militias. Taking direct aim at reformers, a visibly irritated Vizcayan police, still very much in conservative hands, reported that some of the Begoña protesters were "guided undoubtedly by the spirit of partisanship which they [had] displayed for some time," rather than "out of the ideas of economy that they advocate[d]."[125] The provincial government repeated this theme in a frantic late June 1833 warning to central police headquarters in Madrid regarding, among others, the adverse consequences for the militias of liberal participation in the upcoming Vizcayan Juntas. Characteristically, leaving little doubt where it stood politically, an obviously edgy Diputación minced no words in attacking the reformers' intentions and goals: "According to their conversations . . . their first attack will be aimed at destroying or neutralizing the territory's armament because they view it as the foundation of the monarchy; and, afterwards, if they succeed in electing delegates of their persuasion, they will gradually diminish the royalist spirit and substitute it with that of revolution through ever-dangerous innovations."[126] Moreover, just prior to the July General Assembly's opening, in a letter that for unknown reasons was never sent to national police headquarters, the Diputación again sounded an alarm over the damage that liberals would do to the Paisanos, noting that in new hands the province's armament, "whose purpose is to maintain the rights of an absolute monarchy," could eventually take "a turn diametrically opposed to all of these conservative principles."[127] Almost desperate appeals to a less than sympathetic central government, the last-ditch attempts of Vizcayan traditionalists to preserve the militias intact seemed headed for failure. Their fears, nevertheless, were well founded. The 1833 provincial assembly, attended by a *"large number of representatives excluded during the previous ten years,"* began to concern itself with ways of "destroying the nefarious prestige exercised until then by the armed force" by "returning to the townships the responsibility over [the militia] *of which they had been dispossessed illegally.*"[128] The attack against the Paisanos continued, and probably quickened, after the juntas.

Francisco de Hormaeche, a well-informed Vizcayan moderate and a direct participant in many of the period's important events, wrote that *following* the July 1833 gathering, in light of the growing influence of reformers and having elected one of their own (the notorious P. P. de Uhagon) to the post of deputy general for the first time in a decade, a concerted attempt was finally made to disband the Paisanos. Admittedly, this was done in part as a preventive measure to thwart the Carlists' advanced conspiratorial projects.[129] Hormaeche asserts significantly that "some townships, moved by the indirect insinuations of the [Diputación], asked in writing that the [militias] be dissolved as useless in times of peace [and also] costly and bothersome." Just as the resolution on this question was about to be reached, according to Hormaeche, news arrived of Ferdinand's death. In extremis, the Paisanos had been spared an untimely early demise.

Hormaeche's remarks, indeed the thrust of his interpretation, coincide remarkably (and not by accident) with the royal administration's views of, and policies toward, the Basque militias. In 1832, the new captain general of Guipúzcoa, Manuel Llauder, following in his predecessors' footsteps, strongly criticized the diputaciones' control of the local royalist corps. In October of that year, after a surge of proto-Carlist agitation in Bilbao, which included the posting of explicitly anti-Fernandine posters, Llauder sharply reprimanded the Vizcayan Diputación for its ineffectiveness in dealing with the situation, while complaining to the Ministry of War over the situation in his district as a result of the Paisanos' status.[130] Clearly, in the captain general's view, the central administration needed to make profound changes in the militias. Llauder was not alone in his views. Another influential government adviser, General Vicente Quesada, an officer with considerable first-hand knowledge of the Basque provinces, wrote Queen Maria Cristina following the October 1833 uprising: "The recent events of Talavera, Bilbao, and other points . . . justify the foresight with which I indicated the necessity of reforming the corps of royalist volunteers."[131] Finally, perhaps the convergence of the state's interests with those of Vizcayan liberalism was most eloquently illustrated by the rich testimony of P. P. de Uhagon, the acerb critic of the Diputación, who chastised the provincial government in 1834 for having used the "force of bayonets" against "the King's power" during the previous decade.[132] In essence, the bitter attacks on the province's royalist militias by local reformers and royal officials only serve to underscore further the Diputación's unquestionable successes in this key area.

In retrospect, there were undeniable links between the Paisanos and Carlism. The leadership of the Brigadas, for example, went over virtually wholesale to the pretender's side. Foralista stalwarts such as Ventades, Alzaá, Valde-espina, Rotaeche, Urquijo, and others became the political and military chieftains of Vizcayan Carlism. Given their preeminent sociopolitical status and prestige, they were able to drag substantial numbers of Paisanos into the fray. Furthermore, as is shown more fully in the last chapter, the Vizcayan militias—indeed all the Basque royalist corps—played a fundamental role in the October 1833 coup and uprising against the central government. In other words, without their decisive participation at critical moments of the political conjuncture, the insurrection might never have taken place. Addressing the reasons for the successful 1833 movement in the Basque provinces on behalf of Don Carlos, S. E. Widdrington underlined (for the most part rightly) the fact that "the arms [had been] in possession of the Carlist party under the denomination of *realistas*, and that the others were unarmed; the government having no troops in the [Basque] country."[133]

In conclusion, though part of a common political project and strategy, the Vizcayan police and militias followed different courses. In the case of the first, the Vizcayan leadership was able to master the entire body with relative ease. Through an effective police organization, the Diputación achieved impressive levels of penetration and control of the population in general and of liberals in particular. Using the police in this fashion and continually denouncing the alleged enemies of the crown, of orthodox royalism, and of local interests, the provincial government contributed powerfully to the formation of conservative public opinion in the territory during the 1823–1833 decade. The Paisanos, however, provided far greater difficulties and challenges for the provincial government. Toward the royalist corps, the Diputación was forced to proceed as much (and perhaps more) by circumstance than by design. In other words, with respect to the royalist corps, with no master plan readily apparent, and in light of substantial obstacles—internal and external—the political classes acted incrementally and on a trial-and-error basis. Hence, in the case of the Paisanos, a gradual evolution resulted—considerably more so than on the question of the police where, despite uncertainties and pressure from Madrid, the Vizcayan elites quickly gained the upper hand. And yet, despite the makeshift nature of many of the Diputación's actions leading to the formation of the historic September 1827 charter, the very tenacity and hard work displayed by the provincial government (particularly in the

1825–1827 period) enabled it to fashion order out of chaos, discipline out of insubordination, consensus out of disagreement, and uniformity out of disparity. Precisely because of its incessant efforts in militia-related matters, the Diputación garnered important political and ideological victories in the form of continued firm control over the opposition, consolidation of its base and advancement of conservative objectives, including the ever-essential defense of the fueros and local prerogative against centralist temptations. Therefore, the development and growth of the royalist corps were key contributing factors to Carlism. In their training, organization, disciplinary techniques, political orientation against reform, and defense of the cause of the "altar and throne"—instilled and reinforced in the militias by those at the helm of the conservative diputaciones of the era—can be found many of the elements and characteristics of Vizcayan Carlism.

CHAPTER 6

Economic Crisis, Reform, and Class Conflict

How is it that having the exclusive ownership of the
Mines of Somorrostro, possessing in their mountains
such an invaluable wealth and such an inexhaustible substance, and which is superior in quality to the known
ones, [Vizcayans] today find their forges in a primitive
state of backwardness, without other tools than the ham-
mer, without other mechanical power than the sturdy
arm, and without other achievement than that of reducing raw materials to coarse and poorly worked bars?

Victor Luis de Gaminde, Intereses de Bilbao, *1837*.

The profound economic crisis of the 1820s, along
with other important sociopolitical circumstances, created fertile
conditions and incentives for reform in Vizcaya. For the fuerista
political leadership, reform was essentially linked to a long-declining
and now stagnant iron industry, a crucial socioeconomic sector
in dire need of basic improvements and modernization to compete
successfully with foreign imports. However, rather than a complete
overhaul of traditional methods, the governing elites favored limited
changes to make iron production more viable. This way, it would
appear, conservatives hoped to retain full political control under
tolerable—if perhaps not overly prosperous—economic conditions.
For liberals, on the other hand, beyond economic imperative, reform was closely linked to the political and administrative changes
necessary to end proscription from office and secure full public reincorporation. In other words, Vizcayan liberalism perceived reform
as a good vehicle with which to recapture political power and, in

the process, relegitimize an economic predominance long exercised through Bilbao's potent comprador bourgeoisie. The differences of intent between the two bodies of opinion—more precisely, between the contending social forces, groupings, and alliances that each side represented—gave rise to serious class conflict: occasionally overt and violent, but usually latent and largely concealed in the complex relations and social structures of a crumbling old order.

I. AGRICULTURE AND TRADE

With varying intensity, a broad economic crisis affected Vizcaya during the 1823–1833 decade. In large measure, the local crisis stemmed from Spain's colonial losses, from local socio-political discord, from the competition of foreign manufactures, from the worldwide decline in prices following the Napoleonic Era, as well as from complex national factors and unfavorable government policies, particularly in trade-related areas. Significantly, local agriculture was the sector apparently least affected by the economic slump of the 1820s. And this despite the fact that basic agrarian structures—from production to commercialization—had undergone little change since the middle of the eighteenth century. Considerable evidence indicates that Vizcaya continued to be self-sufficient in maize but grossly lacking in wheat. Consequently, as before, roughly half of the wheat consumed locally was imported.[1] Despite sporadic grain shortages in the late 1820s, however, there is little evidence of hunger in Vizcaya. To be sure, in May 1828, a scarcity of maize forced some into begging, but even episodes of this sort do not appear different from indications of endemic impoverishment, vagabondage, and mendicity in the province.[2] More to the point: there were no subsistence or grain-related riots and protests (either in the countryside or in Bilbao) that reveal excessively difficult agricultural conditions. However, largely responsible for this, as noted before, was the Basque provinces' excellent peninsular location, especially their proximity to the Castilian cereal-producing regions.

Not even the protectionist measures of the 1820 Cortes (banning foreign grain and flour in Spain) appear to have adversely affected Vizcaya. Reaffirmed in the aftermath of the 1823 Restoration, notably in February 1824, these policies which were aimed at promoting national agriculture met with little or no opposition among the local ruling classes.[3] In fact, Vizcaya benefited substantially from the central government's protectionist mandates because Castilian wheat was generally plentiful, readily available and, for good measure, could be reexported. In 1828, when Regnaudin ventured southward to better acquaint himself with the "chief source of Bilbao's granaries," the commercial agent encountered numerous agents of the chief commercial firms of the Basque and Cantabrian region contracting briskly after an abundant crop.[4] Perhaps because of this, the price of bread in Bilbao was remarkably stable and low throughout the 1823–1833 decade.[5] And so, while hinterland villages endured occasional grain shortages, not only was Bilbao amply supplied but, in addition, served as an important shipping point for grain destined for other parts of the peninsula and abroad.[6]

Following the Trienio, Vizcayan agriculture appears to have been in some disarray. A 4 June 1823 Vizcayan petition to the Regency, for example, deplored a "decadent agriculture," a likely characterization for a sector that had borne much of the brunt of the recent conflict, notably, through requisitions, forced taxes, and conscriptions of able-bodied males.[7] In 1823 a ranking officer of the French High Command in Spain unfavorably described agriculture in the region between Bilbao and Vitoria. Dauvais felt that the land in this area was poorly cultivated and cared for, but that "cereals would prosper there if the lands were in possession of active and industrious farmers."[8] The officer's harsh remarks, however, were tempered considerably by additional observations that for farmers to prosper it was necessary for them to have access to large, densely populated cities where they might sell their crops. In other words, it was not neglect or indolence which was to blame but rather the survival of subsistence agriculture combined with the insufficient commercialization of local production.[9]

Tellingly, other foreign visitors were extremely impressed by an active and enterprising Basque rural population.[10] Vigorous efforts to alter the Vizcayan landscape, for example, caught the attention of Henry Inglis, who remarked in 1830 that "within the last ten years much wasteland has been brought under cultivation."[11] This, apparently, to replace densely wooded areas with chacolí—a local wine much sought after due to scarcity and high returns—and other crops.[12] As if to underscore the importance of wine production, Domingo de Muruaga, a prominent Bilbao constitutionalist landowner,

in 1830 dedicated a small treatise on the subject to Vizcayan farmers to avert, as he put it, the province's ruin.[13] There was a strong
constitutionalist interest in the countryside (via the commercial development of cash crops) on the part of absentee landlords, living for
the most part in Bilbao.[14] And understandably so in a province where
agricultural profits were considerable as a result of high demand and
limited amounts of arable land.

Although the extent or rate of disentailment of communal lands
is unclear, there is good evidence that the process, begun in the eighteenth century and sharply accelerated by the War of Independence,
continued in 1823–1833 even if perhaps at a diminished pace.[15] The
sociopolitical upheavals of the Trienio also undoubtedly contributed
to the disentailment phenomenon since many Vizcayan localities
divested themselves of commons (and other holdings) to meet pressing obligations: e.g., payment of taxes to both factions.[16] Property
sales continued in the late 1820s as several of the smaller villages,
some possibly already deeply indebted, sold commons to pay for the
uniforms and equipment of the Paisanos Armados. This might well
have contributed to a certain malaise among the population regarding the militias' value.[17]

Emiliano Fernández de Pinedo, a leading specialist of these questions, strongly argues that the disentailment process was an important contributing factor to the gestation of Basque Carlism. In the
author's words, the "contradictions between private interest and col-
lective practices were already frequent before the beginning of the
civil war [of 1833–1839] and were undoubtedly one of its causes."[18]
According to this interpretation, the progressive alienation of the
commons had adversely affected the less competitive rural elements
—small and middle landowners—and had probably strengthened the
hand of the area's larger landholders, sectors sympathetic to political
liberalism and linked to commercial wealth in Bilbao. However, as
Fernández de Pinedo specifically warns, a key problem arises from
our inability to pin down accurately the amount or percentage of
unused lands put under cultivation following their disentailment,
thereby making it difficult to gauge accurately the agricultural consequences of land transfers and changes in status of these properties.[19] Still, land hunger and rising rents indicate that buyers found
these investments profitable. It is therefore safe to conclude that
some of the disentailed lots were actively used in some form or
another by the new owners or tenants.

In a broader perspective, it is apparent that the Vizcayan rural classes in general suffered from communal disentailment.[20] Further local studies in all likelihood will confirm processes of proletarization—proprietors falling into the class and status of wage earners —similar to other widely known contemporary European phenomena. Population growth and the increasing inability to migrate to America may well have also swelled the number of landless in the province. But if the lot of much of the peasantry deteriorated during the first third of the nineteenth century, by contrast, that of the landlords certainly appears to have improved. These socioeconomic developments were not without political significance. Bacon proudly reported that three-fourths of the land in Vizcaya by this time belonged to "anti-Carlists."[21] More to the point: the same author also asserted that "certainly above two-thirds of the rental of the [Basque] provinces belonged to the Constitutionalists."[22] It would of course be important to know which of these rents belonged to Bilbao's commercial bourgeoisie, as well as whether this class was investing heavily in the countryside as a result of difficulties in other sectors at a time of economic crisis.[23]

Regnaudin's first annual report of the 1823 Restoration provided encouraging indications of Vizcayan economic recovery: rise in agricultural production, increase in investment, renewed circulation of currency, and a proliferation of new commercial ventures. According to the agent, Bilbao's chief entrepreneurs reorganized their businesses and ordered substantial quantities of French textiles. Meanwhile, the majority of Bilbao's main export, Castilian wool, was shipped to Great Britain in foreign vessels, particularly English ones.[24] Regrettably, the coming years did much to disprove Regnaudin's early optimism, and for the remainder of the 1823–1833 decade Vizcayan commerce stagnated. During hard economic times wool exports suffered in particular.[25]

The Spanish wool's trade decline was not a recent development. Its collapse was a consequence of the War of Independence and of the postwar substitution of Spanish wools by others—namely those of Saxony, said to be finer, cleaner, longer, and therefore easier to weave—in English markets.[26] According to an authoritative account, Spanish wool shipments to England dropped from 6,062,000 pounds in 1800 to a mere 1,266,000 pounds in 1840.[27] Nor was this all: in addition to the decline in the volume and value of trade in the 1820s, both the price and the quality of Spanish wool fell in the English markets.[28] In sum, the prosperous years at the turn of the century were followed by trying times for Spanish wool merchants, many of whom operated out of Bilbao.[29]

The stagnation of Bilbao's wool trade unquestionably mirrored the national decline. In 1824 and 1825, according to Regnaudin, only about 10,000 bales were shipped yearly through Bilbao. But following the 1825 commercial panic in England and the glutting of British warehouses, 1826 proved even more disappointing when only around 5,000 bales were exported. The pace picked up considerably in 1827 with the shipment of 12,797 bales, but then exports again dropped sharply in 1828 to a mere 8,064 bales, exclusively destined for the British market.[30] These amounts were in stark contrast to the usual 20,000–30,000 bales of the late eighteenth century and well below the impressive (and apparently record) 40,396 bales shipped through Bilbao in the extraordinary year of 1807.[31] Although the effects of the slump in the wool trade among the port's *laneros* (wool merchants) remain largely unknown, there are good indications that the crisis depressed the city's economy, while especially worsening the condition of the working and lower classes.[32]

Another crucial factor in Vizcaya's commercial stagnation was the American Colonies' emancipation movements. Important economic consequences swiftly ensued: loss of outlets for local manufactures, increased foreign competition in the former markets and, naturally, the sudden and extraordinarily significant loss of precious metals and other key colonial revenues.[33] Moreover, the Vizcayan economy, heavily dependent upon overseas trade, was not aided by the general hostility of the central government or by the hard-line pro-fueros stances of the Ominous Decade's diputaciones.[34] Ironically, there was a clear and rare consensus in Vizcaya concerning the colonies' importance. Pointedly, conservative local officialdom persistently requested direct access to the colonies, that is, to what remained of them under Spanish control. At the other end of the political spectrum, Victor Luis de Gaminde's oft-cited *Intereses de Bilbao*, a partisan liberal tract, advanced the view that Vizcayans, through their tightly knit "masonry" in the Americas, could still play an important economic role there, through the new independent states or within the old possessions.[35]

An essential effect of the American convulsions was the interruption in the flow of silver to the peninsula. This in turn produced monetary scarcity and helped to slow down the Spanish economy.[36] The deficiency was partially alleviated by the unintentional influx of French coinage during the 1823 intervention, an act which provided a much-needed medium of exchange in some Spanish regions. Although evidence of a similar dearth in Vizcaya is sketchy, there are periodic allusions to it in Regnaudin's reports. Even so, the local causes of the shortage were complex and might have been due in part to questions of business confidence. A case in point: in January 1825 the French agent informed that the continuing business slump was forcing Vizcayan merchants to transfer their capital abroad.[37] Again in March, Regnaudin reported that bankruptcies were on the rise, banking operations nearly paralyzed, and currency (*numéraire*) extremely rare.[38] This chronic scarcity suggests several possibilities, among them, high rates of hoarding, low levels of trade, or decapitalization via specie transfers abroad—presumably for foreign investment and speculation purposes.[39]

Part of the commercial crisis may well have also been caused by sociopolitical disharmony. This was a pet theme of Spanish and Basque liberals and also of Regnaudin.[40] In August 1825, noting the discriminatory practices and attacks against liberals, the French agent remarked that commerce did "not lend itself to business transactions. . . . Pocketbooks become tighter and tighter, and trust being lost every day, bankruptcies are forecast and awaited."[41] Again in early 1827, Regnaudin emphasized the need of reestablishing a lasting social peace—ending the divisions between "whites" and "blacks" and punishing troublemakers—if business confidence and economic prosperity were to return.[42] To underscore this, the French agent repeatedly denounced royalist threats and attacks against Vizcaya's "honest" and "wise" citizens, many of whom had been identified with the Cortes during the Trienio.[43] Furthermore, most constitutionalists were legally barred from public office and even the Consulado, whose membership was largely constitutionalist, was forced to exclude them for some time from the guild's major posts.[44] Finally, repressive police measures, including constant surveillance, restrictions and limitations on travel, and the curtailment of the right of assembly, unquestionably hampered normal business activity.[45] In essence, discord in the province's political and social fabric probably also contributed to the low level of activity and prosperity of the local moneyed classes, hurting the Vizcayan economy. These facts help to explain why prominent Vizcayans greeted with such unabashed satisfaction the 1828 royal voyage to the Basque provinces, a visit that created a temporary détente among constitutionalists and royalists there.[46] Although the effects of the rapprochement were short lived, there was nevertheless a noticeable decline in tensions between mid-1828 and the 1830 July Revolution. This development might well have been a welcome relief to liberals in particular and to Vizcayan commerce in general. Yet, despite its timid resurgence in public life, liberalism was largely powerless to revive a deeply troubled Vizcayan economy, rapidly nearing in 1832 one of the lowest points of its recessionary phase.[47]

With emphasis on Bilbao, Regnaudin elaborately detailed the "nullity," "stagnation," "inactivity," "crisis," and "tranquillity" of the local economy during the Ominous Decade. Understandably, Regnaudin's correspondence faithfully reflected the numerous frustrations and difficulties of French trade with the Basque region and Spain.[48] While the agent's dispatches attributed much of the blame for this situation to the "disastrously adverse" policies of the Spanish government, doubly injurious perhaps given the valuable Gallic assistance in restoring Ferdinand VII to the throne, several distinct reasons accounted for the decline in French commercial activity.[49] First, an important 17 February 1824 royal order (alluded to earlier) reserved the coasting trade in Spain to national shipping.[50] Second, during the mid-1820s the Spanish government applied a tariff policy favoring imports brought in Spanish ships.[51] Third, to stimulate national production, the Spanish government banned outright certain foreign products, among them popular French brandies.[52] Fourth, other local and Spanish factors also may well have adversely affected French commercial interests: harsh residency requirements in Vizcaya against foreigners, obstacles created by the region's judges of contraband, some of the fueros' restrictive dispositions, and even the partial success of Spanish cloth manufactures.[53] Finally, and perhaps most importantly, the structural disadvantages of the French in northern Spain were a direct outgrowth of British preponderance. That England had been consistently able to dominate trade in the region was not accidental. Great Britain could effortlessly supply the Spanish market with vast quantities of an essential staple, codfish, and with other inexpensive manufactures. In return, the English took back important shipments of wool and occasionally quantities of Basque pig iron. Basically, unable to compete effectively in the wool and codfish trades, the French were condemned to the effects of English commercial superiority.[54]

Despite the apparent economic crisis, Regnaudin reluctantly conceded that business activity in Bilbao would nonetheless remain important. "Trade," he wrote in May 1825, "is paralyzed in comparison to that which was done formerly; however our port is one of the most frequented in Spain and the franchise from tariff duties sustains it."[55] As the agent underscored, the province's location, along with other advantages and considerations—e.g., Basque entrepreneurial expertise and economic initiative—had made Vizcaya the necessary link for important two-way traffic. Precisely for these reasons it seems that the Vizcayan economy, and its driving force of Bilbao, suffered less from the trade slump than might otherwise have been the case.[56] In the absence of reliable trade statistics, Regnaudin's quiet emphasis on the positive aspects of Vizcayan commerce—even if they had a decidedly British stamp—probably suggests that the situation was not nearly as desperate as might appear at first sight.

The persistent contraband trade casts additional doubts on the state of the local economy. In other words, uncertainty about Vizcayan commerce is accentuated by our inability to calculate or even estimate the value and/or volume of contraband goods continually moving through the region. With or without government prohibitions, smuggling was bound to remain lucrative. A case in point: when the central government barred foreign brandies to promote the national distilleries, the articles became the object of a thriving clandestine trade.[57] Tobacco, the item of contraband par excellence, was considered by many the most profitable of all illicit goods. Such was its value that Regnaudin strikingly reported in 1829 that the tobacco smuggled through France into Spain partially offset British commercial superiority in the peninsula.[58] If his figures are correct (admittedly they must be taken with great caution) contraband accounted for up to 40 percent of the value of all French trade in Bilbao.[59] In other words, for all of the problems caused by the judge of contraband's office and other authorities, smuggling was a fundamental part of the Vizcayan economy—the categorical denials of the Diputación notwithstanding. In sum, the *commerce interlope* or fraudulent trade was not only a practical self-defense against the national government's administrative and legal barriers but also a logical (and profitable) response to the province's economic difficulties.[60]

Yet, nationally, as colonial trade plummeted and wool exports reached new lows in the late 1820s and early 1830s, Spanish customs revenues—not reflecting a probable upsurge in smuggling—fell to an all-time low in 1832. From the 200 million reales collected in the late eighteenth century, and the 100 million of 1820, less than 50 million were collected by the Spanish government in 1832.[61] Whether the decline affected all of the peninsula evenly is open to conjecture. Even the normally pessimistic French agent at Bilbao thought not, but royalists and constitutionalists alike described the province's trade in depressingly negative terms. The oft-cited 11 December 1830 petition of the Basque diputaciones to the monarch noted the profoundly sad state of the province's commerce, an opinion shared by liberals although for markedly different reasons.[62] Not until 1833, following the favorable effects of the October 1832 general amnesty (including important ministerial changes) did business activity again pick up, once confidence had been restored and political stability cemented by the massive reincorporation of liberals into the national scene.[63]

II. IRON PRODUCTION: THE NEED FOR REFORM

Probably the part of the Vizcayan economy in deepest trouble during the decade was the manufacturing sector, namely, iron production.[64] Both in price and volume, the province's iron faced stiff and rapidly growing foreign competition. Moreover, the Vizcayan ironworks crisis was aggravated by technological obsolescence— i.e., the outdated production methods of the ferrerías. In other words, it was not that local production had declined precipitously but that, in leveling off during the 1820s, output was progressively falling behind that of the larger and more modern European producers. Hence, Vizcayan iron was confronted with the loss of significant domestic markets to cheaper imports. Most estimates of Vizcayan iron production between the late 1770s and 1800 place the annual output at approximately 80,000 to 100,000 quintales, or about 6,000 to 7,500 tons.[65] Thereafter, production dropped as a result of the Napoleonic invasion. Significantly, two postwar estimates indicate no less than a halving of the output.[66] The 1820s were marked by a noticeable recovery although production in 1827–1828 was slightly below 1800 figures. For example, Regnaudin reported in 1827 that Vizcayan output fluctuated around 80,000 quintales, and the next year Gregorio

González Azaola, a prominent expert in mining and iron manufactures, evaluated it at 94,000.[67] Despite an abundance of iron ore and minor advances in manufacture, the First Carlist War again acted as a brake to increases in production and, in 1840, Julián de Luna, the political governor of Vizcaya, reported that annual output was only around 80,000 quintales.[68] In short, for some time a host of factors cried out for reforms in the province's iron production.

Timidly at first, and with seemingly greater determination later, during the 1823–1833 decade the Vizcayan Diputación attempted to redress the state of local iron production by undertaking a series of studies and experimental reforms. In so doing, the Vizcayan executive was not merely reestablishing or continuing the attempts of the 1816–1819 period, efforts which were discontinued during the Trienio.[69] Both in scope and earnestness, the planned reforms of the mid-1820s were considerably more serious than the prior ones. This, it must be emphasized, was only natural given the new circumstances that increasingly threatened local production. The major problems on the subject were analyzed honestly and in substantial detail in the key *Memoria de la Diputación General sobre el punto de Minería*, a work drafted by Novia de Salcedo and the Marquis de Valde-espina and formally presented to the 1827 General Juntas.[70]

The *Memoria* presented a generally critical view of local iron manufacture and warned of dire consequences without basic improvements in this sector. The outgoing general deputies clearly recognized the economic importance of iron. In a daring pronouncement, the document predicted that iron ore "seems designated, if not as the only one, as the principal foundation upon which the future prosperity of Vizcaya must be based." However, the *Memoria's* authors remarked that local iron processing methods had remained stationary while those of foreigners had improved greatly. For the ferrerías to survive these severe challenges and compete more effectively with foreign iron it was necessary for Vizcaya to modernize. But this could not be achieved without studies detailing the weaknesses of fabrication and, more importantly, fundamental reforms to raise production.

During their 1825–1827 tenure, Novia de Salcedo and Valde-espina had applied themselves (with a fair measure of success) to gathering information concerning the basic operations of the ironworks. In the laborious process, the officials confronted grim realities of the local economic infrastructure which inhibited the growth and progress of iron manufacture; among them, an absence of mineral coal in Vizcaya, poor transportation systems, waste of rich iron deposits, outmoded and inefficient production processes and, naturally, uncompetitive production costs.[71] In addition, the general deputies identified powerful external factors at play, among them, foreign competition, inadequate government tariffs and discriminatory policies and, of course, the loss of the American Colonies.[72] Locally, one of Novia de Salcedo's and Valde-espina's most significant findings was the sharp regional disparity in production costs and prices of raw materials.[73] Clearly, the key items were charcoal and iron ore. Charcoal, for instance, ranged from 52.2 percent to 69.9 percent of production costs (at Carranza and Zornoza, respectively), while iron ore fluctuated between 14.1 percent and 27.2 percent (at Zornoza and Carranza).[74] When combined, the two chief imputs never accounted for less than 77.1 percent nor more than 83.4 percent of production costs (at Vedia and Durango); figures clearly in line with those of Luna's 1840 *Memoria*.[75] Meanwhile, labor costs remained surprisingly constant and modest at approximately 10 percent.[76] As for fixed capital, although it varied somewhat more than labor, in only one region did it exceed 10 percent of production costs. In sum, given the sweeping differentials, location, and other considerations, the cost of production varied widely, the cheapest being at Trucios (69 reales and 15 maravedis per quintal) and the most expensive at Durango (102 reales and 23 maravedis).[77]

Attentive to the essential question of imputs, the 1827 *Memoria* contains lucid observations on the need to improve the exploitation of rich local iron deposits, land and sea transportation, coal production, and associated sectors.[78] And deeply aware of the indispensability of mineral coal in modern production, the Diputación urged immediate efforts to locate it in Vizcaya. Nevertheless, Novia de Salcedo and Valde-espina were primarily concerned with reducing costs at the place of production—i.e., at the forge. To do this they looked for a method that combined the lowest production costs of several Vizcayan ironworks. But this goal could only be achieved through considerable additional research, experimentation, and innovation.[79] Hence, the *Memoria* suggested the creation of a model or pilot school (*escuela normal*) where extensive testing, under expert guidance, would fulfill the desired aims.[80] The rectification of old-fashioned production methods was one of the pilot school's foremost objectives. In another priority, the institution would experiment with various ores and combustible materials to lower costs and raise productivity. Still, Novia de Salcedo and Valde-espina pointedly warned that short-term measures, important as they might be, should not obscure the ultimate purpose of these undertakings: namely, the ability to compete with foreign imports.[81] Consonant with the authors' pragmatic views, the school's director should be someone with some theoretical background but with strengths in practical experience.[82]

In a realistic vein, the *Memoria* candidly admitted that the time had not yet come for fundamental reforms. According to the general deputies, Vizcaya did not yet possess the necessary modern technology to overhaul the traditional ironworks. Consequently, for the time being only local and minor gains were possible. The strongly pragmatic approach charted by the Diputación, notably its limited scope and modest immediate goals, contrasted sharply with the provincial government's own long-range objectives in iron production.[83] But the cautious plan of action envisioned in the *Memoria* was a classic example of piecemeal reform within profound socioeconomic constraints—also a course perfectly in keeping with the Diputación's bedrock conservatism. Consistent with a long-standing desire for self-determination, the document defiantly asserted that Vizcaya must rely only on itself to redress the iron production's disastrous state. Bitterly critical of the central government's policies and neglect, the *Memoria* bluntly concluded (as noted earlier) that any outside solution was "surely inaccessible [and] imaginary."[84]

Much of Novia de Salcedo's and Valde-espina's confidence regarding the eventual possibility of successful competition with foreign iron products was based—correctly no doubt—on the abundance of Vizcayan iron ore.[85] Although poorly exploited, the famous mines of Somorrostro and adjacent areas possessed vast and readily accessible quantities of this mineral. Tellingly, when the central government issued new national guidelines for mining in 1825, the Vizcayan Diputación began a firm and protracted protest against the measures.[86] There were important reasons for the Vizcayan leadership's stubborn resistance. First, as a matter of legal principle, the Diputación wished to protest centralist encroachment and controls that allegedly violated the fueros.[87] Second, the provincial leadership was eager to dominate local resources and supervise their exploitation.

Third, and closely linked to the latter, the leadership understandably wished to preserve the revenue from export taxes on iron ore leaving the province.[88]

In direct response to the central government's mining reform, and in conjunction with the pressing question of improving iron production, the Vizcayan Diputación countered at the 1827 General Assembly with its own charter for the province's mines.[89] Vizcayan defiance led to a characteristically sharp dispute with Madrid in the following years and, although a royal inspector of mines for the Basque provinces was appointed, as of 1830–1831 the outcome remained uncertain.[90] The Diputación's determined efforts to control local resources and improve iron production elicited a favorable evaluation from Regnaudin, for whom the sum of these economic measures represented a welcome step toward reform.[91]

Inexplicably, little was done during the next biennium to implement the important recommendations and decisions aimed at the gradual modernization of iron production. At the July 1829 General Juntas, the Permanent Commission for the Improvement of Iron Fabrication openly attacked official inaction on long overdue reforms.[92] However desirable, the experimental measures advocated in 1827 had regrettably not been enacted. The delay stemmed in part from communication problems between the Vizcayan authorities and Gregorio González Azaola, the noted mineralogist on whom the Diputación had depended heavily for guidance at least since late 1826.[93] A prime candidate for directing the reforms of Vizcayan iron production, González Azaola's national government missions and European travels had prevented him from following up valuable suggestions made earlier to the Diputación, including the establishment of a model school in a ferrería.[94] Possibly, González Azaola's influence and reputation was so great that the Diputación may have been unwilling to proceed without him. Even this plausible hypothesis, however, does not adequately explain the ruling elites' undeniable lethargy in such a vital matter.

Not until July–August 1829 was Francisco Antonio de Echanove officially commissioned by the Diputación to conduct experiments at a still undetermined location.[95] Echanove's first experiments apparently took place in the winter and spring of 1829–1830. An early report of the Permanent Commission—the supervisory body of these operations—while acknowledging minor gains, painted a generally unfavorable picture of the expert's endeavors.[96] From the limited information available, Echanove's trials appear to have been highly conventional, with only minimal variations in machinery and combustibles. Echanove frankly admitted failure to the Diputación; the high expectations had not been fulfilled.[97] Despite the setbacks and under unclear circumstances, Echanove carried out additional experiments the following year.[98] Finding the efforts worthwhile, at the 1831 General Juntas the Permanent Commission recommended that Echanove's results be published as quickly as possible.[99] In light of the issue's pressing nature then, it is difficult to explain the Diputación's indifference towards Echanove's findings, which had still not been published in March 1833 (and, as far as this writer is aware, were never made public).[100]

In conclusion, acutely conscious of the crisis in local iron production, the Vizcayan political leadership realized the imperative need to reform this essential branch of the economy. In preliminary investigations the Diputación tried to determine the comparative regional costs of manufacture, eventually concluding that the prime objective should be a cost reduction to make Vizcayan iron more competitive in the marketplace. Considerable emphasis was therefore placed on the search for more economic production methods and improvements in collateral sectors. Not surprisingly, the Vizcayan government also became aware of the desirability of greater control over local resources, especially the rich iron ore deposits. However, there was a noticeable lack of persistence and determination on the Diputación's part to carry these reforms to term. Predictably, the halfhearted efforts led to meager results at best. In the disappointing process, however, several important lessons were learned, not the least of which was the shocking realization of how far Vizcayan iron production had fallen behind others in this phase of the industrial revolution. Although the ferrerías' conventional methods continued for some time, by the middle of the nineteenth century it was evident that their days were numbered and Vizcaya's future economic wealth lay in modern technology.[101] Finally, it is important to emphasize the extent to which the Vizcayan conservative leaderships, despite their generally antireformist ideological and political orientation, felt compelled to undertake overdue and badly needed local economic improvements. Doubtless a difficult and perhaps even risky project, it was nonetheless a genuine (if ultimately flawed) effort to adapt old structures to new realities.

III. VIZCAYA DIVIDED:
POLITICS AND CLASS CONFLICT

*A. Liberal Reemergence and the Politics of
Administrative and Economic Reform*

Apart from the glaring necessity for them, another reason for the reforms taking place was the reemergence of constitutionalism as an influential political force after 1827–1828.[102] As noted earlier, there are suggestive indications that despite proscription from official participation in public life, Vizcayan liberals actively attempted to steer local politics and the economy in the direction of their interests. In the trajectory between the political repression and intolerance of the post–Restoration Period and the relative sociopolitical conciliation of the late 1820s and early 1830s, two key events worked on Vizcayan liberalism's behalf: the 1828 royal visit to the northern provinces and the 1832 general amnesty. To appreciate the significance of the first, it is important to recall the prior systematic exclusion of liberals from office as well as the multifaceted forms of oppression used against them following constitutionalism's defeat, a state of affairs continually decried by Vizcayan liberals and occasionally by foreign observers.[103] Although the visit failed to end the constitutionalists' exclusion from public office, a policy which lasted until the 1832 general amnesty, the voyage ostensibly enhanced the Vizcayan liberals' sociopolitical standing.[104]

Wherever the monarchs traveled in the Basque provinces and Navarra, the former partisans of the Trienio openly participated in— and apparently helped to finance—the festivities offered the sovereigns.[105] The Diputación and the Bilbao city council spared no cost or effort. In Bilbao preparations were substantial: roads were repaired, houses and streets were cleaned and painted, and the residence of the Mazarredos (a well-known moderate liberal clan) was lavishly readied for the royal family.[106] Regnaudin wrote that the greatest part of the celebrations' participants had been chosen "from among the families that had been prominent under the constitutional system."[107] From the tenuous social rapprochement, some overly optimistic liberals concluded that the royal visit would result in a change in the direction of government—i.e., from absolutism to moderate and representative rule.[108] Although this would not happen for some time, tangible benefits ensued shortly for Vizcayan liberalism from the decline in political tensions. For example, Pedro Pascual de Uhagon, one of its leaders, was commissioned to represent Vizcaya at the September 1828 conferences of the three provinces.[109] Uhagon's participation was undoubtedly good for liberalism since the main item on the agenda was the opening of Bilbao to direct overseas commerce, a measure consistently advocated by constitutionalist reformers.[110] However, as noted before, the parleys soundly rejected the central government's projects which, according to Basque traditionalists, would establish customs offices in Bilbao.[111] Notwithstanding the setback, the events of 1828 probably advanced somewhat liberalism's struggle to secure greater recognition and regain its sociopolitical ascendancy. At the very least, the visit enabled local reformers to put into practice, if perhaps only momentarily, what they had sought for some time: sociopolitical détente and harmony.

During the 1829–1831 period, Vizcayan constitutionalism continued efforts to legally reenter public life and regain office. The results, though mixed, were generally unfavorable to reformers.[112] Yet, even a negative balance sheet shows that liberalism was beginning to present strong challenges and was making headway in local politics. A case in point: At the 1829 General Assembly, several of the delegates (junteros) were noted constitutionalists, some even having served in the Trienio's military corps.[113] Although eventually excluded from the deliberations after royalists questioned their participation, liberals were now engaged in actions almost unthinkable a short while before. Despite the strains generated in the region by the July Revolution and Mina's 1830 adventure, by mid-1831 there were renewed signs of an easing in sociopolitical tensions among Vizcayans. The détente facilitated a new constitutionalist challenge versus the status quo at the 1831 General Juntas leading, ironically, to fresh political skirmishes. In view of the liberals' upsurge, the assembly's conservatives again tried to exclude the former's sympathizers, something they were only able to do with increasing difficulty and after considerable public debate.[114] Quite probably a sign of the Vizcayan leadership's concern about resurgent liberalism is a December 1831 set of instructions to the province's town regarding the coming term's municipal elections.[115] At this juncture the

Diputación stressed the desirability of choosing individuals partial to the fueros and without political blemish, criteria surely designed to ensure the election of trusted royalists.

Vizcayan liberals were visibly frustrated at seeing so many of the provincial and municipal administration posts held by those they considered to be inept or unfit for office.[116] There was an unmistakable element of class prejudice in the resentment of reformers toward those who had excluded from office the so-called productive, enlightened, and educated sectors of society. Therefore, in addition to the gamut of issues that deeply divided Vizcayan society, administrative reform in local government also became a significant point of contention. In essence, Vizcayan liberalism had begun to question the official performance of its conservative opponents.[117]

As early as 1830–1831 local reformers had undertaken a systematic campaign—surreptitious at first, more explicit later—against the incumbents' administration, calling for an efficient, corruption-free government and for a review of the Diputación's handling of public funds.[118] Criticism and debate turned more intense after the 1832 general amnesty once liberalism abandoned its state of semi-clandestinity and legal disenfranchisement for other areas and forms of struggle.[119] As noted previously, liberals advocated thrift in government even if economizing measures meant, as foralista opponents charged, the gradual dismantlement of the Paisanos Armados.[120] At the July 1833 General Assembly, where constitutionalist tendencies predominated for the first time in a decade, reformers who were now openly on the offensive showcased an innovative program of government to meet pressing problems of public administration. In Uhagon's revealing description, the juntas "were conducted with frugality and decorum. Questions were raised that turned up abuses in the previous diputaciones, and the means to correct them were agreed upon. Economic commissions were established to contain and put an end to waste and the poor use of funds. . . . Finally, appropriate principles were laid down for the succeeding administration concerning the deputies who [would] overstep or exceed their faculties."[121] Probably echoing popular local liberal opinion, John Francis Bacon also pointedly accused several members of the 1823–1833 diputaciones of graft and corruption.[122] Largely confirming Uhagon's account of the 1833 juntas, the Vizcayan police, still under traditionalist direction, quickly denounced liberalism's maneuvers: "Yesterday the party clearly unmasked itself and succeeded in seducing the generality of the representatives, obtaining under the flattering slogan of economies that a permanent commission be named to formulate a general budget of all of the revenues of the Señorío and present a new system of revenue administration."[123] During the liberals' brief two-month stint in office—until the 1833 October Carlist uprising—a recently elected General Deputy Uhagon attempted to enact important aspects of his party's platform: a public works program, administrative reform, and the dissolution of the Brigadas.[124] However, during a period of intense political struggle, reform's opponents stepped up assaults on their adversaries, effectively stifling their efforts with charges that liberals were dangerous revolutionaries and that their triumph would damage both the cause of the monarchy and the fueros.[125]

Nevertheless, the decade's record on many of these issues presents striking, if perhaps only apparent, paradoxes and contradictions. For example, how is it possible to account for the fact that the monopoly of political power came so easily to the most conservative segment of the Vizcayan oligarchy when this same group was utterly unable to achieve a similar socioeconomic mastery? And how is it possible to explain the seemingly contradictory situation in which other sectors endowed with considerable wealth and influence—and heavily identified with liberalism—had no apparent political clout? In theoretical terms: how can a social class with vast economic power be so totally lacking in political strength? The interaction of politics and economic and administrative reform suggests revealing answers to these important questions.

During the Ominous Decade the Vizcayan political leadership represented the interests of a broad coalition of agrarian and traditionalist forces. These were for the most part small and middle landowners—with a handful of exceptions such as Valde-espina and a few others who were important property holders—scribes, clerics, and much of the rural and urban lower classes, namely, peasants, tenants, wage laborers, artisans, and shopkeepers. The profoundly conservative nature of the Vizcayan political elite naturally prevented it from undertaking measures detrimental to the interests of any significant sector of its constituency and clientele or, conversely, which might enhance the sociopolitical standing of reform-minded critics. Consequently, even in the face of changing political circumstances and critical economic times, the provincial government—desiring to cling to the fueros—attempted to maintain intact manifestly outdated socioeconomic and legal structures. In essence, the Diputación was caught in an extraordinarily difficult dilemma from which it could not extricate itself without upsetting delicate historical structures and balances. Although the preservation of the status quo was politically expedient to please (and appease) a vocally conservative local following, in a self-defeating manner it also continually pitted the Diputación against the national government in matters vital to the province. In sum, the quest for immobility (for a veritable straitjacketing of society) on the Diputación's part was doomed to failure. Time, historical conditions, and the Vizcayan reality were on the side of those who wished to alter and possibly liquidate the dominant local structures of the ancien régime.

On the other hand, the chief social classes that espoused political liberalism—the commercial bourgeoisie of Bilbao and its land-owning allies in the countryside—had considerable capital and resources, dominating the local economy. Clearly, then, proscription from public office had not totally diluted liberalism's socioeconomic strength. Hence, this *working hypothesis:* From a solid position of economic power, Vizcayan liberalism possessed substantial force to lobby against the diputaciones' conservative policies of the Ominous Decade. If this assumption is correct, it might follow that Vizcayan reformers also had sufficient strength to elicit concessions and perhaps reforms from the ruling elites.[126]

The commercial elites' socioeconomic power, for example, could well have determined the fate of some of the Diputación's pet projects. A case in point: in assessing the meager results of the iron production reforms it is important to note that they did not (and probably could not) receive the full backing of Bilbao's influential entrepreneurial classes since they had little incentive in promoting this sector. In fact, many iron goods were imported at far cheaper prices than local industry produced. Merchants owned no major ironworks; the facilities were primarily held and operated by landed proprietors. They, in turn, most overtly advocated and pressed for reforms in this area. Had Bilbao's merchant oligarchy shown greater concern for Vizcayan iron production and collateral sectors, reforms could well have proven more successful. This presupposes, however, that Bilbao's bourgeoisie could function in a noncompradore capacity to promote domestic iron manufactures—a remote possibility at that time given the inadequacies and underdevelopment of local industry.[127] On the other hand, where the dominant economic elites stood to gain from improvements such as public works, they usually provided firm socioeconomic and political support. An example of this selectiveness was the encouragement and assistance of reformers for the Diputación's road-building and transportation improvement programs, measures consistent with commercial objectives. Indeed, public revenue and private investment converged neatly to maintain an adequate provincial road system. And so, while the commonweal was served, the Vizcayan merchant-capitalist class, a group with strong vested interests in this sector, profited as well from the partnership.[128]

Although murky, the decade-long conflict between the Diputación and Bilbao's economic magnates—including the latter's main association, the Consulado—surely indicates differences of economic policy. Beyond obvious political matters, the Vizcayan government was constantly at odds with the port's merchant elites over a constellation of controversial issues.[129] Key questions during the decade, for example, included the Diputación's insistent monetary requests upon Bilbao's commerce, impositions strenuously resisted by the Consulado until an apparent 1827 standoff.[130] Nor were these the only examples of the Vizcayan government's fiscal difficulties. As if to illustrate the economic might of the local bourgeoisie, in October 1830 the Vizcayan Diputación, overextended as a result of security measures following the July Revolution in France, virtually exacted a forced loan of 2 million reales from Bilbao's reluctant business community.[131]

Despite its impressive economic power, the Vizcayan bourgeoisie lacked the sufficient political leverage to effect crucial reforms in Bilbao's commercial status (and the customs system) even after the ministry had legally enfranchised Bilbao for direct overseas trade in February 1828.[132] During this critical juncture the panorama was bright for local reformers: not only had the central government finally made Bilbao a *puerto habilitado* but, additionally, a committee named by the Consulado to negotiate with the Diputación in March 1828 was heavily staffed with constitutionalists. But, fearing the transfer of the customs houses to Bilbao ("in violation" of the privileges), the fueros' defenders counterattacked vigorously in September–October 1828—an irresistible pressure which, as noted earlier, Vizcayan reformers were unable to withstand.[133] Traditionalists cleverly used the enfranchisement issue to assail politically the powerful elements that supported the measure. Greatly isolated from the mass of Vizcayans, and realizing the limits of their sociopolitical influence, the Consulado's representatives eventually retreated, issuing an unconvincing disclaimer of their intentions, while simultaneously the negotiating committee was dissolved.[134] By blocking a change in Bilbao's status in the name of the fueros and of consumers, however, the Diputación, wittingly or unwittingly, was objectively aiding smuggling interests.

Local reformers demonstrated greater cohesion and determination in the transformation of the Consulado into the *Real Tribunal de Comercio* in 1829–1830.[135] Although the measure presented numerous legal and political problems, the merchant community ably neutralized (exactly how and with what means is unclear) the conservative local opposition, and carried out the apparently beneficial change with no excessive difficulties.[136] Even though the port's status was not at stake, this was no superficial modification. With the new code, the Royal Tribunal of Commerce came under greater royal administrative control than the former Consulado. Reformers stood to gain considerably from the mutation since they were now on somewhat more solid ground and better able to resist the Vizcayan government's pressure. It was one more instance of the tacit crucial alliance and convergence of interests between Vizcayan liberals and royal administrators, both attempting to curtail the considerable power of the diputaciones and local ruling elites.

In assessing the political and economic influence of liberalism, sight should not be lost of the very narrow boundaries under which it was forced to operate until the 1832 general amnesty. Given the unfavorable political conditions and balance of forces, reformers' actions and criticisms by necessity were generally guarded, subtle, and not always readily apparent. Nevertheless, even if political power could not be wielded directly, reformers exercised some measure of power through significant influence in economic and public affairs. Moreover, it is probable that a closer examination of contemporary local political life than this one will reveal a larger and hitherto ignored reformist influence in Vizcaya, seemingly missing because of the provincial government's dominant traditionalism and conservative policies.

In sum, the issues of economic reform and public administration acquired new significance in Vizcaya after 1827–1828. Both questions were part of a larger struggle for sociopolitical supremacy between liberals and royalists, traditionalists and reformers. Political and economic liberalism secured uneven support for specific programs and issues it championed through persistent (and apparently persuasive) criticism of abuses and mismanagement in the provincial administration. At the same time, Vizcayan reformers, for tactical and strategic reasons, repeatedly pressed for harmony and conciliation to end political discrimination, proscription from office, marginalization from decision making, and other repressive practices of the Diputación and of their opponents. Although the socioeconomic power of the bourgeois elite was unmatched by their conservative adversaries, the former's political power was exceedingly limited, being largely in the hands of the tradition-minded sectors which controlled the Ominous Decade's diputaciones with mass rural support. Even so, on balance liberalism managed to make significant inroads in public life—advances that became more perceptible after the 1832 general amnesty. Hence too, the stepped-up attacks of conservatives upon Vizcayan liberals in a frantic last-ditch attempt to stem reform and protect the reputedly endangered Fueros.

B. The Dynamics of Class Conflict

It is certainly not this study's intention to suggest that the era's main socioeconomic and political conflicts in Vizcaya revolved solely or exclusively around the opposition between urban merchant-capitalists and rural gentry. Class and group interplay was considerably more subtle and complex. In fact, different sectors of society had their own strategies based on particular socioeconomic interests, political choices and opinions, cultural reflexes, bodies of ideas, and so forth. In addition, there existed clear class alliances —both permanent and temporary—involving the convergence of individual group strategies against perceived common enemies. For instance, the Vizcayan conservatism of the Ominous Decade (eventually Carlism as well) was a multiclass and consistently logical sociopolitical phenomenon, and it was determined "negatively" in opposition to liberalism, centralism, innovation, and reform. A review of the key Vizcayan groups' and social classes' positions bears out the coherence of their interests and views.

1. Clergy

Most clergy members, particularly those of the regular orders, strongly opposed religious and economic reform. When numerous monasteries and religious institutions were dissolved during the Trienio, clerics swelled the ranks of royalist guerrillas and fought the constitutionalist regime with arms, money, moral encouragement, and other forms of organizational and political support. The episode strongly paralleled the anti-French resistance to the War of Independence and, more specifically, the struggle against "impious" Jacobinism's widespread reforms in the local ecclesiastical structures.[137] In Vizcaya, as elsewhere in much of Spain, the legacy of both conflicts was a long-standing and profound (opponents called it fanatic) opposition among the clergy to centralist projects affecting organized religion's privileges and material interests. The mendicant orders, especially the Franciscans, who had suffered the suppression of convents and who had endured other hardships, became the irreconcilable and outspoken local enemies of liberalism.[138] Predictably, therefore, many Vizcayan clerics showed a marked preference for absolutist political positions during the 1823–1833 decade. In fact, on occasion some ecclesiastics also conspired freely with elements of the ultrarightist opposition in the province.[139]

Unfortunately for their detractors, as countless observers have noted until the present, the Basque clergy enjoyed an enormous ascendancy over a deeply religious, traditionalist population. And in the 1820s, the region's clergy used its material power and moral authority accordingly against foes, real or imaginary. Tellingly, instead of fostering social harmony, certain preachers hurled invectives at liberals and foreigners in their sermons, inciting the population against them.[140] The Vizcayan clergy drew much of its strength from a historical and privileged relationship with the lower classes, particularly the rural ones. Attentive foreign observers reported the important attachment of Basque peasants to priests with whom they shared a close and daily interaction.[141] The Diputación was understandably eager to use the clergy's significant sway among the population to foster the Paisanos' organization and military preparedness.

Clerical influence upon the Paisanos can be clearly discerned during the crucial 1832–1833 period when, according to Uhagon, representatives of the "armed party" in Vizcaya pointedly referred to the queen's government as *liberal, irreligious, and antimonarchical.*"[142] As Ferdinand's reign came to a close, the same ultraroyalist sector in the province simultaneously campaigned (and most probably conspired) for the preservation of absolutism and the *"sanctity of religion."*[143] Two prominent ringleaders of the Vizcayan clerical opposition to reform were Manuel de Landaida, an important future Carlist chieftain, and Manuel Gómez Negrete, known to some simply as the Padre Negrete, a head of the October 1833 Carlist uprising.[144] These and other members of the local clergy consistently demonstrated a clear preference for the royalist paramilitary corps and the provincial liberties the latter were defending. Consequently, during and after the October 1833 uprising, most Vizcayan ecclesiastics sided firmly with the Carlist insurgents, to the point that liberal critics could rightly assert without grossly distorting reality that the Carlist party "with few exceptions [was] composed of lawyers, friars, and peasants."[145] In essence, even before the civil war's start, the organized church in Vizcaya knew that government clerical reforms—such as Godoy's, Joseph's, and the Trienio's—would undermine its privileges, loosen its hold over entailed properties, affect rent collection and tithe gathering, result in the abolition of clerical establishments, and generally weaken its power.[146] Clearly, then, it was in the clergy's interest to oppose centralization and continue to maintain the fueros' totality.

2. Landless Rural Classes

The landless rural classes were comprised of the tenantry and wage laborers. Given the peculiar nature of land tenure and property distribution in Vizcaya, the number of tenants was large and that of rural laborers small.[147] As figures for the Napoleonic period tend to show, around 75 percent of the rural classes were not propertied, although admittedly, many of the tenancies probably amounted to virtual ownerships. This picture is in marked contrast to the highly idealized traditional belief that there were a large number, or high percentage, of small owners in the province. Moreover, as indicated above, much evidence suggests that since the mid-eighteenth century the percentage of landholders in Vizcaya had been steadily declining, and that the downward trend had continued and possibly even accelerated in the first third of the nineteenth century. In addition to the wars and the debts resulting therefrom, rising rents —jacked up by the local gentry, urban landlords, and possibly the church—plus the effects of disentailment, encroachment upon commons, and possibly enclosure, had combined to worsen the condition of the Vizcayan tenantry, making it vastly more precarious. Therefore, it is reasonable to assume that the number of tenants falling into the wage-earning categories was increasing.[148]

To account for the growing mass of rural unemployed and underemployed, a close look at the general indebtedness of the rural communities and the peasantry is in order. Obligations arising from war payments, taxes and donations, borrowing, as well as from high rents and low agricultural prices, resulted in important municipal and private sales—voluntary as well as forced—and, in some instances, displacement from the land. Rural impoverishment and proletarization in Vizcaya, however, may not have been as clear-cut as in certain other parts of the peninsula. For example, severe difficulties in the Vizcayan countryside tended to be compensated for (and, of course, obscured to some extent) by important age-old social mechanisms, in particular a very significant migration (especially of young males) to America and elsewhere in Spain. However, as noted earlier, the colonial emancipation undoubtedly slowed down Basque migration to the New World. As the escape valve closed, there was increasing social tension throughout the Basque provinces. And in Vizcaya, as well as in other parts of the region, there are scattered examples of disgruntled peasants, displaced from their lands and unable to leave the peninsula, trying their lot as artisans and domestics in the cities. The propensity of these individuals to embrace conservative politics should not be underestimated, especially when buyers of disentailed lands were often influential liberals.[149] In other words, the appeal of Carlism to many present and former peasants then, might have been based on the movement's defense of the political status quo and resistance to economic change in the face of new conditions which, among others, spelled dispossession for the more disadvantaged rural sectors.

In all likelihood, the turnover in landownership had benefited the more prosperous sector of the rural bourgeoisie and of the urban propertied classes, particularly merchants, with substantial interests in the countryside. Many of the province's new proprietors, in fact, were outside landlords who found it convenient to leave the management of their rural estates to local middlemen and administrators. Consequently, there existed an undeniable dependency of tenants and wage laborers upon affluent absentee landlords, many of them from Bilbao. Naturally, the unequal social relationship was not without strong political overtones: to wit, by a strong dislike on the poorer rural classes' part towards those heavily identified with the constitutionalist-reformist cause.[150] Basically, there was a classic opposition between the lower-class rural proponents of the old order and the partisans of economic liberalism. The first sought to

preserve a paternalistic socioeconomic system based on an unbroken association with the land and the past—however increasingly
tenuous—while the second attempted to disentail and thereby overcome key obstacles to forward-looking policies and an increased
commercialization of the land, whatever the social consequences
and costs.[151]

Nor were these the only important issues dividing the peasantry
and Vizcaya's socioeconomic elites. As repeatedly indicated, the latter perceived little need to oppose the establishment of customs
houses since a considerable portion of their businesses, especially
the usually vigorous import-export trade, lay outside the province,
notably in Castile and abroad. As such, economic liberalism saw
little need to protect local consumers from possible government tariffs. Nevertheless, the fueros permitted the duty-free importation of
nearly every conceivable good, except those expressly banned by the
central government and, at times, by the Diputación.[152] In terms of
cheap merchandise (particularly clothes) this privilege was beneficial
to the mass of Vizcayans but not, it should be emphasized, to local
manufactures which, devoid of protection, could not yet compete
effectively with foreign imports. For example, according to Bacon
the "freedom from customs duties on goods imported from foreign
countries" was noticeable in the "comfortable and decent clothing
of the Vizcayan peasantry."[153] The franchises' role in assuring very
reasonable prices for foreign goods in Vizcaya was noted by others as
well.[154] In addition, salt was tax-free, there were no stamp duties on
paper and legal documents, and tobacco could be bought in Vizcaya
with a fraction of the duty levied on it elsewhere in Spain—no doubt
an important incentive for professional smugglers and moonlighting
peasant-smugglers.

Against the tangible advantages of the fueros for most Vizcayans,
liberals showed a callous disregard for the population's well-being by
advancing their own exclusive commercial aspirations and interests.
Victor Luis de Gaminde, for instance, in refuting the conservative
argument that the establishment of customs houses by the sea would
seriously hamper Vizcayan commerce, openly argued that the only
harm of such a measure would be to the provincial or local consumption, which he scornfully dismissed as being "of little importance."[155]
But that provincial market, admittedly of small value to large merchants given the population's economic self-sufficiency and limited
purchasing power, was precisely the vital zone franche where the

Vizcayan peasantry purchased duty-free goods. Immediate reforms in the customs administration without improvements in manufactures would have had adverse consequences for the rural classes and for most Vizcayans, although this was something that economic liberalism denied, claiming that the commercial franchises resulting from the region's fueros were more costly for the province than their benefits—an important and suggestive assertion, which awaits serious investigation.[156]

There were also sociogeographic reasons for the secular opposition between the rural lower classes and the province's Bilbao-based bourgeois strata. Gaminde, with characteristic hyperbolic flare, exclaimed, "what greater clash can ever exist than the actual one between Bilbao and Vizcaya?"[157] Another passage described the peasantry's resentment against the port city's merchant-capitalists more graphically and vividly: "The farmer (*labrador*) naturally hates him, who, without exposing himself to the rigors of the seasons, gathers his own capital and lives in abundance; [and the farmer] believes that he who does not suffer like himself . . . employed dishonest means in the acquisition of his fortune."[158] Finally, as Bacon observed, "there [was] a wonderful feeling of equality among the northern peasantry of Spain," a fact that the author, interestingly enough, attributed to the church.[159] "Proud" and "free" Basque peasants would naturally tend to resent undue outside controls, be they from Bilbao or from Madrid. These questions must be kept in mind when examining the eventual social alignment of Carlism, and why such an overwhelming part of the peasantry went over to the pretender's camp when the conflict erupted in 1833.

3. Landowners

Landowners comprise an extremely problematic class to examine given its complex makeup and the limited body of research available (except of course Fernández de Pinedo's solid work).[160] Consequently, some of the following schematic observations are speculative and should be considered as such.

a. *Large landowners.* Probably hoping to consolidate past gains and aiming at future communal and clerical disentailment to enhance their holdings, there are good indications that some of the "chief landholders" in the Basque provinces favored liberal rule.[161] The example of Baracaldo seems to bear this out. As Manuel González Portilla has shown, the town's largest property owners in the 1830s were liberal absentee landlords from Bilbao.[162] A number of important owners, including the powerful Uhagon family, had obtained lands through communal disentailment in 1809–1811, 1828, and 1834–1835. Many were winegrowers who had profited handsomely from chacolí. Moreover, since some of the large landowners were merchants, their ties to Bilbao's commercial and capital circuits provided additional incentives to a greater commercialization of the land at the expense of tenants and dependents through higher rents, shorter contracts and leases, and other economic mechanisms.

Considerable evidence indicates that these landowners, especially the liberals, were quite unpopular among the peasantry. The continual transfer of lands—private, communal, and clerical—undoubtedly affected the rural classes' lower echelons, making their situation more precarious. Since those who benefited more often than not were members of the urban and rural bourgeoisie, they were naturally perceived by the peasantry, landless or not, as objective enemies. Although much of this socioeconomic and political tension was not resolved until after the First Carlist War (which, ironically, accelerated the disentailment process much to the detriment of the peasantry and the church), the land-owning bourgeoisie was already in command of the Vizcayan countryside well before then.[163]

There were notable exceptions, however, to the large landholders' nearly exclusive allegiance to the liberal political cause: notably, the two archconservative leaders of the Ominous Decade, Valde-espina and Novia de Salcedo. It is not unlikely that there may have been a handful of other wealthy Vizcayan landed proprietors among the Carlists—e.g. the Casa Eguías, the Zavalas, and possibly others—therefore leaving the question open to discussion. Nevertheless, it is interesting to note that Bacon, in an obvious attempt to discredit the Carlists, obscrvcd that "with the exception of Novia, Valdespina [sic] and two or three others, the Carlist leaders were men who had nothing to lose."[164] While this may or may not have been true for the movement's direction, there was a much wider sector for whom certainly a lot was at stake, namely, that of the rank and file peasant fighters for whom the victory or defeat of the Carlist cause would signify either the possible reclamation of lands (and the reversal of the expropriation tendencies), or their definitive loss, accompanied by additional impoverishment.[165]

b. *Middle and small landowners.* Since they may well have been close to the lower rural sectors, especially the tenantry, the middle and small landowners were in opposition to the province's affluent classes. Tellingly, numerous middling Vizcayan gentry demonstrated pronounced antireformist leanings during the 1823–1833 decade and, eventually, Carlist sympathies as well. As Fernández de Pinedo correctly points out, they became the insurrection's directors.[166] Perhaps these modest proprietors were being eased out of social influence and economic power at the local level by nouveau riche constitutionalist elements in the countryside. Were this to be the case, as some have suggested, it would certainly help to explain the rise of Carlism among the region's middle and small owners. In other words, the phenomenon may well have been a logical sociopolitical reaction against the replacement of the older rural elites by the newer ones. Whatever the specific reasons, many of these entail holders and small owners strongly resisted centralization and reform, and clearly preferred tradition, clericalism, and the fueros.[167]

4. Artisans

Throughout the 1823–1833 decade artisans, particularly in Bilbao and the larger towns, manifested a staunch royalism in defense of the province's institutions and liberties. Several reasons account for this important sociopolitical development. First, local artisans often found themselves pitted against the merchant-capitalists who controlled the province's economic life. Not only were the latter the main employers and landlords, but much of their trade involved foreign imports to the detriment of domestic products—always a sensitive issue to Vizcayan foundry workers and others employed in the elaboration of iron. Not coincidentally, most of the forges' laborers eventually found themselves squarely in the Carlist camp. Second, local artisans sought and obtained protection from the Diputación against foreign craftsmen. For instance, taking advantage of a prevalent xenophobic royalism against "liberal" France, the Vizcayan authorities pressured Gallic artisans to leave the province due to the latter's inability to provide blemish-free lineages to meet stringent local residency requirements.[168] Fundamentally, behind the

Diputación's official exclusionary policies lay the persuasive lobbying power of artisans whom, after all, it was necessary to please in light of their unwavering loyalty to the royalist paramilitary corps.[169] Third, one may certainly assume that some of these individuals were displaced peasants and farmers who had succumbed to economic pressures and social processes fostered by their political adversaries.[170] Fourth, many artisans, as indeed the majority of the peasantry, defended the fueros not abstractly or as ideological constructs, but because they felt that without them their socioeconomic situation would be more difficult. The absence of commercial franchises, for example, would have meant higher living costs and quite probably new taxes. And without the fueros, artisans and many others among the population would be subject to the national military service, normally a burden weighing most heavily upon the lower classes. Fifth and last, artisans were well aware that the liberal credo strongly opposed the guilds' monopolies and entrenched interests. In conclusion, Vizcayan artisans aligned themselves solidly behind the aegis of royalism, the privileges, and the local authorities' paternalism against economic liberalism and political reform. Much of what has been said about artisans probably applies as well to the status and problems of local shopkeepers and other members of the urban lower classes.[171]

5. Lawyers and Notaries Public

Even though a small and not homogenous socioprofessional category, lawyers and notaries public were highly influential in public life.[172] For reasons which have yet to be adequately explained and which lie beyond the scope of this study, Vizcayans as a whole were quite a literate population, and in all likelihood somewhat more so than the other Spanish peoples. In fact, the limited size of the local government was unable to accommodate and absorb an abundance of well-educated and capable Vizcayans. Therefore, though numerous Vizcayans and other Basques traditionally left their homes for bureaucratic employment in the royal administration and clergy, they were still a surplus in the province, where most resisted change. Several reasons account for this behavior.

First, some of them—particularly the lawyers—regarded themselves as the legal guardians and interpreters of the fueros and of tradition.[173] Second, the socioprofessional standing of lawyers and notaries public was continually enhanced by the Vizcayans' propensity to sue in court and engage in legal battles. Bacon correctly observed that "the peasantry are as litigious as the Normans; for the merest trifle they may go to law with each other."[174] Third, profiting from this state of affairs, these *letrados* defended corporatist interests against reform, liberal or otherwise. For instance, a provision of the 1812 Constitution (reinstated in 1820) created the post of peacemaker or ombudsman (*juez de conciliacion*) in each of the nation's districts. His role was to reconcile the respective parties and thus prevent them from spending money in possibly futile lawsuits.[175] Afraid to lose their business, according to Bacon many lawyers and notaries public "became staunch absolutists."[176] Even the normally conservative Diputación and General Assembly took up the matter in May 1824, acknowledging the existence of 110 notaries public in the province when apparently only 65 would suffice. Despite a recommendation to reduce the number, there is no evidence that the measure was carried out.[177] Even though a handful were in the liberal camp, most lawyers and notaries public sided with the Carlists once the conflict began.[178]

6. Merchants and Capitalists

Merchants and capitalists include those deriving their income primarily from large-scale trade (overseas and national) and other capitalist enterprises: banking, insurance companies, and certain types of manufacture such as shipbuilding. Along with some of the most important landowners, these bourgeois classes directed the Vizcayan economy. Operating largely out of Bilbao, the hub of an extensive system of commercial, family, and personal relationships spanning the Old World and the New, this capitalist oligarchy enjoyed great social cohesion, common economic interests, and a deep awareness of its own identity that, because of political persecution and its status as a minority, made it more coherent than the royalist alliance of forces.[179] Fundamentally, then, common interests and strong bonds enabled the capitalist oligarchy to traverse the perilous Ominous Decade without any appreciable loss of socioeconomic power.

Instead of defending the old and the traditional, merchants and capitalists were open to innovation and reform; and, in this sense, there were crucial convergences between their objective interests and those of the central government in engineering administrative reform and economic change. Likewise, whereas Vizcayan conservatism was thoroughly imbued with regionalism, exclusivism, and even protoseparatism, bourgeois liberalism on the other hand saw itself as both cosmopolitan and part of a national collectivity.[180] And in accordance with contemporary European trends, Vizcayan capitalists for the most part were far from adverse to Spanish political unification, state building, and the integration of the regional economy into a national market where, for the time being at least, most of their interests lie. Consistent with these views, Vizcayan liberals vehemently denounced and actively opposed exclusive privileges, alleged royalist abuses of power, conservative ideologico-religious manifestations, and those sectors of society that purportedly blocked the route to progress. The furious invectives of reformers against "clerical obscurantism" and the supposed irrationality of the fueros and their defenders are prime examples of the self-appointed, "enlightened" missionary approach to society adopted by the representatives of the new bourgeois order.[181] Their laissez-faire doctrines and practices, however, were correctly perceived as a threat by the supporters of the ancien régime—in this case, the vast majority of Vizcayans.

One of the most striking and original aspects of the dynamics of class conflict, whose origins and development led to Carlism, is that while the fundamental opposition between the lower and the upper classes remained intact in Vizcaya, this social contradiction manifested itself in unusual politico-ideological forms. That is, the province's lower classes were oriented toward the political right while the upper classes embodied liberal-reformist positions— the conservatives representing the broad masses of the population, the reformers but a tiny minority of the province. With the Carlist War already in progress, Bacon vividly described this lower-class "tyranny": "The superior classes are oppressed by the furious and fierce fanaticism of myriads of proletarii, led on with perfect unity of purpose by a skillfully organized hierarchy."[182] In terms of social forces, on the side of the "oppressors" was a motley confederation of clerics, most of the peasantry and artisans, led by a handful of gentry, lawyers, and ecclesiastics—all of them the uncompromising adversaries of liberalism and reform.[183] These anticentralist sectors favored an all-out defense of the fueros and provided unconditional support to the legitimist cause. The "oppressed," meanwhile, were a relatively small (though socioeconomically compact and affluent) group of merchants, capitalists, and of course wealthy landowners, tightly bound by economic liberalism, administrative and political reform, and a pro-central government stance in essential matters of reciprocal interest.[184]

CHAPTER 7

Carlists, Liberals, and the October 1833 Uprising

Now, in virtue of the amnesty, the liberals believe they have carte blanche to openly display their great desire of regeneration and consider themselves the only [ones] capable of ruling.

Communication of the Vizcayan police to central headquarters, 24 June 1833.

Vizcayans: persevere as all good Spaniards in your courageous determination. The Diputación which leads you will give the signal to your zeal and enthusiasm; and when your efforts, in unison with those of the rest of Spain, will have succeeded in placing our most beloved monarch D. Carlos V on the throne of Saint Ferdinand, [how great] will be your happiness!

Proclamation of the Carlist Vizcayan Diputación, Bilbao, 5 October 1833.

This is a revolution of classes, of principles, not of any particular region.

Letter of the liberal Diputación and Junta Particular of Alava to the Queen, Vitoria, 21 November 1833.

I. SURGE OF THE CARLIST OPPOSITION (1832–1833)

After 1828 a semblance of sociopolitical peace appears to have prevailed in Vizcaya. Remarkably, the detente was not even troubled by the July Revolution and other contemporary events.[1] However, that the calm was both fragile and deceptive was conclusively demonstrated by the aftermath of the crucial September 1832 events of La Granja[2] and the general amnesty granted by the queen the following month.[3] These closely related occurrences, coupled with the change in direction of the national government which was now headed on a moderately liberal course, upset the precarious status quo and launched the Vizcayan political factions once again into open and bitter struggle. The 1832 amnesty, marking the official reincorporation of liberalism into public life, met with stiff resistance from Vizcayan hard-core royalists now solidly grouped under Don Carlos's apostolic banners.[4] Simultaneously, the purportedly threatened Carlists began to actively oppose the queen's followers or *Cristinos*.[5] The generally liberal authors of the *Galería militar contemporanea* correctly linked the episode of La Granja and the amnesty to the upsurge of Carlist agitation in Bilbao.[6]

But even before official word of the amnesty reached the city, Carlist activity was much in evidence. On the night of 18 October, for example, an extraordinarily revealing Carlist libel—replete with suggestive local, national, and international allusions—was posted in several public places:

> To arms Carlists!
> Long live Religion, long live the Inquisition!
> Long live Carlos V, long live Don Miguel!
> Long live their valiant defenders, Novia,
> The Marquis [de Valde-espina], Epalza, and Mati!
> Long live Calomarde and Alcudia!
> Long live the faithful of the Cuartel de la Ronda!
> Death to France and to England!
> Death to the Neapolitan whore!
> Death to the gouty one, death to Cafranga!
> Death to the Corregidor and Castelló!
> Death to the *pancistas* Unceta, Gurbista, and Gómez!
> Death to all the blacks and *fernandistas*![7]

Naturally, Carlist stirrings became more intense after the amnesty was officially known. On the nights of 24 and 25 October there were significant disturbances in Bilbao which the Diputación consciously downplayed and largely left unpunished even after the military governor of Guipúzcoa, General Llauder, reprimanded the Vizcayan leadership for its failure to preserve public order. The officer's strong reaction appears to indicate that the episodes were far more serious than the provincial government was willing to admit.[8] More ominously still, by early November 1832 Regnaudin was reporting on the existence of a clandestine Carlist club in Bilbao that met at the Convent of San Mamés.[9] Some measure of Carlist sentiment had also begun to filter down from a small circle of committed activists to the rest of the population, particularly to the lower classes. Indicative of this, a certain Juan de Lasagabaster (a part-time iron worker and a royalist veteran of the Napoleonic Era and the 1821–1823 civil war) was arrested while drunk (on 25 November 1832) in the town of Ochandiano after crying out "death to the king, death to the queen, and long live Carlos!"[10] Similar seditious expressions against the monarchs, accompanied by cries of admiration for Don Carlos and the so-called whites, were heard in Bilbao on 27 January 1833.[11] Significantly, some of the port's common folk were involved in the disturbances, including the barber of General Deputy José Ramón de Rotaeche, an ultraconservative leader of the 1823–1833 decade and a commander in the Paisanos. There were additional incidents during this period. According to the Vizcayan police, another subversive libel surfaced in mid-February—also with "highly offensive expressions" toward the monarchs and containing other "alarming" items.[12] Again in early March at a town council meeting in Begoña, a suburb of Bilbao, a participant (doubtless a Carlist given the political context) reportedly made offensive expressions "to the august and sovereign right of His Majesty and the authority of his delegates."[13] The sum of these events strongly suggests that well before the October 1833 uprising, consistent with long-held antiliberal and antireformist sympathies, some members of the Vizcayan artisan and urban lower strata already openly embraced Carlist positions. In addition to dynastic preference, ideological conviction, religious opinion, political choice, and socioeconomic interest, two important sets of events contributed powerfully to the rise of Vizcayan Carlism: the military purges after La Granja and the nomination of a new corregidor in November 1832.

First, following the extensive removal from the army of unreliable conservative commanders, many of them were exiled, reassigned, or retired to the Basque provinces "where, upon their arrival, they began to preach rebellion and became known as its true apostles."[14] The disgruntled officers—"disaffected to the legitimate heiress," according to Uhagon—frequented the Diputación and "bitterly censured" the recent changes in Madrid.[15] In essence, the central government's mishandling of the affair, resulting in the sizeable presence of Carlist officers in the Basque region, would be deeply regretted by liberalism, both local and national. Second, the appointment of Juan Modesto de la Mota (a committed liberal) as corregidor also fueled the growth of Vizcayan Carlism.[16] Much to the traditionalists' displeasure, de la Mota, apparently a politically inexperienced and ill-informed magistrate, immediately sided unconditionally with Vizcayan liberals. The corregidor's brash actions quickly proved glaringly counterproductive for himself and his liberal allies. So much so, in fact, that de la Mota and his friends were severely criticized by none other than Bacon for not being "fully acquainted with the extent of the Carlist organization of the [Basque] Provinces," or for underrating its strength.[17] Predictably, therefore, de la Mota himself became a focal point of contention and a political pawn in the intense factional struggle.[18] In sum, the close relationship between the corregidor and prominent liberals such as Pedro Pascual de Uhagon —especially after the latter was elected general deputy in July 1833 —discredited them in Carlist quarters and undermined their political effectiveness at a critical moment. Carlists were growing weary of the significant new presence and respectability of Vizcayan liberalism. Even though the numbers are not known, between February and April 1833, the Vizcayan police forwarded to Madrid no fewer than six lists of political amnestees residing in the province.[19]

Nor were liberals the only objects of Carlist ire. Eventually, Vizcayan moderate royalists also became the prime targets of sharp political criticisms. Witness the vicious attacks against prominent moderates—Unceta, Gurbista, and Gómez—and "Fernandistas" in the seditious October 1832 libels at Bilbao. As in much of Spain, Vizcayan royalism had split early into two main factions: that of the "ultras" or "apostolics," and that of the moderates. Though not much is known about the nature of the schism, socioeconomic differences may have partly accounted for the divisions. The Carlist sector included the local militias' commanders, members of the regular clergy, and sectors of the lower classes, both urban and rural. Moderate royalists, on the other hand, apparently belonged to some of the more privileged and economically advantaged (if not the wealthiest) provincial interests.[20] Worth underscoring, the scission was accentuated by the 1828 royal visit, after which some moderate royalists began a noticeable sociopolitical—and economic?—rapprochement with local liberals. Ideological and religious divisions among local royalists were also well in evidence when moderates were accused by Carlists of opposing the Inquisition's reestablishment.[21]

Both among the leadership and the rank and file, Carlism enjoyed a considerable following in the royalist militias. Led by staunch legitimist-absolutists, the 12,000 to 14,000 Vizcayan royalists, of whom Bilbao and some adjacent towns alone had well over 1,500, were a continual source of intimidation for liberals. However, in 1832–1833 the latter finally began to organize a coherent strategy to gradually neutralize and curtail these bodies' military and political force.[22] In so doing, Vizcayan liberalism appears to have followed a yet undefined but growing governmental trend to undertake the orderly disarmament of the royalist volunteer corps, said to number around 300,000 nationally.[23] In late 1832, General Llauder joined in the chorus of administration officials complaining about the central government's inaction toward the Basque militias—warnings which, as he bitterly admitted, went largely unheeded.[24] With painfully little help from Madrid, Vizcayan reformers would have to deal with the paramilitary corps. Carlism's increasing strength, the close ties of noted Carlists to (and within) the militias, and their unreliability toward Ferdinand's designated succession, indeed had convinced local liberals that the time to move against them had finally arrived. In early March 1833, Regnaudin reported that the forthcoming General Juntas would tackle the issue of the militias' disarming.[25] Concurring, Uhagon, the future general deputy, asserted that the Paisanos' reform was an essential and immediate part of his agenda of government.[26] Soon after the July 1833 general assembly, General Federico Castañón, the recently appointed military commander of Guipúzcoa, visited Vizcaya where Carlist agitation was on the rise. Castañón warned the authorities of Carlist designs and, significantly, offered government troops to disarm the ever-dangerous Bilbao royalist corps.[27] However, the suggestion was refused by de la Mota and Uhagon. The latter, according to Bacon, was unwilling "to increase his unpopularity by bringing troops into the Señorío . . . alleging that he did not wish to infringe the Fueros."[28] Instead of insisting, the general returned to San Sebastián and nothing more was done by the central government about the Vizcayan militias. The matter was now in Uhagon's and de la Mota's very fragile political hands. Despite strenuous efforts, intricate schemes, and the orchestration of a public campaign against the militias' "tyranny," much to

Vizcayan liberalism's misfortune, the corps were neither disarmed nor reformed.[29] Fundamentally, the reformers' inability to disarm or otherwise counteract the militias facilitated Carlism's plans.

Prior to these events, to counter Carlist rumblings and to consolidate the authority of his office, in early May General Castañón had written the Vizcayan Diputación, urging its unconditional acceptance of the hereditary rights of Princess Isabel.[30] While containing vows of fidelity to the fueros, Castañón's letter voiced fears of subversion and warned that efforts to undermine public order or run counter to governmental policies would be actively opposed. To underscore his determination, several days later the general addressed a proclamation to Vizcayans with similar observations.[31] Castañón's actions strongly corroborate Carlism's growing political appeal and strength. In fact, as early as mid-May 1833, observers on the French-Spanish border were already reporting on Carlist preparations for a projected insurrection and possible war.[32] Despite being a minority in a manifestly disadvantageous correlation of political forces, Vizcayan liberalism was active with its own brand of militancy. A case in point: after arguing unsuccessfully against a municipal project in Begoña to clothe the Paisanos with public funds, liberals posted seditious libels in May 1833 attacking the approved allocation.[33] Deep concern prompted the Council of Ministers on 28 June to summon to court on an emergency basis Corregidor de la Mota (in Valladolid at the time) for instructions concerning the upcoming Vizcayan Juntas. Moreover, the magistrate was ordered to proceed forthwith to Guernica.[34] Significantly, before the general assembly's opening, the Vizcayan police denounced the actions of liberals, who, in preparation for the parley, allegedly practiced large-scale bribery to secure representation and votes.[35] But counterattacking liberals suggested that Vizcayan conservatives hid behind a smokescreen of slander due to fears that power would be wrested from them permanently.[36] Vizcayan political life, substantially altered by a considerable reformist presence, was about to experience an open confrontation. The stage was set for a major political skirmish, one which in key ways was a fitting preview of a much larger looming conflict. In conclusion, the Carlist opposition was growing more articulate, vocal, and well organized in late 1832–early 1833. Carlist networks were becoming more widespread and sophisticated.[37] The struggle between Carlism and liberalism, already strong after the 1832 general amnesty, had become distinctly more intense as the 1833 Vizcayan Juntas approached. The lines were now sharply drawn for head-on political battles.

II. THE JULY 1833 JUNTAS AND THEIR AFTERMATH

In the inaugural address to the Vizcayan Juntas delivered on 4 July, Corregidor de la Mota appealed for unity and peace, stressing the hope that public tranquility not be disturbed.[38] The royal official then promptly instructed the gathering's delegates to follow a moderate and conciliatory line, one exempt from partiality or personal interest. Undoubtedly, de la Mota's remarks were intended to defuse tensions and calm a thoroughly conflictive situation. Still, in an early session Manuel José de Epalza, a notorious and influential Carlist from Bilbao, strenuously challenged several delegates whose mandates had been obtained by substitution, a long-standing (though controversial) procedure by which powerful Vizcayans "replaced" delegates from the smaller or needier villages through strong-arm tactics or questionable enticements, including outright bribes. Given the context, Epalza's criticism was a patent assault on liberalism's purported subterfuges to illegally secure representation at the parley. After intricate maneuvers, which apparently included concessions by liberals, the issue seems to have been largely resolved in their favor despite strong Carlist pressure.[39] Guided by liberalism's strong hand, some political compromises began to emerge. For instance, substitutions were henceforth forbidden (an allowance to Carlists?) but more importantly, property and monetary qualifications for candidacy to the highest provincial offices were raised substantially.[40] Powerful landowners, most of them Cristinos (liberal followers of Ferdinand VII's wife, Maria Cristina), were in all likelihood the intended beneficiaries of the changes. Still greater victories were in store for Vizcayan liberalism, especially in finances and administration.

Reformers secured recognition of war debts incurred during the Trienio—for supplies and equipment to constitutionalists—which had been voted down by the Ominous Decade's diputaciones.[41] And capitalizing on suspicions of mismanagement of funds by the outgoing Diputación, liberalism finally realized a prime objective: the creation of a permanent commission to (1) draw a general budget and (2) establish a plan of administration for all provincial revenues. According to reformers, the commission would handle public funds more economically to relieve villages of heavy tax burdens.[42] Carlists, however, understandably viewed the measure as a clever stratagem to undermine the militias' strength and sap the conservatives' political power, opinions that liberals undoubtedly shared in private. Also indicative of the rising liberal tide was the establishment of an "auxiliary permanent commission for the improvement of agriculture."[43] Close scrutiny of the commission's composition reveals a considerable liberal participation, including that of Mariano de Eguía, one of Vizcaya's wealthiest Cristino landholders, a good indication that reformers intended to make the body responsive to their interests.

Matters were proceeding well at the gathering for the liberal party until unforeseen difficulties arose over Pedro Pascual de Uhagon's naturalization papers or *vizcainía*. For years the French-born Uhagones had been struggling hard for recognition as vizcaínos, but had encountered stiff opposition from local traditionalists envious of the family's enormous socioeconomic and political success and the manner in which it had been secured.[44] In essence, as foreigners and nouveaux riches, the Uhagones were viewed apprehensively by some Vizcayans. The royal order of Uhagon's vizcainía, dated 18 October 1831, was now presented to the juntas. In addition to granting him (and his brothers) all of the rights of Vizcayans, the decree legally enabled the family to hold public office again.[45] Although heeded by the previous corregidor, the royal order had met with local opposition and had apparently not been fully enforced.[46] The document was well received at the assembly except for a lawyer named Velasco from the town of Sestao, who spearheaded opposition against acceptance of Uhagon's vizcainía.[47] If at the outset the incident had the connotations of a personal vendetta, it soon acquired political proportions when Uhagon's antagonists sided with Velasco, united disgruntled royalist elements, and led a skillful campaign to embarrass the newly elected general deputy.[48] The episode's ramifications—lasting of course beyond the juntas—were extremely significant for Uhagon and his political constituency. Fundamentally, Velasco's open defiance directly challenged and therefore diminished the leader's prestige and authority.[49] According to one account, "the rebellion existed in the hearts of men, and Velasco's resistance to the corregidor's orders . . . proved that it was not out of the question to imagine an uprising that would go unpunished."[50] More than a sour note, the affair was an ominous foreboding for Vizcayan liberalism. Nevertheless, in comparison to liberalism's achievements, conservative triumphs at the parley were meager and, except for Zavala's election as general deputy, bordered at times on the symbolic.[51]

A high point for Vizcayan liberalism came on 14 July when, at the urging of representatives from Galdámes, the juntas "spontaneously and unanimously hailed" Princess Isabel as the heiress to the "State of Vizcaya in lieu of a male heir to Ferdinand."[52] The session was lavish in praise of Cristina's handling of power during the king's recent illness. Possibly in an attempt to ingratiate itself further to the crown, the assembly apologized for not having pledged allegiance earlier to Isabel, explaining (correctly) that it had been necessary, as prescribed by tradition and law, to first convene juntas.[53] These must have been sad and disappointing moments for Don Carlos's Vizcayan followers and, as if to underscore their defeat, the letter from the general deputies and the corregidor informing Ferdinand VII of the gathering's important decisions contained references to the fueros that in this critical juncture were probably unacceptable to traditionalists.[54] Reformers capped a decade-long uphill struggle by securing the election of prominent liberals to the Diputación, although this was not achieved without adverse political consequences—particularly in Uhagon's case.[55] Uhagon's unpopularity was well known and, in Bacon's words, "constitutionalists themselves regretted the election" of the general deputy.[56] Resentment against Uhagon produced a swift and unfavorable reaction that was easily exploited by adversaries to weaken the officeholder's power precisely when liberals needed it most.[57] In fact, when Uhagon and Zavala were inaugurated on 31 July 1833 the pro-Carlist holdovers from the previous administration "paid the usual ceremonious visit . . . very ungraciously."[58] Not surprisingly, "soon after the election, the suspicions of the corregidor as to the designs of the Carlists, became aroused."[59] However, in early August Uhagon and Zavala—in their first joint police communiqué to Madrid—reported that public order and tranquility reigned in the province.[60] The calm, as Uhagon admitted later, was extremely deceptive. In Uhagon's words, "the armed party" disapproved of the Diputación's pledge of allegiance to Isabel, and "immediately set out to nullify its effects, accusing the government of Her Majesty of reformism."[61]

Also of immediate concern to the liberal leader was how to deal with a fellow general deputy, Fernando de Zavala, a well-known ultra-conservative royalist. Zavala's recent behavior appeared both moderate and reasonable. However, Hormaeche paints a vastly different picture, claiming that Zavala was "of a vacillating and weak character," and that "he pretended opinions and feelings that his bosom did not harbor, or which he later abandoned."[62] Uhagon seems to have solved the thorny political matter by making Zavala privy to sensitive matters (which ones it is not known) thereby assuring himself of his colleague's complicity through a kind of flattery.[63] There remained nevertheless an irreducible political and ideological contradiction between them. Pirala summed it up best: "Uhagon and Zavala personified [the] war in the Diputación" between liberalism and Carlism.[64] Upon taking office, the new Diputación faced a host of pressing problems. Led by a determined Uhagon, the provincial leadership acted upon three prime areas of concern to liberalism: administrative and economic reform, public works, and the ever-present issue of the Paisanos.[65] Even in extraordinarily difficult circumstances the general deputy believed that reform ideas were progressing rapidly—unquestionably an overly optimistic assessment.[66]

To its misfortune, however, Vizcayan liberalism would only have a two-month time span to enact its platform of government. Furthermore, in mid-September the Diputación was suddenly confronted with an incident reminiscent of the Velasco affair. This time, a royalist militia captain named Cantaló, accused of excesses by the township of Deusto, was removed by the Diputación and replaced with another officer. The provincial leadership's action angered the battalion's commander, Francisco Javier de Batiz, an ultraroyalist and future Carlist chieftain, who complained strongly. But "the Diputación upheld its decision and . . . in this way attempted the reforms that had to be carried out in the armed corps of the señorío."[67] The executive's firm stance toward Cantaló alienated the Carlist opposition even more and deepened political divisions. Significantly, the Cantaló episode coincided with rumors of the king's poor health. There were already numerous signs of sedition in Vizcaya.[68]

Carlist agitation—covert and overt—was increasing in the second half of September. According to Uhagon, Father Negrete used a Franciscan convent for private meetings with the brass and the rank and file of the local royalist militias.[69] Another clandestine Carlist club met under the auspices of Eusebio de Larumbe, the Dipu-

tación's official printer. Carlist agitation was plainly in sight elsewhere. Epalza, the notary public alluded to earlier, and Clemente
de Zalvide, a traditionalist lawyer, reportedly held openly seditious
meetings at their respective workplaces.[70] Meanwhile, elements of
the royalist corps were said to circulate insultingly in Bilbao, and
alarmist news and rumors were the order of the day.[71] The flurry of
activity had placed the Diputación and the corregidor in a delicate
political position. Essentially, a growing isolation made the Vizcayan authorities vulnerable to the rapidly advancing Carlist tide. The
situation had become so critical that, in a change of heart and despite
legal and institutional drawbacks, Uhagon and de la Mota requested
troops from the captain-general of Guipúzcoa but none were sent.[72]
Arguably too late anyway, the Vizcayan authorities were soon to be
overtaken by the rush of events.

The Diputación's difficult position was accentuated by a powerful "fifth column" fully dedicated to the pretender's cause.[73] The
group was headed by Miguel de Artiñano, the senior police official
in the province who, along with other important bureaucrats in the
Diputación, actively opposed Uhagon, de la Mota, and their allies.
Uhagon's hands were completely tied, for no matter how strongly
he may have wanted to reform the government's personnel, the ap-
pointments of hostile elements had been confirmed at the recent
juntas.[74] There is ample reason to believe that during Uhagon's brief
incumbency Artiñano's faction worked from within to undermine
the general deputy's policies. Also contributing to the debilitation
of the Vizcayan authorities was the central government's seeming
indecision or indifference even in the face of the provincial government's desperate situation.[75] Perhaps Uhagon summed it up best:
"Everything which surrounded the Diputación was mined."[76] In a
last-ditch attempt to forestall the impending rebellion, the Diputación sought the assistance of prominent Vizcayans. Novia de Salcedo, for instance, was approached by the provincial government and
asked to use his influence among the militias to head off an "impru-
dent struggle."[77] Although he promised to act efficaciously—an important pledge given his rank as colonel in Bilbao's militias—Novia
de Salcedo's efforts yielded no apparent results.[78] Hence, devoid of external and internal aid, a paralyzed Diputación and corregidor could
only watch helplessly as the dramatic October 1833 events neared.
The Carlists, as the central government well knew, were ready to
rise "as soon as the king died."[79]

III. THE INSURRECTION

While some conservatives have tended to stress the "spontaneous" character of the October 1833 Carlist insurrection, liberals—commentators, historians, and protagonists—have emphasized its organized and conspiratorial aspects.[80] Goicoechea, Hormaeche, the *Observaciones'* anonymous author and, of course, Pirala stand out among the most forceful proponents of the latter view.[81] However, the most specific references to a conspiracy in Bilbao to proclaim Don Carlos king are in Uhagon's important account.[82] Uhagon wrote that by mid-1833 there were clear signs "of a sedition prepared in Vizcaya to support the alleged rights of the Infante D[on] Carlos."[83] Without mincing words, the general deputy strikingly observed that "advanced preparations were made for the uprising, and everything was organized to hoist the banner on the mournful day that the king's death was known."[84] Uhagon also charged that the Paisanos' commanders were systematically involved in the plot since "unless there was a prearranged combination among them, it is not normal that there had existed the simultaneity of action with which all of them concurred to support the treason promulgated in Bilbao on the third of October."[85] But suggestive evidence also comes from the Carlist camp. An admiring Father Negrete approvingly spoke of the uprising's "conspirators" (*conjurados*).[86] An analysis of the insurrection casts light on this essential question.[87]

News of Ferdinand VII's death reached the Diputación in the early hours of 2 October. Acutely aware of the situation's gravity, the provincial government immediately convened at the corregidor's residence and adopted urgent measures to preserve order, among them the dispatch of a communication to the captain-general of Guipúzcoa requesting troops, the seizure at Deusto of the gunpowder deposit, and the convocation of the mayor of Bilbao and the commander of the city's royalist Guardia to urge them to quietly gather a small company before daybreak in order to contain disorders.[88] The orders were quickly disregarded, however, and the first major act of disobedience began with the consent of the municipal authorities and the militias' officers.[89] First, "they sounded a general call that was immediately followed by a similar alarm and formation . . . at Begoña and Abando." Then, a "drum roll calling to formation was heard, and without informing the Diputación," according to Uhagon, two "battalions occupied the main streets of the city."[90] The corps' insubordination would have far-reaching consequences since, once assembled, the Diputación and local authorities would be utterly powerless to disperse them. Still, Uhagon and de la Mota stubbornly attempted to defuse the mounting insurrection through numerous orders calling for the militias' demobilization, but all met with determined resistance and ultimately floundered.[91] The Diputación's unsuccessful efforts were largely due to the lack of effective authority over the detachments' officers. Yet another factor looms as important, namely, the almost certain disobedience of some of the rank and file against their commanders' orders. Without discounting a possible duplicity on the officers' part to gain valuable time, some of them (notably Novia) informed the Diputación that commands had been issued to prevent the militias' "total collusion," but in vain "since the latter refused to heed the orders to return home."[92] Such then, was the apparent strength of the revolt from below. Although no pro–Don Carlos proclamation had been issued, the Diputación, facing a spreading military revolt, was scarcely in control. The balance of the rebellion's first day can be summed up thusly: the Diputación, though not completely defeated, was feebler and more isolated than before, while the city's fate was in the hands of royalist units which had seized the initiative and propelled themselves into the movement's armed vanguard. The defiant militias would determine the sedition's success.

One of the most suggestive aspects of the first day's events—something that applies to the revolt's early stages—was the absence of disorderly conduct among the population. There were, to be sure, the elements of confusion, noise, excess, and violence present in nearly every upheaval or revolutionary situation.[93] Despite this, significantly, there is nevertheless broad agreement among widely divergent narratives that public tranquility was generally preserved in Bilbao during the uprising's otherwise extremely heated and agitated initial moments.[94] Strikingly, as far as is known, the authorities issued no orders to control crowds or contain popular riots. Instead, the Diputación's commands concentrated solely upon the dispersal of the militias, the only ones said to be disturbing the peace. This is largely explained by the fact that the 2 October Carlist revolt was not a mass popular movement. Rather, the rebellion was inspired and led by a small sector representing the militias. The majority of Vizcayans were unaffected by the first insurrectionary thrust and would only be involved in the struggle later on. Popular participation in the events, however, was not totally lacking. It should not be forgotten that the lower social strata—artisans, shopkeepers, domestics, peasants, and others—comprised the majority of the armed bodies. But, ironically, obscured by their formal membership in these corps' structure and organization, these social elements have tended to be hidden from the historian. Basically, then, military hierarchy and discipline—admittedly disregarded at times by some of the armed elements—effectively forestalled and checked unrestrained behavior on the rebels' part. This, in turn, helps to explain the relative absence of disorder and violence, a surprising development given the pronounced antagonisms fostered in the previous decade.

During the insurrection's first days, for instance, there was isolated and sporadic looting in Bilbao, but certainly nothing on a significant scale. Even the *Galería militar's* authors—no friends of Carlism—asserted with astonishment that business establishments and offices "remained closed after the first moments of the alarm, and they remained in this state until they were opened again personally by their rightful owners."[95] Organized Carlism, however, made various impositions upon Bilbao's wealthy liberal community. But even this "grand larceny" could well be viewed as a transfer of property from one power bloc to another, or as the expropriation of a particular class by its social and political adversaries.[96] In other words, these requisitions—made through force to be sure—were not made to enrich an individual or satisfy another's vendetta, but to collectively bolster the rebel cause. As Uhagon suggestively stated, the Carlists "took over as many objects as would facilitate an increase in their power and in their subversive plans."[97] Simply put, if there was little spontaneous looting, there existed nonetheless a higher (and more significant) level of utilitarian appropriation by the Carlists.

Although reports abound of violence against reformers and their allies, many of these are uncritical repetitions of previous exaggerated accounts. Close scrutiny of the documentation actually reveals strikingly few physical assaults and overt aggressions.[98] Apart from the assassination on 2 October of Uhagon's brother-in-law, Cándido de Aréchaga, by an officer of the Guardia, the identities of only three liberals apparently wounded in the uprising have been verified.[99] There is little evidence to support Uhagon's assertions of other deaths and casualties.[100] That constitutionalists were set upon and beaten by Carlists, as Regnaudin and Bacon attest, is beyond question, but the attacks, except for Aréchaga's—which resulted in the only known death—hardly exceeded the intensity and level of violence attained in the mid-1820s disturbances in Bilbao. Again, in view of the deep-seated political divisions and personal animosities, rebel violence on the whole was stunningly light and scattered, particularly after the Carlists had gained the upper hand over a disorganized liberal party.

Even as the balance of forces was tilting rapidly toward the insurgents, a sizeable number of "patriotic" bilbaínos—some 150 to 200 liberals—volunteered their services to the Diputación. The governing body, however, now in a decidedly defensive position, refused the offered assistance to avoid a premature and potentially disastrous showdown against the 1,500 militiamen controlling Bilbao and some of its surrounding towns.[101] By the morning of 3 October the units' pressure had become unbearably intense, and Bilbao was rife with rumors of an imminent move to proclaim Don Carlos.[102] As the day progressed, Uhagon received confidential reports that the pronouncement would take place at 5:30 in the afternoon. Ominously, too, the general deputy and the corregidor learned that a decision had been made to assassinate them.[103] Apparently clinging to the hope of receiving assistance from Guipúzcoa, Uhagon and the corregidor did everything possible to postpone the proclamation of Don Carlos by the militias. Attempting to neutralize the assembled militia companies, a courageous Uhagon even left the Diputación building to walk among his antagonists, but to little avail. No longer able to count on the Miqueletes who guarded the seat of government, Uhagon and de la Mota turned in desperation to Zavala just minutes before the final uprising. Asked "to place himself at the head of the battalions of the adjoining district," Zavala agreed and left the building, according to some accounts, offering to "repel all of the insurgents in Bilbao."[104] Tellingly, no sooner had Zavala made this pledge—unquestionably in bad faith—than the Diputación was stormed by the Carlists. Bacon and Uhagon sketched vivid accounts of the dramatic attack, one that came amid cries of "Long live Carlos V! Death to the Corregidor! Death to the Deputy Uhagon!"[105] While the marked men fled over the rooftops to avoid assassination, abandoning their posts and touching off a massive manhunt, the victorious rebels finally proclaimed Don Carlos king.

There is documentary unanimity that the militias proclaimed the new king. In fact, the episode has all the trappings and characteristics of a military pronouncement and not those of a mass-based movement. Zavala's first police report on 4 October following the previous authorities' ouster, was unequivocal: "The armed force of this city yesterday proclaimed Don Carlos King of Spain and Lord of Vizcaya."[106] Revealingly, the same communiqué spoke of "the pronouncement of the armed force." Similar views and interpretations are found in the *Galería militar*, the *Fastos Españoles*, Bacon, Hormaeche, and Uhagon.[107] A determined, compact, and well-armed minority had dictated its terms to the rest of Vizcayans, doing so swiftly and with remarkably little violence.[108] By the nightfall of the third, the rebels were proudly displaying a standard in the Arenal of Bilbao bearing the inscription *"Viva Dn Carlos V."*[109] The following day, according to Bacon, "Charles V was proclaimed in form; the [municipal] corporation and Diputación took [an] oath of allegiance; and the proclamation was issued."[110] The Carlist takeover of Bilbao was complete. The pretender's followers were now the city's and the province's undisputed masters, a position they would retain until dislodged by the queen's troops (commanded by General Sarsfield) in late November 1833.

In short, the Carlist insurrection triumphed for these essential though not exclusive reasons: (1) the strength of the royalist militias and the military weakness of the liberal camp;[111] (2) the absence of government troops in the province; (3) a Carlist organization whose preparations—including clandestine meetings—and coherence must be measured against the material disorganization and political isolation of the liberal-reformist sectors; (4) the irresistible convergence of Carlist aspirations and objectives, a key factor that helped to overcome the differences between the royalist militias' rank and file and their commanders, and which resulted in a remarkable degree of unity among the insurgents;[112] (5) the division among the constituted authorities, most notably between Uhagon and de la Mota on one hand, and Zavala on the other—Zavala's crucial defection clearing the road for the final rebel onslaught; (6) the desertion of the Miqueletes, the last peace-keeping force at the Diputación's disposal; and (7) the effective ideological, political, and material aid of the regular and secular clergy.[113]

IV. MOTORS OF THE UPRISING

Unquestionably, the chief driving political and ideological force behind the October uprising was legitimism. Juan Antonio Zaratiegui correctly observed that "the war begun . . . in 1833 did not have other object than the defense of the rights of . . . Don Carlos Maria Isidro to the Crown."[114] The pretender's claim to the Spanish throne had been and would continue to be the cornerstone of Carlism. A harbinger of things to come, a Carlist proclamation circulated in Guipúzcoa in late 1832 or early 1833 which savaged María Cristina's government, ended with this stirring appeal: "To arms, royalist volunteers! Long live the absolute king, with Carlos V as regent and with legitimacy!"[115] The fundamentally legitimist character of the Vizcayan October 1833 insurrection is amply illustrated by two key proclamations issued by Carlists during the initial days of Bilbao's seizure: the first, a document that has simply come to be known as "Valde-espina's Proclamation," dated 5 October; the second, the *Demostración del incontestable derecho que el Sr. D. Carlos de Borbón tiene al Trono de España*, dated 7 October, signed with the pen name of *"El Restaurador"* and most probably the work of Father Negrete, the noted Franciscan cleric.[116] Valde-espina's brief proclamation, written in the terse language of the 1823 restoration, violently denounced the "antireligious and antimonarchical faction" which had purportedly taken control of the king's will during his long illness to introduce revolution and anarchy—all familiar themes of Carlism. The piece claimed that reformers were trying to wreck the kingdom's ancient and fundamental laws of succession. Finally, the proclamation's signers— Valde-espina, Batiz, and Zavala—urged Vizcayans to remain faithful to the cause of Don Carlos, the "legitimate sovereign" and recently proclaimed monarch in Bilbao. Father Negrete's *Demostración*, by comparison, was a lengthy and elaborate document detailing the reasons—legal, historical, ideological, religious, and political—validating Don Carlos's claim to the throne. Negrete's opus, however long-winded and cumbersome, never departed from basic legitimist premises.[117] Nor was the thrust of Colonel Ibarrola's laconic proclamation (issued at Orduña on 4 October) different in legitimist substance.[118] Along with dynastic legitimism, and as close corollaries to it, were absolutism and traditionalism. Under the aegis of historical precedent and custom, the Carlists not only called for the preservation of an absolute monarchy but also appealed to the "ancient laws," the "fatherland's laws," and the "fatherland's freedoms."[119] Moreover, traditionalism in Vizcaya (as this narrative has endeavored to show) was heavily identified with the provincial liberties and fueros, which Carlism also wished to preserve.

Xenophobia and nationalism were likewise integral components of the Carlists' body of ideas.[120] Notwithstanding the provincial or particularist nature of the Carlist appeals—e.g., aimed specifically at the Vizcayans—there were significant and repeated references in the proclamations to the need of defending a national entity.[121] In fact, a nationalism which can only be characterized as Spanish was continually articulated by the Carlists. This should come as no surprise since, after all, legitimism was not a local problem but a national one. Hence, during the Vizcayan rebellion's initial stages, paradoxically perhaps, strong nationalist tendencies prevailed over regionally based considerations. Possibly for similar reasons, the preservation of "religious sanctity," an issue that distinctly transcended local concerns, was also a guiding cause of the October insurrection. From the very outset, therefore, the movement had all the trappings of a religious crusade. The enthusiastic response of the Vizcayan clergy on the Carlist rebels' behalf is unanimously attested to in the insurrection's numerous accounts, both friendly and hostile.[122] Whatever may have been the Vizcayan clergy's aims and aspirations, from the revolt's early moments the alliance between religion and legitimism would prove one of Carlism's most effective motors as well as one of its most enduring legacies.

Finally, consideration must be given to the fueros' role in the uprising proper. As noted before, it is this author's firm belief that Carlism in Vizcaya and in other parts of the Basque provinces and Navarra was directly tied to the defense of important provincial freedoms, to the economic benefits these conveyed, and to the political institutions that maintained them. Distinctions must be made, however, in the fueros' significance at different historical junctures to avoid misrepresentations of their importance during the October 1833 insurrection, such as José de Presas's caricatural account.[123] As has been stressed at length, especially in chapter 3, the fueros' preservation was a major preoccupation of Vizcayan conservatism. In the process, therefore, at numerous levels—national, regional, and local—the privileges became a focal point of contention between the proponents and opponents of reform. When reformers augmented their political influence and pressure in 1832–1833, the province's traditionalists stepped up the defense of the allegedly endangered fueros while accusing liberals of trying to destroy them. According to Hormaeche, the Carlists skillfully wielded powerful arguments that played upon profound Vizcayan fears: "The liberals will proclaim the 1812 Constitution, they will suppress your institutions, subjecting you to the ruinous uniformity that you have never consented to."[124] Equally significant, following the 1833 July juntas, Carlists effected a crucial link between the liberties' maintenance and absolutism's continuation, arguing that to conserve the fueros "it was also imperative to maintain in the monarchy an absolutist government."[125] Although it is difficult to weigh the political consequences of the campaign, it is reasonable to assume that it probably capitalized on Vizcayans' apprehension that the privileges might be altered or abolished. If Carlism built any political momentum around this issue, however, it was not apparent during the uprising when, interestingly, hardly a reference to the fueros was made.

Part of the answer to this apparent puzzle is contained in Pirala's striking (if much overlooked) observation that in the struggle's start "nobody remembered the fueros because nobody threatened them."[126] Suggestively, none of the voluminous documentation of the 1833 Carlist uprising in Vizcaya consulted by this author contains explicit references to the freedoms and, to my knowledge, only Verastegui's proclamation at Vitoria (7 October) and Alzaá's manifesto at Oñate (8 October) make reference to the Basque privileges.[127] Hence, except perhaps for these references, Boislecomte's important assertions on this question are fundamentally correct:

> The insurrection was done in the name of Don Carlos and of religion. These were the only two themes which were effectively heard, and it is worth noting that in the countless proclamations circulated in the provinces no allusion has been made to their fueros nor to local circumstances. To the contrary, all of the proclamations were imbued with the astonishing spirit of nationality and monarchy in the purely Spanish sense.[128]

Did the privileges, then, play little or no part in the Carlist seizure of power? Despite the previous remarks, the answer is negative. Ironically, Boislecomte's own perceptive comments rebut other assertions of his and, in fact, clearly confirm the fueros' role in the general context of the uprising.

For instance, it was the author of the *Ensayo histórico* who pointedly wrote that the Basque provinces and Navarra, "adherents of the ancient system, and with the means to sustain it *and not lose their fueros*, taking advantage of the existent organization of voluntary royalists, and enjoying the general cooperation of the nation, rebelled and took up arms."[129] Boislecomte added significantly that the Basque provinces looked upon "the conservation of their privileges as inherent in Don Carlos's interests."[130] Yet, subtly tempering his arguments as well, Boislecomte cautioned against attributing too much importance to the freedoms: "They entered [into the rebellion] only as a condition, as a means. The true goal was a national goal; it was the preservation of the general institutions, of the faith, and of the customs of the country."[131] But even "as a means" (to use this author's language) the privileges were no less important. In fact, long before the uprising, Vizcayan conservatism had incorporated the freedoms' preservation into traditionalist concerns, and the key bond between the fueros and Carlism—as in the case of religion —would have lasting consequences beyond the immediate October events.

In conclusion, if the insurrection's motors were indeed dynastic legitimism—and its political adjunct, absolutism—along with the defense of the traditional religious and social order, the fueros then were an important though ultimately secondary consideration. Consequently, it should come as no surprise that little mention was made of the privileges during the crucial October 1833 juncture. After all, the fueros, while clearly important, were essentially local questions, while the most pressing and acute issues were primarily of a national political and socioeconomic significance. In other words, most directly at stake was the character and form of the nation's government—structure, substance, and political orientation—and the country's future socioeconomic direction. It was at these basic levels that there arose the most profound contradictions between the ancien régime's proponents on the one hand, and the bourgeoisie on the other: a bourgeoisie avid for restructuring society under the general label of reform along the lines of private property, free enterprise and economic liberalism, individual freedom, political and administrative change, and a constitutional monarchy. The moving force, and veritable raison d'être of the devastating Carlist War that erupted in 1833 was the profoundly rooted and sharply antagonistic opposition between sociopolitical classes and forces whose fundamental interests, objectives, and ideology (including of course religion) brought them into open and violent conflict with one another.

CHAPTER 8

Conclusion

Almost without exception, the study of Carlism —Spanish, Basque, and Vizcayan alike—has been characterized almost exclusively by political, dynastic, and ideologico-religious approaches. Not only have these emphases regrettably tended to obscure significant aspects of Carlism's roots, but worse yet, major factors in its formation and development have been omitted altogether. This work's intention has been to challenge traditional views of Carlism since, in Vizcaya at least, it is impossible to comprehend the movement's genesis and complexity without a thorough understanding of the socioeconomic context and the political processes that preceded it. More to the point: beyond the now familiar interpretations of conservatives versus liberals, of country versus city, of peasants versus merchants, of proclericals versus anticlericals, and of Carlists versus Cristinos, strikingly little has been written of the profound class conflict in pre-industrial Vizcaya—a class conflict which encompasses important class alliances and interrelationships. There is a direct and ascertainable link between this class conflict and the rise of Vizcayan Carlism.

During the first third of the nineteenth century, the Vizcayan upper classes—merchants, entrepreneurs, large landowners, and some professionals—were constantly at odds with the middle and lower classes—middle and small landowners, peasants, tenants, rural wage laborers, artisans, shopkeepers, smugglers, notaries public and, of course, the clergy—over a broad array of fundamental questions. The first camp was generally constitutionalist-liberal and favored reforms in policy, society, and the economy. Consistent with their material interests and world view, the Vizcayan upper classes clearly supported and promoted disentailment and the redistribution of property (communal and clerical) and administrative and economic reforms (in government and trade) to enhance their power and to adapt to changing circumstances. Therefore, while not attacking the provincial freedoms head-on, it became clear during the Ominous Decade that important sectors of the Vizcayan upper classes and entrepreneurial strata were willing to forego or modify some of the fueros and acquiesce to centralism in return for economic and political advantages.

The middle and lower classes, on the other hand, with the clerical establishment's firm support, remained staunchly committed to traditional society and the provincial privileges. Unified politically around extremely conservative diputaciones, these social strata strenuously opposed state intervention, particularly if it entailed (1) reforms, (2) changes in the fueros, (3) modifications in the Vizcayan government and local institutions, or (4) basic alterations in the privileged historical relationship between the province and the crown. In other words, if a seemingly compatible royalism characterized the restored leaderships in Vizcaya and in Madrid, numerous critical issues troubled their relations throughout much of the period under consideration. As each party strove to uphold and defend special prerogatives, important conflicts inevitably arose between the central government and the Vizcayan Diputación. In detailing the sources and nature of this conflictive interaction, this study casts light on another sorely (and strangely) neglected factor in the formation of Vizcayan Carlism, namely, state-Vizcaya relations. Military conscription, taxation, trade (including vital questions concerning customs, tariffs, and smuggling) and, naturally, the liberties, contributed to continual tension between the province and the royal administration. The Vizcayan leadership strongly defended provincial and regional prerogatives against centralizing, uniformizing, and incorporationist efforts—in essence, against the state's dreaded universal leveling (nivelación universal). Shielding itself effectively with the provincial privileges and enjoying the confidence and assistance of most of the local population, the Diputación attempted to preserve, largely intact, traditional socioeconomic, legal, and institutional structures.

In the tug-of-war between Vizcayan conservatives and the royal administration, Vizcayan liberalism sometimes sided with the central government in political matters and trade. Particularly welcome to local reformers were state measures to curtail the diputaciones' purportedly arbitrary powers, to palliate repression and political abuses, and to end the proscription from office that liberalism suffered following the 1823 Restoration. However, Vizcayan traditionalists, deeply distrustful of Madrid's and liberalism's objectives, eventually rallied to the rightist sectors of the royalist-absolutist party to safeguard age-old national and local institutions, among them, the fueros. Regarded as costly and bothersome feudal atavisms by the central government and by Vizcayan liberalism, the freedoms nonetheless enjoyed widespread popular support in the province. Even if possibly detrimental in certain respects, most Vizcayans drew tangible benefits from the fueros: exemption from military conscription and numerous government taxes, a generally high standard of living on account of the region's commercial franchises and an enclave economy, and the almost limitless capacity to engage in smuggling. In sum, Vizcayans had a solid stake in the liberties' preservation.

Following the 1820–1823 constitutional experience, the Vizcayan ruling elite organized an extraordinarily efficient police, and an impressive paramilitary corps known as the Brigadas de Paisanos Armados. Rooted in the peasantry and in the urban middle and lower classes, especially among the artisan strata, the militias became an effective counterrevolutionary force. More specifically, during the 1823–1833 political reaction, the police and the Paisanos handily served the conservative diputaciones as agents of repression: the police by providing a hitherto unknown level of penetration into, and control of, personal activities; the royalist corps by functioning as the provincial leadership's exclusive military arm to intimidate the political opposition. Furthermore, if notoriously unruly and undisciplined at times (notably in Bilbao during the turbulent 1823–1825 period) the militias nonetheless provided an imposing armed defense for the Vizcayan laws and institutions. Finally, in numerous ways—organizationally, in terms of discipline and training, political indoctrination, and in their counterrevolutionary ideological orientation—the militias were an important breeding ground for Carlism. Predictably, therefore, Vizcayan liberalism attempted to disarm and dismantle the paramilitary corps well before the October 1833 insurrection. Had they succeeded, reformers might well have prevented—or at least delayed—the Carlist uprising.

After 1823 liberals were barred from public office. This was patently advantageous to the conservative Vizcayan leadership, giving it a free hand to dictate policy and to determine the use of public funds. Still, the Vizcayan rulers were unable to match their political success in economic matters. Multiple adverse factors—among them, the loss of the American Colonies, unfavorable government policies, the stagnation of Vizcayan iron production, an international decline in prices, and pronounced sociopolitical divisions—created a deep crisis in key sectors of the provincial economy. To redress this situation, the Vizcayan Diputación tried several limited reforms (primarily in iron manufacture) but, to its great disappointment, with marginal results at best. Undoubtedly, the projected reforms' failure lay in circumstances beyond the ruling elite's control. For instance, the Vizcayan leadership had to contend with the vested interests and vast socioeconomic influence of the local commercial bourgeoisie, a class generally unresponsive to certain domestic economic concerns. Given the lack of effective protection for home manufactures —largely as a result of the fueros and the high cost of domestic production—the Vizcayan compradore bourgeoisie found it more profitable and convenient to rely on foreign imports. Additionally, the reduced importance of the Vizcayan market reinforced this orientation since the commercial bourgeoisie was far more interested in penetrating national outlets, preferably through legal means, than in merely supplying goods to a self-reliant and numerically small population. Hence, too, the desire of Vizcayan merchants for direct overseas trade even if this possibly meant the establishment of customs bureaus within the provincial territory in violation of the liberties.

In reaction to the previous political upheavals and changes, the predominantly conservative nature of the 1814–1820 and 1823–1833 restorations enabled the Vizcayan leaderships to effectively maintain, and perhaps expand, the provincial and regional privileges—often, it should be underscored, with the explicit support of the Alavese and Guipúzcoan ruling elites. This led as well to a de facto regional alliance or confederation among the Basque provinces against unpopular centralist measures. The common front strategy was undoubtedly one of the conditioning agents and contributing factors to the rise of Carlism. In fact, the sharpening of tensions between the diputaciones and the central government—possibly felt most acutely during the Ominous Decade—clearly put the Basque region and the state on an inexorable collision course. The clash, however, would only begin in earnest following the important political mutations of 1832—events of La Granja, change of ministry, general amnesty, and liberalism's return to public life—which caused influential Vizcayan and Basque traditionalists to fear significant reforms, including changes in the provinces' laws and institutions. Therefore, to safeguard the status quo, regional interests and local political power, Vizcayan Carlists (along with their Spanish counterparts) began to prepare a political exchange solution at the highest levels. The scheme's objective was to ensure the installation on the throne of Ferdinand VII's brother Don Carlos instead of Queen Maria Cristina and her daughter Isabel—the latter eventuality extremely distasteful to ultraroyalists who foresaw the dangers, real or imaginary, of a liberal-controlled regency.

Finally, although the evidence remains inconclusive, the October 1833 uprising at Bilbao appears to have formed part of a prearranged national movement and conspiracy to maintain traditional government, authority, and the interests of the church. A careful examination of the insurrection reveals beyond doubt that it was inspired, led, and carried to term by a compact minority, and that it had the classic characteristics of a military coup—the Vizcayan royalist militias ensuring the rebellion's successful takeover of Bilbao. Furthermore, there is substantial evidence that the Vizcayan fueros, even if for the most part not directly invoked by the Carlists during the uprising, nevertheless had a significant—if secondary—role in the general context of the revolt.

Abbreviations

The abbreviations included in this list are used extensively in the notes section that follows.

AC	Archivo de las Cortes, Madrid
ACJG	Archivo de la Casa de Juntas de Guernica, Vizcaya
ADV	Archivo de la Diputación de Vizcaya, Bilbao
AGP	Archivo General del Palacio, Madrid
AGS	Archivo General de Simancas
AHN	Archivo Histórico Nacional, Madrid
AMAE	Archives du Ministère des Affaires Étrangères, Paris
ANP	Archives Nationales, Paris
APG	Archivo de la Presidencia de Gobierno, Madrid
CC	Archives du Ministère des Affaires Étrangères, Paris Correspondance Consulaire, Bilbao
CD	Archives du Ministère des Affaires Étrangères, Paris Correspondance Diplomatique, Espagne
CDC	*Colección de los decretos y órdenes generales expedidos por las Cortes*
CD	*Colección de Decretos del rey don Fernando VII*
DSC	*Diario de las sesiones de Cortes*
ESR, 1983	*European Studies Review*, vol. 13, no. 3, 1983
OCSV	Órdenes Circulares del Señorío de Vizcaya
RAH	Real Academia de la Historia, Madrid
SHAT	Service Historique de l'Armée de Terre, Vincennes, France

Notes

Preface

1. Excellent examples of this are the recent studies of Pablo Fernández Albadalejo, Emiliano Fernández de Pinedo, Manuel González Portilla, and others that have appeared in the past decade. To their credit, these authors have been among the first to recognize the necessity of filling in glaring socioeconomic gaps in Basque history.

2. From a documentary standpoint, a notable exception was my inability to gain any semblance of reasonable access—try as I did—to private archival collections. This proved an important obstacle toward securing data on the specific personal and family histories of some of the period's chief protagonists. Had more of this information been available, for example, it would have been far easier to reconstruct the socioeconomic and political background of the Vizcayan elites both liberal and conservative and quite probably ascertain their concrete interests and aspirations in much greater detail.

3. See, for example, Jaime del Burgo's multivolume *Bibliografía de las Guerras Carlistas y de las luchas políticas del siglo XIX*, 5 vols. (Pamplona: Diputación Foral de Navarra, Institución Príncipe de Viana, 1953–1966).

4. A recent example of a somewhat different and more modern approach in John F. Coverdale, *The Basque Phase of Spain's First Carlist War* (Princeton: Princeton University Press, 1984). Unfortunately, this book appeared after the bulk of my present study had been completed. Consequently, it was difficult to incorporate its findings and conclusions. Though regrettable, in another sense it is probably better this way since Dr. Coverdale's work on Carlism deserves a far more serious and thorough critique than any treatment that could have been cursorily offered here.

5. Some of the more salient exceptions to this are the authors cited in note 1.

6. I shall never forget the humorous mixture of surprise and disbelief of a major specialist in this era, when I recounted in some detail how the Carlist forces had taken over Bilbao during the October 1833 insurrection. Clearly, sticking to a traditional (and highly erroneous) interpretation, he had always believed that, despite repeated sieges, the Carlists had never gained control of the city. Probably in an effort to acknowledge that his earlier opinions

had been incorrect, some time later he generously forwarded to me exceedingly interesting data concerning the aftermath of the Carlists' conquest of Bilbao.

7. On some of these important questions—e.g., core and periphery relations in the pre-industrial era, nation building, and the consequences of political incorporation—Michael Hechter's *Internal Colonialism. The Celtic fringe in British national development, 1536–1966* (Berkeley and Los Angeles: University of California Press, 1977) provides suggestive comparisons between England and Spain. See in particular chaps. 1–4. However, despite its impressive scholarly and theoretical strengths, this work's general analysis must be applied to Spain with the utmost care given the numerous differences between the Basque provinces and the English areas that Hechter identifies as the Celtic fringe. To name but one critical disparity, while the Celtic fringe included traditionally underdeveloped pastoral highland societies and economies, by contrast (as is abundantly known) the Basque provinces and Catalonia (and, for that matter, other parts of the Spanish periphery) contained some of the peninsula's more socioeconomically advanced structures. Because of these considerations, the relation between London and the Home Counties to the Celtic fringe was bound to be at sharp variance with that which existed between Castile and its peripheral regions. In sum, precisely for these reasons, Hechter's central thesis of internal colonialism in the British case does not seem to apply to Spain and the Basque provinces.

Chapter 1: Structures and Antecedents

1. Henry Swinburne, *Travels Through Spain, in the years 1775 and 1776,* 2d ed., 2 vols. (London: Printed by J. Davis for P. Elmsly, 1787), vol. 2, p. 272. Additional interesting remarks in pp. 273–278 passim. In particular, see p. 276.

2. Alexandre Laborde, *A View of Spain Comprising a Descriptive Itinerary, of Each Province, and a General Statistical Account of the Country,* 5 vols. (London: Printed for Longman, Hurst, Rees, and Orme, 1809), vol. 2, p. 341. For the same reference in the earlier French edition, see *Itinéraire descriptif de l'Espagne et tableau élémentaire des différentes branches de l'administration et de industrie de ce royaume,* 5 vols., plus atlas of map. (Paris: Chez H. Nicolle et Lenormant, 1808), vol. 2, p. 105.

3. See the *Censo español executado de orden del rey, comunicada por el excelentísimo señor conde de Floridablanca, primer secretario estado y del despacho, en el año de 1787* (Madrid: Imprenta Real, 1787), and the *Censo de la población de España de el año de 1797, executado de orden del Rey en el de 1801* (Madrid: Imprenta de Vega y Compañia, 1801). The Floridablanca Census gives Vizcaya a population of 114,863, while that of 1797 (known as that of Godoy) shows a decline of approximately 3–3.5 percent, and a total of only 111,436. These figures do not include the regular clergy. When the latter's numbers (and those of dependents) are included, the 1787 and 1797 figures would be 116,042 and 112,371, respectively. The regular and

secular clergy in Vizcaya, including domestics and dependents, accounted for 1.5 percent of the total Vizcayan population at the end of the eighteenth century.

4. See Archivo de la Diputación de Vizcaya, Bilbao (hereafter cited as ADV), Guernica, *Copiador de Oficios y Representaciones del año de 1813*, letter of the Vizcayan Diputación to the Jefe Político, 11 February 1814. This communication states that the population of Vizcaya was 101,396. However, conscious Vizcayan undercounting should not be ruled out, especially since these totals appear to have been drawn up for tax purposes. Also, the chaos and disorganization of the post-war period could well have influenced these totals, making them seem lower than they really were. Still, whatever the causes, this low figure would certainly seem to suggest some demographic stagnation.

5. See Juan Ramón de Iturriza y Zabala, *Historia General de Vizcaya y Epítome de las Encartaciones*, Angel Rodríguez Herreo, ed., 2 vols. (Bilbao: Gran Enciclopedia Vasca, 1967), vol. 1, p. 199.

6. Real Academia de la Historia, Madrid (hereafter cited as RAH), 9/6255. According to Floridablanca's Census, Bilbao's population was 9,611.

7. See Renato Barahona, "Basque Regionalism and Centre-Periphery Relations, 1759–1833," *European Studies Review*, vol. 13, no. 3, (1983), (hereafter cited as *ESR*, 1983), p. 273; and Davydd J. Greenwood, "Continuity in Change: Spanish Basque Ethnicity as a Historical Process," in Milton J. Esman, ed., *Ethnic Conflict in the Western World* (Ithaca and London: Cornell University Press, 1977), pp. 86–98.

8. ADV, Guernica, *Reales Ordenes Generales. De 1755 a 1800*. This volume contains considerable data that was not included in the 1797 census published in 1801.

9. See Emiliano Fernández de Pinedo, *Crecimiento económico y transformaciones sociales del País Vasco (1100–1850)* (Madrid: Siglo XXI de España Editores, 1974), pp. 478–482 (hereafter cited as *Crecimiento*). This is one of the most lucid contemporary historical works on the socioeconomic structures of the Basque provinces during the ancien régime.

10. Additional information on these important occupations in Julio Caro Baroja, *Los Vascos*, 2d edition (Madrid: Ediciones Minotauro, 1958). See, for example, pp. 230–245 on miners and iron workers; pp. 208–211 on lumbermen and charcoal makers; and pp. 215–227 and 247–253 on fishermen and what the author calls the "nautical complex."

11. See Barahona, *ESR*, 1983 passim.

12. See Fernández de Pinedo, *Crecimiento*, pp. 350–353 and 470–482 passim.

13. The figures for this paragraph have been drawn primarily from three sources: the 1787 and 1797 censuses (cited in note 3), and the unpublished partial data for the 1797 census at the ADV (cited in note 8).

14. See note 3.

15. ADV, Corr[egimiento], leg[ajo]. 785, exp[ediente]. 34: *"Desde el pobre jornalero al cavallero más distinguido y poderoso."*

16. ADV, Corr., leg. 244, exp. 29.

17. *Reglamento criminal para la sustanciación y determinación de las causas de robos, hurtos, muerte en despoblado o de noche, en el M.N. y M.L. Señorío de Vizcaya, aprobado por S.M. en 18 de Diciembre de 1799* (Bilbao: Eusebio de Larumbe, 1815).

18. *Extractos de las Juntas generales celebradas por la Real Sociedad Bascongada de los Amigos del País en la ciudad de Vitoria por Setiembre de 1777* (Vitoria: Tomás de Robles y Navarro, Impresor, n.d.), p. 19. In the Sociedad's words: *"el aumento que en estos últimos tiempos ha adquirido la labranza en el país bascongado (singularmente en Guipúzcoa y Vizcaya) llega a ser increible."*

19. Archivo Historico Nacional, Madrid (hereafter cited as AHN), Consejos, leg. 3068, exp. 2: *"la agricultura en Vizcaya está en el más alto grado de perfección, sin embargo de la aspereza y debilidad de sus terrenos."*

20. See note 18.

21. José María de Areilza, "La economía vizcaína a fines del siglo XVIII," *Boletín de la Real Sociedad Vascongada de Amigos del País*, Año II, (1946), cuaderno 2, p. 134. The anonymous description cited by Areilza asserts: *"a medida que su población ha ido en aumento, la misma necesidad de su sustento, les ha precisado a quebrantar hasta las mismas cumbres de los montes."*

22. Ibid.

23. Ample evidence of this in Fernández de Pinedo, *Crecimiento*, pp. 153–230 passim.

24. Fernández de Pinedo, *Crecimiento*, p. 171.

25. Fernández de Pinedo, *Crecimiento*, pp. 183–185. See also Guillermo Bowles, *Introducción a la Historia Natural, y a la Geografía Física de España*, 2d ed. (Madrid: Imprenta Real, 1782), p. 307ff. for a brief but interesting description of chacolí.

26. On this point a wide array of sources is virtually unanimous. For one thing, iron production was the only manufacturing sector that could significantly help to offset the deficits resulting from the massive imports of foodstuffs and other necessities. Or, as Fernández de Pinedo rightly notes about the Basque provinces: *"Región agrícolamente pobre, mantenía su equilibrio inestable merced a la fabricación y exportación de hierro,"* (*Crecimiento*, p. 318).

27. See Fernández de Pinedo, *Crecimiento*, pp. 322–330 passim; and Archivo de Casa de Juntas de Guernica, Vizcaya (hereafter cited as ACJG), Expedientes y Escrituras Varias, 1817–1823, reg[istro]. 4: *"Exposición verdadera sobre el censo de frutos, manufacturas, artes y fábricas de esta Prov[inci]a de Vizcaya, y respuesta a la reflexiones hechas sobre ello."* Undated and unsigned, it seems to be the work of Miguel de Antuñano, an influential Vizcayan traditionalist of the period. See also Francisco Carreras y Candi, *Geografía General del País Vasco-Navarro*, 6 vols. (Barcelona: Editorial Alberto Martín, n.d.), vol. 5, p. 593.

28. More on these questions in chapters 2 and 4 of this book.

29. "Estado de las Rentas anuales que constituyen la riqueza territorial de particulares; de propios de pueblos, clero, y comercio de todo el Gobierno,

que comprende las tres Provincias de Vizcaya, Guipúzcoa y Alava," *Suplemento a la Gazeta del Gobierno de Vizcaya*, San Sebastián, 23 June 1810, no. 38. An apparently complete collection of the *Gazeta* (in three volumes) is in the library of the ADV. This data, along with the 1787 census, is also the source for the next two tables.

30. A good example is the report submitted by Corregidor Paz y Merino from Bilbao on 16 August 1782, immediately after the completion of the juntas: AHN, Consejos, leg. 3487, dossier entitled *"1782. El Corr[egido]r D[o]n Juan Ant[onio] Paz y Merino sobre los abusos que hay en el mismo Señorío, en la celebración de Juntas para las elecciones de Diputados generales, Regidores, Síndicos, y Escribanos, del mismo."*

31. The best work on the Diputación remains that of Darío de Areitio, *El Gobierno Universal del Señorío de Vizcaya. Cargos y personas que los desempeñaron. Juntas, Regimientos y Diputación* (Bilbao: Junta de Cultura de Vizcaya, 1943).

32. In addition to these offices, Vizcaya possessed an unofficial senior advisory council of elders that met at the Diputación's urging on an ad hoc basis when the circumstances required it. Its members were known as *padres de provincia*, and membership in this elite group was restricted to those who had held the post of general deputy. It was a creative way of continuing to make use of the talent and expertise of former leaders.

33. The best account of the Consulado is that of Teófilo Guiard Larrauri, *Historia del Consulado y Casa de Contratación de Bilbao y del Comercio de la Villa*, (hereafter cited as *Consulado*) 2 vols. (Bilbao: Imprenta y Librería de José de Astuy, 1913–1914).

34. Guiard, *Consulado*, vol. 2, pp. 101–105.

35. Juan de Junta, Impresor de Libros: Burgos, 1528. The fueros (or fuero) were republished numerous times in the next centuries with few modifications. For the 1865 version of the Vizcayan privileges, with a recent introduction by Adrián Celaya Ibarra, see *Fuero Nuevo de Vizcaya* (Leopoldo Zugaza: Durango, 1976).

36. More on this question, and on center-periphery relations, in Barahona, *ESR*, 1983 passim.

37. See Renato Barahona, "Histoire d'une révolte en Biscaye: Bilbao, 1631–1634" (Paris: École Pratique des Hautes Études, 1971), unpublished. This monograph is currently undergoing revision for publication. See also Fernández de Pinedo, *Crecimiento*, pp. 68–77 and 391–405; and J. H. Elliott, "La resistencia periférica," in *La España de Felipe IV*, vol. 25 *Historia de España* (Madrid: Espasa-Calpe, 1982), pp. 427–436. Despite these authors' excellent descriptions, considerable work remains to be done on seventeenth- and eighteenth-century social movements in the province.

38. A bitter polemic on this subject raged until well into the last quarter of the nineteenth century. See, for example, the introduction by Antonio Cánovas del Castillo to Miguel Rodríguez Ferrer's *Los vascongados, su país, su lengua, y el Príncipe L.L. Bonaparte* (Madrid: Imprenta de Nogueira, 1873). For the reply to Canovas, see Fermín de Lasala y Collado, *La separación de Guipuzcoa y la Paz de Basilea* (Madrid: Fontanet, 1895). Finally,

see the extremely suggestive remarks of Pierre Vilar in "Quelques aspects de l'occupation et de la résistance en Espagne en 1794 et au temps de Napoleon," in *Occupants-Occupés, 1792–1815* (Brussels: Université Libre de Bruxelles, Institut de Sociologie, 1969), pp. 221–256.

39. Andrés Muriel, *Historia de Carlos IV*, edited, with a preliminary study, by Carlos Seco Serrano, 2 vols., *Biblioteca de Autores Españoles*, vols. 114–115 (Madrid: Atlas, 1959), vol. 114, pp. 222–223.

40. AHN, Estado, leg. 3240/2–3241.

41. The most complete works on the Zamacolada are those of Camilo de Villavaso, *La Questión del Puerto de la Paz, y la Zamacolada* (Bilbao: Imprenta de Juan E. Delmas, 1887), and of Javier de Ybarra y Bergé, *Datos relativos a Simón Bernardo de Zamacola y la Zamacolada* (Bilbao: Imprenta Provincial de Vizcaya, 1941). See also Fernández de Pinedo, *Crecimiento*, pp. 446–453.

42. Juan Antonio Llorente, *Noticias históricas de las tres provincias vascongadas, en que se procura investigar el estado civil antiguo de Alava, Guipúzcoa y Vizcaya, y el origen de sus fueros*, 5 vols. (Madrid: Imprenta Real, vols. 1–4: Imprenta de Luciano Vallín, vol. 5, 1806–1808), (hereafter cited as *Noticias históricas*). Llorente was extremely proud of this effort; in his words, a work "*écrite par l'ordre du gouvernement ancien, avec l'objet de préparer l'opinion publique a recevoir, sans scandale des provinces exemptes, l'uniformité de législation, si désiré[e] a present, heureusement établi dans notre precieuse constitution; grâces au grand Napoleon.*" See Adolphe Morel-Fatio, "D. Juan Antonio Llorente," *Bulletin Hispanique*, vol. 23, (1921), pp. 118–119.

43. Abundant evidence of the central government's many-sided attacks against the Vizcayan (and Basque) fueros in AHN, Estado, leg. 201/2. In the increasingly volatile political atmosphere of late 1807–early 1808, these attempts against the regional liberties could well have contributed to undermining Godoy's own authority and standing in government.

44. ADV, Guernica, *Representaciones y Confirmaciones de Fueros de el Año 1808 y 1814.*

45. See ADV, Guernica, *Noticias Históricas de Vizcaya*, vol. 1, pp. 146–173.

46. "*Los fueros particulares de las Provincias de Navarra, Vizcaya, Guipúzcoa y Alava se examinarán en las primeras cortes para determinar lo que se juzgue más conveniente al interés de las mismas provincias y al de la nación,*" in Carlos Sanz Cid, *La Constitución de Bayona* (Madrid: Talleres Tipográficos de la Editorial Reus, 1922), p. 474. The French original is at the Archives Nationales de Paris (hereafter cited as ANP), AF IV, 1609, Plaq. 1.

47. See a set of unbound documents under the name "Acuerdos de la Junta Gubernativa del Señorío de Vizcaya del mes de Agosto de 1808," contained inside the *Libro de Decretos y Diputación y Juntas Generales, 1808–1810*, no. 68, in the ADV, Guernica.

48. See Archives du Ministére des Affaires Étrangères, Paris (hereafter cited as AMAE), Correspondance Diplomatique (CD), Espagne, vol. 676,

letter of Ambassador Laforest, Vitoria, 20 August 1808; and letter of the
Consular Agent Francine, Bayonne, 29 September 1808.

49. See Service Historique de l'Armée de Terre, Vincennes, France (hereafter cited as SHAT), C8/179, report no. 39 of General Thouvenot, 5 February
1809: "*La prestation de serment se fait partout dans la province [de Gui-
puzcoa], avec lenteur et avec une Répugnance marquée: on obéit mais le
coeur n'y est pour rien.*" For the taking of the oath of allegiance at Bilbao,
see SHAT, C8/21, letter of General J. J. Avril to Wagram, 7 February 1809.

50. SHAT, C8/179, report no. 201 of General Thouvenot, 27 April 1809:
"*Amorós vient de former un tribunal Spécial pour juger les crimes relatifs
aux circonstances dans lesquelles se trouve l'Espagne.*" More on this question in A. Morel-Fatio, "Don Fracisco Amorós, Marquis de Sotelo, Fondateur
de la Gymnastique en France," *Bulletin Hispanique*, vol. 26, no. 3, (1924)
pp. 209–240.

51. Some measure of the guerrillas' later growth and impressive sophistication in SHAT, C8/206, report no. 172 of General Thouvenot, 14 April
1812.

52. Albert Jean Michel Rocca, *Memoirs of the War of the French in Spain*,
(London: J. Murray, 1815), pp. 193–194.

53. Barahona, *ESR*, 1983, pp. 284–285.

54. More on the circumstances of, and reaction to, these major changes
in Joseph Bonaparte, *Mémoires et Correspondance Politique et Militaire
du Roi Joseph, publiés, annotés et mis en ordre, par A[lbert] Du Casse,*
10 vols. (Paris: Perrotin, Libraire-Éditeur, 1853–1854), vol. 7, p. 148ff. A so-
called Vizcayan *Conseil de Province* was officially installed by the French
on 6 March 1810.

55. Even Thouvenot was forced to admit privately on several occasions
that the taxes he had instituted were far beyond Vizcaya's means.

56. Some of the guerrillas' families were deported and incarcerated in
France during the war. Mina's relatives, among others, suffered from this
repression. Numerous dossiers on these matters exist at the SHAT. More on
the question of hostage taking in Bonaparte, *Mémoires et Correspondance
Politique*, vol. 7, pp. 263–264 and 270–271. A very good recent treatment
of French counterinsurgency methods during the war in Don W. Alexander,
Rod of Iron (Wilmington, Delaware: Scholarly Resources Inc., 1985). Many
of this author's conclusions regarding Aragon and Catalonia have striking
parallels in the Basque provinces and Navarra.

57. The seizure and sale of the properties of the clergy and of town commons were in part intended to serve as payment to local entrepreneurs for
services and supplies. As for the confiscation of forbidden goods in Bilbao
and elsewhere, the local merchant community bitterly attacked the practice
as contrary to business ethics and interests. Significantly, some Vizcayan
afrancesados also viewed the harsh seizures as politically counterproductive,
undercutting, as they did, the French's already weak support in the region.

58. The resurgence of this counterpolitical power would have profound
consequences on the war's course. See SHAT, C8/96, letter of the Intendant-

General Bessières to the Duke of Feltre, Vitoria, 27 May 1812. See also SHAT, C8/211, report no. 383 of General Thouvenot, 18 November 1812. Observed the general: *"Parmi les moyens de séduction que Mendizabal employe envers les trois Provinces de Biscaye, il rétablit les anciennes députations et les flatte de les faire jouire de nouveau de leurs privilèges."*

59. Unfortunately, these important projects have not received the attention they rightly deserve. Napoleon's designs on the Basque province certainly merit closer scrutiny. See, for example, Bonaparte, *Mémoires et Correspondance Politique*, vol. 7, p. 342ff. See also SHAT, C8/201, reports 15 and 19 of General Thouvenot, 10 and 14 January 1811, respectively. Other French military and political records are replete with similar allusions.

60. Archivo de las Cortes (hereafter cited as AC), leg. 18, exp. 27.

61. *Actas de las sesiones secretas de las Cortes generales extraordinarias de la nación española* (Madrid: Imprenta de J. A. García, 1874), p. 810.

62. SHAT, C8/214, report no. 108 of General Thouvenot, 12 April 1813.

63. The remonstrances paint an extraordinarily gloomy picture of the province at war's end. See ADV, Guernica, *Copiador de Representaciones al Gobierno*, passim. This register covers the period November 1813–July 1816.

64. ADV, Guernica, *Libro de Decretos y Diputación y Juntas Generales, 1810–1814*, no. 69.

65. Several issues of this newspaper in the library of the ADV, call no. F. 3,883.

Chapter 2: Restoration, Constitution, and Civil War

1. The transition from the Diputación *Provincial* to the *General* was smooth and without opposition. In fact, some of the key members of the new diputación, installed on 20 May 1814, had also belonged to the previous one. This body acted in a caretaker capacity until the General Assembly of September 1814, when a new diputación was properly elected according to tradition for the coming biennium. See Darío de Areitio, *El Gobierno Universal del Señorío de Vizcaya*, section entitled "Cargos y Personas," pp. 128–129.

2. ADV, Guernica, *Representaciones y Confirmaciones de Fueros de el Año 1808 y 1814*.

3. Tomás González, *Colección de cédulas, cartas-patentes, provisiones, reales órdenes y otros documentos concernientes a las Provincias Vascongadas, copiados de orden de S.M. de los registros, minutas y escrituras existentes en el Real Archivo de Simancas, y en los de las Secretarías de Estado y del Despacho y otras oficinas de la Corte*, 6 vols. (Madrid: Imprenta Real, vol. 1–5; Imprenta de Miguel de Burgos, vol. 6), vol. 2, p. 471 (hereafter cited as *Colección*).

4. *Órdenes Circulares del Señorío de Vizcaya* (hereafter cited as *OCSV*), 1814, speech by Martín León de Jáuregui at the General Assembly of Vizcaya, 1 September 1814.

5. AC, leg. 19, exp. 4, petition of the Diputación Provincial to the Cortes, 4 March 1814.

6. ADV, Corr., leg. 983, exp. 11.

7. ADV, Guernica, *Copiador de Oficios y Representaciones del año de 1813*, communication number 739 of the Diputación Provincial to the provincial governor of the province, 30 October 1813.

8. *OCSV*, 1814, communication of General Eguía to the Vizcayan Diputación, 16 June 1814. The order was reproduced in a circular of the Vizcayan government dated 23 June 1814.

9. ACJG, Expedientes, reg. 3, petition dated 14 November 1816.

10. *OCSV*, 1814, circular of the provincial governor of Vizcaya, 18 February 1814.

11. ACJG, Policía, reg. 30, dispatch no. 98 from the Vizcayan police to central headquarters in Madrid, 6 August 1824.

12. See chapter 1, note 17 for the charter's complete title.

13. ADV, Guernica, *1813 y 1814, 15 y 16. Copiador de Representaciones al Gobierno*, petition of the Diputación to the king, 28 March 1815.

14. ADV, Guernica, *1816 y 1818. Memoriales y Oficios Presentados en las Juntas de Guernica*. See the petition of the *arrieros* and *viajantes* dated 14 July 1818.

15. ADV, Guernica, *1813 y 1814, 15 y 16. Copiador de Representaciones al Gobierno*, memorial dated 12 September 1814.

16. Ibid.

17. ADV, Corr., leg. 790, exp. 18.

18. Teófilo Guiard Larrauri, *Historia de la Noble Villa de Bilbao*, 4 vols. (Bilbao: Imprenta de José de Astuy 1905–1912), vol. 4, pp. 248–255 (hereafter cited as *Villa*).

19. SHAT, C8/221, letter from Thouvenot to the French Minister of War, 15 October 1813.

20. Guiard, *Villa*, vol. 4, p. 272.

21. José Luís Comellas García-Llera, *Los primeros pronunciamientos en España* (Madrid: Consejo Superior de Investigaciones Científicas, 1958), pp. 128–129, 140, 142, and 187. However, in several instances during the 1817–1818 period, Bilbao's authorities denied the existence of masonic lodges (*logias*) in that city. See Archivo General de Palacio, Madrid (hereafter cited as AGP), *Papeles reservados de Fernando VII*, vol. 17, documents 19–20 and 22–27. More convincing evidence on the existence of political and freemasonry efforts in Vizcaya, in a copy of a letter purportedly written by the exiled Vizcayan afrancesado, Juan Antonio de Zamacola to Pedro Pascual Fernandez Sardineau, Auch, France, 2 or 3 April 1817: *"Renovales hace lo mismo por su parte en Vizcaya y me consta que en Vilbado (sic) tenemos de nuestra parte una porción de hermanos que entran por momentos en la Congregación,"* (ANP, F 7, 11996).

22. ADV, Guernica, *1813 y 1814, 15 y 16. Copiador de Representaciones al Gobierno*, petition of the Diputación to the king, 30 December 1815.

23. Considerable information on these matters in ADV, Guernica, *1816 a 1818. Copiador de Oficios Particulares de la Diputación*. See also AHN,

Consejos, leg. 3475, exp. 2, for a request by the port of Lequeitio for permission to import a sizeable amount of Castilian wheat. The town's request was dated 28 February 1817.

24. ADV, Corr., leg. 191, exp. 4, report of the *síndico* to the Diputación, 27 February 1815.

25. Ibid.

26. Ibid. To the obvious satisfaction of the town, which was now able to dispose of its properties to meet its debts and other obligations, permission for the sale was granted on 14 August 1815.

27. ADV, Corr., leg. 1055, exp. 25, 26, and 27.

28. An excellent treatment of the communal disentailment process in Emiliano Fernández de Pinedo, "La entrada de la tierra en el circuito comercial: la desamortización en Vascongadas. Planteamiento y primeros resultados," in Jordi Nadal and Gabriel Tortella, eds., *Agricultura, comercio colonial, y crecimiento económico en la España contemporanea* (Barcelona: Ariel, 1974), pp. 100–128 (hereafter cited as "La entrada de la tierra"). See pp. 114–124 in particular. Of the same author, consult *Crecimiento*, pp. 313–317. On the question of rents, consult the latter work, p. 276 passim.

29. ADV, Guernica, *1813 y 1814, 15 y 16. Copiador de Representaciones al Gobierno*, petition of the Diputación to the king, 15 April 1816.

30. ACJG, Expedientes, reg. 4 (1817–1823), document entitled "*Estado de los frutos, ganados, y primeras materias de las artes de la Provincia.*"

31. ACJG, Ferrerías, reg. 2, report presented to the Juntas Generales on 16 July 1816.

32. ADV, Guernica, *1816 a 1818. Copiador de Oficios Particulares de la Diputación*, letter of the Vizcayan executive to Consulado, notifying it of the decree prohibiting the importation of foreign iron in Vizcaya, 15 April 1817. The Diputación's decree carried the same date.

33. ADV, Guernica, *1816 y 1818. Memoriales y Oficios Presentados para las Juntas de Guernica.* See in particular the petition of the *maestros toneleros* which, although undated, is most probably from the mid-1818 period.

34. ACJG, Ferrerías, reg. 1, document entitled "*Plan que los dueños, arrendatarios de las ferrerías comprendidas en el distrito de Arratia, correspondiendo a la más celosa y laudable invitación de la Diputación General proponen con los más ardientes deseos de que se consiga el importantísimo objeto de mejorar la fundición y calidad del fierro y sus manufacturas en las ferrerías del país,*" 20 December 1819.

35. Royal order of 13 August 1819, communicated to the judge of contraband at Bilbao by the minister of finance, José de Ymaz. The order was reproduced in a circular of the Vizcayan Diputación dated 29 September 1819; in *OCSV*, 1819.

36. Naturally, the colonial question was constantly in the minds of Vizcayans. See, for example, the allusions in the petition cited in note 22 above.

37. *OCSV*, 1819, circular of the Vizcayan Diputación dated 7 December 1819 that contains some of the history of the so-called Permanent Commission. The commission was created on 16 July 1816. More on this body in ACJG, Ferrerías, reg. 2.

38. Archivo General de Simancas (hereafter cited as AGS), Consejo Supremo de Hacienda, leg. 285, exp. 13, dossier entitled *"Expediente formado acerca de la exposición del Director del Real Gabinete Físico y Químico sobre el abandono en que están las ricas minas de fierro del Valle de Somorrostro y Providencia que propone a S.M."*

39. ADV, Guernica, *1816 y 1818. Memoriales y Oficios Presentados para las Juntas de Guernica*, petition dated July 1818, and signed by a number of *"dueños y arrendatarios de las fábricas de curtidos de este . . . Señorío."*

40. Ibid., memorial dated 11 July 1818.

41. Ibid.

42. Guiard, *Consulado*, vol. 2, p. 784.

43. Gónzalez, *Colección*, vol. 2, p. 377, *"Real Orden mandando que las Aduanas del cordón del Ebro continuen como lo estaban en Abril de mil ochocientos ocho,"* 9 September 1814.

44. ADV, Guernica, *1813 y 1814, 15 y 16. Copiador de Representaciones al Gobierno*, letter from the Vizcayan Diputación to Miguel de Antuñano, 27 September 1814.

45. A manuscript copy of the junta's final report in the AHN, Estado, libro no. 62, from which I am quoting. For a printed version of the final report see the *Copia del Informe de la Junta de Reforma de Abusos de Real Hacienda de las Provincias Vascongadas, creada en Real Orden de 6 de Noviembre de 1815* (Madrid: Oficina de Tomás Jordán, 1839).

46. Guiard, *Consulado*, vol. 2, pp. 658–659, February 1817 letter of Miguel de Antuñano to the Consulado (?).

47. ADV, Guernica, *1813 y 1814, 15 y 16. Copiador de Representaciones al Gobierno*, petitions of the Vizcayan Diputación to the monarch dated 21 November and 1 December 1815. When the junta submitted its recommendations in 1819, Campuzano was among the signers of the final report.

48. See note 45 above for complete references to the junta's final 2 April 1819 report.

49. Gregorio de Balparda, *Don Martín de los Heros y el Progresismo Vascongado de su Tiempo* (Bordeaux: Feret & Fils, 1925), p. 29.

50. González, *Colección*, vol. 2, pp. 385–386, *"Real orden ampliando la jurisdicción del Juez de contrabando de Bilbao a todo el territorio, costas y puertos de Vizcaya, y creando oficina para la expedición de Guías y depósito de géneros, para los objetos y en la forma que se expresa,"* 2 April 1817.

51. ADV, Guernica, *1813 y 1814, 15 y 16. Copiador de Representaciones al Gobierno*, petitions of the Vizcayan Diputación to the king, 17 May and 14 July 1816. For a much-romanticized version of Longa's activities during this period, see Michael J. Quin, *Memoirs of Ferdinand VII, King of the Spains, by Don *** Advocate of the Spanish Tribunals*, translated from the original Spanish manuscript by Michael J. Quin (London: Hurst, Robinson and Co., 1824), pp. 211–213.

52. González, *Colección*, vol. 2, p. 387, *"Real orden declarando que el aceite que salga de Castilla para consumo de las Provincias exentas pague derechos de extracción en la forma que se expresa,"* 9 July 1817.

53. Ibid., pp. 388–389, *"Real orden mandando formar registros de todo*

lo que se conduzca a las Provincias exentas: que se entreguen a los Jueces de contrabando de Bilbao y San Sebastián, y que se expidan las guías de referencia, según y en la forma que se previene," 10 July 1817.

54. *(Colección de) Decretos del Rey don Fernando VII,* 18 vols. (Madrid: Imprenta Real, 1816–1834), vol. 6, pp. 2–3, royal order dated 4 January 1819. (Hereafter this work will be cited as *CD.*)

55. González, *Colección,* vol. 2, pp. 391–392, *"Real orden mandando llevar a debido efecto el establecimiento de la oficina de reconocimiento en Bilbao, y ampliación de la jurisdicción del Juez de contrabando a toda Vizcaya en la forma que se expresa."*

56. AHN, Estado, libro no. 17, *Actas Originales del año 1816,* session of the Council of State, 17 September 1816.

57. Ibid., session of 22 October 1816.

58. Ibid.

59. Archivo de la Presidencia de Gobierno, Madrid (hereafter cited as APG), *Actas del Consejo de Ministros* (hereafter cited as *Actas*), session of 10 October 1829; also 22 May 1830. The *Actas* of these two sessions contain considerable background information on military-related matters in the Basque provinces and Navarra from 1818 on.

60. Ibid., session of 10 October 1829. See also ADV, Guernica, *Conferencias de las Provincias Bascongadas. 1812 a 1833,* sessions of 7–8 December 1817.

61. Even though Vizcayans had been in the forefront of colonial activity, they had been excluded from the Spanish overseas commercial monopolies. This had forced the vizcaínos to seek other (often illegal) arrangements and channels of trade. Thus, it is quite conceivable that Vizcayans (and, by extension, much of the Basque leadership) were not interested in reconquering territories which, no matter how important, had never fully belonged to them. Whatever may have been the reasons, it is worth underscoring that these positions were sharply at variance with the strenuous plans and efforts by the period's conservative national governments to recover the lost overseas territories by force. Clearly, this is an area in need of considerable further research.

62. Guiard, *Villa,* vol. 4, p. 260.

63. See the untitled dossier-like pamphlet published by Pedro Antonio de Apraiz in Bilbao, in 1820, that simply begins with the words *"LA OBEDIEN-CIA DEBIDA A NUEVE REALES ÓRDENES."* This twenty-four-page piece contains much of the official documentation and history of this episode.

64. Ibid., petition of the consulado to the king, 16 May 1820, p. 10. The royal orders lifting the barriers are in González, *Colección,* vol. 2, pp. 419–420 and 422–423. They are dated 8 January and 19 February 1820, respectively.

65. Federico Suárez Verdeguer, *Martín Garay y la reforma de la Hacienda,* 2 vols. (Pamplona: Universidad de Navarra, *"Documentos del reinado de Fernando VII,"* no. 4, 1967), vol. 1, p. 349, session of the Council of State dated 1 or 4 May 1817. See also ADV, Guernica, *1816 a 1818. Copiador de Oficios Particulares de la Diputación,* letter of the Diputación to Casimiro de Lóizaga, 17 May 1817.

66. AMAE, Correspondance Consulaire (hereafter cited as CC), Bilbao, vol. 3, letter from Auguste Regnaudin to the Ministry of Foreign Affairs, wrongly dated 2 April 1819; in fact, it should clearly be 1820. The French delegation at Bilbao did not enjoy the status of a consulate. It was merely a commercial bureau. This is why I refer to Regnaudin as a commercial agent and not a consul. His reports to the ministry are generally only signed with his last name. His full name was Augustin Marie Pierre Regnaudin.

67. Unsigned article in the *Miscelanea de Comercio, Artes y Literatura*, Madrid, no. 70, 10 April 1820. The piece, written in Bilbao, was dated 4 April 1820. And Regnaudin pointedly wrote on 30 April 1820: "*Le nouveau système constitutionnel s'établit dans ces provinces avec tranquilité et sans enthousiasme*," (AMAE, CC, Bilbao, vol. 3).

68. *El Constitucional*, Madrid, no. 378, 21 May 1820. This was the first of a two-part article signed with the pen name of *el buen Vizcaíno*. A more detailed account of these issues, and of the transition to constitutionalism in Vizcaya, in my essay "Politics, Ideology and the Fueros in Vizcaya During the Initial Phase of the Liberal Triennium (1820)" in *Basque Politics: A Case Study of Ethnic Nationalism*, William A. Douglass, editor (Associated Faculty Press Inc., and Basque Studies Program: University of Nevada, Reno, Nevada, 1985), (hereafter cited as *Basque Politics*, 1985).

69. The constitution of 1812, reestablished in 1820, had created the office of *Jefe Político* (literally translated, Political Boss). This official, designated and appointed by national government in Madrid, thus became the highest centralist representative in the provinces. Given his wide-ranging functions and responsibilities, however, I have opted for the English nomenclature in the text rather than for the more literal translation which, interestingly, was also used in the English language political literature of the period.

70. Bilbao, 24 April 1820; in *OCSV*, 1820.

71. See the article in *El Constitucional* cited in note 68. The author endeavored to demonstrate that despite the erroneous policies of absolutism during the previous six years, Vizcaya had maintained the substance of its fueros: "*de manera que en esta parte se han respetado y mantenido sus franquezas en todo su vigor.*"

72. A lengthy discussion of this in Barahona, *Basque Politics*, 1985.

73. See the article in the *Miscelanea* cited in note 67.

74. Ibid. See also Guiard, *Villa*, vol. 4, pp. 273–274.

75. Guiard, *Villa*, vol. 4, pp. 273–279. See also AMAE, CC, Bilbao, vol. 3, letter of Regnaudin, 2 April 1820 (cited in note 66).

76. *OCSV*, 1820, circulars of the provincial governor. In particular, see that of 3 April 1820 addressed to the Vizcayan municipal authorities. Vedia urged the towns to comply quickly with the recent orders from Madrid.

77. *OCSV*, 1820. This information is found in several printed circulars issued by the respective provincial governors in March–April 1820.

78. The sources for these first elections are as follows: circulars of the provincial governor issued on 22 April and 23 May 1820 (*OCSV*, 1820); and Areitio, *Gobierno Universal*, p. 132.

79. Ibid. An excellent description of the new Diputación Provincial's conservatism and the reasons for this in a joint petition of the municipality of

Bilbao and consulado to the Cortes, dated 18 July 1820, in Fidel de Sagarmí-naga, *El gobierno y Régimen Foral del Señorío de Vizcaya desde el reinado de Felipe segundo hasta la mayor edad de Isabel segunda*, 8 vols. (Bilbao: Tipografía Católica de José de Astuy, 1892), vol. 7, pp. 271–272, (hereafter cited as *Gobierno*.)

80. Guiard, *Villa*, vol. 4, pp. 279–280.

81. More on the grande équivoque in Renato Barahona [Arévalo], "The Making of Carlism in Vizcaya (1814–1833)," (2 vols. Doctoral dissertation: Princeton, 1979), vol. 1, pp. 53–55 and 72 (hereafter cited as *Making*). See also *Basque Politics*, 1985.

82. ACJG, Expedientes, reg. 4, dossier entitled "*Representaciones, y otros papeles relativos al establecimiento de la capital de Vizcaya en la villa de Bilbao.*"

83. *OCSV*, 1820, joint circular of the provincial governor and the Diputación Provincial, Bilbao, 5 June 1820.

84. *OCSV*, 1820, proclamation with the heading "*Nobles, leales, pacíficos y laboriosos habitantes de Lequeytio*," Lequeitio, 8 April 1820.

85. *OCSV*, 1820, proclamation to the Basques by the Intendant, Bilbao, 29 December 1820.

86. Barahona [Arévalo], *Making*, pp. 55–60.

87. Arnold R. Verduin, *Manual of Spanish Constitutions, 1808–1931. Translations and Introductions* (Ypsilanti, Michigan: University Lithographers, 1941), p. 34.

88. AMAE, CC, Bilbao, vol. 3, letters of 2 and 30 April 1820.

89. ADV, Guernica, *Oficios de Varias Clases. De 1820 a 23*. The provincial governor replied in a report dated 5 June 1820, entitled "*Informe del Jefe Político de Vizcaya, con arreglo a la orden de la Dirección General de Hacienda Pública de 29 de Abril último.*"

90. Guiard, *Consulado*, vol. 2, p. 670.

91. *OCSV*, 1820, joint petition of the provincial governor and Diputación Provincial, Bilbao, 22 September 1820.

92. Ibid.

93. *Colección de los decretos y órdenes generales expedidos por las Cortes* (hereafter cited as *CDC* followed by the volume number), 10 vols. (Madrid: Imprenta Nacional, vols. 1–9; and Imprenta de Tomás Albán y Compañía, vol. 10, 1820–1823), vol. 8, pp. 63–65, decree of 18 December 1821 entitled "*Sobre aduanas y contrarregistros.*" More on the establishment of the customs bureaus and the checkpoints in *CDC*, vol. 6, pp. 315–325, decree of 8 November 1820 entitled "*Establecimiento de aduanas y contrarregistros,*" and in ibid., vol. 6, pp. 347–348, decree dated the same day entitled "*Establecimiento de Aduanas e Intendencias en las Provincias Vascongadas.*" See, in particular, article 1 of this last decree. Finally, more on this question in ibid., vol. 6, pp. 170–179, decree of 5 October 1820 entitled "*Se establece un arancel general de aduanas,*" article 8.

94. *Actas de las sesiones secretas de las Cortes ordinarias y extraordinarias de los años 1820 y 1821, de las de los años 1822 y 1823, y de las celebradas por las Diputaciones permanentes de las mismas Cortes ordinarias* (Madrid: Imprenta de J. A. Garcia, 1874), p. 20.

95. *CDC*, vol. 6, pp. 315–325, decree of 8 November 1820: "*Estableci-miento de aduanas y contrarregistros.*"

96. See the proclamation cited in note 85 and AMAE, CC, Bilbao, vol. 3, letters of Regnaudin dated 30 April and 26 November 1820.

97. See Barahona, *ESR*, 1983 and *Basque Politics*, 1985.

98. AMAE, CC, Bilbao, vol. 3, 1820 annual report, 11 January 1821.

99. Ibid.

100. Guiard, *Consulado*, vol. 2, p. 668. See also *Diario de las sesiones de Cortes* (hereafter cited as *DSC* followed by the year, page number[s], and date of the Cortes's session when necessary), 16 vols., (Madrid: Imprenta de J. A. García [all volumes, except for April–December 1823, which has the following imprint: Madrid: La Imprenta Nacional, 1858], 1871–1885), 1821, pp. 1262–1270 and 1338–1353, sessions of 25 and 30 April 1821, respectively.

101. Guiard, *Consulado*, vol. 2, p. 669. See also ADV, Guernica, *Representaciones a las Cortes*, petition of the Vizcayan Diputación Provincial entitled "*Suplica a las Cortes se sirvan llevar a efecto el citado convenio celebrado entre el señor Intendente de las Provincias Vascongadas y los comisionados del comercio de esta villa [de Bilbao],*" 23 March 1821.

102. A suggestive literary portrait of him in an anonymous pamphlet entitled *Condiciones y Semblanzas de los Diputados a Cortes para la legislatura de 1820 y 1821* (Madrid: Imprenta de Juan Ramos y Compañía, 1821), pp. 112–113. The commentary stresses Yandiola's financial abilities: "*Este es el amo del dinero,*" and "*lo que quiere es mucha plata en las arcas.*"

103. *DSC*, 1821, p. 1343, session of 30 April. Yandiola steadfastly defended the Consulado and the commercial classes of Bilbao despite bitter attacks from those who favored Santander or were simply opposed to Bilbao and Vizcaya.

104. AMAE, CC, Bilbao, vol. 3, letter from Regnaudin, 20 October 1820. In the same register see the letter from Regnaudin's assistant, Sobry, dated 29 March 1821. The latter made the significant observation that despite the enfranchisement of Bilbao for direct colonial trade, the turmoil in the New World practically nullified (for the time being at least) all possible advantages derived from overseas trade.

105. AMAE, CC, Bilbao, vol. 3, 1820 annual report, 11 January 1821.

106. I owe some of these formulations to Stanley J. Stein, who found the correct expressions for something that I had been trying to set forth in a much less satisfactory manner. The expression "compradore bourgeoisie" as my idea, however, warrants a clarification. While this term generally has been applied to certain Third World economic trading elites (especially in Asia), the term appears appropriate in the text since I wish to refer mainly to that sector of the Vizcayan commercial bourgeoisie dedicated exclusively (or even primarily) to import-export activity, and not to domestically generated wealth in general, or to manufactures and industry in particular. In other words, as the commercial intermediaries for products and activities originating beyond the province (be it abroad or in the rest of the peninsula), it is my contention that such Vizcayan bourgeois strata objectively functioned in much the same way as their Third World comprador counterparts. (See my observations in chapter 6 in this book and in note 127 of that chapter).

107. Letter from Sobry cited in note 104.

108. Guiard, *Villa*, vol. 4, p. 286 passim.

109. Several long lists of members of the Voluntary Militia are in ibid., vol. 4, pp. 298–301. More on the constitutionalists' cohesion around the Voluntary Militia in ADV, Corr., leg. 1009, exp. 9.

110. AMAE, CC, Bilbao, vol. 3, letter from Regnaudin, 20 October 1820.

111. A list of the members of the Compania can be found in the newspaper *El Verdadero Patriota*, Bilbao, no. 58, 26 September 1822.

112. This militia, whose proper name was in fact *Milicia Nacional Local*, was created on 31 August 1820, see *CDC*, vol. 6, pp. 64–79 (*"Reglamento provisional para la Milicia nacional local"*). There was an addendum to this militia's charter on 4 May 1821, see *CDC*, vol. 7, pp. 66–71 (*"Reglamento adicional al de 31 de Agosto de 1820 para la Milicia nacional"*).

113. Guiard, *Villa*, vol. 4, p. 289.

114. Ibid., vol. 4, pp. 280–281.

115. Ibid., vol. 4, p. 322.

116. See, for example, Regnaudin's observations in the 27 July 1822 dispatch to his superiors (AMAE, CC, Bilbao, vol. 3). This report also contains extremely interesting remarks on the conflicts between the Regular and Voluntary militias.

117. AHN, Estado, libro no. 51, consulta of 23 August 1820.

118. Ibid.

119. Ibid.

120. Most Council members favored naming one intendant for the three Basque provinces and another for Navarra, while a minority believed that there should be one intendant per province. As noted earlier, the first proposal was the one that was eventually adopted.

121. Secret session of 11 October 1820. For a complete reference, see note 94.

122. *CDC*, vol. 6, pp. 289–291, *"Repartimiento de ciento veinte y cinco millones de reales de contribución,"* and pp. 291–293, *"Repartimiento de veinte y siete millones de reales por contribución a las capitales de provincia y puertos habilitados."*

123. Ibid., vol. 6, pp. 347–348, decree of 8 November 1820 entitled *"Establecimiento de Aduanas e Intendencias en las Provincias Vascongadas."*

124. Ibid. Fourth and last article of the decree.

125. ACJG, Constitución, 1820, letter from José Canga Arguelles to the Diputación Provincial. In this communication Canga Arguelles speaks of a 9 November decree of the Cortes which, I believe, is an error. To my knowledge, the only decrees that dealt with these matters were those of 8 November, already alluded to earlier.

126. Ibid., letter to the Vizcayan Diputación Provincial informing it of the content of a separate letter—also of Canga Arguelles—to the intendant of the Basque provinces dated on the same day (25 November 1820).

127. AMAE, CC, Bilbao, vol. 3 (previously cited letter of 29 March 1821).

128. AHN, Consejos, leg. 51,554, dispatch no. 13, Bilbao, 3 March 1821: *"esta provincia, a pesar de [la] tranquilidad aparente, no está contenta en lo general con las nuevas instituciones."*

129. See Barahona, *Basque Politics*, 1985, particularly the attacks against this development by the traditionalist who wrote clandestinely under the pseudonym el buen Vizcaíno—not to be confused with the constitutionalist correspondent by the same pen name alluded to previously.

130. *CDC*, vol. 6, p. 233, decree of 21 October 1820. More on this in ACJG, Constitución, 1820, among the correspondence of the provincial governor Vedia.

131. *OCSV*, 1820, circular of the Diputación Provincial of Vizcaya, 13 June 1820. See also *DSC*, 1820, pp. 2036 and 2164–2165, sessions of 2 and 7 November, respectively; and *CDC*, vol. 6, pp. 309–310, order of 8 November 1820. A list of petitioners for these posts in AGP, *Papeles reservados de Fernando VII*, vol. 82, document no. 15.

132. *DSC*, 1820, p. 62, session of 12 July.

133. AC, leg. 38, no. 64. A printed version in *OCSV*, 1821.

134. Vizcaya was not alone in this situation. See, for example, the petition of the Diputación Provincial of Catalonia to the Cortes (dated 17 April 1821) which, significantly, was reprinted in Bilbao by Eusebio de Larumbe, the official printer of the Vizcayan Diputación.

135. See AHN, Consejos, leg. 51,554, letter of the provincial governor Vedia to the Ministry of the Interior, 16 June 1821. Angrily reported the governor: *"hay en Vizcaya grande apariencia y muy poca realidad en el cumplimiento de las órdenes."*

136. AC, leg. 37, no. 52. Bilbao's petition was apparently not acted upon until 29 December 1821.

137. In point of fact, there were strong pro-religion expressions in Vizcaya even before the Cortes adopted important measures against the clergy. See Barahona, *Basque Politics*, 1985, especially the remarks of the anti-constitutionalist el buen Vizcaíno.

138. *CDC*, vol. 6, pp. 155–159, *"Supresión de monacales y reforma de regulares."*

139. *CDC*, vol. 7, pp. 118–119 and 245–249, decrees of 28 May and 29 June 1821, respectively. More on the consequences of these actions in Marqués de Miraflores, *Apuntes histórico-críticos para escribir la historia de la Revolución de España desde el año 1820 hasta 1823* (London: Ricardo Taylor, 1834), p. 70, (hereafter cited as *Apuntes*). Two excellent discussions of some of these issues and other fiscal matters during liberal rule in Jaime Torras Elías, "En torno a la política tributaria de los gobiernos del Trienio Constitucional (1820–1823)," *Moneda y crédito*, no. 122 (September 1972), pp. 153–170; and Joaquín del Moral Ruiz, "La presión fiscal en el Trienio Constitucional (1820–1823)," *Hacienda Pública Española*, no. 27 (1974), pp. 47–72.

140. See Joaquín del Moral Ruiz, *Hacienda y sociedad en el Trienio Constitucional (1820–1823)* (Madrid: Instituto de Estudios Fiscales, 1975), pp. 121–122. He estimates that more than half of Spain's convents and monasteries were suppressed by the Cortes. In 1820 there were approximately 1,928 such establishments, but only 873 by 1822.

141. AMAE, CC, Bilbao, vol. 3, 17 January 1822.

142. Ibid.

143. Guiard, *Villa*, vol. 4, p. 294.

144. AHN, Consejos, leg. 51,554, dispatch no. 13, 3 March 1821.

145. Guiard, *Villa*, vol. 4, p. 294.

146. AHN, Consejos, leg. 51,554, dispatch of the provincial governor of Vizcaya, 17 March 1821.

147. On the question of arms caches, see AHN, Consejos, leg. 51,554, confidential dispatch of the provincial governor of Vizcaya, 21 April 1821. For more on government actions against the Vizcayan clergy, including the suppression of convents, see the following: *DSC*, 1822: p. 1618, session of 30 May; p. 1788, session of 9 June; and p. 2010, session of 19 June. See also *CDC*, vol. 9, p. 417, 19 June 1822; Guiard, *Villa*, vol. 4, pp. 328 and 339; AHN, Estado, leg. 124, no. 5: *"Consejo de Estado de 8 de Febrero de 1823:"* and *El Verdadero Patriota* no. 58, 26 September 1822.

148. AHN, Consejos, leg. 51,554, confidential dispatch no. 29 of the provincial governor of Vizcaya, 14 April 1821; and AMAE, CC, Bilbao, vol. 3, letter of Regnaudin, 22 April 1821.

149. AHN, Consejos, leg. 51,554, dispatch no. 30 of the provincial governor of Vizcaya, 17 April 1821.

150. AMAE, CC, Bilbao, vol. 3, letter of Regnaudin, 26 April 1821.

151. ANP, F 7, 6642, letter no. 142 of Descalone to the central police (?), 5 May 1821.

152. *OCSV*, 1822, joint circular of the provincial governor of Vizcaya, Antonio Seoane, and the Diputación Provincial, dated September 1822.

153. See the following: AHN, Consejos, leg. 51,554, dispatch of the provincial governor of Vizcaya, 16 June 1821; order of the provincial governor of Vizcaya dated 9 August 1822 (and reproduced in Guiard, *Villa*, vol. 4, pp. 335–337); and *OCSV*, 1822, circular of the provincial governor, 11 September 1822.

154. See Pío de Montoya, *La intervención del clero vasco en las contiendas civiles (1820–1823)* (San Sebastián: Txertoa, 1971), pp. 191–220, 299 passim, and 436–439.

155. For the clerics' political orientation, see AHN, Consejos, leg. 51,554, confidential reports nos. 60 and 66 of the provincial governor of Vizcaya, dated 20 November and 29 December 1821, respectively. For the August 1822 events and their aftermath, consult AMAE, CC, Bilbao, vol. 3, letter from Sobry, 14 September 1822; Guiard, *Villa*, vol. 4, p. 331, with a list of those deported to Santoña; *El Verdadero Patriota*, no. 47, 18 August 1822, with an even longer list of the deportees; and ADV, Corr., leg. 1009, exp. 6 and leg. 134, exp. 12.

156. In the ANP there are numerous lists of Spanish royalist refugees in the French southern districts. See in particular F 7, 11,984, the *liasse* entitled *"Correspondance relative aux Royalistes Espagnols refugiés en France,"* (1821–1823). More lists in F 15, 3250.

157. AHN, Consejos, leg. 51,554, dispatch no. 701 of the provincial governor of Vizcaya, 25 December 1821.

158. See *Condiciones y semblanzas de los Sres Diputados a Cortes para los años de 1822 y 1823* (Madrid: Imprenta del Zurriago, 1822), p. 23. See

also the pamphlet entitled *Diputados por la península, para la legislatura de los Años de 1822 y 1823* (Seville: Por la Viuda de Vázquez y Compañía, 1822).

159. AHN, Consejos, leg. 51,554, confidential dispatch no. 66 of the provincial governor of Vizcaya, 29 December 1821.

160. *OCSV*, 1822, circular dated 11 September 1822.

161. Inaugural speech of Seoane before the municipality of Bilbao, 31 August 1822 (in Guiard, *Villa*, vol. 4, pp. 332–334). The new governor, apparently a non-Vizcayan, was a colonel in the cavalry corps.

162. *El Verdadero Patriota*, nos. 47 and 58, dated 18 August and 26 September 1822, respectively. Another excellent example of anticlericalism is in ADV, Corr., leg. 1009, exp. 9. One of the accused in this case, a constitutionalist militiaman named Domingo de Leoz (alias El Navarro), was overheard saying that he would kill three priests, and similar expressions.

163. See Joaquín del Moral Ruiz, *Hacienda y sociedad*, pp. 102–118 for an excellent analysis of rural and agricultural problems during the Trienio. Although he does not specifically deal with Vizcaya, he examines carefully the situation in some of Spain's northern regions—areas that have strong similarities with Vizcaya. Therefore, much of what he says about Navarra and Guipúzcoa could well apply by extension to Vizcaya.

164. AHN, Consejos, leg. 51,554, dispatch no. 37 of the provincial governor of Vizcaya, 28 April 1821. See also his 16 June 1821 dispatch.

165. AMAE, CC, Bilbao, vol. 3, letter of Sobry, 29 March 1821.

166. Guiard, *Villa*, vol. 4, pp. 293–296.

167. AHN, Consejos, leg. 51,554, dispatch no. 707 of the provincial governor of Vizcaya, 25 December 1821; and confidential dispatch no. 66, 29 December 1821. According to Miraflores: "*en fin de Diciembre las Provincias Vascongadas y Navarra estaban infestadas de facciosos, que se llamaban defensores del Altar y del Trono,*" (*Apuntes*, p. 122).

168. Guiard, *Villa*, vol. 4, pp. 313–314. See also ANP, F 7, 6644, anonymous letter from Bilbao, dated 30 December 1821. More on these events in *El Liberal Guipuzcoano*, no. 158, 4 January 1822.

169. For the link between the royalist guerrillas and smuggling, see ADV, Corr., leg. 884, exp. 20 and 23. See also Guiard, *Villa*, vol. 4, pp. 319–321; and AHN, Consejos, leg. 51,554, dispatch no. 258 of the provincial governor of Vizcaya, 27 April 1822.

170. ANP, F 7, 6644, anonymous letter dated 9 May 1822.

171. AMAE, CC, Bilbao, vol. 3, letter of Regnaudin, 17 January 1822.

172. ANP, F 7, 12,011, letter to the French minister of the interior, 25 July 1822. It is worth noting that for information after May 1822 it is necessary to rely heavily on French documentation in light of the discontinuation—termination? interception?—of the dispatches of the provincial governor of Vizcaya.

173. In addition to the materials cited in note 155 above, see the following for the conspiracies and arrests: ANP, F 7, 6644, letter of Peche (?), undated, and whose only identification is a notation that reads "*Madrid le 25 Juillet 1822;*" AMAE, CC, Bilbao, vol. 3, letter of Regnaudin, 27 July

1822; and Guiard, *Villa*, vol. 4, pp. 328–329. The extent of the unrest at Bilbao underscores the fact that opposition to constitutionalism was far from confined to the rural areas of Vizcaya. As further evidence of this, see the pointed observations of John Bramsen, an English traveler who visited the region in mid-1822, *Remarks on the North of Spain* (London: Printed for G. and W. B. Whittaker, 1823). Bramsen noted that "by their conversation" many of Bilbao's inhabitants were "much adverse" to the current state of affairs (p. 63).

174. Guiard, *Villa*, vol. 4, pp. 330–331; and AMAE, CC, Bilbao, vol. 3, letter of Regnaudin, 27 July 1822.

175. See notes 155 and 173 for complete references to these events.

176. *El Verdadero Patriota*, no. 47, 18 August 1822.

177. AMAE, CC, Bilbao, vol. 3, letter of Regnaudin, 20 September 1822, and Guiard, *Villa*, vol. 4, pp. 331–342.

178. Miraflores, *Apuntes*, p. 188. Significantly, even the extraordinarily militant royalist chieftain, Domingo de Guezala, was forced into exile as a result of the powerful government offensive; see ANP, F 7, 6644, document entitled "*Etat Nominatif de 50 Espagnols . . .*" at Mont-de-Marsan (Préfecture des Landes), 26 February 1823.

179. William Walton, *The revolutions of Spain, from 1808 to the end of 1836*, 2 vols. (London: Richard Bentley, 1837), vol. 1, pp. 283–284. This matter was of course of great interest to the French authorities. See the communication of the sous-préfet of Bayonne to the minister of the interior, 18 March 1823, in ANP, F 7, 11,981, dossier 28, document no. 512.

180. Guiard, *Villa*, vol. 4, pp. 352–362.

181. Ibid., p. 357.

182. See ADV, Corr., leg. 884, exp. 20; AHN, Consejos, leg. 51,554, confidential dispatch no. 58 of the provincial governor of Vizcaya, 6 November 1821; also dispatch no. 258, 27 April 1822; and Guiard, *Villa*, vol. 4, p. 315.

183. See note 169.

184. *OCSV*, 1822, circular of the provincial governor of Vizcaya, 18 September 1822. See also AHN, Consejos, leg. 51,554, confidential dispatch no. 51 of the provincial governor of Vizcaya, 1 September 1821.

185. *El Verdadero Patriota*, no. 35, 7 July 1822; *El Liberal Guipuzcoano*, no. 158, 4 January 1822; and ADV, Corr., leg. 578, exp. 1 and leg. 539, exp. 13.

186. *El Verdadero Patriota*, no. 39, 21 July 1822. Class accusations of this kind abound during the Trienio, particularly from the merchant classes and authorities toward their lower-class royalist antagonists.

187. Abundant information on the role of retired military officers in the royalist resistance is in the oft-cited dispatches of the provincial governor (AHN, Consejos, leg. 51,554). They are far too numerous to detail separately.

188. Many conservative Vizcayan administrators and political leaders spent time in exile because of opposition to constitutionalism, among them Basaguren, Larumbe, Polanco, Batiz, and others. See, for example, ADV, Corr., leg. 13, exp. 12, and leg. 824, exp. 5. Finally, see Guiard's interesting observations: "*los constitucionales tachaban particularmente de enemigos*

al Diputado . . . Batiz . . . a Basaguren, y a los oficiales de la Diputación"
(*Villa*, vol. 4, p. 330).

189. Clearly, Eguía and Batiz—and probably several others—could be included in this category despite having been alluded to in the first two.

190. AHN, Consejos, leg. 51,554, in particular the following communications of the provincial governor of Vizcaya: unnumbered dispatch, 24 July 1821; confidential dispatch no. 48, 21 August 1821; and confidential dispatch no. 60, 20 November 1821. See also ANP, F 7, 12,003, dossier 398e, and F 7, 6644, dossier entitled "*41. Affaires d'Espagne. Rapports du Commissaire spécial de Police de Bayonne, 1821–1822.*"

191. Both Rafael Gambra, *La primera guerra civil en España (1821–1823). Historia y meditación de una lucha olvidada*, 2d ed. (Madrid: Escelicer, 1972), and José Luis Comellas García-Llera, *Los realistas en el Trienio Constitucional (1820–1823)* (Pamplona: Universidad de Navarra, "*Colección histórica,*" no. 1, 1958) tend to discount the importance of the Basque fueros during this civil war. See, in particular, Gambra, p. 37, note 7; and Comellas García-Llera, pp. 80–81. For a considerably different interpretation, based partly on traditionalist sources, see Barahona, *Basque Politics*, 1985.

192. AHN, Consejos, leg. 51,554, dispatch dated 16 June 1821.

193. As was nearly inevitable, some elements clearly expected greater results from the sociopolitical changes. This may account in part for the growth of the radical tendencies within the constitutionalist camp. Whatever the reasons, there is evidence that impatient local exaltados were highly critical of the purportedly timid measures of the provincial governor and the Diputación Provincial of Vizcaya.

194. See *Hacienda y sociedad*, pp. 102–118, and articles cited in note 139.

195. It should be stressed that the economic crisis was part of a long-term process and not, strictly speaking, a conjunctural affair. Thus, while in no way denying the potentially adverse effects of the Cortes's legislation, I believe that the general economic and political processes of the period were primarily responsible for the contraction in Vizcaya.

196. Sagarmínaga, *Gobierno*, vol. 7, pp. 311 and 319.

Chapter 3: Conservatism and the Fueros

1. Much of what follows in this first section is derived from the chapter entitled "French Intervention and Local Counter-Revolution in the Early Stages of the 1823 Restoration" in Barahona [Arévalo], *Making*, pp. 149–206. (A complete reference to this work in chapter 2, note 81.) Specifically, the restoration of the authorities in Vizcaya is dealt with on pp. 150–167 in the fourth chapter of the dissertation.

2. See Guiard, *Villa*, vol. 4, pp. 365–366 and *Le Moniteur Universel*, 3 May 1823. The consulado was perhaps the body that posed the greatest difficulties to the restorationists. See in particular Guiard, *Consulado*, vol. 2, pp. 853–854; *Villa*, vol. 4, pp. 377–379; and ADV, Guernica, *Reales Ordenes*

Generales. De 1814 a 1830. This register contains important transcripts of the efforts to reestablish the traditional authorities while excluding known constitutionalists.

3. Excellent examples of repressive measures that mainly affected the constitutionalists in Guiard, *Villa,* vol. 4, pp. 398 and 405–407, ordinances of the municipality of Bilbao dated 16 August and 16 December 1823, respectively. Significantly, both came on the heels of important disturbances in the city. A more detailed account of the general context of oppression against constitutionalists in the immediate wake of the Trienio in Barahona [Arévalo], *Making,* pp. 176–186.

4. *OCSV,* 1823, circular of the Corregidor Eguiluz, 5 July 1823 (articles 3–6).

5. Petition to the Regency, 26 September 1823, in Guiard, *Villa,* vol. 4, pp. 400–402.

6. See Barahona [Arévalo], *Making,* pp. 168–183 passim. During the vicious December disturbances, royalists in Bilbao lynched a constitutionalist shoemaker named Valentín Muñuzuri who, at the time, was under the temporary joint custody of the French-Spanish authorities.

7. See Barahona [Arévalo], *Making,* pp. 157–162, 167–169, and 177–178. The first of these bodies, the *Guardias de Honor,* organized in a fashion strongly reminiscent of the constitutionalist Voluntary Militia three years earlier, was the brainchild and tool of the Bilbao city government—the other three the work of the Diputación.

8. A detailed discussion of military organization in Vizcaya during the Ominous Decade in chapter 5 in this book, section II.

9. Numerous tough communications of the French command to the Vizcayan Diputación in ADV, Guernica, *Oficios del General Francés. 1823 a 24.* The proud local authorities clearly resented being constantly admonished about their duties by the French.

10. Barahona [Arévalo], *Making,* pp. 171–174. The Vizcayan authorities bitterly opposed the ordinance. See, for example, ADV, Guernica, *1823. Representaciones al Rey y otras autoridades,* petition of the Diputación to the Regency, 14 August 1823. Not surprisingly, the municipality of Bilbao too was strongly dissatisfied with the measures of the French command, in particular its patrols of the streets (see Guiard, *Villa,* vol. 4, pp. 395–399).

11. The 16 August 1823 ordinance of the Bilbao city government, alluded to earlier, was an excellent illustration of this. Among others, it limited the size of public gatherings after dark to five persons and enforced stricter curfews. Constitutionalists repeatedly complained that decrees of this kind unfairly obstructed the normal conduct of public activities and business. As is shown in chapter 5, the sympathizers of the Cortes were hit with numerous other repressive regulations and measures in the course of the Ominous Decade.

12. AMAE, CC, Bilbao, vol. 3, letters of Regnaudin dated 12 June, 12 July, and 31 July 1823.

13. Barahona [Arévalo], *Making,* pp. 177–178. See Sagarmínaga, *Go-*

bierno, vol. 7, pp. 394–395. According to this source, the Diputación reestablished the so-called *Partida de Miqueletes* on 6 November 1823.

14. See in particular ADV, Guernica, *Oficios del General Francés. De 1823 a 24*. The relevant dispatches are numerous.

15. AMAE, CC, Bilbao, vol. 3, letter dated 12 July 1823.

16. Substantially complete transcriptions of the proceedings of the important May 1823 Vizcayan Juntas in Sagarmínaga, *Gobierno*, vol. 7, pp. 329–368. This documentation can be occasionally complemented with other sources—e.g., with accounts that appeared in *Le Moniteur Universel*.

17. See Guiard, *Consulado*, vol. 2, pp. 680–682; ADV, Guernica, *Escrituras Originales. De 1821 a 1823* and Sagarmínaga, *Gobierno*, vol. 7, pp. 342–343, 353–354 and 359–361.

18. Sagarmínaga, *Gobierno*, vol. 7, p. 344: "*Que la Diputación represente con la mayor energía a la Junta Provisional de Gobierno que se digne mandar que se trasladen las aduanas y registros establecidos en el Señorío a los puntos donde antes estuvieron.*" More on the sensitive question of the bureaus' transfer in chapter 4 of this book, section IV. Finally, another indication of the strong foralista sentiment at the assembly in AMAE, CC, Bilbao, vol. 3, communication of Regnaudin to the ministry, 12 June 1823. Reported the agent: "le retour des anciens privilèges a été agitè tumultuesement."

19. Important political and legal positions emerged from the Vizcayan freedoms. For example, protofederalism, particularism, regionalism, and separatism—along with other politico-legal and economic views—flowed from, or had their basis in, the provincial liberties. More on this in Barahona, *ESR*, 1983 passim, and in chapter 1, section IV of this book.

20. For example, see the petition of the Bilbao city council to the monarch (dated 6 February 1824), requesting the reestablishment of the Inquisition. This suggestive document, probably authored by Pedro Novia de Salcedo, can be consulted in ADV, Library, F-3,220 of the *Sección Vascongada*. Guiard alludes to the petition in *Villa*, vol. 4, pp. 410–411. Another excellent example of conservative thought and terminology in the same work, vol. 4, p. 437.

21. While clearly favoring liberal rule, Vizcayan constitutionalists had never opted for an outright republican system of government. Most simply desired a constitutional monarchy—king and Cortes—as during the 1812–1814 and 1820–1823 periods. In other words, well within the mainstream of the opposition, local constitutionalists could not be accused of political extremism.

22. AMAE, CC, Bilbao, vol. 4, letter dated 3 October 1830 and vol. 3, letter dated 30 June 1825.

23. See note 20 above for complete reference. Nor was this the only Vizcayan request for the Inquisition's return. Earlier, royalists at Orduña (the customs house town) had made a similar demand; see Luis Alonso Tejada, *Ocaso de la Inquisición en los últimos años del reinado de Fernando VII. Juntas de Fé, Juntas Apostólicas, Conspiraciones Realistas* (Algorta: Zero, 1969), p. 70. The Orduña petition was dated 20 October 1823. And later, the

Vizcayan Diputación also asked for the return of the Holy Office; see ADV, Guernica, *1823. Representaciones al Rey y otras autoridades*, petition to the monarch, 26 June 1824.

24. See note 12 above. Extremely interesting and useful observations on the state of the clergy in Bilbao several years later by the English traveler Henry D. Inglis, in *Spain in 1830*, 2 vols. (London: Whittaker, Treacher and Co., 1831), vol. 1, pp. 1–34 passim.

25. AMAE, CC, Bilbao, vol. 3, letter of 18 March 1824. See also the agent's yearly report for 1824, dated 1 January 1825, in volume 4 of the collection.

26. *OCSV*, 1824, circular of the Corregidor, 8 March 1824. Among others, the official castigated the *"revolucionarios"* of the Trienio for what he called *"la más triste desmoralización pública"* in the province.

27. Ibid., 1825, circular of the Vizcayan Diputación, 28 October 1825.

28. ADV, Guernica, *R[eales] Cedulas y Reales Ordenes Dirigidas al Senor Corregidor*, order dated 7 December 1826. It is not altogether clear who ordered the calendar's confiscation although it appears to have been a certain Antonio de la Parra of the *Subdelegación de Imprentas* at Valladolid.

29. ADV, Corr., leg. 508, exp. 3. The prosecutor's tough summation is dated 4 January 1825.

30. *OCSV*, 1824. See also Sagarmínaga, *Gobierno*, vol. 7, pp. 435–436.

31. An excellent, if brief, general overview of right-wing conspiracies against the Spanish government during the 1823–1833 decade in Josep Fontana Lázaro, *La crisis del Antiguo régimen, 1808–1833*, 2d ed. (Barcelona: Crítica [Grupo editorial Grijalbo] 1983), pp. 186–196, (hereafter cited as *La crisis*). Opposition to Ferdinand VII's rule from those labeled by Fontana as "ultras" was clearly linked to the rise of Spanish Carlism.

32. AMAE, CC, Bilbao, vol. 4, letter of Regnaudin, 25 August 1825. This is one of the earliest explicit references to pro–Don Carlos political sentiment in Vizcaya. The commercial agent described in some detail the conspiratorial goings-on in the province, particularly in Bilbao. Partial corroboration of all this in M.F.M. de Vargas, *La guerra en Navarra y Provincias Vascongadas* (Madrid: N.p., 1848), as quoted by Guiard, *Villa*, vol. 4, pp. 430–431. See also P[edro] P[ascual] de Uhagon, *Informe evacuado por Don . . . sobre los crímenes cometidos en el aciago alzamiento de 3 de Octubre de 1833* (Bilbao: Imprenta de los Hijos de R. Martín y Cortázar, 1871), p. 46 (hereafter cited as *Informe*). Henceforth, I shall always refer in the text to Ferdinand VII's brother, Carlos María Isidro de Borbón, either as Don Carlos, or simply as the Pretender. The only exceptions to this will be in direct quotes. In these instances, I have opted for leaving intact the original nomenclature, however it may read.

33. See, for example, Barahona [Arévalo], *Making*, p. 335; and chaps. 6 and 7 passim in this book.

34. From the petition of the Bilbao city council requesting the reestablishment of the Inquisition. See note 20 above for the complete reference.

35. AHN, Consejos, leg. 12,278, letter from the Vizcayan general depu-

ties, Novia de Salcedo and Valde-espina, to the superintendent of police, 16 April 1827.

36. To the historian's delight, the Vizcayan police dutifully reported local reaction to national political events in its dispatches to central headquarters in Madrid. A detailed discussion of the organization, activities and aims of the provincial police in chapter 5, section I.

37. ADV, Guernica, *1824 a 1830. Yndice de Oficios a la Superintendencia*, dispatch no. 778 of the Vizcayan police to central headquarters, 4 December 1826.

38. Ibid., dispatch no. 478 of the Vizcayan police to central headquarters, 21 July 1826.

39. See, for example, John Francis Bacon, *Six Years in Biscay* (London: Smith, Elder and Co., Cornhill, 1838), p. 81; and Guiard, *Villa*, vol. 4, pp. 440–441.

40. Local sources tend to confirm Regnaudin's remarks on the poor treatment of the French. For instance, see Guiard, *Villa*, vol. 4, p. 409; and ACJG, Policía, reg. 27, letter of the municipal authorities of Luyando to the Vizcayan police, 18 October 1830. For the sources of the commercial agent's repeated expressions of discontent, see note 42 below.

41. Sagarmínaga, *Gobierno*, vol. 7, pp. 413–414.

42. The French commercial agent at Bilbao strongly believed that this was the case. Among others, see AMAE, CC, Bilbao, vol. 4, yearly reports for 1824, 1825, and 1826. Also consult AMAE, CPC, Espagne, vol. 5, letter of Regnaudin, 21 October 1832. More on this subject in Bacon, *Six Years in Biscay*, p. 81; Victor Luis Gaminde, *Intereses de Bilbao. Ecsamen de lo perjudicial que sería la permanencia del sistema foral en el siglo XIX al comercio e industria del país, y a los liberales de Vizcaya* (Bilbao: Imprenta de Adolfo Depont, 1837), pp. 24–25 (hereafter cited as *Intereses*) and Pedro de Lemonauría, *Ensayo crítico sobre las Leyes Constitucionales de Vizcaya* (Bilbao: Imprenta de Nicolás Delmas, 1837), pp. 4–5 (hereafter cited as *Ensayo crítico*.) The latter three authors of course offer a liberal critique of the Vizcayan residency requirements.

43. See the letter of the Vizcayan police to the Corregidor of Vizcaya, 24 November 1832, concerning the state of public order in the province (ACJG, Policía, reg. 4); as well as dispatch no. 28 of the Vizcayan police to central headquarters, 1 February 1833 (ibid., reg. 31).

44. Charles Frederick Henningsen, *The most striking events of a twelvemonth's campaign with Zumalacárregui in Navarre and the Basque Provinces*, 2 vols. (London: John Murray, 1836), vol. 2, pp. 13–18. See also ADV, Guernica, *1826 a 1829. Libro de Armamento*, letter of the Vizcayan Diputación to the Inspector-General of the Spanish Royalist Volunteers, 29 January 1827; and the letter of the same body to the authorities of the Council of Zalla, 23 March 1827. Many other examples of this brand of conservative ideology could be summoned forth.

45. AMAE, CC, Bilbao, vol. 4, letter to the sous-préfet of Bayonne, 12 May 1823.

46. Pedro Novia de Salcedo, *Defensa histórica, legislativa y económica del Señorío de Vizcaya*, 4 vols. (Bilbao: Librería de Delmas e Hijo, 1851–1852), vol. 4, pp. 1–18 (hereafter cited as *Defensa*). There are extremely interesting passages railing—often sarcastically—against "modernism," "lights," "philosophers," and "modern erudites" (*modernismo, luces, filósofos, eruditos modernos*). Other suggestive opinions of Vizcayan traditionalists in ADV, Guernica, *1825 al 1829. Representaciones. Ministerio de Gracia y Justicia*, petition of the Vizcayan Diputación to the monarch, 5 January 1829.

47. See in particular Novia de Salcedo, *Defensa*, vol. 1, pp. i–vii (Introduction), and vol. 4, pp. 1–18 and 232–243. See also a Vizcayan conservative attack upon innovation and reform in ADV, Guernica, *1823. Representaciones al Rey y otras autoridades*, document entitled "*Felicitación a S.M. por medio del S[eñ]or Marqués de Valde-espina*," 11 October 1823.

48. See Novia de Salcedo, *Defensa*, vol. 1, pp. i–vii (Introduction), and vol. 4, pp. 9–18. In addition, see this author's sharp accusations against the conclusions of the *Junta de Reforma de Abusos*. According to Novia de Salcedo, among the junta's goals was the achievement of a *"nivelación general,"* vol. 4, pp. 141–145).

49. See, for example, ADV, Guernica, *1825 al 1829. Representaciones Ministeriales. Hacienda*, petition of the Vizcayan Diputación to the king, 26 November 1825. In this document the Vizcayan authorities severely criticized the "levelers" in Madrid. Numerous other Vizcayan attacks upon *niveladores* and *nivelación* could be cited.

50. Novia de Salcedo, *Defensa*, vol. 2, p. 399. Interesting observations of traditionalists regarding Vizcayan independence from Castile in the 5 January 1829 petition of the Diputación to the king cited in note 46.

51. Novia de Salcedo, *Defensa*, vol. 2, p. 401. See also vol. 4, pp. 238–239.

52. Good examples of Novia de Salcedo's political separatism in ibid., vol. 2, pp. 397–416 passim. In some of these passages the author raises Vizcaya and the Basque provinces to the level of wholly independent states and political entities.

53. See ADV, Guernica, *Conferencias de las Provincias Bascongadas. 1812 a 1833*.

54. It is interesting to note that neither ethnocultural and racial considerations in general, nor the Basque language (Euskera) in particular, scarcely occupied any space in conservatives' arguments to define and underscore the region's uniqueness. In fact, despite this period's numerous contentious issues between the Basque provinces and the central government (detailed in chapter 4), at no point was the Basque language a source of conflict. Why this was the case awaits a detailed demonstration. Still, certain observations regarding this important question are perhaps in order. First, there was little reason for Vizcayans to challenge Castilian, the dominant (written) politico-administrative language. Indeed, for many *provincianos*, Castilian was a crucial vehicle for social advance, especially in bureaucracy and business. Second, the Basque elites appear to have been fully bilingual and bicultural. Hence, here too, there would be little to gain from a monolingual agenda.

Third, only later in the century, with the rise of Vizcayan political national-ism (birth of the PNV, etc.) did the question of the Basque language—along with education and the preservation of the region's cultural heritage in the face of Castile's alleged imperial/colonial domination—become an ardent issue for many Vizcayans. In sum, in the early nineteenth century sociocul-tural and political conditions in Vizcaya were not yet ripe for the emergence of the Basque language as an issue in itself.

55. Novia de Salcedo, *Defensa*, vol. 4, p. 237. In fact, the entire third volume of this work is devoted to an in-depth description and passionate defense of Basque legislation.

56. González, *Colección*, vol. 2, pp. 428–430, royal order of 16 February 1824. Somewhat ironically, the services of the Basque provinces to the roy-alist cause were generously acknowledged by the ruler in this order—the same one that established the bases for the important Basque *donativo*, the subject of considerable controversy during the 1823–1833 decade. More on this question in chapter 4 of this book, section I.

57. AMAE, CC, Bilbao, vol. 4, yearly report for 1825, 1 January 1826.

58. Some political skirmishes around the provincial freedoms and insti-tutions had already taken place during the Trienio; see my essay in *Basque Politics*, 1985. Later, Gaminde's important and polemical *Intereses* would certainly raise both the quality and the tone of the debate concerning the advantages and disadvantages of the Basque privileges. Of course, as a com-mitted liberal, Gaminde felt that the liberties were an impediment to pro-gress—economic or otherwise—in the region.

59. More on the fueros and their effects upon Vizcayan society in chap-ter 1, section IV, and chapter 6, section III.

60. A lengthy discussion of many of these issues in chapter 4.

61. ANP, F 7, 12,011, letter of the sous-préfet of Bayonne to the minister of the interior, 29 July 1827; and AMAE, CD, Espagne, vol. 744, letter of Regnaudin to the minister of foreign affairs, 30 July 1827. Not only were foreign observers keenly aware of this expansionism; see Antonio Pirala, *Historia de la guerra civil y de los partidos liberal y carlista, escrita con presencia de memorias y documentos inéditos*, 5 vols. (Madrid: Estableci-miento Tipográfico de Mellado, 1853–1856), vol. 1, pp. 135–136 (hereafter cited as *Historia*).

62. For example, see P. P. de Uhagon's pointed remarks against the Viz-cayan *fueristas* cited in chapter 4 of this book.

63. AGS, Consejo Supremo de Hacienda, leg. 20. These remarks are from a prosecutor's legal brief (*dictamen fiscal*) dated 7 September 1829.

64. APG, *Actas*, 3 September 1825.

65. ADV, Guernica, *1825 a 1829. Oficios de Alta Clase*, letter dated 5 November 1825.

66. APG, *Actas*, 28 November 1829. The four royal orders for Cavani-lles' projected—and eventually aborted—mission can be consulted in AHN, Consejos, leg. 3827, exp. 27. More on this episode in chapter 4 in this book.

67. APG, *Actas*, 14 December 1825.

68. ADV, Guernica, *1825 a 1829. Oficios Alta Clase*, letter dated 7 January 1826.

69. Still, Vizcaya—as indeed the entire Basque region—had good reason to be worried. After all, as noted in chapter 1, Godoy's review of the freedoms and Llorente's *Noticias* had accompanied important institutional political reforms in Vizcaya. More on the circumstances and origins of González's *Colección* in chapter 4.

70. APG, *Actas*, 5 September and 14 December 1825.

71. Ibid., 16 June 1827 and 31 March 1830.

72. ADV, Guernica, *Conferencias de las Provincias Bascongadas*, 27 June 1827 (at Vitoria). The two orders in question regarding military substitution were those of 8 February and 21 May 1827. See also Sagarmínaga, *Gobierno*, vol. 7, p. 497.

73. ADV, Guernica, *Conferencias de las Provincias Bascongadas. 1812 a 1833*, 1 June 1828 (at Bilbao), and 11–13 March 1830 (also at Bilbao). More on the March 1830 petition in Sagarmínaga, *Gobierno*, vol. 8, pp. 51–58.

74. ADV, Guernica, *Conferencias de las Provincias Bascongadas. 1812 a 1833*, 22–24 September 1828.

75. Ibid., 14–16 January 1829. Actually, this procedure was not entirely new. The groundwork had already been laid at the September 1828 conferences in Vitoria. See the previous note.

76. More on these questions in chapter 4.

77. APG, *Actas*, 15 January 1828.

78. AHN, Consejos, leg. 3784, exp. 4, letter of Calomarde to the dean of the royal council, 21 March 1828. See also Calomarde's 8 February 1828 letter to the dean. Both of these documents became the object of substantial administrative proceedings, many of which are detailed in the same dossier.

79. Ibid. This dossier contains several inventories of the documents finally submitted to the council of state, including one signed by Valentín Pinilla, dated 12 May 1829. The bulk of this documentation can be consulted in AHN, Estado, leg. 198/1 through 211.

80. APG, *Actas*, 20 December 1828. During this session Ballesteros, the minister of finance, noted that he had communicated the monarch's "sovereign resolution" (regarding González's undertaking) to the other ministers and heads of department on 30 October 1828. He then asked them if they had "received and circulated" the said document. All replied affirmatively.

81. Ibid.

82. Royal order of 13 May 1829. This order is reproduced several times in the *Colección*.

83. AGS, Consejo Supremo de Hacienda, leg. 20. The quote is from an undated *minuta* of the council, which is unidentifiable except for indications that it is clearly connected to other materials that concern Basque mining.

84. AHN, Estado, libro no. 40, *Actas Originales del año 1830*, 4 August 1830.

85. ADV, Guernica, *1825 a 1829. Oficios Alta Clase*, letter of the Vizcayan Diputación to Novia de Salcedo, 25 August 1829. Novia de Salcedo's

work had been sent to the diputaciones of Alava and Guipúzcoa in May of the same year. Apparently, the Guipúzcoan authorities did not feel that the publication of the *Defensa* was a timely idea, and they so informed their Vizcayan counterpart. As noted earlier, the *Defensa* did not appear until 1851–1852.

86. APG, *Actas*, 10 October and 23 December 1829, and 31 March 1830. The transcripts of these sessions contain detailed information of Basque, fueros-based opposition to the central government's military measures.

87. This is worth noting because there is strong evidence that the Spanish state was wary of revolutionary activity in the northern regions well before the July Revolution in France after which, as is well known, many Spanish liberals migrated to that country from England. Led by Mina, some of them eventually launched an ill-fated invasion of Navarra in October 1830. More on these questions in chapter 4.

88. APG, *Actas*, 31 March 1830.

89. Ibid., 7 June 1830.

90. AHN, Estado, libro no. 40, *Actas Originales del año 1830*, 9 August 1830. For a brief follow-up to this matter, in the same register see the session of 16 August 1830.

91. APG, *Actas*, 21 August 1830.

92. Ibid., 28 August 1830.

93. Bacon, *Six Years in Biscay*, p. 79. The emphasis is Bacon's.

94. Pirala, *Historia*, vol. 1, p. 136.

95. AHN, Estado, libro no. 42, *Actas Originales del año 1832*, 9 January 1832. The minutes leave no doubt that the council was again at work on Basque materials: "*Mientras se resuelve el expediente general que está examinando el Consejo sobre los fueros de Vizcaya.*"

96. APG, *Actas*, 14 January 1832.

97. AHN, Estado, libro no. 42, *Actas Originales del año 1832*, 6, 13, and 20 February 1832.

98. Ibid., no. 42, 21 March 1832, and no. 43, 28 January 1833.

99. Ibid., no. 43, 28 January 1833. It is of course possible that the Council of State, in the March 1832–January 1833 interval, was awaiting the arrival of an important dossier dealing with military matters in the Basque region, namely, one that the monarch had ordered sent to this body in July–August 1830. But even if this was the case—the crucial *expediente* not reaching State until January 1833—the body possessed other voluminous documentation on the Basque provinces for its review. In sum, at this point, there is no adequate explanation for the 1832–1833 gap, a situation similar to that which followed the mid-1830 crisis brought about by the July Revolution in France.

100. Ibid., no. 43.

101. Ibid., no. 43, 18 February 1833. "For greater clarity and instruction," the council ordered that a "detailed extract" be drawn by the staff concerning the military parts of González's *Colección*. This was clearly designed to facilitate the work of the *consejeros* unfamiliar with the publication.

102. APG, *Actas*, 8 March 1833. Next to the Council of Ministers' recommendation is an entry on the margin that reads, *"Aprobada esta resolución por S.M."*

103. AHN, Estado, libro no. 43, *Actas Originales del año 1833*, 11 March 1833.

104. Among others, the decree may be consulted in Jaime del Burgo, *Origen y fundamento del régimen foral de Navarra* (Pamplona: Diputación Foral de Navarra, Institucion Príncipe de Viana, 1968), p. 123, note 242.

105. In addition to the brief comments on the question of local reforms in chapter 4, a far more extensive discussion on this and related issues in chapter 6, section II.

106. More on this episode and its political ramifications in chapter 4, section IV.

107. Uhagon, *Informe*, pp. 10–11.

108. More on this and related problems in Samuel Edwards Widdrington, *Sketches in Spain during the years 1829, 30, 31, & 32*, 2 vols. (London: Thomas and William Boone, 1834), vol. 1, pp. 329–330.

109. Uhagon, *Informe*, p. 7.

110. *OCSV*, 1830, circular dated 20 October 1830.

111. Sagarmínaga, *Gobierno*, vol. 8, p. 131. Also at this time, as the municipal elections approached, the Vizcayan Diputación issued another circular urging the electorate to keep in mind that the province's laws and fueros were "its most precious property," (in ibid., 1831, 9 December 1831). Identifying royalism with local patriotism, the circular was a clear attempt to keep liberals or sympathizers of reform from reaching public office.

112. Ibid., 1832, *alocución* of the Vizcayan Diputación to the Paisanos Armados, 31 March 1832.

113. Uhagon, *Informe*, p. 13. See also the kind of argument that Francisco de Hormaeche, a prominent Vizcayan moderate liberal, attributes to a local conservative of mid-1833 in the extremely important article "De las causas que más inmediatamente han contribuido a promover en las Provincias Bascongadas la guerra civil," *Revista de Madrid*, 2d series, no. 1 (1839), p. 339 (hereafter cited as "De las causas").

114. Uhagon, *Informe*, p. 13. Chapter 7, section I of this book examines some of the earthier and more popular manifestations of Carlism prior to the October 1833 uprising.

Chapter 4: The State and Vizcaya During the Ominous Decade

1. González, *Colección*, vol. 2, pp. 428–430. For the central government's rationale in requesting this contribution, see Ballesteros's 1826 ministerial report, which is reproduced in its entirety in Federico Suárez Verdeguer, *López Ballesteros y la hacienda entre 1823–1832*, 5 vols. (Pamplona: Universidad de Navarra, "Documentos del reinado de Fernando VII," no. 6, 1970), vol. 3, pp. 15–208 (hereafter cited as *Ballesteros*). On the Basque provinces' donation, see pp. 52–55.

2. ADV, Guernica, *Conferencias de las Provincias Bascongadas. 1812 a*

1833, session of 30 March 1824 (at Bilbao). See also Sagarmínaga, *Gobierno*, vol. 7, pp. 398–399.

3. ADV, Guernica, *Conferencias de las Provincias Bascongadas. 1812 a 1833*, session of 12 June 1824. For a discussion of the donation issue at the May 1824 Vizcayan Juntas, see Sagarmínaga, *Gobierno*, vol. 7, pp. 401–407 passim. A copy of the 12 June 1824 Basque petition to the monarch, in ADV, Guernica, *1823. Representaciones al Rey y otras autoridades.*

4. APG, *Actas*, session of 5 September 1825. See also Sagarmínaga, *Gobierno*, vol. 7, p. 499. More on this question in chapter 3 of this book, and note 70 of that chapter. The royal order summoning the Basque representatives to Madrid is dated 13 September 1825.

5. APG, *Actas*, session of 20 October 1825.

6. Ibid., session of 14 December 1825.

7. See Josep Fontana Lázaro, *Hacienda y estado en la crisis final del Antiguo régimen español: 1823–1833* (Madrid: Instituto de Estudios Fiscales, 1973), pp. 90–91, 131–132, 141–154 passim, 188–192 passim, 260–264 passim, 303–309 passim, and 328.

8. AHN, Estado, libro no. 29, *Actas Originales del año 1826.* See my remarks in chapter 3 of this book.

9. See note 1 for complete reference. The report is dated 3 February 1826.

10. Suárez Verdeguer, *Ballesteros*, vol. 3, p. 43.

11. See, for example, ADV, Guernica, *1825 al 29. Representaciones Ministeriales. Hacienda*, petition of the Vizcayan Diputación to the king, 31 August 1827 (partly cited as an epigraph to this chapter). More on these questions in chapter 3 of this book.

12. ADV, Guernica, *1825 al 29. Representaciones Ministeriales. Hacienda*, petition of the Vizcayan Diputación to the king, 13 June 1826.

13. Suárez Verdeguer, *Ballesteros*, vol. 3, p. 241. See in particular the *Informe del Consejo de Estado sobre la Memoria presentada por el Ministro de Hacienda en Febrero de 1826*, dated 20 May 1826, reproduced in pp. 209–242 of this volume. More on the question in AHN, Estado, libro no. 29, *Actas Originales del año 1826*, session of 20 May 1826.

14. The issue of royal armed intervention in the Basque provinces during the Ominous Decade is not a simple affair. That central government troops were stationed in the region is, of course, not in doubt. A small royal garrison at San Sebastián served as the headquarters of the *Capitanía General de Guipúzcoa*. The question of Vizcaya, however, is more complicated. Except for a very brief period at the start of the 1823 Restoration, I have not found solid evidence that royal troops were stationed in Vizcaya before 1831. See, for example, Guiard, vol. 4, *Villa*, p. 446. Between 1824 and 1831 the royal detachments were generally located on the southern flank of the Ebro, a situation that seems to have begun to change around 1830. See APG, *Actas*, session of 31 March 1830. Significantly, there is a striking lack of Vizcayan petitions requesting the withdrawal of royal forces from the province. In other words, extremely attentive to the freedoms, the Vizcayan government would have certainly requested the corps' removal. Again, it is possible that some royal troops may have been temporarily stationed in the province; e.g.

at Orduña, as Guiard points out. Still, as is noted in chapter 7 of this book, the absence of government troops in Vizcaya would have far-reaching consequences during the October 1833 Carlist uprising.

15. There are allusions to this document—and extended paraphrases of it as well—in ADV, Guernica, *1825 al 29. Representaciones Ministeriales. Hacienda*, petition of the Vizcayan Diputación to the king, 31 August 1827. More on the 30 June 1827 royal order in Sagarmínaga, *Gobierno*, vol. 7, pp. 499–500.

16. Sagarmínaga, *Gobierno*, vol. 7, pp. 512–513. See also AMAE, CD, Espagne, vol. 744, letter of Regnaudin to the minister of foreign affairs, 30 July 1827. More on the province's important military projects in chapter 5, section II of this book.

17. ADV, Guernica, *1825 al 29. Representaciones Ministeriales. Hacienda*, petition of the Vizcayan Diputación to the king, 31 August 1827.

18. In particular, see Jaime Torras Elías, *La Guerra de los Agraviados* (Barcelona: Universidad de Barcelona, Publicaciones de la Cátedra de Historia General de España, 1967).

19. ADV, Guernica, *Conferencias de las Provincias Bascongadas. 1812 a 1833*, session of 13 November 1827 (at San Sebastián).

20. APG, *Actas*, session of 15 January 1828. Additional materials on this (and related matters) in AHN, Estado, leg. 221, no. 14, dossier entitled *"Expediente relativo a los fueros y exenciones y privilegios de las Provincias Vascongadas."* See also AHN, Estado, libro no. 36, *Actas Originales del año 1828*, session of 14 February 1828. Finally, see also Sagarmínaga, *Gobierno*, vol. 7, pp. 570–575, for a review of some of these questions at the July 1829 Vizcayan Juntas.

21. Suárez Verdeguer, *Ballesteros*, vol. 4, pp. 75–76. The official's *Memoria* is dated 11 October 1829. It comprises pp. 21–149, volume 4 of *Ballesteros*.

22. *Memoria Ministerial Sobre el Estado de la Real Hacienda, de 12 de Diciembre de 1829*, in ibid., vol. 4, pp. 211–312, and 280. This ministerial report contained other harsh remarks against the Basques. More on these questions in Fontana, *Hacienda y estado*, p. 286.

23. See Fontana, *Hacienda y estado*, pp. 298–303 for a lucid discussion on this matter.

24. The report of the Junta de Jefes de Hacienda is reproduced in Suárez Verdeguer, *Ballesteros*, vol. 5, pp. 85–156. The junta's report is dated 28 February 1831, an excellent indication of the swiftness and urgency under which its members operated—the body having only been created on 9 January 1831. See note 157 for the junta's second report.

25. In ibid., vol. 5, p. 197. Ballesteros's first 1831 ministerial report is reproduced in pp. 157–233 of volume 5, with more on this issue on p. 182.

26. Ibid., vol. 5, pp. 287–341.

27. Ibid., vol. 5, p. 318.

28. Ibid., vol. 1, p. 404, session of the Council of Ministers dated 19 April.

29. CD, 1824, vol. 9, pp. 445–447, *"Circular para que se proceda al sorteo de 36,000 hombres, a fin de reorganizar el ejército."*

30. Sagarmínaga, *Gobierno*, vol. 7, pp. 401–403.

31. See ADV, Guernica, *1823. Representaciones al Rey y otras autorida-des*, and ADV, Guernica, *Conferencias de las Provincias Bascongadas. 1812 a 1833*. As noted earlier, the Basque petition is dated 12 June 1824. According to the transcript of the session dated the same day, the Basque provinces demanded the strict preservation of their military exemptions: "*[se pedía] se las declarase libres y exentas de contribuir al reemplazo del ejército.*"

32. To date, the only evidence of governmental activity in 1824–1826 with respect to the reemplazo issue is a 30 September 1824 consulta of the Council of War, which may well have ruled against Basque objections to compulsory national military service; see ADV, Guernica, *Reales Ordenes Generales. De 1814 a 1830*, 13 January 1830 royal order transmitted by the Minister of War Zambrano, to the Vizcayan Diputación. This important document, to which repeated reference will be made, contains considerable background on these issues. Unfortunately, I have been unable to consult two of the diputación's petitions, which may well have touched on problems of military service. Dated 21 May 1825 and 13 June 1826, both remonstrances are mentioned in the very significant 31 August 1827 petition of the Vizcayan leadership to the monarch; see ADV, Guernica, *1825 a 1827. Representaciones al Ministerio de la Guerra*, document with an annotation on the margin that reads: "*Sobre el reemplazo para el Ejército pedido a este Señorío.*"

33. Royal orders dated 8 February and 21 May 1827; see ADV, Guernica, *Conferencias de las Provincias Bascongadas. 1812 a 1833*, session of 27 June 1827 (at Vitoria). See also ADV, Guernica, *1825 a 1827. Representaciones al Ministerio de la Guerra*, petitions of the Vizcayan Diputación to the Ministry of War and to the king, dated 1 June and 31 August 1827, respectively. More on this in Sagarmínaga, *Gobierno*, vol. 7, pp. 499–515 passim; in AMAE, CD, Espagne, vol. 744, communication of Regnaudin to the minister of foreign affairs, 30 July 1827; in APG, *Actas*, sessions of 10 October 1829 (with a detailed summary of reemplazo-related questions during this period), and of 31 March and 22 May 1830 (also with important information germane to the issues); and, finally, in the 13 January 1830 royal order transmitted by Zambrano to the Vizcayan Diputación, cited in the previous note.

34. The quote is not from the 21 May 1827 royal order proper, but rather, is an apparently faithful paraphrase from the 1 June 1827 Vizcayan petition alluded to in the previous note. Concerning the 1818 compromise (or *convenio*), see chapter 2 in this book.

35. ADV, Guernica, *Conferencias de las Provincias Bascongadas. 1812 a 1833*, session of 27 June.

36. Sagarmínaga, *Gobierno*, vol. 7, pp. 499–515 passim. See also Regnaudin's dispatch of 30 July 1827, cited in note 33.

37. See, for example, the language and imagery of the 31 August 1827 petition of the Vizcayan Diputación to the king; in ADV, Guernica, *1825 a 1827. Representaciones al Ministerio de la Guerra*.

38. Ibid.

39. Ibid.

40. For post-summer 1827 governmental activity, see the 13 January 1830 royal order (fully referenced in note 32). According to this document, at least three different royal orders related to this were issued in the latter part of 1827. They are dated 15 and 18 October and 3 December.

41. For these parleys, see ADV, Guernica, *Conferencias de las Provincias Bascongadas. 1812 a 1833*. Regarding the Barcelona petitions and their aftermath, see note 20, and chapter 3 in this book.

42. Judging from a wide variety of Vizcayan and governmental sources, the silence does not appear to be the result of documentary gaps. Rather, I believe that the central government chose not to press home its demands in 1828–1829, hoping perhaps that the Council of State would offer assistance in resolving the matter. Moreover, the important issue was not to be forgotten in Madrid, and the plausible argument might be advanced that the ministry brought back the question of the Basque reemplazo in August 1829 as a prelude and/or preparation for the 1830 quinta which, undoubtedly, was already in the works.

43. Most of the following information is from the 10 October 1829 session of the Council of Ministers, in APG, *Actas* and from the much-cited 13 January 1830 royal order to the Vizcayan Diputación transmitted by the Ministry of War.

44. APG, *Actas*, session of 10 October 1829. In fact, if the council seemingly favored some form of compromise and adjustment for the sums owed, the session's transcript also tends to show that the body was only willing to make temporary concessions to the Basques, while subjecting these matters to additional (and perhaps troublesome) scrutiny.

45. ADV, Guernica, *Reales Ordenes Generales. De 1814 a 1830*. See in particular the passage that reads: "*Ha tenido a bien S.M. . . . . desestimar las reclamaciones que las Provincias Vascongadas y la Diputación . . . de Navarra han hecho a consecuencia de lo mandado en la Real Orden de 21 de Mayo de 1827.*" Next, the 13 January 1830 royal order reaffirmed in toto the recommendations of the 10 October 1829 session of the Council of Ministers.

46. See Sagarmínaga, *Gobierno*, vol. 8, pp. 7–49 passim; and AMAE, CC, Bilbao, vol. 4, communication of Regnaudin to the minister of foreign affairs, 27 February 1830.

47. Sagarmínaga, *Gobierno*, vol. 8, p. 49. See also ANP, F 7 12,011, letter of the sous-préfet of Bayonne to the minister of the interior (?), 8 March 1830.

48. ADV, Guernica, *Conferencias de las Provincias Bascongadas. 1812 a 1833*. See also Sagarmínaga, *Gobierno*, vol. 8, p. 51.

49. Sagarmínaga, *Gobierno*, vol. 8, pp. 51–58.

50. APG, *Actas*, session of 31 March 1830, where the 13 March 1830 Basque petition and other matters were discussed.

51. More on the question of royal troops movements in the north—and the stationing of such corps in Vizcaya—in chapter 3 of this book. See also chapter 4, (note 14 in particular).

52. APG, *Actas*, 31 March 1830. Ballesteros had recently referred favorably to González's work in the 1829 ministerial report, voicing the hope that the newly published volumes of the *Colección* would clarify the fueros' legitimacy—or lack thereof (see note 22).

53. APG, *Actas*, session of 22 May 1830.

54. AMAE, CD, Espagne, vol. 752, letter of the Vicomte de Saint Priest to Polignac, 1 June 1830.

55. APG, *Actas*, session of 7 June 1830.

56. APG, *Actas*, session of 7 June 1830. Again, see chapter 3 in this book, passim.

57. APG, *Actas*, session of 21 August 1830. More on this matter in Sagarmínaga, *Gobierno*, vol. 8, pp. 69–75. The order in question—whose exact date is unknown to me—was received in Vizcaya on 27 August. It would therefore appear that it was drafted on or about 21 August. See also APG, *Actas*, session of 4 September 1830, where the Basque delegates' arrival was eagerly awaited in the council.

58. APG, *Actas*, session of 11 September 1830. Nevertheless, the council instructed the delegates to meet with the minister of war at the latter's house the following day, a Sunday.

59. Sagarmínaga, *Gobierno*, vol. 8, p. 72.

60. APG, *Actas*, session of 18 September 1830. The royal order with these stipulations is dated 21 September. The 15 September session also contains tangential references to the military situation in the Basque region.

61. See Sagarmínaga, *Gobierno*, vol. 8, p. 75; and ADV, Guernica, *Conferencias de las Provincias Bascongadas. 1812 a 1833*, sessions of 4–5 October 1830 (at Vitoria).

62. See in particular chapter 3 of this book.

63. For an interesting defense of Basque positions concerning military service on the heels of the Ominous Decade, see the anonymous *Observaciones sobre la necesidad de examinar el régimen administrativo de las Provincias Vacongadas, para fallar con acierto en esta materia* (Madrid: Imprenta de Miguel de Burgos, 1834), pp. 5–9 (hereafter cited as *Observaciones*).

64. More on the problems of Vizcayan iron in chapter 1 of this book, and chapter 6, section II; Barahona, *ESR*, 1983, p. 278. See also Bacon's interesting remarks on these particulars in *Six Years in Biscay*, p. 75.

65. ADV, Guernica, *1823. Representaciones al Rey y otras autoridades*.

66. Sagarmínaga, *Gobierno*, vol. 8, p. 64.

67. González, *Colección*, vol. 2, pp. 437–438. More on this in Sagarmínaga, *Gobierno*, vol. 7, p. 478.

68. ADV, Guernica, *1825 a 1829. Oficios Alta Clase*, letter of the Diputación to Novia de Salcedo, 17 January 1826.

69. AHN, Estado, libro no. 29, *Actas Originales del año 1826*, session of 11 March 1826.

70. See the following: ADV, Guernica, *1825 a 1829. Oficios Alta Clase*, letter of the Vizcayan Diputación to the general intendant of the principality of Asturias (at Oviedo), 8 May 1826; *1824 a 1830. Yndice de Oficios a la*

Superintendencia, dispatches of the Vizcayan police to central headquarters, nos. 303 and 355, dated 12 May and 2 June 1826, respectively; *1825 al 29. Representaciones Ministeriales. Hacienda*, letter-petition of the Vizcayan Diputación to the Ministry of Finance, 15 May 1826; and, AHN, Estado, leg. 214/1, dossier 18.

71. ADV, Guernica, *1824 a 1830. Yndice de Oficios a la Superintendencia*, dispatch of the Vizcayan police to central headquarters, no. 371, 9 June 1826. Follow-ups on this and related matters, in AHN, Estado, libro no. 30, *Actas Originales del año 1826*, sessions of 8 and 21 August 1826.

72. A more complete discussion of this important *Memoria* in chapter 6 of this book. (See note 70 of chapter 6 for a complete reference.) All quotes are from the printed version.

73. *Memoria*, pp. 15–16.

74. *Memoria*, p. 17. Emphasis added.

75. See AMAE, CC, Bilbao, vol. 4, Regnaudin's 1827 annual report, dated 24 January 1828.

76. See ADV, Guernica, *1825 al 29. Representaciones Ministeriales. Hacienda*, and *1825 a 1827. Representaciones al Ministerio de la Guerra*.

77. In addition to the sources in notes 20 and 41, see Uhagon, *Informe*, pp. 8–9.

78. See chapter 4 in this book.

79. See the following: ACJG, Policía, reg. 12, dispatch no. 133 of the Vizcayan police to central headquarters, 9 May 1828; AMAE, CD, Espagne, vol. 748, communication of Regnaudin to the minister of foreign affairs, 11 May 1828; and ADV, Guernica, *Conferencias de las Provincias Bascongadas. 1812 a 1833*, session of 17 June 1828. During their 1828 stay in Bilbao —more on this in chapter 6 of this book—the monarchs were presented with petitions regarding important questions, among them some that were related to local iron production. Uhagon succinctly describes these demands; see Uhagon, *Informe*, p. 9. Significantly, the Vizcayan Diputación even offered to make the iron balcony for the Prado Museum in return for the duties' repeal; see ADV, Guernica, *1825 a 1829. Oficios Alta Clase*, letter of the provincial government to Gabriel José de Aizquibel, its agent at court, 7 November 1828.

80. See ADV, Guernica, *Conferencias de las Provincias Bascongadas. 1812 a 1833*, sessions of 14–16 January 1829 (at Mondragón); and ACJG, Ferrerías, reg. 2, 16 February 1829 session of the Permanent Commission for the Improvement of Iron Fabrication.

81. AHN, Estado, libro no. 39, *Actas Originales del año 1829*, session of 22 September.

82. Sagarmínaga, *Gobierno*, vol. 8, pp. 51–59.

83. See note 66.

84. ADV, Guernica, *Conferencias de las Provincias Bascongadas. 1812 a 1833*, session of 11 December. See also Sagarmínaga, *Gobierno*, vol. 8, pp. 85–88.

85. Sagarmínaga, *Gobierno*, vol. 8, p. 99. A commission report assailed the duties levied on Vizcayan products upon entering Castile, and charged

that local production was rapidly becoming less competitive on account of the tariffs.

86. AHN, Estado, libro no. 43, *Actas Originales del año 1833*, session of 4 February 1833.

87. ADV, Guernica, *1824 a 1826. Copiador de Oficios*, letters of the Vizcayan Diputación to the judge of contraband, 7 and 9 February 1824.

88. González, *Colección*, vol. 2, pp. 439–440, royal order of 9 November 1825. This directive reaffirmed the judge of contraband's earlier prerogatives.

89. AMAE, CC, Bilbao, vol. 3, communication to the minister of foreign affairs, 26 February 1824.

90. Considerable information on these matters in the following sources: (a) González, *Colección*, vol. 2, pp. 432–434; (b) OCSV, 1825, 21 January 1825 circular of the Vizcayan Diputación; (c) ADV, Guernica, *1825 al 1829. Representaciones. Ministerio de Gracia y Justicia*, letter of the Vizcayan Diputación to the ministry of that name, 12 August 1826. More on this particular episode in ADV, Guernica, *1824 a 1830. Yndice de Oficios a la Superintendencia*, dispatch no. 358 of the Vizcayan police to central headquarters, 14 August 1826; (d) ADV, Guernica, *1825 al 29. Representaciones Ministeriales. Hacienda*, petition of the Vizcayan Diputación to the minister of finance, 1 May 1827; (e) ADV, Guernica, *Competencia entre la Anteiglesia de Deusto con el Juez de Contrabando*. In particular, see the materials of June–July 1827. A related follow-up of this in ADV, Guernica, *1825 a 1829. Oficios Alta Clase*, letter of the Vizcayan Diputación to the corregidor, 31 July 1827; (f) APG, *Actas*, session of 7 November 1829; (g) AMAE, CC, Bilbao, vol. 4, communications of Regnaudin to the minister of foreign affairs, of 26 January 1829 and 27 February 1830, respectively; and (h) Gaminde, *Intereses*, pp. 4 and 7–17 passim. Among others, this fundamental work provides an excellent liberal interpretation of the judge of contraband's functions and attributes.

91. ADV, Guernica, *1824 a 1830. Yndice de Oficios a la Superintendencia*, dispatch no. 193 of the Vizcayan police to central headquarters, 25 April 1825.

92. All three can be consulted in *CD*, 1824, vol. 9, pp. 216–222.

93. Ibid., pp. 219–222: "*Real orden en que se prescriben las reglas que deben observarse para dar guías de géneros, y evitar el contrabando que se hace por las lineas de Aduanas de Cantabria, y las de las fronteras de . . . Soria, Aragón y Navarra.*"

94. Sagarmínaga, *Gobierno*, vol. 7, p. 425.

95. *Guía de la Real Hacienda*, 1825, pp. 73–103: "*Reglamento provisional para las columnas móviles de tropa activa que S.M. se ha dignado establecer en todos los distritos militares por vía de ensayo para perseguir y exterminar el contrabando.*" Dated 11 February 1825, the *Reglamento* carried Ballesteros's signature.

96. See notes 67 and 88 to this chapter, respectively.

97. ADV, Guernica, *1825 al 29. Representaciones Ministeriales. Hacienda*, petition of the Vizcayan government to the king, 26 November 1825. See also APG, *Actas*, session of 14 December 1825.

98. Suárez Verdeguer, *Ballesteros*, vol. 3, p. 92.

99. See the following: AHN, Estado, libro no. 28, *Actas Originales del año 1826*, session of 17 February 1826; *CD*, 1826, vol. 11, pp. 62–63, royal order of 7 March 1826; and [Estanislao de Kotska Bayo], *Historia de la vida y reinado de Fernando VII de España*, 3 vols. (Madrid: Imprenta de Repullés, 1842), vol. 3, pp. 280–281.

100. ADV, Guernica, *Conferencias de las Provincias Bascongadas. 1812 a 1833*, sessions of 14–16 January 1829. See also ACJG, Contrabando, dossier entitled "*Años 1826–29*" with interesting information.

101. *CD*, 1829, vol. 14, pp. 73–111. The *Cuerpo de Carabineros de Costas y Fronteras* was created by the royal decree of 9 March 1829. Considerable background material on this issue in ACJG, Carabineros, dossier no. 6.

102. ADV, Guernica, *1825 a 1829. Oficios Alta Clase*, letter of the Vizcayan Diputación to the General Direction of Revenues, 25 September 1829.

103. See ACJG, Carabineros, dossier no. 6, and Sagarmínaga, *Gobierno*, vol. 8, pp. 119–121.

104. See chapter 3 in this book, and chapter 4 passim.

105. Cavanilles's instructions are reproduced in Sagarmínaga, *Gobierno*, vol. 7, pp. 592–596. A slightly different version—though not significantly so—in ADV, Guernica, *Documentos Históricos Relativos al Señorío de Vizcaya*, vol. 1 (?). In particular see an unbound manuscript inside this volume entitled "*Ministerio de Hacienda-Reservado-Corte y Vizcaya 1829 y antecedentes.*" Worth underscoring, Cavanilles was also given two volumes of Tomás González's recently published *Colección*.

106. See Uhagon, *Informe*, p. 6.

107. See, for example, ADV, Guernica, *1825 al 29. Representaciones Ministeriales. Hacienda*, two petitions of the Vizcayan Diputación to Ferdinand VII, of 17 August and 7 December 1829, respectively. Extensive documentation concerning the Patiño Convention (and related matters) in González, *Colección*, vol. 2, pp. 317–349, section entitled "*Capitulados de 1727, 1728, 1729 y 1748.*"

108. See the previous note for a complete reference. See also Novia de Salcedo, *Defensa histórica*, vol. 4, pp. 72–145 passim and 211–219 for more on these issues. Completed in May 1829—though not published at that time—the essential *Defensa* distinctly influenced the Vizcayan leadership's opinions.

109. ADV, Guernica, *1824 a 1826. Copiador de Oficios*, letter of the Vizcayan Diputación to its Guipúzcoan counterpart, 24 December 1824.

110. González, *Colección*, vol. 2, pp. 435–437, royal order of 11 July 1825. In this document the central government cited numerous antecedents in support of its policies.

111. See the following: APG, *Actas*, session of 14 December 1825; Ballesteros's 1826 ministerial report, in Suárez Verdeguer, *Ballesteros*, vol. 3, pp. 52–55; and AHN, Estado, libro no. 29, *Actas Originales del año 1826*, session of 11 March 1826.

112. Suárez Verdeguer, *Ballesteros*, vol. 3, p. 55.

113. Ibid. See also *CD*, 1825, vol. 10, pp. 338–339, royal order of 21 December 1825; and Guiard, *Consulado*, vol. 2, p. 790.

114. Suárez Verdeguer, *Ballesteros*, vol. 3, p. 55.

115. See the following: ACJG, Expedientes y Escrituras Varias. 1823 a 1829, reg. 5, dossier entitled *"Expediente relativo a la habilitación de los Puertos de Bilbao y San Sebastián para el Comercio de América. 1828;"* Guiard, *Consulado*, vol. 2, pp. 790–794; ADV, Guernica, *Conferencias de las Provincias Bascongadas. 1812 a 1833*, sessions of June 1828 and January 1829; Uhagon, *Informe*, pp. 6–7; and *Gaceta de Madrid*, supplement to the 26 February 1828 issue.

116. ACJG, Policía, reg. 12, dispatch no. 56 to central headquarters, 29 February 1828.

117. Liberal P. P. de Uhagon of course favored the port's enfranchisement; see *Informe*, pp. 6–7. More on the positions of traditionalists and reformers in Guiard, *Consulado*, vol. 2, pp. 790–794. For a later view on this problem from an extreme liberal perspective, see Gaminde, *Intereses*, pp. 18–21.

118. Guiard, *Consulado*, vol. 2, pp. 790–794.

119. Ibid., p. 791: *"Había fijado el Consulado por base de sus gestiones 'el inalterable principio de habilitación sin contrafuero.'"*

120. ADV, Guernica, *Conferencias de las Provincias Bascongadas. 1812 a 1833*, sessions of 22–24 September 1828 (at Bilbao). See also Uhagon, *Informe*, pp. 6–7.

121. ADV, Guernica, *Conferencias de las Provincias Bascongadas. 1812 a 1833*, session of 14–16 January 1829.

122. See chapter 3 in this book, and chapter 4 passim.

123. See the following: Sagarmínaga, *Gobierno*, vol. 7, pp. 578–589 passim; ADV, Guernica, *1825 a 1829. Oficios Alta Clase*, letters of the Vizcayan Diputación to its commissioners in Madrid, 28 August, and 1 and 7 September 1829; *1825 al 29. Representaciones Ministeriales. Hacienda*, petitions of the Vizcayan Diputación to the king, 17 August and 7 December 1829; ACJG, *Diputación General. Correspondencia y Cuentas de los Diputados y Agentes en Madrid, Valladolid y Burgos, No. 1, Años de 1812 a 1838*; and AMAE, CC, Bilbao, vol. 4, communication of Regnaudin to the minister of foreign affairs, 13 July 1828.

124. AGS, Consejo Supremo de Hacienda, leg. 20, document entitled *"Minuta de Consulta de 25 de Septiembre, relativa a la exposición hecha por parte del Señorío de Vizcaya al cumplimiento de la R[ea]l or[de]n de 18 de Mayo de 1829."* On the whole, this dossier is extremely adverse to the Basque petitions. Unfortunately, I have been unable to consult the complete versions of the Supreme Council of Finance's important 19 August and 25 September 1829 consultas, although both are well summarized in the Council of Ministers' deliberations (see the next note).

125. APG, *Actas*, session of 7 November 1829.

126. Ibid.

127. Deeply aware of this, the Diputación revived the matter in a 24 November 1829 session of the provincial government; see Sagarmínaga, *Gobierno*, vol. 7, p. 591. Doubtless, as a result of this, the Diputación chose to press its earlier demands, doing so by way of the 7 December 1829 petition to the king which, in reality, merely restated the previous 17 August 1829 requests.

128. See APG, *Actas*, session of 28 November 1829; and AHN, leg. 3827, no. 47. Both sources contain the royal orders issued for Cavanilles's mission.

129. Uhagon, *Informe*, p. 9. See also Guiard, *Villa*, vol. 4, p. 446.

130. See notes 105 and 128.

131. Sagarmínaga, *Gobierno*, vol. 7, pp. 592–593. Several articles specifically zeroed in on the privileges and on their allegedly unreasonable interpretation by the Diputación.

132. A complete reference to this important piece in note 123.

133. Ibid.

134. See Uhagon, *Informe*, pp. 10–11; Sagarmínaga, *Gobierno*, vol. 7, p. 596; and chapter 3 in this book.

135. Sagarmínaga, *Gobierno*, vol. 8, p. 64. No date is given in this work for the order.

136. See chapter 4 in this book.

137. See ADV, Guernica, *Conferencias de las Provincias Bascongadas. 1812 a 1833*, sessions of 11 December (at Tolosa); and Sagarmínaga, *Gobierno*, vol. 8, pp. 85–88.

138. Sagarmínaga, *Gobierno*, p. 87. The document is dated 11 December 1830.

139. Ibid.

140. Ibid., p. 92.

141. Royal order of 14 November 1832; see ADV, Guernica, *Conferencias de las Provincias Bascongadas. 1812 a 1833*, sessions of 21–23 March 1833 (at Vitoria); Sagarmínaga, *Gobierno*, vol. 8, pp. 152–158; and AMAE, CPC, Espagne, vol. 5, Regnaudin's 1832 annual report, dated 14 March 1833. Finally, see José Múgica, *Carlistas, Moderados y Progresistas (Claudio Antón de Luzuriaga)* (San Sebastián: Biblioteca Vascongada de los Amigos del País, 1950), pp. iv–vi and 72–97 passim, for interesting information regarding the controversies in Guipúzcoa caused by the 1832 *habilitación*.

142. Sagarmínaga, *Gobierno*, vol. 8, pp. 154–155.

143. See chapter 3 in this book. Recall that a rollback had also occurred in 1814 after the War of Independence; see chapter 2.

144. See Suárez Verdeguer, *Ballesteros*, vol. 4, p. 264. Ballesteros left little doubt that important mutations had been in the offing earlier. Wrote the minister to the monarch: *"Bien comprenderá V.M. que hablo de la traslación de las aduanas al Pirineo por la frontera de Navarra; medida importantísima ya concebida por V.M. en los primeros años de su restitución al Trono."*

145. AMAE, CC, Bilbao, vol. 4, communication of Regnaudin to the minister of foreign affairs, 13 July 1828.

146. ADV, Guernica, *1825 a 1829. Oficios Alta Clase*, letter of the Vizcayan Diputación to the head of the customs administration of Cantabria, 12 August 1828.

147. See Rodrigo Rodríguez Garraza, *Navarra de Reino a Provincia (1828–1841)* (Pamplona: Universidad de Navarra, "Colección histórica," no. 21, 1968), pp. 88–93; and del Burgo, *Origen y fundamento del régimen foral de Navarra*, pp. 355–357.

148. The French government was understandably concerned with possible changes in the customs administration next door, and therefore followed events in Spain closely. In fact, French sources on this issue—particularly between 1828 and 1830—are too numerous to detail adequately here. Worth underscoring, however, there is considerable documentation in the ANP, F 7, 12,011, notably, in the correspondence of the sous-préfet of Bayonne to the French Ministry of the Interior.

149. AMAE, CC, Bilbao, vol. 4, communication to the minister of foreign affairs, 26 January 1829. The agent had recently voiced similar opinions; see AMAE, CD, Espagne, vol. 750, communication to the same party, 11 January 1829.

150. ADV, Guernica, *Conferencias de las Provincias Bascongadas. 1812 a 1833*, sessions of 14–16 January 1829. See also Sagarmínaga, *Gobierno*, vol. 7, pp. 563–565.

151. Sagarmínaga, *Gobierno*, vol. 7, pp. 563–565.

152. *OCSV*, 1829, circular dated 12 March 1829. See also, ADV, Guernica, *1824 a 1830. Yndice de Oficios a la Superintendencia*, dispatch no. 85 of the Vizcayan police to central headquarters, 13 March 1829.

153. Suárez Verdeguer, *Ballesteros*, vol. 4, p. 265. The ministerial report, as noted before, was dated 12 December.

154. Ibid., vol. 5, pp. 212 and 227. This report, as noted earlier, was dated 28 March.

155. Fontana, *Hacienda y estado*, pp. 298–303.

156. Suárez Verdeguer, *Ballesteros*, vol. 1, p. 393.

157. See notes 23–24, and Suárez Verdeguer, *Ballesteros*, vol. 5, pp. 253–286, document entitled *Informe que da en 3 de Septiembre de 1831 la Junta de Jefes de Hacienda, creada por R.O. de 9 de Enero y reunida de nuevo por otra de 22 de Julio [de 1831]*. In particular, see pp. 270–271. This was the second report of this junta.

158. Suárez Verdeguer, *Ballesteros*, vol. 5, pp. 277–279 and 285.

159. Ibid., vol. 5, p. 303. See also pp. 327, 329, and 336.

160. Ibid., vol. 1, p. 404. See note 28.

161. Another rare voice, raised in defense of the Basque provinces against the proposed shift in the customs bureaus, was that of Alcudia. See Suárez Verdeguer, *Ballesteros*, vol. 5, pp. 343–409, *Memoria* of the Count, dated 13 April 1832. In particular, see pp. 360–362 and 395.

162. See note 141.

163. Vizcayan liberalism for some time consistently had favored the transfer of the customs houses to the sea as a necessary measure to regulate and systematize trade, and to end the constant harassment by the judge of contraband at Bilbao. See Gaminde, *Intereses*, pp. 3–21 passim. Significantly, according to Francisco de Hormaeche, P. P. de Uhagon was unpopular among local traditionalists because he favored Bilbao's enfranchisement—a measure which, at least in some circles, was tantamount to asking for the establishment of customs houses there; (see the informative and suggestive "De las causas," p. 342). An excellent nineteenth-century liberal discussion of the purportedly beneficial aspects of the final transfer of the customs sites

in Pirala, *Historia*, vol. 1, pp. 127–128. Finally, brief and insightful observations on the customs issue and the consequences of the transfer of the offices in Javier Corcuera Atienza's excellent recent *Orígenes, ideología y organización del nacionalismo vasco, 1876–1904* (Madrid: Siglo XXI, 1979), pp. 37–44. Among other important comments, Corcuera Atienza remarks: *"Sobre todo, la década de los cuarenta va a ver inciarse la moderna industria siderúrgica"* (p. 43).

Chapter 5: Instruments of Counterrevolution

1. *Gaceta de Madrid*, supplement to the 13 January 1824 issue. The Basque provinces' objections to the order are recorded in a series of printed documents dated 30 April 1824, and which can be consulted in *OCSV*, 1824. For the earliest Vizcayan objections to the national police plan, see ADV, Guernica, *1823. Representaciones al Rey y otras autoridades*, petition of the Diputación to the monarch, 23 January 1824: *"Al Rey solicitando que la Diputación sea la que entienda en la Policía y empleados de esta."*

2. This point was clearly made in the Vizcayan Diputación's 23 January 1824 petition cited in note 1. See also *OCSV*, 1824, 30 January 1824 legal opinion of the Diputación's syndic, where similar objections were raised. Finally, the remarks of Talaru, the French ambassador to Madrid, are very much worth taking into consideration; see AMAE, CD, Espagne, vol. 726, letter to Châteaubriand, 1 March 1824.

3. The 23 January 1824 Vizcayan petition to the king demanded that the Diputación be recognized as the province's supreme police authority: *"que sea reconocida su Diputación general como Yntendente nato de Policía."* See also the 26 April 1824 royal order reproduced in *OCSV*, 1824, which is unequivocal: *"Solicitaron las tres provincias se las encargase a ellas exclusivamente el ramo [de policía] en sus respectivos distritos."*

4. 30 April 1824 printed documents cited in note 1. Emphasis added.

5. See ADV, Guernica, *1823. Representaciones al Rey y otras autoridades*, petition of the Basque diputaciones to the king, 12 June 1824; and ADV, Guernica, *1825 al 1829. Representaciones. Ministerio de Gracia y Justicia*, petition of the Vizcayan Diputación to the monarch, 1 September 1827.

6. *OCSV*, 1824, document entitled *"Reglamento de Policía del M.N. y M.L. Señorío de Vizcaya,"* 36 pp., with 140 articles divided into 18 chapters. This is certainly the code summarized in Sagarmínaga, *Gobierno*, vol. 7, pp. 399–400. Most Vizcayan police ordinances (and other printed police materials) can be consulted in ADV, Guernica, in a two-volume collection entitled *Circulares de Policía*. The first covers the years 1824–1827; the second, 1828–1830. Many of these documents, however, are also in *OCSV*, where I have consulted the majority of them.

7. See *OCSV*, 1824, circular of the Vizcayan Diputación, 15 June 1824. The ordinance's preamble clearly demonstrates the interim nature of some of the measures. See also Sagarmínaga, *Gobierno*, vol. 7, pp. 435–436, police ordinances dated 1 and 17 July 1824.

8. See ADV, Guernica, *Circulares de Policía* and *OCSV*.

9. Sagarmínaga, *Gobierno*, vol. 7, p. 435, police ordinance dated 1 July 1824.

10. Ibid., pp. 399–400. Further orders for the formation of a Vizcayan census in *OCSV*, 1825, police circular dated 26 August 1825.

11. The Bilbao and Lequeitio censuses, for example, are sheer gems of detail and exactitude. Both can be consulted in the ACJG. Unfortunately, the completed census for the province was forwarded to the central government, and I have been unable to locate it.

12. *OCSV*, 1825, circular of the Vizcayan Diputación, 30 August 1825. See also Sagarmínaga, *Gobierno*, vol. 7, pp. 476–477.

13. Same sources in the previous note. Interestingly, constitutionalist women were deemed sufficiently important and/or dangerous to warrant the formation of a separate political index: "*El índice de las mujeres se hará en papel separado que se titulará* Indice de las mujeres" (article 6).

14. Same sources as in the previous two notes (article 8).

15. ACJG, Policía, reg. 31, dispatch no. 129 of the Vizcayan police to central headquarters, 12 April 1833. All of the *Indices Inversos*—and related confidential materials in the Vizcayan police's possession—were sent to Madrid.

16. On rare occasions the Vizcayan police issued passports for travel on national soil.

17. *OCSV*, 1825. See also the original 8 May 1824 police charter cited earlier; in ibid., 1824, and in Sagarmínaga, *Gobierno*, vol. 7, pp. 399–400. Discussing the *cartas de seguridad*, S. E. Widdrington argued for their French origin; see *Sketches*, vol. 1, p. 204.

18. *OCSV*, 1824, police circular dated 22 September 1824. See in particular the passage that reads "*El pasaporte en regla debe tener las circunstancias siguientes,*" nos. 1–4.

19. *OCSV*, 1825, police circular dated 14 January 1825.

20. Ibid. See article 9, part 5.

21. See *OCSV*, 1824, police circular dated 25 August 1824, and *OCSV*, 1825, police circular dated 18 January 1825. Henry Inglis perceptively noted the important role of eating societies in Bilbao. His remarks illustrate well how these *tertulias* and *sociedades* could be organized along political lines; see *Spain in 1830*, 2 vols. (London: Whittaker, Treacher and Co., 1831), vol. 1, p. 25.

22. ACJG, Policía, reg. 22. The request was simply dated February 1825. In addition to Portugalete, the elder Uhagon had requested permission to travel to Plencia, Guecho, and Santurce—locations that the provincial authorities had recently made off-limits to constitutionalists without special documents (see note 21). Uhagon's request was finally approved by the Vizcayan police on 6 September 1825.

23. ACJG, Policía, reg. 22. Many of the requests can be consulted in this register. Through such petitions much can be learned of the leisure habits and property locations of notable Bilbao constitutionalists.

24. Ibid., petition of Ceferino Salazar, 6 February 1827.

25. ACJG, Policía, reg. 33, draft of a confidential letter of the Vizcayan

police to the director of the French police, 29 July 1824. In another suggestive instance of international cooperation, requesting the same vigilance as that accorded P. P. de Uhagon, in September 1824 the Vizcayan police notified Bayonne authorities of the imminent arrival there of Nicolás de Urcullu, a noted constitutionalist and allegedly one of the first to enroll in Bilbao's voluntary militias; see the same register, draft of a letter to the sous-préfet of Bayonne, 7 September 1824.

26. Important materials regarding these questions in ANP, F 7, 12,011.

27. See AHN, Consejos, leg. 12,333, reports for the period January–August 1827.

28. ACJG, Policía, reg. 23, dispatch no. 34 to central headquarters, 31 January 1831.

29. However, other measures also restricted the liberal community's movements. Significantly, there is evidence that late in the Ominous Decade absolutism's opponents were occasionally confined to a designated town or area (*asignación a residencia*). See, for example, the case of Antonio María de Barbara, a noted constitutionalist military commander who was confined in 1830 to the Valley of Llodio after having resided in Bilbao; in ACJG, Policía, reg. 13, dispatch no. 414 of the Vizcayan police to central headquarters (?), 6 December 1830. This officer's plight strongly paralleled that of Ildefonso de Sancho, the sometimes unruly Bilbao liberal lawyer, who in September 1824 had been restricted to the town of Munguía by the Vizcayan authorities.

30. See the following: (*a*) 8 May 1824 police charter (cited in note 6); (*b*) 1 July 1824 police ordinance (cited in note 7); and (*c*) 14 December 1825 police ordinance; in *OCSV*, 1825 and in Sagarmínaga, *Gobierno*, vol. 7, pp. 481–484. In the last ordinance the reference to "*posaderos . . . secretos*" might be an allusion to brothels although, admittedly, this is conjectural.

31. 14 December 1825 police ordinance, article 1 (cited in the previous note.)

32. Ibid., article 8. See also the 17 July 1824 police ordinance, article 2, (cited in note 7).

33. ACJG, Policía, reg. 22, letter of the police agent to the Vizcayan Diputación, 8 January 1827.

34. See ACJG, Policía, reg. 1. More on the surveillance of royalists in the following note. Given the stern prohibitions on certain kinds of meetings (in accordance with the 25 August 1824 ordinance cited earlier), special permission from the authorities was necessary. Many such requests can be consulted in ACJG, Policía, reg. 22. Some of the petitions were ostensibly for the organization of social clubs, conversation groups, billiards playing, and other recreational activities.

35. ACJG, Policía, reg. 1. The creation of this post was approved by the central government on 2 December 1824. Apparently an unsuccessful experiment, the effort was discontinued in October 1825. In the instructions given to Elias Storm, the Vizcayan police (among others) directed him to conduct surveillance of ultraroyalists who purportedly introduced political divisions in the population.

36. ACJG, Policía, reg. 27, letter of the mayor of the Concejo to the Vizcayan Diputación, 6 September 1830.

37. See, for example, the 14 December 1825 police ordinance, article 13 (cited in note 30). Other articles of the ordinance also urged the population to inform.

38. *OCSV*, 1828, police circular, 23 April 1828 (also in Sagarmínaga, *Gobierno*, vol. 7, pp. 552–553); and Sagarmínaga, *Gobierno*, vol. 8, pp. 140–143, document dated 2 July 1832. Unfortunately, the author does not inform the reader whether this last document was the product of the Vizcayan police, as seems likely.

39. Almost without exceptions, the use of firearms and gunpowder was a royalist monopoly during most of the 1823–1833 decade. The principal regulations and ordinances governing firearms and gunpowder are contained in the following documents: (*a*) 22 April 1823 circular of the Junta Provisional de Gobierno; Guiard, *Villa*, vol. 4, p. 377; (*b*) 2 September 1823 ordinance of the Corregidor in Vizcaya, Tiburcio de Eguiluz; ibid., p. 394; (*c*) 8 May 1824 police charter; *OCSV*, 1824 and in Sagarmínaga, *Gobierno*, vol. 7, pp. 399–400; (*d*) 25 August 1824 police ordinance; Sagarmínaga, *Gobierno*, vol. 7, pp. 438–439; (*e*) 30 September 1824 police ordinance; ibid., pp. 439–440; (*f*) 12 October 1824 police ordinance; ibid., pp. 440–442; (*g*) 18 January 1825 police ordinance; *OCSV*, 1825, *Circulares de Policia*, vol. 1; and (*h*) 5 June 1825 police ordinance; Sagarmínaga, *Gobierno*, vol. 7, p. 449. Other arms-related matters will be detailed accordingly.

40. See (*d*) in the previous note.

41. See (*e*) in note 39, articles 1 and 3.

42. *OCSV*, 1825, 18 January 1825 police ordinance, article 10.

43. Bacon, *Six Years in Biscay*, p. 74. "Allende" and "Salazar" are probably erroneous references to the Allendesalazar family, a prominent Vizcayan household.

44. Sagarmínaga, *Gobierno*, vol. 8, p. 159. The Diputación's decision was in direct response to a 26 March 1833 royal order. The measure marked a sharp departure from policies of the recent past. More on these matters in chapter 7 of this book.

45. On the Vizcayan police's early difficulties, see ACJG, Policía, registers 22 and 30. The latter register in particular has considerable information on the provincial police's initial May 1824 measures. In addition to the Vizcayan Diputación's protests and those of the other provinces (see notes 1–5) the Bilbao city council had also initially opposed the police; see Guiard, *Villa*, vol. 4, p. 424. The municipal corporation had strongly favored the reestablishment of the Inquisition, and this may have accounted for its resistance to the police. See also S. E. Widdrington's interesting remarks on the creation of the Spanish police, where, among others, he declares the new body to be "political inquisition"; *Sketches*, vol. 1, pp. 198–199.

46. AMAE, CC, Bilbao, vol. 4, communication to the minister of foreign affairs, 3 October 1830.

47. For a list of employees of the Vizcayan Diputación, among them police officials, see Sagarmínaga, *Gobierno*, vol. 7, pp. 591–592.

48. See Gaminde, *Intereses*, p. 34; Bacon, *Six Years in Biscay*, pp. 74–76; and Bayo, *Historia*, vol. 1, p. 135. Another classic liberal criticism against the Vizcayan police in Lemonauria, *Ensayo crítico*, pp. 43–44.

49. APG, *Actas*, session of 10 October 1825. See also the important petition of the Vizcayan Diputación to Ferdinand VII of 1 September 1827; in ADV, Guernica, *1825 al 1829. Representaciones. Ministerio de Gracia y Justicia*. This remonstrance basically requested that the provincial police continue under the Diputación's authority and control. More on these questions in Sagarmínaga, *Gobierno*, vol. 7, pp. 543–545.

50. Sagarmínaga, *Gobierno*, vol. 7, pp. 543–545; and *OCSV*, 1827, circular of the Vizcayan Diputación which reproduces the 4 October 1827 royal order (at Tarragona).

51. APG, *Actas*, session of 7 March 1829.

52. Ibid., session of 24 October 1829.

53. Ibid., sessions of 10 July and 28 August 1830, and 16 June 1832.

54. See Sagarmínaga, *Gobierno*, vol. 7, p. 329, 27 April 1823 "*reglamento para la persecución de malhechores*." For the creation of the corps at the national level, see Federico Suárez Verdeguer, "Los cuerpos de Voluntarios Realistas. Notas para su estudio," *Anuario de Historia del Derecho Español* (1956): pp. 47–88. The corps were established on 10 July 1823.

55. Sagarmínaga, *Gobierno*, vol. 7, pp. 419–421. Lest there be any confusion about this, although the 26 February 1824 charter for the royalist volunteers was communicated to the provincial government by the military governor of Guipúzcoa, the document originated in Madrid. This charter was apparently in operation until the 8 June 1826 code went into effect (about which more will be said below.)

56. Sagarmínaga, *Gobierno*, vol. 7, pp. 419–421, 25 May 1824 charter (article 1): "*El armamento de los pueblos de Vizcaya no puede tener otro caracter que el prescrito por su especial reglamento criminal, ni diversa denominación que la de paisanos armados*."

57. Importantly, the 25 May 1824 charter for the Paisanos reaffirmed an important clause of the 24 May 1823 code, namely, that the Diputación was the commander-in-chief of the provincial militias. See article 9 of the 24 May 1823 document and article 5 of the 25 May 1824 regulations; in Sagarmínaga, *Gobierno*, vol. 7, pp. 363 and 420, respectively.

58. *OCSV*, 1824, 24 August 1824 session of the provincial government. The measures adopted this day were printed separately and circulated by the Diputación. Although much responsibility was seemingly placed on the local authorities' shoulders, it is clear that the Vizcayan executive remained very much in charge.

59. See, for example, AMAE, CD, Espagne, vol. 726, document entitled "*Coup d'oeil sur l'Espagne au 30 Janvier 1824*." The author, a certain "Mr. de Caze"—possibly Francois de Caze, later Regnaudin's assistant at Bilbao —remarked sarcastically that public disorder in the Basque provinces was so great that one tended to think that a region was actually calm when it was not in total turmoil or revolution. Numerous reports of the French military command at Vitoria (Division du Haut Ébre) attest to those areas' extreme

sociopolitical volubility. Many of these reports can be consulted in ANP, F 7, 12,011. See also the following: Guiard, *Villa*, vol. 4, pp. 415–426 passim; ADV, Guernica, *1824 a 1830. Yndice de Oficios a la Superintendencia*, dispatches nos. 27, 39, and 54 of the Vizcayan police to central headquarters, 21 June, 2 July, and 16 July 1824, respectively. For more on these disorders, see ACJG, Policía, reg. 30. The central government was understandably concerned by the disturbances. See, for instance, Calomarde's letter to the corregidor in Vizcaya expressing the king's concern over the "frequent alteration" of "public tranquility" in Bilbao by the Guardia de Honor; in ADV, Guernica, *Reales Cédulas y Reales Órdenes Dirigidas al Señor Corregidor*, 6 October 1824. For the Vizcayan response, see ADV, Guernica, *1823. Representaciones al Rey y otras autoridades*, letter of the Diputación to Calomarde, 12 October 1824.

60. ANP, F 7, 12,011, report from the general commander to the French minister of war, 14 April 1824 (at Toledo). This register contains considerable information on these matters, in particular an important dossier on the Spanish royalist militias and the problems of disarmament in the Basque provinces.

61. Guiard, *Villa*, vol. 4, pp. 415–418. See also ANP, F 7, 12,011, letter of the sous-préfet of Bayonne to the French minister of the interior, 26 June 1824.

62. Guiard, *Villa*, vol. 4, pp. 420–421. Guiard fails to inform the reader as to the document's destination—if any. Among the signers was the ubiquitous Matías de Landa, an influential ultraroyalist and future Carlist.

63. The principal sources for the study of this riot are the following: Guiard, *Villa*, vol. 4, p. 419; AHN, Consejos, leg. 3744, exp. 25, (this dossier contains important reports from the Vizcayan police and the corregidor); ADV, Guernica, *Gestión política en el Señorío del Marqués de Villarías*, passim; ADV, Guernica, *1823. Representaciones al Rey y otras autoridades* letter of the Vizcayan Diputación to Calomarde, 12 October 1824, (cited in note 59); and, finally, AMAE, CC, Bilbao, vol. 4, reports of the French commercial agent in Bilbao for the period in question.

64. Interesting (though limited) information on the Miqueletes in ACJG, Policía, reg. 30, dispatch no. 98 of the Vizcayan police to central headquarters, 6 August 1824. Used primarily as mountain soldiers to track down smugglers and maintain order in the countryside, this corps was also used in Bilbao to protect the seat of the provincial government, to whom they were directly and ultimately accountable. Apparently created in 1814, the Miqueletes were a small force—some fifty men in 1824—and do not appear to have held a clear-cut political orientation or preference. In fact, on this occasion they do not seem to have opposed the Paisanos for political and ideological reasons, having only moved against the troublemakers at the Diputación's request and for no other apparent reasons. More on their significance in chapter 7 of this book.

65. AHN, Consejos, leg. 3744, no 25. See in particular the Vizcayan police's report dated 1 October 1824, and the corregidor's dated the next day. According to Guiard, *"se clamó sin rebozo, 'Muera el Marqués de Villa-*

rías!'" The hastily drawn 30 September 1824 police ordinance on the use of firearms was a direct consequence of this event and a concession to the rioters.

66. ADV, Guernica, *Gestión política en el Señorío del Marqués de Villarías*, rough draft of a letter of the Marquis to León de Jáuregui, 6 October 1824. On attempts to vindicate and rehabilitate Villarías—which dragged on for years—see Sagarmínaga, *Gobierno*, vol. 8, pp. 62–63, and AHN, Consejos, leg. 3744, exp. 25.

67. ADV, Guernica, *1824 a 1830. Yndice de Oficios a la Superintendencia*, dispatch no. 179 of the Vizcayan police to central headquarters, 8 October 1824. Note the possible confusion arising from these corps' overlapping names and nomenclatures.

68. ADV, Guernica, *Gestión política en el Señorío del Marqués de Villarías*, letter to the Marquis, 9 October 1824 (from Bilbao).

69. Guiard asserts that the charter of the Guardia was modified; see *Villa*, vol. 4, p. 418. This passage contains brief details on the changes in the militias' chain of command.

70. For a vivid description of the passionate atmosphere among Bilbao royalists, see Guiard, *Villa*, vol. 4, pp. 424–425. Additional evidence of strong royalist esprit de corps and sociopolitical cohesion in ACJG, Policía, reg. 1. This register contains lists of royalist *tertulias* and social gatherings in Bilbao around 1825.

71. Sagarmínaga, *Gobierno*, vol. 7, p. 466, session of 14 July 1825. See also pp. 472–473.

72. Admittedly in part a conjecture, this assertion is not without foundation. Whether liked or not by Vizcayan royalists, the French had contributed substantially to the preservation of order in Bilbao. Hence, their imminent departure might have created fears among royal administrators that an important vacuum was about to occur—one perhaps not adequately filled by the Vizcayan makeshift militias.

73. ADV, Guernica, *1824 a 1830. Yndice de Oficios a la Superintendencia*, dispatch no. 198, 22 October 1824: *"Se dirige a V.Y. el estado del número de Voluntarios Realistas de este Señorío conocidos en el con el nombre de Paisanos Armados de Guardias de Honor."* Again, it is well to emphasize how the terminology used to describe the corps lends itself to considerable confusion.

74. For the role of the Vizcayan royalist corps in the disorder of June–July 1825, see Guiard, *Villa*, vol. 4, pp. 425–426. See also the reports of Elías Storm, the Vizcayan police's secret agent, which have abundant and interesting information on the mid-1825 disturbances in Bilbao (ACJG, Policia, reg. 1). Extensive and detailed descriptions of these disturbances in AHN, Consejos, leg. 3702, nos. 35 and 36. In addition, these dossiers—particularly no. 36—contain important information on opposition to the central government's militia-related measures in the other Basque provinces. See also APG, *Actas*, sessions of 24 and 29 June, 1, 9, and 10 July, 30 August, and 1 and 3 September 1825. The new charter of the Guipuzcoan royalist corps (dated 28 July 1825) caused noticeable apprehension among royal aides,

some of whom expressed strong reservations about the emphasis given in the document to the provincial fueros. An original copy of the charter can be consulted in the dossier no. 36 cited above.

75. APG, *Actas*. Although the council seems to have existed earlier, the body's proceedings are only conserved from 1825 on. There are also unsolved questions regarding materials that were apparently misplaced or lost.

76. APG, *Actas*, session of the same date. Similar dispositions were adopted by the council in a 13 October 1825 meeting.

77. AHN, Consejos, leg. 3702, exp. 36: "*Estado que manifiesta la fuerza efectiva de las pártidas de a veinte hombres de los Paisanos Armados . . . conforme al decreto de la Junta General de 25 de Mayo, del año de 1824.*" The "*Estado*" is signed by Martín León de Jáuregui and is dated 10 July 1825 (at Guernica). (This official is almost certainly the same one that sometimes simply went by the name of León.)

78. ACJG, Policía, reg. 30, dispatch no. 264 of the Vizcayan police to central headquarters (?), 29 November 1824.

79. APG, *Actas*, session of 3 September 1825. Unless noted otherwise, the minister's remarks that follow are from this meeting of the council.

80. S. E. Widdrington expressed strikingly similar remarks later. Speaking of the Basque provinces, the author observed that the "territory of republicans [had] fifty thousand men . . . armed ready to turn out in an instant to fight the troops of their sovereign, should any attempt be made by the Castilians on their *fueros* or privileges;" in *Sketches*, vol. 1, pp. 120–121.

81. APG, *Actas*, session of 3 September 1825. The emphasis is the minister's. Salazar used the suggestive term "*milicia aforada*" to describe the Basque royalist corps.

82. APG, *Actas*, sessions of 24 June and 5 September 1825. More on these questions in the council's meetings cited in note 73.

83. See in particular ADV, Guernica, *1826 a 1829. Libro de Armamento.* More on this question in ADV, Guernica, *1825 a 1829. Oficios al Capitán General de Guipúzcoa.* See also the 22 December 1826 questionnaire circulated by the Diputación throughout the province requesting information on the Paisanos' armament and state of readiness; in *OCSV*, 1826. More in note 86 on the Vizcayan government's vigorous efforts to secure armament for its under-equipped Paisanos.

84. ACJG, Brigadas de Paisanos Armados, reg. 9. See in particular the dossier entitled, "*Expediente donde resulta todo lo obrado a consecuencia del Real Decreto de 1 de Mayo de 1826 . . . por el que se dispone que la misma Diputación quede encargada de la subinspección de las fuerzas que voluntariamente se hallan inscritas en el y se inscriban en adelante.*"

85. *Adición al Reglamento para los Voluntarios Realistas del Reino correspondiente a las Provincias Vascongadas* (Madrid: Imprenta de Don José del Collado, 1826). Both this addendum and the charter are dated 8 June 1826. In the future the central government and the Basque leaderships would continually refer to the *Adición*—the royal administration stressing the desirability of modifying it or annulling it altogether, the diputaciones attempting to preserve it in its entirety.

86. In addition to the materials cited in note 83, see ADV, Guernica, *1825 a 1827. Representaciones al Ministerio de la Guerra*, petition of the Vizcayan Diputación to the king, 1 April 1826. Among others, the provincial government requested 4,000 rifles that were deposited at Santoña. See also ADV, Guernica, *1824 a 1830. Yndice de Oficios a la Superintendencia*, dispatch no. 424 of the Vizcayan police to central headquarters, 26 June 1826.

87. Even before 1826, the Diputación had already adopted certain precautions. See, for instance, the 24 August 1824 measures of the provincial government (alluded to earlier) after a series of disturbances and invasion attempts at Tarifa. Many of them dealt with problems of coastal defense; see Sagarmínaga, *Gobierno*, vol. 7, pp. 437–438. More recently, on 17 March 1826, the Diputación had also taken preventive measures to forestall an invasion by sea; ibid., vol. 7, p. 485. Additional references to coastal issues below, notably in the Paisanos' various charters.

88. An excellent example of this in ADV, Guernica, *1824 a 1830. Yndice de Oficios a la Superintendencia*, dispatch no. 45 of the Vizcayan police to central headquarters, 22 January 1827.

89. Both quotes are from the preamble to the interim 29 January 1827 charter of the Paisanos, a copy of which can be consulted in *OCSV*, 1827. A summarized version of the code in Sagarmínaga, *Gobierno*, vol. 7, pp. 492–494. The preamble also contains important information on local political and military affairs. The document's conservative prose and ideology bear the unmistakable imprint of the Novia de Salcedo–Valde-espina Diputación. In addition to the signatures of the general deputies, the charter carries those of the corregidor Eladio Alonso Valdenebro, the syndic Miguel Antonio de Inunciaga, and the secretary of the provincial government, Diego Antonio de Basaguren. The document is dated at Bilbao. An interesting rationale for the interim charter in ADV, Guernica, *1826 a 1829. Libro de Armamento*, letter of the Vizcayan Diputación to the inspector general of royalist volunteers, 29 January 1827.

90. Nine pages long and unnumbered, the 29 January 1827 charter is divided into three chapters and forty articles. The chapters are entitled (1) *"Reunión de veitenas para la formación de compañías,"* (2) *"Formación de compañías de Artilleros para el servicio de Baterías de la costa,"* and (3) *"Reunión de compañías por distritos y Delegados de ellos."*

91. Articles 32–40. The charter also saw the appearance of a *"Delegado de Distrito,"* a post which, as far as I know, was not in existence before. The *delegado* was to be the liaison between the Diputación and the leaders of the Paisanos at the local township level (article 34). It is highly probable that the *delegado* was the direct forerunner of the future *Jefes de Brigada*, section or district commanders, of whom there would be six in all.

92. See the Vizcayan Diputación's 29 January 1827 letter cited in note 89. As stated previously, the purported Vizcayan specificity was a favorite theme of local conservatives. Through this leitmotiv, traditionalists defended the province's privileges, autonomy, and in this case also its military organization.

93. See ACJG, Brigadas de Paisanos Armados, reg. 9 (in particular a large table-like composite dated March 1827); and ADV, Guernica, *1826 a 1829. Libro de Armamento,* "*Estado general de la fuerza organizada en el Señorío,*" March 1827.

94. ANP, F 7, 12,011, letter of the sous-préfet of Bayonne to the French minister of the interior, 5 February 1827. This letter apparently served as the basis of a report of the police chief Franchet to the French minister of foreign affairs, 11 February 1827 (in AMAE, CD, Espagne, vol. 744). See also the 15 May 1827 proclamation of General Blas de Fournas, captain general of Guipúzcoa, carrying out the central government's instructions for the disarmament of the Guipuzcoan royalist corps (a copy of which can be consulted in ANP, F 7, 12,011). More on the last issue in a letter of the sous-préfet of Bayonne to the French minister of the interior, 26 May 1827 (ANP, F 7, 12,011), and below in note 95.

95. ANP, F 7, 12,011, letter of the sous-préfet of Bayonne to the French minister of the interior, 29 July 1827. Remarked this official: "It cannot be concealed that in calling the people to arms the [Vizcayan] general assembly might not have also searched for the means with which to shelter the province from a military operation similar to that with which General Fournas recently struck Guipúzcoa."

96. See, for example, ANP, F 7, 12,011, letters of the sous-préfet of Bayonne to the French minister of the interior, 1 and 10 February 1827. The last document in particular stressed the Vizcayan authorities' military preparations. Important information on this period's matters in Baron de Montevilla, "El Armamento General del Señorío de Vizcaya (1804–1833)," *Revista Internacional de Estudios Vascos,* vol. 22 (1931), pp. 420–435 passim (hereafter cited as "Armamento").

97. ADV, Guernica, *1825 a 1829. Oficios de Pueblos,* letter of the Diputación to the province's ecclesiastical authorities, 10 March 1827. More on this question in Montevilla, "Armamento," pp. 425–427.

98. See the Council of State's important 24 May 1830 consulta which traces the chronology of the dispute; in AHN, Estado, libro no. 56. More information on these matters in AHN, Estado, libro no. 40, *Actas Originales del año 1830,* sessions of 17 May and 23 August 1830; as well as in the council's 23 August 1830 consulta; in ibid., no. 56. The Vizcayan Diputación naturally backed the Guipuzcoan claims and positions against centralist controls; see Sagармínaga, *Gobierno,* vol. 8, pp. 114–115.

99. ACJG, Brigadas de Paisanos Armados, reg. 9. In particular see the table-like composite dated July 1827. As before, the percentage of well-armed personnel remained at almost exactly 60 percent.

100. For this gathering's military measures, see Sagarmínaga, *Gobierno,* vol. 7, pp. 513–542 passim, and *OCSV,* 1827.

101. *OCSV,* 1827, report of the *Comisión del punto de armamento* to the juntas, 17 July 1827. The quote is from a kind of preamble or foreword to the main body of recommendations.

102. In other words, in addition to Ibargoitia and Rotaeche, of the fourteen individuals who signed the 17 July 1827 report, five others would be-

come influential leaders of the Paisanos: Labarrieta, Arazamendi, Batiz, and Pedro Antonio and Agustín de Ventades.

103. *OCSV*, 1827. The document carries the signatures of the four original members of the Permanent Commission: Valde-espina, Novia de Salcedo, Ibargoitia, and Rotaeche. The charter was printed and circulated by the Vizcayan Diputación, which, at the time, was headed by Marcos Joaquín de Retuerto and Francisco Javier de Batiz, the general deputies. The printed copy also carries the names of the corregidor, Eladio Alonso de Valdenebro, and of the new syndic, José Manuel de Murgoitio. It is twenty-four pages long.

104. The degree of integration of Bilbao's militias into the general organization of the Paisanos remains an open question. However, in 1830 a royalist contingent from that city—the first battalion of the Guardia de Honor—was sent to Hernani to repel Mina's invasion of Navarra; see Guiard, *Villa*, vol. 4, pp. 437–438. More on Bilbao's paramilitary corps during this period in ibid., pp. 360–459 passim.

105. Emphasis added.

106. Interesting information on these questions in Montevilla, "Armamento," which concentrates on the Brigadas' fourth section under Valde-espina's leadership. The Diputación strongly encouraged the Paisanos to acquire better military skills; see, for example, the provincial government's two 31 March 1832 directives. One was addressed to the Paisanos, the other to the Vizcayan townships. Both can be consulted in *OCSV*, 1832, and in Sagarmínaga, *Gobierno*, vol. 8, pp. 134–138.

107. *OCSV*, 1832. The Spanish text is extremely ambiguous because of the term *país*, which means country in the sense of nation, but also region or province in the sense of native land.

108. The August 1833 figure is from Montevilla, "Armamento," p. 435. The October 1833 one is from Bacon, *Six Years in Biscay*, p. 94: "A short time after the outbreak in 1833, I was informed at the diputacion that the number of royalists on the muster rolls in Biscay was 14,276." Earlier, Bacon writes that according to the *Guia de Forasteros*, published in 1833, Vizcaya could raise 14,658 men, a figure I have been unable to confirm; ibid., p. 10. Considerable additional information on these matters in the same work, pp. 93–104 passim.

109. Bacon, *Six Years in Biscay*, p. 94: "An immense number, in proportion to the population, being nearly one-half of those able to bear arms."

110. Montevilla, "Armamento," p. 433. The passage is apparently from a draft of a letter of the Marquis to an unknown party, 20 June 1832 (at Ermua). Emphasis added.

111. AMAE, CPC, Espagne, vol. 5, communication of the commercial agent to the French minister of foreign affairs, 11 November 1832.

112. See the following for the 1827 events: *OCSV*, 1827, circular of the Diputación, 12 October 1827; AHN, Consejos, leg. 3849, no. 20; ACJG, Policía, reg. 4; ADV, Guernica, *1826 a 1829. Libro de Armamento*, letter of the Diputación to the inspector general of royalist volunteers, 8 October 1827; ADV, Guernica, *1825 al 1829. Representaciones. Ministerio de Gracia y*

Justicia, letter of the Diputación to Calomarde (?), 15 October 1827; Sagar-mínaga, *Gobierno*, vol. 7, pp. 545–547; and, finally, *OCSV*, 1827, letter of Minister of War Zambrano to the Diputación, 19 October 1827, thanking the provincial government for its extraordinary efforts in smashing Lausa-garreta's band. The communication explicitly mentioned the services rendered by the Vizcayan Paisanos. For the Vizcayan ramifications of the July Revolution and Mina's ill-fated 1830 invasion of Navarra, see Sagarmínaga, *Gobierno*, vol. 8, pp. 63–83 passim; ACJG, Expedientes, reg. 6, dossier entitled *"Estractos de los espedientes relativos a la Ynvasión verificada por los revolucionarios refugiados en Francia"*; ACJG, Policía, reg. 13; Guiard, *Villa*, vol. 4, pp. 437–438; Montevilla, "Armamento," p. 427; and *OCSV*, 1830, circulars of the Diputación, particularly those of 21 September, 16 October, and 27 November 1830.

113. APG, *Actas*, session of 24 October 1829.

114. AHN, Estado, libro no. 40, *Actas Originales del año 1830*, session of 17 May 1830. See also the Council's 24 May 1830 consulta to the monarch; ibid., libro 56.

115. See note 112.

116. More on the Paisanos in chapter 6 of this book, passim.

117. ADV, Guernica, *1825 al 1829. Representaciones. Ministerio de Gracia y Justicia*, letter-report of the Diputación to the ministry of that name, 22 December 1826.

118. ADV, Corr., leg. 390, exp. 2. The artisan, Eizaguirre, was 23 or 24 years old.

119. Ibid.

120. Ibid.

121. ACJG, Policía, reg. 27, letter from the authorities of Gordejuela to the Vizcayan Diputación, 24 October 1830.

122. See, for example, Lemonauría, *Ensayo*, p. 44; Hormaeche, "De las causas," pp. 339–344; the anonymous *Observaciones*, p. 23; and Uhagon, *Informe*, passim. Finally, see Bacon's numerous disparaging remarks in *Six Years in Biscay*, pp. 74–104 passim.

123. Uhagon, *Informe*, p. 11.

124. Ibid.

125. ACJG, Policía, reg. 31, dispatch no. 164 to central headquarters, 13 May 1833. More on the reformers' theme of economy in dispatch no. 239, 12 July 1833, which I return to below (in the same register).

126. ACJG, Policía, reg. 32, rough draft of an unnumbered letter of the Diputación to central headquarters, 24 June 1833. In this register, see also a letter of the Vizcayan police to the corregidor, dated the same day, expressing similar fears regarding the liberals' participation in the upcoming juntas.

127. ACJG, Policía, reg. 32, letter to central headquarters, 1 July 1833. This communication was properly written, but the signatures at the end are crossed out. Perhaps another one, similarly written, was sent in its place. However, at this point this is conjectural.

128. Uhagon, *Informe*, p. 12. The emphasis is in the text, though it is difficult to know whether it is the author's or the editor's.

129. Hormaeche, "De las causas," p. 343. More on this key question in chapter 7.

130. Sagarmínaga, *Gobierno*, vol. 8, pp. 146–148. More on this in Manuel Llauder, *Memorias documentadas del teniente general don Manuel Llauder, Marqués de Valle de Ribas* (Madrid: I. Boix, 1844), p. 82 of the text and pp. 36–37 of the appendix (document no. 27). Again, additional information on this important matter in chapter 7.

131. *Galería militar contemporanea, o sea coleccion de biografías y retratos*, 2 vols. (Madrid: Sociedad Tipográfica de Hortelano y Companía, 1845–1846), (hereafter cited as *Galería*), vol. 1, p. 75, letter of 9 October 1833.

132. Uhagon, *Informe*, p. 6.

133. Widdrington, *Sketches*, vol. 1, pp. 329–330. The last remark was clearly an overstatement. Of course there were some, if few, royal troops in the region, notably in Guipúzcoa.

Chapter 6: Economic Crisis, Reform, and Class Conflict

1. ADV, *1825 a 1829. Oficios de Alta Clase*, letter of the Vizcayan Diputación to the Royal Junta on Tariffs, 2 September 1828. For the clear predominance of maize in Vizcaya, see Fernández de Pinedo, *Crecimiento*, pp. 171–172.

2. ACJG, Policía, reg. 12, dispatch no. 127 of the Vizcayan police to central headquarters, 2 May 1828. See also ADV, Guernica, *1824 a 1830. Yndice de Oficios a la Superintendencia*, dispatches 94 and [unnumbered] of the Vizcayan police to central headquarters, dated 12 January and 29 June 1827, respectively. Numerous ordinances enacted during this era dealt with the problems of transiency and beggary. For example, see the following circulars of the Diputación: 25 November 1825, in Sagarmínaga, *Gobierno*, vol. 7, p. 479; 30 September 1828, ibid., vol. 7, pp. 560–561; 14 May 1830, ibid., vol. 8, pp. 60–61; 4 October 1831, ibid., vol. 8, p. 130; 6 August 1833, *OCSV*, 1833 (apparently not in Sagarmínaga). The corregidor in Vizcaya also could legislate in these general areas. See the eight-point ordinance (*bando*) issued by the corregidor on 8 March 1824 (at Bilbao), in *OCSV*, 1824.

3. González, *Colección*, vol. 2, pp. 431–432, *"Real orden dictando varias providencias para impedir la introducción de géneros extrangeros."* See also ADV, Guernica, *1825 a 1829. Oficios de Pueblos*, letter of the Vizcayan Diputación to Tomás de Cortezena, 27 May 1826. In the communication, the provincial government expressed disapproval of grain imports at Bermeo.

4. AMAE, CC, Bilbao, vol. 4, letters to the minister of foreign affairs, 1 October and 3 November 1828, respectively.

5. See the price series of the Convent of Saint Augustin at Bilbao, in AHN, Clero, reg. 18,169 and 18,170. On the collapse of Spanish agricultural prices during this period, see Fontana, *Hacienda y estado*, pp. 332–333. The author suggests important connections between the impoverishment of small farmers and the rise of Carlism.

6. There is considerable evidence of this throughout the 1823–1833 de-

cade. See AMAE, CD, Espagne, vol. 745, letter of Regnaudin to the minister of foreign affairs, 6 September 1827; and AMAE, CC, Bilbao, vol. 4, letter of the commercial agent to the same party, 26 January 1829. Finally, consider the interesting testimony in *El Correo, Periódico Literario y Mercantil*, [Madrid] no. 90, 6 February 1829.

7. ADV, Guernica, *1823. Representaciones al Rey y otras autoridades.*

8. SHAT, Mémoires Historiques, no. 805/1, document entitled "*Notice Sur la Campagne d'Espagne de 1823 Par Mr Dauvais, commandant d'État-major,*" Strasbourg, 9 March 1824.

9. Fernández de Pinedo's massive work contributes substantially to the elucidation of these hitherto little-studied questions. See in particular *Crecimiento*, chaps. 8–9.

10. See, for example, Capefigue, *Récit des opérations de l'Armée en Espagne, sous les ordres de S.A.R. Mgr Duc d'Angouleme. Accompagné de notices biographiques et géographiques et suivi de considérations sur les résultats politiques de cette guerre* (Paris: E. Gide, 1823), pp. 73–75. Other similar accounts could be summoned forth. One of the most lavish in praise of Basque agriculture is that of Edward Bell Stephens, *The Basque Provinces: Their Political State, Scenery, and Inhabitants With Adventures Amongst the Carlists and Christinos*, 2 vols. (London: Whittaker and Co., 1837), vol. 1, pp. 15–16, 18–19, 60–62, 124–126, 138–139, 177–178, and 205. This testimony is all the more suggestive inasmuch as it occurs in the midst of the Carlist War.

11. Inglis, *Spain in 1830*, vol. 1, pp. 38–39. For a far more extensive modern treatment of land reclamation in the Basque region, see Fernández de Pinedo, *Crecimiento*, pp. 192–212 and 227–230.

12. AMAE, CC, Bilbao, vol. 4, Regnaudin's 1827 annual report, 24 January 1828.

13. *Colección de lo más indispensable y precioso para el cultivo de la viña. Y modo de hacer y gobernar el vino por Don . . . Dedícala a los honrados labradores del M.N. y M.L. Señorío de Vizcaya a quienes demuestra en un discurso preliminar la necesidad de aplicarse al cultivo de la vid si se ha de evitar la ruina del País* (Bilbao: Eusebio de Larumbe, 1830).

14. See Manuel González Portilla's unpublished master's thesis entitled *La población en la zona minera y la Ría de Bilbao en el siglo XIX. Baracaldo un ejemplo del paso de una demografía de Antiguo régimen a la Revolución industrial* (University of Valencia [Spain], 1969–1970), passim, in particular appendices numbered 10, 13, 15, and 16.

15. Fernández de Pinedo, "La entrada de la tierra," p. 114: "*entre la guerra de Independencia y la Carlista el ritmo de ventas parece ser que menguó, sin por eso cesar.*" Of the same author, see *Crecimiento*, pp. 313–317.

16. Fernández de Pinedo, "La entrada de la tierra," pp. 114–115.

17. Ibid., pp. 120–121.

18. Ibid., p. 117. See also p. 100.

19. Ibid., pp. 123–124.

20. Ibid., pp. 100 and 125. For popular protests against enclosure, see pp. 117–118.

21. Bacon, *Six Years in Biscay*, p. 74.

22. Ibid., p. 103.

23. These key questions will hopefully be answered by future studies in socioeconomic history.

24. AMAE, CC, Bilbao, vol. 3, 7 January 1824.

25. In addition to Regnaudin's voluminous reports which often touch on this question, see Pascual Madoz, *Diccionario geográfico-estadístico-histórico de España y sus posesiones de ultramar*, 16 vols. (Madrid: Imprenta del Diccionario geográfico-estadístico-histórico de Don Pascual Madoz, 1845–1850), vol. 16, pp. 385–386. Interesting observations on the effects of the wool trade decline upon Bilbao, in Inglis, *Spain in 1830*, vol. 1, p. 23.

26. See Josep Fontana Lázaro, "Colapso y transformación del comercio exterior español entre 1792 y 1827. Un aspecto de la crisis de la economía del Antiguo régimen en España," *Moneda y crédito*, no. 115, (December 1970), p. 12.

27. Edward Baines, *Account of the Woollen Manufacture of England*, with a new introduction by K. G. Ponting (New York: A. M. Kelley, 1970), p. 79. Other relevant information in pp. 76–79 passim, and p. 107.

28. Numerous first-hand examples of this in the *Report from the Select Committee of the House of Lords, appointed to take into consideration the state of the British wool trade, and to report to the House, together with the minutes of evidence taken before the said Committee, and an appendix and index thereto. Ordered to be printed 27th June 1828* (N.p., n.d.). For clear evidence of a drop in the price of Spanish wool during the 1820s, see William Hurt, *History of the Woollen Trade in the Last Sixty Years* (Leeds: Printed by S. Moody, 1844), part 1, p. 38; part 2, pp. 12–13; and part 3, p. 25.

29. Among the most prominent was Benito Felipe de Gaminde, patriarch of an important *lanera* family, who in 1827 published a suggestively entitled *Memoria sobre el estado actual de las lanas merinas españolas y su cotejo con las extranjeras, causas de la decadencia de las primeras y remedio de mejorarlas* (Madrid: Imprenta de E. Aguado, 1827). For the most part, however, the *Memoria* provides impressions rather than hard facts and statistics.

30. See the following: AMAE, CC, Bilbao, vol. 4, Regnaudin's 1826, 1827, and 1828 annual reports (the last of these is dated 26 January 1829); and *Report from the Select Committee of the House of Lords*, pp. 330–335 (cited in note 28 above).

31. Nicolás Delmas, *Guia de Vizcaya*, (1863), cited by Fernando de la Quadra Salcedo, *Economistas vascongados y artículos varios sobre problemas destacados de la economía vizcaína* (Bilbao: Editorial El Pueblo Vasco, 1943), p. 80. See also Vicente Palacio Atard, *El comercio de Castilla y el puerto de Santander en el siglo XVIII, notas para su estudio* (Madrid: Consejo Superior de Investigaciones Científicas, Escuela de Historia Moderna, 1960), p. 185.

32. For the social effects of the commercial slump, see AMAE, CD, vol. 745, letter of Regnaudin to the minister of foreign affairs, 6 September 1827. More on this later in this chapter.

33. See the following: Josep Fontana Lázaro, *La quiebra de la monarquía absoluta (1814–1820). La crisis del Antiguo régimen en España* (Barcelona: Ariel, 1971), pp. 53–57; Fontana, *La crisis*, pp. 197–206; 2 July 1827 *Memoria* of Valde-espina and Novia de Salcedo, pp. 15–16 (see note 70 below in this chapter for a complete reference); my observations on these questions in chapter 4 of this book; and, finally, my paper entitled "Los vascos y la pér- dida de las colonias americanas (1810–1840): aproximación a un problema," (Simposio Hispano-Luso-Norteamericano de Historia, Madrid, June 1985).

34. These questions have been examined at length in chapter 4 and, to a lesser extent, also in chapter 3.

35. Gaminde, *Intereses*, pp. 18–19.

36. Fontana, *Hacienda y estado*, pp. 76–77; Fontana, *La quiebra*, p. 56.

37. AMAE, CC, Bilbao, vol. 4, 1824 annual report, 1 January 1825.

38. Ibid., letter to the minister of foreign affairs, 13 March 1825. Numerous contemporary reports of the French commercial agent indicate a scarcity of currency and capital. The documents are filed in the same register.

39. I owe some of these suggestions to Stanley J. Stein.

40. See, for example, [Bayo], *Historia*, vol. 3, p. 275.

41. AMAE, CC, Bilbao, vol. 4, letter to the minister of foreign affairs, 25 August 1825.

42. Ibid., 1826 annual report, 28 January 1827.

43. See AMAE, CD, Espagne, vol. 739, and CC, Bilbao 4, Regnaudin's reports of 17 December 1826 and 28 January 1827, respectively.

44. See Barahona [Arévalo], *Making*, pp. 155–156; chapter 2 in this book.

45. An extensive discussion of these matters in chapter 5, section 1 of this book. The merchants of Bilbao encountered business difficulties when forbidden by the police to assemble in groups at the Arenal, a popular promenade and gathering place used by the business community as an informal stock exchange.

46. See the following: ANP, F 7, 12,011, letter of the sous-préfet of Bayonne to the minister of the interior, 15 May 1828, AMAE, CD, Espagne, vol. 748, letter of Regnaudin to the minister of foreign affairs, 22 June 1828; ANP, F 7, 12,011, letter of the sous-préfet of Bayonne to the minister of the interior, 29 June 1828; and AMAE, CD, Espagne, vol. 744, letter of the minister of the interior to his counterpart at Foreign Affairs, 5 July 1828. More on this in chapter 7 of this book.

47. On the reemergence of liberals in public life, see chapter 5, section III in chapter 6, and most notably sections I and II in chapter 7 passim. On the economic significance of 1832, see Fontana, *Hacienda y estado*, p. 106. In wait of additional evidence and research, I have taken the liberty of extrapolating this author's conclusions to Vizcaya.

48. See in particular the "*Tableau de commerce de la France avec l'Espagne de 1821 à 1834*," which certainly tends to validate the commercial agent's observations for Bilbao; in ANP, F 12, 2,663.

49. See in particular Regnaudin's 1826 and 1827 annual reports cited in notes 42 and 12 of this chapter, respectively.

50. See note 3 above for the complete reference. See in particular article 3

of the royal order, which read in part, "*no podrá hacerse este comercio como todo el de cabotage, sino en buques españoles.*"

51. See AMAE, CC, Bilbao, vol. 4, Regnaudin's reports of 28 January and 1 October 1827, and 23 February and 14 March 1833.

52. AMAE, CC, Bilbao, vol. 4, Regnaudin's 1826 annual report. However, this report contains suggestive observations on the numerous subterfuges —outright violations in some instances—used by local shippers and merchants to sidestep these prohibitions. More on these matters in the agent's 26 January 1829 and 27 February 1830 reports in the same register.

53. (*a*) On the residency question, see chapter 3 and chapter 6. (*b*) On the judgeship of contraband, see chapter 4 passim, and other allusions to this office interspersed throughout the passages on trade. (*c*) On the issue of the Vizcayan privileges and the province's trade, see chapter 3 and chapter 4, section IV passim. (*d*) See Regnaudin's 1826 annual report, which observed that the Spanish consumption was declining on account of the new high tariffs upon them, but also because of the relative success and partial advance of national cloths manufactured in Navarra, Aragon, Catalonia, and Castile.

54. See in particular Regnaudin's remarks in the 1826 annual report. In fact, nearly all of the agent's dispatches, especially the annual reports, contain telling information on British commercial preponderance in the region.

55. AMAE, CC, Bilbao, vol. 4, letter to the sous-préfet of Bayonne, 12 May 1825. At least in this case, Regnaudin was forced to admit that the Vizcayan freedoms played a positive role in Bilbao's trade. However, as noted before, this was not necessarily the rule.

56. See AMAE, CC, Bilbao, vol. 4, Regnaudin's 1826 and 1827 annual reports. Also suggestive remarks along these lines in the agent's 1831 annual report, 23 February 1832 in the same register.

57. See in particular AMAE, Bilbao, CC, vol. 4, Regnaudin's 1826 and 1827 annual reports. More on this question and related matters, in chapter 4, section IV.

58. AMAE, CC, Bilbao, vol. 4, 1828 annual report.

59. Ibid.

60. AMAE, CC, Bilbao, vol. 4, 1832 annual report, 14 March 1833. This document strongly suggests these interpretations.

61. Fontana, *Hacienda y estado*, p. 332. See also pp. 97 and 106.

62. Sagармínaga, *Gobierno*, vol. 8, pp. 85–88.

63. Good evidence of the economic upturn in the document cited in note 49.

64. Although this section concentrates almost exclusively on the plight of Vizcayan iron production, it is well to emphasize that a host of other local manufactures suffered from identical problems. For instance, see Sebastián de Miñano y Bedoya, *Diccionario geográfico-estadístico de España y Portugal*, 10 vols. (Madrid: Imprenta de Pierart-Peralta, 1828), vol. 10, pp. 40–44, with important information regarding the crisis of all Vizcayan manufactures, not only iron. See also Gaminde, *Intereses*, pp. 21–28 passim, which also paints an extremely bleak picture of local industry. A committed liberal, the author understandably attributes the sad state to the supposedly

erroneous policies of the generally traditionalist Vizcayan diputaciones and to the sway of the fueros.

65. These figures are based on these sources: (a) ANP, A.A.E., B III, 334, document entitled *"Description de la Seigneurie de Biscaye,"* with the further identification of *"Joint à la lettre de M. d'abadie à Bilbao le 22 Février 1777,"* production is estimated at 100,000 quintales; (b) AHN, Consejos, leg. 3068, no. 2, report of the corregidor Josef Colón de Larreátegui, Bilbao, 21 May 1786: *"se labran solo en ellas [Vizcaya y Encartaciones] como 90,000 quintales, poco más o menos";* (c) Julián de Luna, *Memoria que contiene una Estadística sucinta de Vizcaya* (Bilbao: Imprenta y Litografía de Nicolás Delmas, 1842): *"el año de 1790 . . . se elaboraban de noventa a cien mil quintales de hierro;"* (d) Juan Ramón de Iturriza y Zabala, *Historia General de Vizcaya y Epítome de las Encartaciones,* 2 vols., Angel Rodríguez Herrero, ed. (Bilbao: La Gran Enciclopedia Vasca, 1967), vol. 1, p. 27: *"[se] labran de 80 a 90,000 quintales de fierro"* [1793]; (e) *"Copia la relación entregada a don Antonio Regas a principios de [Octu]bre de 1795 para el Sr dn Francisco de Zamora del Consejo Real,"* in José María de Areilza, "La economía vizcaína a fines del siglo XVIII," *Boletín de la Real Sociedad Vascongada de Amigos del País,* Año II, 1946, Cuaderno 20., pp. 131–147. The anonymous author estimates production at 80,000 to 100,000 quintales per year; (f) *Geografía General del País Vasco-Navarro,* 6 vols. (Barcelona: Establecimiento Editorial Alberto Martín, n.d.), vol. 5, p. 393. This passage, apparently the work of Carmelo de Echegaray, places production in 1796 at 90,000 quintales; (g) AHN, Estado, leg. 205/2, petition of Mariano Josef de Urquijo to the monarch, 19 May 1801. Urquijo puts the province's iron production at about 100,000 quintales; (h) Sotero de Goicoechea, *A Luminous Guide for the British Cooperative Forces in Spain on the Principal Subjects connected with particular information relative to the Basque Provinces* (Bayonne: [Lamaignère], 1936), pp. 22–23. Without providing an exact date, the author affirms in 1836 that the Vizcayan *ferrerías* "in regular times . . . manufactured upwards of 100 thousand quintales (called macho of 152 liv) of wrought iron." More on this in Fernández de Pinedo, *Crecimiento,* p. 330. My conversion of quintales to tons is based on Bacon's assertion that one *quintal macho* equaled 150 English pounds (*Six Years in Biscay,* p. 89), an observation confirmed by Goicoechea. Thus, it would take approximately 13,333 quintales to make up one ton of 2,000 pounds. Significant corroborative information in Pascual Madoz: *"el quintal macho de que se sirven en la prov[incia de Vizcaya] para pesar el hierro, tiene 146 lib[ras] de 17 onzas en Bilbao, que equivalen a 155 1/8 libras castellanas de 16 onzas,"* *Diccionario,* article "Vizcaya," vol. 16, p. 397.

66. For 1816, see *Geografía General del Pais Vasco-Navarro,* vol. 5, p. 393. The article's author estimates output at around 50,000 quintales. And for 1819, see Luna, *Memoria, "Los estragos causados por la guerra de independencia alcanzaron a las ferrerías en términos que . . . solo existían 117, que producían de cincuenta a cincuenta y cinco mil quintales."* The *Memoria's* pages are unnumbered. See rubric entitled *"Ferrerías."*

67. AMAE, CC, Bilbao, vol. 4, 1827 annual report. The commercial agent

calculated local production at between 78,660 and 82,800 quintales. As for 1828, see ACJG, Ferrerías, reg. 2, dossier entitled "*1816 a 1831. Sobre la Fabricación de fierro*," letter of González Azaola (from Paris) to the Vizcayan Diputación, 1 November 1828. See Inglis's interesting 1830 observations concerning the decline of Vizcayan iron exports. He attributed much of the problem to competitive Swedish imports; in *Spain in 1830*, vol. 1, pp. 23–24.

68. Luna, *Memoria*.

69. For the reforms of the pre-Trienio era, see chapter 2 in this book. See also chapter 4, section III for more on these matters. The Permanent Commission for the Improvement of Iron Fabrication was established on 25 May 1824 (see the charter for the exploitation of mines cited in note 73 in this chapter, [p. 28 of the document]).

70. Allusion to this important document has been made in chapter 4 of this book. I am using the printed version of the *Memoria*, which is contained in pp. 12–28 of the accords of the 1827 General Juntas. Bound according to year, the acts are in the ADV, Guernica, in a collection entitled *Juntas Generales de Vizcaya*. The *Memoria*, dated 2 July 1827, was signed by the outgoing general deputies, Valde-espina and Novia de Salcedo. From other materials, it is my strong belief that the document was primarily the work of the latter official. The manuscript copy (apparently the final version before publication) may be consulted in ACJG, Ferrerías, reg. 2, dossier cited in note 67. All the references here, however, will be from the printed version.

71. *Memoria*, pp. 13–14 and passim. See also S. E. Widdrington, *Sketches*, vol. 2, p. 79.

72. A discussion of many of these matters in chapter 4, section III passim. See also my paper cited in note 33. Additional information on this important question in González Azaola's 1 November 1828 communication to the Vizcayan Diputación (cited in note 67); in Sagarmínaga, *Gobierno*, vol. 7, pp. 509–512; and, finally, in the newly enacted Vizcayan charter for the exploitation of the mines, dated 4 April 1827, pp. 28–47 of the printed accords of the 1827 juntas.

73. *Memoria*, pp. 22–24.

74. Extremely detailed information on this in ACJG, Ferrerías, reg. 1, dossier entitled "*Noticias relativas a la mejora y adelantamientos en la Fabricación del Fierro*." The calculations seem to be largely the work of Novia de Salcedo.

75. Ibid. See also the oft-cited *Memoria . . . sobre el punto de Minería*, p. 23.

76. By the time of Luna's *Memoria*, however, labor accounted for only 5.5 percent of total cost—a noticeable drop from Valde-espina's and Novia de Salcedo's figures. Two factors may well have come into play in a relatively short period of time: first, as Luna points out, an improvement in production methods and, second, a population increase may well have lowered the cost of labor.

77. See notes 73 and 74.

78. *Memoria*, pp. 20–22.

79. See the preamble to the charter for the exploitation of Vizcayan mines (cited in note 72), in particular pp. 30–31.

80. *Memoria*, pp. 23–25. According to the authors, the experimental school should be financed by the Diputación and located in an existent *ferrería* close to Bilbao for greater convenience. In the deputies' words, *"los ferrones tendrán sin riesgo en esta ferrería una utilísima escuela,"* p. 24.

81. *Memoria*, p. 24.

82. Ibid., pp. 18 and 25.

83. Ibid., pp. 22–24.

84. Ibid., pp. 13–17 passim, and in particular p. 17. See the passage that reads *"pero Vizcaya debe contar para el [remedio] solo consigo misma: remedio que penda de otras manos es seguramente inaccequible, imaginario."*

85. Ibid.

86. See the charter-like document entitled *"Sobre el laboreo y beneficio de Minas,"* dated 4 July 1825, in *Guía de la Real Hacienda*, 1825, pp. 284–286.

87. See, for example, the preamble to the Vizcayan charter for the exploitation of the mines cited in note 72. In particular, see pp. 28–29.

88. The usual duty at this time was twenty-five maravedis per quintal of iron imported. See, for example, Sagarmínaga, *Gobierno*, vol. 8, pp. 99–100 (with information from the 1831 General Juntas). That the Diputación intended to use the proceeds from iron ore exports for its own purposes was clearly demonstrated at the 1829 general assembly; see ibid., vol. 7, p. 576. There is evidence that the duty was not fixed and that it could vary according to circumstance; see Bacon, *Six Years in Biscay*, p. 89. Understandably, the provincial government kept an eye on fraudulent iron ore exports; see ACJG, Minería, reg. 1 and 2 with information on legal proceedings against violators of the 1827 Vizcayan charter.

89. See note 72. A summarized version of the charter in Sagarmínaga, *Gobierno*, vol. 7, pp. 509–512. The code regulating Vizcayan mining was divided into three chapters and comprised sixty-one articles.

90. Considerable material on this and related matters in AGS, Consejo Supremo de Hacienda, leg. 20. A good example of the central government's irritation in the second epigraph to chapter 3 in this book. I have not found any evidence that the inspector named by the royal administration in July 1830 ever exercised his post; see ADV, Guernica, *Reales Ordenes Generales. De 1814–1830*.

91. AMAE, CC, Bilbao, vol. 4, 1827 annual report. The commercial agent praised *"le vif désir dont la Seigneurie est animée pour l'amélioration de cette partie industrielle et de l'impulsion nouvelle qu'elle cherche a lui donner."* The Diputación was of course deeply aware of the need to end abuses in mining and improve the province's transportation networks. For forceful statements on these questions, see the 1827 *Memoria* of Valdeespina and Novia de Salcedo, pp. 20–22.

92. Sagarmínaga, *Gobierno*, vol. 7, pp. 575–576.

93. See ADV, Guernica, *1825 a 1829. Oficios de Pueblos*, letter of the Diputación to González Azaola, 17 December 1826. This is the earliest contact between the parties of which I am aware.

94. Some of the expert's work may be consulted at the ACJG, Ferrerías, reg. 2. In particular, see González Azaola's two *Memorias* entitled *1a. Sobre las Minas de Hierro de Somorrostro, Propias del M.N. Señorío de Vizcaya*, dated 28 February 1827; and *2a. Sobre la importancia y urjencia de mejorar la elaboración del Hierro en Vizcaya y medios de conseguirlo*, 19 March 1827 (both written at Santander). To my knowledge, they have not been published.

95. See Sagarmínaga, *Gobierno*, vol. 7, pp. 575–577. The accords of the 1829 Vizcayan Juntas clearly indicate that the decision had been made not to wait for González Azaola any longer, thereby setting the stage for Echanove. See also ACJG, Ferrerías, reg. 2, dossier entitled "*1816 a 1831. Sobre la Fabricación de fierro*," where much of the pertinent information regarding the Permanent Commission for the Improvement of Iron Fabrication is contained, and to which repeated reference will be made below.

96. ACJG, Ferrerías, reg. 2, dossier cited in notes 67 and 95, report of the permanent commission, 19 May 1830. In passing, this document strikingly details the numerous difficulties confronting Vizcayan iron production.

97. Ibid. In particular see Echanove's 26 May 1830 *Memoria*, which carried a cover letter addressed to the Diputación. The document's dominant tone, especially the letter, is one of bitter disappointment.

98. Ibid. The experiments apparently lasted until June 1831. There is no evidence that they continued after that.

99. Sagarmínaga, *Gobierno*, vol. 8, pp. 99–100. Some of Echanove's handwritten work can be consulted in the ACJG, Ferrerías, reg. 1 and 2.

100. ACJG, Ferrerías, reg. 2, letter of the Vizcayan Diputación to Echanove (who was in Madrid), 15 March 1833, asking him to submit his manuscripts for publication. Echanove responded immediately (on 25 March), promising to forward the materials. There is unfortunately no way of knowing what happened after this, and any conjectures would necessarily be highly tentative. However, the episode certainly raises questions concerning the Diputación's commitment to the dissemination of materials related to the reform of iron production.

101. As I emphasize in this chapter, when assessing the projected reform's outcome, it is necessary to keep in mind the vested socioeconomic interests—from woodland owners to commercial importers, to name but two—which, for distinctly different reasons, may have opposed basic innovations and technological improvements. See, for example, Gaminde, *Intereses*, pp. 27–28.

102. See note 47 above. The apparent recovery of Vizcayan liberalism during the late 1820s and early 1830s is an extremely important topic. In fact, it is one sorely in need of additional research well beyond the work presented in this section. Some of the most glaring shortcomings stem in large part from documentary limitations encountered in the course of my investigation. More to the point: while researching Vizcayan liberalism—and, to a

considerable extent, Carlism too—I was continually hampered by the seeming unavailability of, and outright inaccessibility to, key source materials —e.g., personal and official correspondence, diaries, business and financial accounts, as well as other relevant private and public records. However, with time, perseverance, and patience, it should be possible to reconstruct satisfactorily the political and socioeconomic trajectory of local liberalism during the Ominous Decade, especially during the crucial phase that started with the royal visit to Vizcaya in mid-1828. In sum, while I remain confident that the broad outline and interpretation below are fundamentally correct, I am equally convinced that much more remains to be done on this question to overcome what some might rightly consider embarrassing historiographic gaps.

103. See note 44 above.

104. For other references to the 1828 royal visit, in addition to those in this chapter, see chapters 3 and 4.

105. See in particular the following French sources: (*a*) AMAE, CD, Espagne, vol. 748, letter of Regnaudin to the minister of foreign affairs, 11 May 1828; (*b*) ANP, F 7, 12,011, letter of the sous-préfet of Bayonne to the minister of the interior, 15 May 1828; (*c*) ibid., letter of the same to the same party, 14 June 1828; (*d*) AMAE, CD, Espagne, vol. 748, confidential report drafted by the *Division du Cabinet* of the Ministry of the Interior to the Ministry of Foreign Affairs, 21 June 1828; (*e*) ibid., letter of Regnaudin to the minister of foreign affairs, 22 June 1828; (*f*) ANP, F 7, 12,011, letter of the sous-préfet of Bayonne to the minister of the interior, 29 June 1828; and (*g*) AMAE, CD, Espagne, vol. 744, letter of the minister of the interior to his counterpart at foreign affairs, 5 July 1828.

106. For considerable additional information on the 1828 royal visit to Vizcaya and its sociopolitical effects, see the following Spanish sources: (*a*) Sagarmínaga, *Gobierno*, vol. 7, pp. 553–557; (*b*) ADV, Guernica, *1824 a 1830. Yndice de Oficios a la Superintendencia*; (*c*) ACJG, Policía, reg. 12, dispatch no. 130 of the Vizcayan Police to central headquarters; (*d*) *La célebre década de Bilbao, o sea Memoria de los festejos con que su Muy Ilustre Ayuntamiento ha procurado obsequiar a SS. MM. los Reyes Nuestros Señores, D. Fernando Séptimo y Doña Josefa María Amalia, durante su permanencia en esta M.N. y M.L. Villa de regreso para la Corte* (Bilbao: Imprenta de Basozabal, 1828), an anonymous work generally attributed to Francisco de Hormaeche, the prominent Vizcayan moderate liberal; (*e*) *Relación de los festejos con que han sido obsequiados los Reyes y Señores Don Fernando Séptimo y Doña María Josefa Amalia, en el M.N. y M.L. Señorío de Vizcaya, desde el día 14 de Junio de 1828, en que pisaron su suelo, Hasta el 21 del mismo en que salieron para la Ciudad de Vitoria* (Bilbao: Imprenta de Basozabal, 1828), an account which, to my knowledge, has not been attributed to any author; and (*f*) Uhagon, *Informe*, p. 8: "*[la visita] dió a conocer que el Gobierno propendía a destruir las disensiones civiles y olvidar los estravíos anteriores.*"

107. See (*e*) in note 105 for the complete reference. The royal visit to San Sebastián, as José Múgica reports, had extremely similar consequences to

those at Bilbao, creating a rapprochement among those who until then had held opposing political opinions; see Múgica, *Carlistas*, p. 62.

108. See (*c*) in note 105 for the complete reference. More on this in (*d*) of the same note.

109. ADV, Guernica, *Conferencias de las Provincias Bascongadas. 1812 a 1833*.

110. See Uhagon, *Informe*, pp. 6–7; Gaminde, *Intereses*, pp. 14–28 passim; Guiard, *Consulado*, vol. 2, pp. 791–797; and chapter 4 of this book, section IV passim.

111. ADV, Guernica, *Conferencias de las Provincias Bascongadas. 1812 a 1833*, sessions of 22, 23, and 24 September 1828 at Vitoria.

112. See Gaminde, *Intereses*, p. 51. The author places the following words in the mouth of an imaginary wise man: "*[fueron los liberales] escluidos hasta el año 20 de la dirección del país, expulsados del 23 al 32 de toda corporación, y de tomar parte activa en su gobierno.*"

113. Sagarmínaga, *Gobierno*, vol. 7, pp. 567–575 passim. See also ANP, F 7, 12,011, letter of the sous-préfet of Bayonne to the minister of the interior, 18 September 1829. However, as noted several times before, it should be emphasized that the conservative Vizcayan diputaciones were not opposed to liberalism's participation in consultative matters. The tripartite parleys of the Basque provinces are a good example.

114. Sagarmínaga, *Gobierno*, vol. 8, pp. 90–127 passim.

115. *OCSV*, 1831, circular of the Diputación, 9 December 1831. It is also in Sagarmínaga, *Gobierno*, vol. 8, pp. 131–132.

116. See Uhagon, *Informe*, pp. 7–12. The author sharply criticizes traditionalists for barring liberals from "*de toda intervención en los asuntos de la república, dejando por este medio separados de su conocimiento a todas las clases útiles del Estado, y el gobierno de los pueblos en las manos de arbitristas y proletarios.*" More on these matters in Gaminde, *Intereses*, pp. 33–39 passim.

117. This is made even more interesting by the fact that the provincial administration enjoyed an excellent reputation for dedication, honesty, and efficiency that cut across political opinions. In addition to my remarks in chapter 1 passim of this book, see for example Gaminde, *Intereses*, pp. 42–43; Hormaeche, "De las causas," p. 355; the anonymous *Observaciones*, pp. 9–18 passim; and, of course, Novia de Salcedo, *Defensa histórica*, passim. The provincial government's financial methods and know-how in particular earned it high praise—even from liberals.

118. Uhagon, *Informe*, pp. 13–14.

119. See in particular the relevant passages in chapter 7. Some of these matters are also addressed within a larger sociopolitical context in chapter 3 of this book.

120. See chapters 5 and 7 in this book. According to Hormaeche, "*algunos ayuntamientos, movidos por las insinuaciones indirectas de la propia corporación pidieron por escrito que se disolviesen los tercios como inútiles en tiempos de paz, dispendiosos y molestos,*" "De las causas," p. 343. Finally, recall Regnaudin's pointed observation that the Paisanos were more

a matter of local pride than a useful instrument; (see AMAE, CD, Espagne, vol. 739, letter to the minister of foreign affairs, 17 December 1826).

121. Uhagon, *Informe*, pp. 13–14.

122. Bacon, *Six Years in Biscay*, p. 90.

123. ACJG, Policía, reg. 31, dispatch no. 239 to central headquarters, 12 July 1833.

124. Uhagon, *Informe*, pp. 13–18 passim.

125. See chapters 3 and 7 passim of this book.

126. On the other hand, there is little evidence of liberalism among the provincial leaderships of the Ominous Decade, as the Baron of Boislecomte suggestively asserts in the generally perceptive *Ensayo histórico sobre las Provincias Vascongadas (Alava, Guipuzcoa, Vizcaya y Navarra), y sobre la guerra que actualmente sostienen*, 2 vols., translated by Pedro Martínez López (Bordeaux: Cl. Dulac, 1836), vol. 1, p. 50. Boislecomte reemphasizes this point by affirming that the Basque region, despite the 1823 Restoration, had more seeds of liberalism than the rest of the monarchy; ibid., vol. 1, p. 68. Occasionally, there is liberal praise for certain Vizcayan general deputies, but even this is very thin evidence; see for example Uhagon, *Informe*, p. 8, and Lemonauría, *Ensayo crítico*, pp. 43–44.

127. More on the concept of compradore bourgeoisie as applied to Basque entrepreneurs, in Fernández de Pinedo, *Crecimiento*, pp. 348 and 351. In the main, I concur with this author's opinion. See, for example, my remarks in chapter 1 and chapter 2, note 106 in chapter 2 in particular.

128. See ADV, Guernica, *"Plan de Iguala"* [see bibliography for a complete reference]. The commission which drafted the general road plan for Vizcaya had been created on 12 July 1831 at the General Juntas. The project was approved by the central government on 4 February 1833. See also Gaminde, *Intereses*, p. 43; Uhagon, *Informe*, pp. 15–17; and *Observaciones*, p. 14. Capitalist involvement in road building dated back to the seventeenth and eighteenth centuries.

129. See, for example, chapter 4 in this book. See also Guiard, *Consulado*, vol. 2, pp. 679–683.

130. Sagarmínaga, *Gobierno*, vol. 7, pp. 451, 500, 541, and 573. See also Guiard, *Consulado*, vol. 2, p. 683.

131. See *OCSV*, 1830, circular of the Vizcayan Diputación, 16 October 1830; Sagarmínaga, *Gobierno*, vol. 8, p. 76, for more on the "loan"; and AMAE, CPC, Espagne, vol. 1, letter of Regnaudin to the minister of foreign affairs, 28 October 1830.

132. See chapter 4 in this book.

133. Guiard, *Consulado*, vol. 2, pp. 791–794.

134. Ibid.

135. Ibid., pp. 856–859.

136. Ibid., pp. 858–859. The Diputación may possibly have been placated by being awarded interim control of the Tribunal until the change was fully realized.

137. See chapter 1 in this book. With an eye toward a later period, see Henningsen's insightful remark "that all the classes that have espoused the

interests of [Don Carlos] are precisely the same as those who, during the war of independence resisted so energetically to the French usurpation," in *Zumalacárregui*, vol. 1, pp. 176–177.

138. See in particular chapter 2, section III passim. See also chapters 3 and 7. Finally, see Bacon, *Six Years in Biscay*, p. 20, and AMAE, CC, Bilbao, vol. 4, letter of Regnaudin to the minister of foreign affairs, 16 September 1830.

139. See chapter 3 in this book. Other interesting information regarding the Bessières episode in Vizcaya, in Uhagon, *Informe*, p. 46.

140. ANP, F 7, 12,011, letter of the sous-préfet of Bayonne to the minister of the interior, 1 February 1825. Similar information in some of Regnaudin's reports, such as the one cited in note 138.

141. See Bacon, *Six Years in Biscay*, pp. 21–53 passim, 61 and 77; Henningsen, *Zumalacárregui*, vol. 1, pp. 11–12; and S. E. Widdrington, *Sketches*, vol. 1, p. 329.

142. See chapter 3 in this book. Emphasis in text.

143. Uhagon, *Informe*, pp. 14–15. Emphasis in text.

144. See chapter 7 in this book.

145. Bacon, *Six Years in Biscay*, p. 75.

146. However, it does not seem that the *economic* power of the Vizcayan clergy was very great. In 1810 the French had estimated that only 9 percent of the rents in the province belonged to the clergy; (see chapter 1 in this book). See also Fernández de Pinedo, *Crecimiento*, p. 481. Clearly, the clerical reforms (and other related measures) of the previous decades had weakened the church's economic standing.

147. See chapter 1 in this book.

148. See this chapter passim.

149. See González Portilla's unpublished master's thesis (cited in note 17), and Fernández de Pinedo's work (cited in notes 15–20).

150. See chapters 3 and 5 in this book. It was Bacon who pointedly reported—a point upon which I shall return below—that Uhagon was "probably the most obnoxious to the peasantry" of the liberals. Finally, according to Thomas Roscoe—in an intriguing assertion I have neither been able to confirm nor refute—it was the peasantry which gave the name of *negros* to liberals and Cristinos; see *The Tourist in Spain. Biscay and the Castiles* (London: Robert Jennings and Co.), p. 27.

151. For an excellent period description of the opposition between the peasantry on the one hand, and the Vizcayan aristocratic and bourgeois elites on the other, see Bacon, *Six Years in Biscay*, pp. 22–53 passim. See also Fernández de Pinedo's suggestive remark, *"para la generalidad de los labriegos, y muy en especial para los más pobres, el liberalismo solo tenía desventajas,"* *Crecimiento*, p. 455.

152. See, for example, Barahona [Arévalo], *Making*, p. 219, note 37.

153. Bacon, *Six Years in Biscay*, p. 72.

154. See Michael Burke Honan, *The Court and Camp of Don Carlos, being the results of a late tour in the Basque Provinces, and parts of Catalonia, Castile, and Estramadura* [sic] (London: John Macrone, 1836), p. 235.

155. Gaminde, *Intereses*, p. 7.

156. Cursory remarks on these matters in chapter 3. For an in-depth discussion of the customs houses and enfranchisement issues, see chapter 4, section IV passim.

157. Gaminde, *Intereses*, p. 17.

158. Ibid., p. 12.

159. Bacon, *Six Years in Biscay*, p. 26. See also pp. 61 and 65.

160. Fernández de Pinedo's *Crecimiento* has contributed substantially to our understanding of these questions. See in particular chapter 9.

161. See Bacon, *Six Years in Biscay*, pp. 103–104; and Fernández de Pinedo, *Crecimiento*, pp. 264–317 and 479–482.

162. See note 14.

163. Fernández de Pinedo, *Crecimiento*, p. 478.

164. Bacon, *Six Years in Biscay*, p. 147.

165. Ibid., p. 78: "The peasant was taught to look upon his landlord (if a Constitutionalist) as his direct foe; that faithful attachment to the cause of the altar and the throne should be rewarded *by his elevation in rank from tenant to freeholder.*" Emphasis added.

166. Fernández de Pinedo, *Crecimiento*, p. 473.

167. The Vizcayan Diputación was a strong and consistent defender of entails, particularly in the late 1820s and early 1830s when the central government attempted to place limits on them; see AHN, Estado, libros, no. 42, *Actas Originales del año 1832*, session of 9 January. More on this in chapter 3 of this book.

168. See chapter 3.

169. Ibid. See also chapter 5; and AMAE, CC, Bilbao, vol. 4, letter of Regnaudin to the minister of foreign affairs, 17 December 1826. According to the agent, nearly all of the Paisanos came "from the class of proletarians and artisans."

170. See my earlier remarks on these questions in this chapter.

171. A possible additional cause for the opposition between liberals and royalists in the urban milieu could well have been the fact that the former owned large properties in Bilbao. Having the more modest urban classes in an economically disadvantageous position—through high rents and other mechanisms—could easily have made liberals the obvious and immediate target of artisans, shopkeepers, coffeehouse and tavern owners, many of whom demonstrated pronounced conservative tendencies during the Ominous Decade.

172. The term *escribano* is probably best translated as notary public—in light of his legal functions and attributes—rather than as scribe, a misleading synonym that, in fact, does not fully describe and explain the profession.

173. As far as I am aware, all—or at the very least most—of the Diputación's consultores were lawyers or individuals with strong legal backgrounds; see chapter 1.

174. Bacon, *Six Years in Biscay*, p. 88. My long periods of research at the Chancillería de Valladolid, notably in the Sala de Vizcaya, in the main confirm Bacon's remarks.

175. This is well explained in Bacon, *Six Years in Biscay*, pp. 77–78.

176. Ibid., p. 78.

177. Sagarmínaga, *Gobierno*, vol. 7, pp. 426–433 passim.

178. See, for example, Uhagon, *Informe*, pp. 18–19. Some lawyers and notaries public were instrumental in the October 1833 Carlist uprising at Bilbao, along with important bureaucrats of the Diputación with whom they shared a deep-rooted traditionalist orientation.

179. Gaminde's *Intereses* is a masterful articulation of the Vizcayan bourgeoisie's interests and aspirations.

180. Ibid. Numerous examples of this in pp. 5, 17–19, 24–25, 28, and 50–51. See in particular the crucial passage in p. 28. Another important example of liberalism's self-image in Uhagon, *Informe*, pp. 10–14 passim.

181. Liberal literature of the era—both in Vizcaya and in the rest of Spain —is replete with examples of anticlericalism and the alleged obscurantism of the lower classes. See, for instance, Gaminde, *Intereses*, pp. 6, 24, 29, 34, 36, and 49, to mention but some of this work's most flagrant cases. See also Uhagon, *Informe*, p. 13, and Bacon, *Six Years in Biscay*, pp. 21–53 passim.

182. Bacon, *Six Years in Biscay*, p. 53.

183. It is well to keep in mind that smugglers, be they "professionals" or "part-timers," were closely linked to the peasantry and that, as such, they too had much to gain from the preservation of the socioeconomic and political status quo while, conversely, much to lose from administrative and economic reform.

184. A neat summary of this relation of forces, which could also well apply to Vizcaya, in Jean-Marie Duvergier de Hauranne, *Coup-d'oeil sur l'Espagne* (Paris: Baudouin Frères, 1824), pp. 4–5. Later, the author significantly observed, "*nulle part la lutte des vieux abus et de la réforme politique n'est plus animée qu [en] Espagne*," p. 41.

Chapter 7: Carlists, Liberals, and the October 1833 Uprising

1. See *Galería*, vol. 1, p. 262. For an excellent recent analysis of the political and social consequences of the July Revolution in Spain, see Fontana, *Hacienda y estado*, pp. 289–303 passim.

2. The so-called *sucesos de la Granja*, as the events have come to be collectively known, occurred in mid-September 1832 at the royal resort of this name in the province of Segovia. With the king gravely ill, and with the succession to the throne in considerable doubt due to contradictory Bourbon measures on this question, Ferdinand VII was persuaded—in effect coerced —by prominent traditionalists to rescind a recent measure which, if maintained, would have effectively blocked his brother's accession to the crown. At stake were at least two fundamental and closely interrelated issues—one legal, the other political. The first involved long-standing (and widely divergent) legal interpretations on whether both males and females could succeed to the throne. That females could inherit the crown was seldom in serious doubt until the Bourbons established Salic Law in Spain (Act of 1713).

However, this ruling was apparently overturned through the enactment of the Pragmática Sanción in 1789, a measure voted upon by the Cortes but (inexplicably) not published at the time. The act was reaffirmed—this time officially—on 29 March 1830, shortly after Ferdinand's fourth marriage to his young Italian niece, María Cristina (23 years old at the time of the wedding), and following the birth of Princess Isabel, henceforth the most likely heiress. Refusing to accept the female succession (and in essence capitulate), Don Carlos and his partisans held their ground and kept alive his claims to the throne. The crisis of La Granja, not a totally unforeseen situation given the ruler's very poor condition, then seemed to at long last provide an ideal opportunity for the Pretender. In other words, at this critical junction the second important question, the political one, fully intersected with the legal one. According to a composite of contemporary accounts, Ferdinand, under considerable pressure, secretly revoked the Pragmática Sanción, in effect paving the way to his brother's rule. Nevertheless, while Carlists were already making preparations—quite prematurely as it turned out—for the aftermath of Ferdinand's rule, a surprisingly resilient monarch recovered and María Cristina and her advisers, now firmly supported by powerful moderate liberals, mounted a successful defense and then counterattacked—a coup d'état according to Federico Suárez—to derail the Carlist challenge. In extremely short order, important political measures followed. Of course the chief beneficiaries of these actions were the liberals: a new government was installed on 1 October, an amnesty was issued on the fifteenth of the same month and, finally, the act revoking the Pragmática Sanción was in turn derogated by the monarch on 31 December 1832. In essence, the political tide turned against the Carlists. Liberalism, albeit of a respectable and moderate variety, had secured control of the national government. An excellent discussion of the La Granja affair in Josep Fontana, *La crisis*, pp. 207–217. See also Federico Suárez, *La crisis política del antiguo régimen en España (1800–1840)*, 2d ed. (Madrid: Rialp, 1958), pp. 181–218 passim. By this author, see the earlier and more extensive *Los sucesos de La Granja* (Madrid: Consejo Superior de Investigaciones Científicas, 1953). Another good discussion on La Granja and its aftermath in Miguel Artola, *La España de Fernando VII* (Madrid: Espasa-Calpe, 1968), pp. 923–947. Finally, see the important account of Encima y Piedra cited in the next note.

3. For the conception, planning, and enactment of the amnesty, see the interesting and authoritative account of Victoriano de Encima y Piedra, *De los sucesos del Real Sitio de San Ildefonso o La Granja, a fines del año de 1832; de las disposiciones tomadas por el ministerio que se nombró el 1 de Octubre del mismo año, y de las causas inmediatas del estado actual de España* (Paris: Librería de Rosa, 1837), pp. 53–55. More on this in Luis Bordas, *Historia de la revolución y guerra civil de España, o sea hechos memorables acaecidos desde la última enfermedad de Fernando VII hasta la conclusión de la guerra en los campos de Vergara* (Barcelona: Librería de Manuel Sauri, Imprenta Hispana, 1847), pp. 18–19. For early Carlist attacks against the amnesty in Guipúzcoa, see Pirala, *Historia*, vol. 1, pp. 77–78.

Finally, for a good brief overview of the political situation in Spain during 1832–1833, see Miguel Artola, *La burguesía revolucionaria (1808–1869)* (Madrid: Alianza Editorial, 1973), pp. 52–53.

4. See Francisco de Paula Madrazo, *Historia militar y política de Zumalacárregui, y de los sucesos de la guerra de las provincias del Norte, enlazados a su época y a su nombre* (Madrid: Imprenta de la Sociedad de Operarios del Mismo Arte, 1844), pp. 64–65. For other important consequences of the 15 October 1832 amnesty, see Suárez, *La crisis*, pp. 222–227.

5. See AMAE, CPC, Espagne, vol. 5, letter of Francine to the minister of foreign affairs, 29 October 1832, and Uhagon, *Informe*, p. 12. For the Vizcayan Diputación's response to the amnesty, see Sagармínaga, *Gobierno*, vol. 8, pp. 145–146.

6. See *Galería*, vol. 1, p. 262 and Hormaeche's "De las causas," p. 339.

7. This version of the 18 October libel is a composite of two different documents. One is in Llauder's *Memorias*, appendix 27, pp. 36–38; the other is in a letter of Regnaudin to the minister of foreign affairs, 21 October 1832, in AMAE, CPC, vol. 5. Since each contains nearly verbatim similarities (and yet elements absent in the other), the two versions would appear to be complementary. Space unfortunately prevents a detailed analysis of the libel's interesting references. Most, however, are self-evident. For those unfamiliar with modern common political parlance, the term *pancista* refers to egoists, opportunists, fence sitters, or those who try to maintain good relations with those in power—whatever the latter's political views and opinions.

8. See the following: Uhagon, *Informe*, p. 12; Sagармínaga, *Gobierno*, vol. 8, pp. 146–147; Llauder, *Memorias*, p. 82 (text), and pp. 36–38 (appendix 27); AMAE, CPC, Espagne, vol. 5, letter of Regnaudin to the minister of foreign affairs, 28 October 1832.

9. AMAE, CPC, Espagne, vol. 5, letter to the minister of foreign affairs, 11 November 1832.

10. ARCV, Sala de Vizcaya, leg. 1670, no. 6.

11. AMAE, CPC, Espagne, vol. 5, Regnaudin's 1832 annual report, 14 March 1833.

12. ACJG, Policía, reg. 31, dispatch no. 54 of the Vizcayan police to central headquarters, 18 February 1833.

13. Ibid., dispatch no. 78 of the Vizcayan police to central headquarters, 8 March 1833.

14. Hormaeche, "De las causas," p. 340. See also *Galería*, vol. 1, p. 271 for more detailed information on those who were reassigned in Vizcaya.

15. See Uhagon, *Informe*, p. 13, and Bacon, *Six Years in Biscay*, pp. 129–130.

16. Sagармínaga, *Gobierno*, vol. 8, p. 149.

17. Bacon, *Six Years in Biscay*, p. 130.

18. Ibid. See also Hormaeche's praise of de la Mota in "De las causas," p. 342.

19. ACJG, Policía, reg. 31, dispatches nos. 31, 49, 59, 66, 88, and 118; dated 1, 15, 22, and 25 February; 15 March; and 5 April 1833, respectively. Unfortunately, with one or two exceptions, these copies of the lists do not provide the names of those amnestied.

20. *Galería*, vol. 1, pp. 261–262, and Guiard, *Villa*, vol. 4, pp. 430–431. Guiard cites several passages of M.F.M. de Vargas's *La Guerra en Navarra y Provincias Vascongadas* (Madrid: n.p., 1848), a work I have not been able to consult. Additional information on the split among Spanish royalists in Suárez, *La crisis*, pp. 106–130 passim.

21. AMAE, CPC, Espagne, vol. 5, letter of Regnaudin to the minister of foreign affairs, 21 October 1832.

22. For information on the numerical strength of the Vizcayan militias, see chapter 5. For liberal attempts at neutralizing the military force of local royalists, see chapters 5 and 6, and chapter 7 passim.

23. See Suárez, *La crisis*, pp. 228–230; and Zaratiegui, *Zumalacárregui*, p. 23. The latter's remarks on the question are excellent.

24. Llauder, *Memorias*, p. 82 (text), and pp. 36–38 (appendix 27).

25. AMAE, CPC, Espagne, vol. 5, 1832 annual report, 14 March 1833.

26. Uhagon, *Informe*, pp. 12, 14–17, 20–22, 37–38, and 45.

27. Bacon, *Six Years in Biscay*, pp. 131–132.

28. Ibid.

29. Uhagon, *Informe*, p. 14 passim. Timely comments on this important point in Hormaeche, "De las causas," pp. 339 and 343; and in Bacon, *Six Years in Biscay*, pp. 131–132.

30. Sagarmínaga, *Gobierno*, vol. 8, p. 160. The officer's letter was dated 7 May 1833 (at San Sebastián).

31. Ibid., pp. 160–161. The *alocución* was dated 11 May 1833 (at San Sebastián).

32. AMAE, CD, Espagne, vol. 759, document entitled, "*Copie de la lettre addressée au Gén[ér]al Harispe par le S[ieur] Nicolás de Castro le 16 mai 1833*," sent from Bayonne.

33. ACJG, Policía, reg. 31, dispatch no. 164 of the Vizcayan police to central headquarters, 13 May 1833. Additional symptoms of liberal agitation in Bilbao, in dispatch no. 165 (dated the same day and to the same destination).

34. APG, *Actas*, session of 28 June 1833.

35. See in particular ACJG, Policía, reg. 32, letter central headquarters, 24 June 1833. Even Victor Luis de Gaminde obliquely admitted that there was something suspiciously peculiar about liberalism's success at the 1833 juntas; see *Intereses*, p. 38.

36. See Hormaeche, "De las causas," pp. 339–343; and Uhagon, *Informe*, pp. 12–15.

37. APG, *Actas*, sessions of 18 and 20 November 1832.

38. Sagarmínaga, *Gobierno*, vol. 8, pp. 163–164. Most of the materials on the 1833 juntas used in this section are from Sagarmínaga, pp. 163–207.

39. Ibid., pp. 166–168.

40. Ibid., pp. 168–195 passim.

41. Ibid., pp. 188 and 195–197.

42. Ibid., p. 189. This commission, as noted below, was openly criticized by the Vizcayan police, a body still very much in conservative hands.

43. Ibid., pp. 201–202.

44. See *Galería*, vol. 1, p. 263; Hormaeche, "De las causas," pp. 341–342; and Bacon, *Six Years in Biscay*, p. 131.

45. Sagarmínaga, *Gobierno*, vol. 8, pp. 190–191.

46. Ibid.

47. *Galería*, vol. 1, pp. 263–264. More on this in Pirala, *Historia*, vol. 1, p. 405.

48. *Galería*, vol. 1, pp. 263–264 and 269.

49. Ibid.

50. Ibid., vol. 1, pp. 263–264.

51. Sagarmínaga, *Gobierno*, vol. 8, pp. 192–193 and 201.

52. Consult the following: (a) letter of the new General Deputies Zavala and Uhagon and the Corregidor de la Mota, to Ferdinand VII, 3 August 1833, in [Juan Antonio Suárez], *Fastos españoles o efeméridas de la guerra civil desde Octubre de 1832*, 2 vols. (Madrid: Imprenta de Ignacio Boix, 1839–1840), vol. 1, pp. 408–409 (hereafter cited as *Fastos*); (b) Pirala, *Historia*, vol. 1, p. 93; (c) Sagarmínaga, *Gobierno*, vol. 8, pp. 200–201; (d) Uhagon, *Informe*, pp. 13–14; and (e) Bayo, *Historia de la vida y reinado de Fernando VII de España*, vol. 3, p. 418.

53. Sagarmínaga, *Gobierno*, vol. 8, p. 201.

54. See (a) and (b) in note 52 above.

55. Hormaeche, "De las causas," pp. 341–342.

56. Bacon, *Six Years in Biscay*, p. 131. See also Pirala, *Historia*, vol. 1, p. 105.

57. Hormaeche, "De las causas," p. 342.

58. Bacon, *Six Years in Biscay*, p. 131.

59. Ibid.

60. ACJG, Policía, reg. 31, dispatch no. 262 to central headquarters, 2 August 1833.

61. Uhagon, *Informe*, pp. 12–13.

62. Hormaeche, "De las causas," p. 342. See also Uhagon, *Informe*, p. 14.

63. Uhagon, *Informe*, p. 17: "*Le halagaba extraordinariamente ver su nombre escrito a la cabeza de todo lo que pareciese grande, y esto bastaba para estimularle y atraerlo a mi objeto.*"

64. Pirala, *Historia*, vol. 1, p. 105.

65. Uhagon, *Informe*, pp. 13–16.

66. Ibid.

67. Ibid., pp. 17–18.

68. Ibid., p. 18.

69. Ibid. Although incorporated into the organization of the Paisanos Armados (in Bilbao at least), these corps were still known as the Guardia de Honor.

70. Ibid.

71. Ibid.

72. Ibid., pp. 18–19.

73. Ibid., pp. 18–19. See also Hormaeche, "De las causas," pp. 342–343.

74. Ibid., p. 17.

75. Ibid., pp. 19–20. Similar strong criticisms of the central government's inactivity and neglect toward the Basque provinces in Hormaeche, "De las causas," pp. 340–341, and in the anonymous 1834 pamphlet entitled *Observaciones*, p. 21.

76. Uhagon, *Informe*, p. 19.

77. Ibid., p. 20.

78. Ibid., pp. 20–21.

79. [Suárez], *Fastos*, vol. 1, p. 473. See also p. 478. In sum, given the mass of evidence, it is impossible to agree with the interpretation of Miguel Artola in *La burguesía revolucionaria*, pp. 54–55.

80. For example, see Henningsen's claim that royalists were without organization prior to Ferdinand's death, in *Zumalacárregui*, vol. 1, pp. 33–34.

81. Goicoechea, *Luminous Guide*, pp. 8–9; Hormaeche, "De las causas," pp. 339–344 passim; *Observaciones*, p. 23; and Pirala, *Historia*, vol. 1, p. 92.

82. Uhagon, *Informe*, p. 3. Despite Uhagon's bitter resentment caused by the Carlists' persecution, which included three weeks in hiding and thirty days in a public jail, on the whole the author's narrative is rather straightforward, informative, and contains remarkably little rhetoric.

83. Ibid., p. 12.

84. Ibid., p. 15. Other unmistakable references to a plot in pp. 25–29 passim.

85. Ibid., pp. 15–16.

86. See his *Demonstración del incontestable derecho*, in *Fastos*, vol. 1, p. 544.

87. For the outbreak of the October Carlist rebellion I have relied on these sources: (a) Uhagon, *Informe*, passim; (b) Bacon, *Six Years in Biscay*, pp. 129–143 passim; (c) *Fastos*, vol. 1, pp. 487–489, letter of the Vizcayan Diputación and the corregidor to the queen, 30 November 1833; (d) Pirala, *Historia*, vol. 1, pp. 105–106; (e) *Galería*, vol. 1, pp. 267–273; (f) Hormaeche, "De las causas," pp. 343–345; (g) José F. Acedo, Melchor Ferrer, and Domingo Tejera, *Historia del tradicionalismo español*, 30 vols. (Sevilla: Editorial Católica Española [vols. 1–2], Ediciones Trajano [vol. 3], 1941–1942), vol. 3, pp. 187–190 (hereafter cited as *Tradicionalismo*); (h) Goicoechea, *Luminous Guide*, pp. 8–9; (i) Guiard, *Villa*, vol. 4, pp. 453–477 passim; (j) Bordas, *Historia de la revolución y guerra civil de España*, p. 27; (k) AMAE, CPC, Espagne, vol. 6, dispatches nos. 3, 4, and 5 of Regnaudin to the minister of foreign affairs, dated 3, 6, and 7 October 1833, respectively; and (l) ACJG, Policía, reg. 31, dispatch no. 340 of the Vizcayan police to central headquarters (labeled "*Extraordinario*"), 4 October 1833.

88. [Suárez], *Fastos*, vol. 1, p. 487; *Galería*, vol. 1, pp. 267–268; and Uhagon, *Informe*, pp. 22–24.

89. Uhagon, *Informe*, pp. 23–34. More on the militias' refusal to heed the Diputación's orders in *Galería*, vol. 1, pp. 267–270; [Suárez], *Fastos*, vol. 1, p. 487; and Pirala, *Historia*, vol. 1, p. 105.

90. [Suárez], *Fastos*, vol. 1, p. 487.

91. Uhagon, *Informe*, pp. 24–26 and 28; [Suárez], *Fastos*, vol. 1, p. 487; *Galería*, vol. 1, p. 268; Hormaeche, "De las causas," p. 343; and Pirala, *Historia*, vol. 1, p. 105.

92. Uhagon, *Informe*, p. 24.

93. Bacon, *Six Years in Biscay*, pp. 132–138 passim.

94. For example, see *Galería*, vol. 1, p. 270; Hormaeche, "De las causas," pp. 343–344; and, of course, Regnaudin's early October 1833 reports—

see (k) in note 87 above for complete references—which definitely suggest surprisingly little social disorder and upheaval during the Carlist rebellion's beginning.

95. *Galería*, vol. 1, p. 270.

96. See the following: Uhagon, *Informe*, pp. 47–48; Bacon, *Six Years in Biscay*, pp. 137–146 passim; *Galería*, vol. 1, pp. 270–271; [Suárez], *Fastos*, vol. 1, p. 488; Pirala, *Historia*, vol. 1, p. 106; and AMAE, CPC, Espagne, vol. 6, dispatch no. 5 of Regnaudin, 7 October 1833.

97. Uhagon, *Informe*, pp. 47–48.

98. See the following: Uhagon, *Informe*, pp. 43–51 passim; *Galería*, vol. 1, pp. 269–270; Bacon, *Six Years in Biscay*, pp. 132–138 passim; [Suárez], *Fastos*, vol. 1, pp. 488, 504, 508, and 527–528; Pirala, *Historia*, vol. 1, p. 105; Hormaeche, "De las causas," p. 344; Acedo, Ferrer, and Tejera, *Tradicionalismo*, vol. 3, pp. 187–188; and AMAE, CPC, Espagne, vol. 6, dispatch no. 5 of Regnaudin, 7 October 1833.

99. The names are drawn from these sources: Uhagon, *Informe*, pp. 43–44 (Landeza and Velasco); *Galería*, vol. 1, p. 269 (Mena); and Bacon, *Six Years in Biscay*, p. 135 (Landeza). In Uhagon's account, Landeza's name is misspelled twice as Landeta—an obvious mistake of transcription.

100. Uhagon, *Informe*, p. 44.

101. Ibid., p. 25.

102. [Suárez], *Fastos*, vol. 1, p. 487, and Uhagon, *Informe*, p. 26.

103. Uhagon, *Informe*, pp. 26–27.

104. [Suárez], *Fastos*, vol. 1, pp. 487–488. Essentially, the same description in Uhagon, *Informe*, p. 28.

105. Bacon, *Six Years in Biscay*, pp. 133–134, and Uhagon, *Informe*, p. 29. The quote in the text is Uhagon's. On the Miqueletes' complicity with the rebels, see ibid., pp. 18–19 and [Suárez], *Fastos*, vol. 1, p. 488. In the latter passage, the Miqueletes' collusion with the Carlists is more pronounced. See also Hormaeche, "De las causas," p. 344, and Regnaudin's dispatches of 6 and 7 October 1833.

106. See (l) in note 87 above.

107. *Galería*, vol. 1, pp. 270–272 (with at least three references in this respect); [Suárez], *Fastos*, vol. 1, p. 487 (the rubric introducing the Carlist uprising at Bilbao reads, "*Pronunciamiento a favor de D[on]. Carlos en Bilbao*"); Bacon, *Six Years in Biscay*, pp. 132–138 passim; Hormaeche, "De las causas," p. 344; and Uhagon, *Informe*, passim. Uhagon's numerous remarks on the insurrection leave little doubt that he considered the movement a kind of military coup and pronouncement. See also Louis de Carné, "De l'Espagne au dix-neuvième siècle," *Revue des Deux Mondes*, 4th series, no. 8 (1836), p. 649.

108. For possible indications of Vizcayan resistance to the Carlists' seizure of power, see [Suárez], *Fastos*, vol. 1, pp. 528–535. It should be underscored, however, that both accounts have a patently anti-Carlist bias.

109. AMAE, CPC, vol. 6, dispatch of Regnaudin, 7 October 1833. See also Bacon, *Six Years in Biscay*, "A white flag, bearing his device, was hoisted in the Arenal" (p. 135).

110. Bacon, *Six Years in Biscay*, p. 135. These important observations indicate that the proclamation of the previous day (3 October) had been more or less "informal," and that now Carlists moved swiftly to legitimize and make official their seizure of power.

111. See Charles Louis Lesur, *Annuaire historique universel ou histoire politique pour 1818–1861* (Paris: A. Thoisnier-Desplaces and others 1821–1866), p. 516; Henningsen, *Zumalacárregui*, vol. 1, p. 38; Uhagon, *Informe*, p. 25; and S. E. Widdrington's pointed remarks on this question in *Sketches*, vol. 1, pp. 329–330.

112. Interesting remarks along these lines in the *Galería*, vol. 1, p. 272.

113. For the important role of the Vizcayan clergy in the insurrection, see the following: Uhagon, *Informe*, pp. 42–49 passim; [Suárez], *Fastos*, vol. 1, pp. 487–489, 571–572, and 603; APG, *Actas*, session of 6 December 1833, (the letter read at this session was most probably that of the liberal Vizcayan Diputación dated 30 November 1833, reproduced in *Fastos*); Bacon, *Six Years in Biscay*, p. 135; and S. E. Widdrington, *Sketches*, vol. 1, pp. 329–330.

114. Zaratiegui, *Zumalacárregui*, p. 9.

115. Pirala, *Historia*, vol. 1, pp. 77–78.

116. For the first, I have used an original copy which Regnaudin forwarded to the minister of foreign affairs along with his letter of 9 October 1833, in AMAE, CPC, Espagne, vol. 6. This document may also be consulted, among other places, in the Marquis de Miraflores's *Memorias del Reinado de Isabel II*, 3 vols., Biblioteca de Autores Españoles, nos. 172–174, edited with a preliminary study by Manuel Fernández Alvarez (Madrid: Atlas, 1964), vol. 1, no. 172, pp. 212–213. For the second, see [Suárez], *Fastos*, vol. 1, pp. 536–546. See also Bacon, *Six Years in Biscay*, pp. 132–133.

117. [Suárez], *Fastos*, vol. 1, p. 537.

118. Ibid., vol. 1, p. 503. More on Ibarrola's "pronunciamiento" in the same work, pp. 496–498.

119. The first expression is from Valde-espina's proclamation; the second is attributed by Uhagon to the Carlists (*Informe*, p. 13); and the third is from Valentin de Verastegui's famous proclamation issued at Vitoria on 7 October 1833. This important document is reproduced in vol. 172 of the Biblioteca de Autores Españoles, pp. 213–215. See note 116 for a complete reference.

120. See Bacon, *Six Years in Biscay*, p. 135; Pirala, *Historia*, vol. 1, pp. 77–78; [Suárez], *Fastos*, 1, pp. 536 and 545; and my earlier remarks on xenophobia in chapter 3. Don Carlos's Spanish extraction was certainly to his political advantage, while the queen's foreign origin proved a strong liability, especially among traditionalists.

121. See in particular Manuel Gómez de Negrete, *Demostración del incontestable deracho que el Sr. D. Carlos de Borbón tiene al Trono de España* (Bilbao: n.p., 1833), passim; Valde-espina's and Verastegui's proclamations, passim; as well as Ibarrola's proclamation which was pointedly addressed to the "Soldados del ergército español," in [Suárez], *Fastos*, vol. 1, pp. 503–504.

122. Liberalism was understandably eager to underscore the clergy's enormous influence over an allegedly ignorant and fanatic population. In addition

to the sources detailed in note 113 above, see the following: Goicoechea, *Luminous Guide*, pp. 9–11 and 23–24; and the manifesto of the liberal Alavese Diputación to the queen, dated 21 November 1833, in [Suárez], *Fastos*, vol. 1, pp. 523–532 and 552–555 passim.

123. *Cronología de los sucesos más memorables ocurridos en todo el ámbito de la Monarquía Española, desde el año de 1759 hasta 1836* (Madrid: Imprenta de M. Calero), p. 119.

124. Hormaeche, "De las causas," p. 339. Additional important remarks on p. 340.

125. Uhagon, *Informe*, pp. 14–15. Similar observations along these lines in the *Galería*, vol. 1, pp. 260–261 and 264–265.

126. Pirala, *Historia*, vol. 1, p. 136.

127. In Miraflores's *Memorias*, pp. 213–215; and in [Suárez], *Fastos*, vol. 1, p. 550, respectively.

128. Boislecomte, *Ensayo histórico*, vol. 1, p. 90.

129. Ibid., vol. 1, p. 98. Emphasis added.

130. Ibid., vol. 1, p. 230.

131. Ibid., vol. 1, p. 231. Other interesting remarks related to this on pp. 238–239. Also, on the importance of the Basque fueros, consider Hormaeche's significant observations in "De las causas," pp. 337 and 345; as well as Zaratiegui's in *Zumalacárregui*, p. 22.

Selected Bibliography

Manuscript Sources

Archives du Ministère des Affaires Étrangères, Paris (AMAE):
    Correspondance Consulaire, Bilbao (CC); Correspondance
    Diplomatique, Espagne (CD)—this section also goes by the title of
    Correspondance Politique; Correspondance Politique des Consuls,
    Espagne (CPC); Mémoires et Documents, Espagne (M&D).
Archives Nationales, Paris (ANP).
    Administration générale de la France: F 7—Police générale; F 11—
    Subsistances; F 12—Commerce et industrie; F 15—Hospices et secours.
    Archives des Affaires Étrangères: B I—Correspondance consulaire; B III
    —Affaires commerciales.
    Archives du pouvoir exécutif de 1789 à 1815: AF I, II, III, IV, and V.
Archivo de la Casa de Juntas de Guernica, Vizcaya (ACJG): Agentes y
    Diputados en Corte; Brigadas de Paisanos Armados; Carabineros;
    Constitución. Expedientes y Ordenes del Tiempo de la Constitución,
    1820; Corregimiento; Diputación General; Elecciones; Expedientes.
    Expedientes y Escrituras Varias (title varies slightly according to
    volume); Exposiciones y Representaciones al Rey, sus Ministros,
    Diputación de Vizcaya, etc.; Ferrerías; Granos; Minería; Molineros;
    Policía.
Archivo de la Diputación de Vizcaya, Bilbao (ADV): Biblioteca;
    Corregimiento; Sala de Guernica. (This section is also referred to as the
    "Sala [de] Villarías" since the room where the materials are housed also
    serves as the depository for the archive of the family by that name. I
    have opted for the title of Guernica because the overwhelming majority
    of documents in this section come from the former seat of government
    and Diputación of the province. In addition, Guernica has often been
    regarded as the capital and seat of government of Vizcaya.)
Archivo de la Presidencia del Gobierno, Madrid (APG): Actas del Consejo
    de Ministros (Actas).
Archivo de la Real Academia de la Historia, Madrid (ARAH): Population
    census known as that of Aranda; Population census known as that of
    Floridablanca; Colección Vargas Ponce.
Archivo de la Real Chancillería de Valladolid (ARCV): Sala de Vizcaya.
Archivo de las Cortes, Madrid (AC).

Archivo General del Palacio, Madrid (AGP): Papeles reservados de
    Fernando VII.
Archivo General de Simancas (AGS): Consejo Supremo de Hacienda;
    Dirección General de Rentas; Secretaría y Superintendencia de
    Hacienda.
Archivo Histórico Nacional, Madrid (AHN): Sección de Clero Secular y
    Regular (Clero); Sección de Consejos Suprimidos (Consejos); Sección de
    Estado.
Biblioteca Nacional de Madrid (BNM): Sección Manuscritos.
Service Historique de l'Armée de Terre, Vincennes, France (SHAT): Armée
    d'Espagne, 1808–1814 (C/8); Mémoires et reconnaissances; Mémoires
    historiques.
Private collections:
Archive and Library of José María de Areilza, Count of Motrico (Madrid).
Archive and Library of Juan Ramón Urquijo (Bilbao).

Public Documents

*Actas de las sesiones secretas de las Cortes generales (y) extraordinarias
    de la nación española, que se instalaron en la Isla de León el dia 24 de
    setiembre de 1810, de las celebradas por la Diputación permanente de
    Cortes, instalada en la propia ciudad el dia 9 de dicho mes, y de las
    secretas de las Cortes ordinarias, que se instalaron en la misma ciudad
    el 25 del propio mes, y trasladadas a Madrid, fueron disueltas en su
    segunda legislatura el 10 de Mayo de 1814.* Madrid: Imprenta de J. A.
    García, 1874.
*Actas de las sesiones secretas de las Cortes ordinarias y extraordinarias de
    los años 1820 y 1821, de las de los años 1822 y 1823, y de las
    celebradas por las Diputaciones permanentes de las mismas Cortes
    ordinarias.* Madrid: Imprenta de J. A. García, 1874.
*Adición al reglamento para los voluntarios realistas del reino,
    correspondiente a las Provincias Vascongadas.* Madrid: Imprenta de José
    de Collado, 1826.
Calendario manual y guía de forasteros en Madrid. Madrid: Imprenta Real,
    1825–1827 and 1829–1834. (This collection is sometimes catalogued
    under the title of *Guía Oficial de España.*)
*Censo de la población de España de el año 1797, executado de orden del
    Rey en el de 1801.* Madrid: Imprenta de Vega y Compañía, 1801.
*Censo español executado de orden del rey, comunicada por el
    excelentísimo señor conde de Floridablanca, primer secretario estado y
    del despacho, en el año de 1787.* Madrid: Imprenta Real, 1787.
Colección de los decretos y órdenes generales expedidos por las Cortes.
    10 vols. Madrid: Imprenta Nacional [and others], 1820–1823. (The title
    presented here has slight variants in some of the volumes. The
    collection covers the Cortes's legislation from 24 September 1810 to
    11 May 1814, and from 6 June 1820 to 19 February 1823. The
    abbreviation for it in this text is *CDC.*)

Copia del Informe de la Junta de Reforma de Abusos de Real Hacienda de las Provincias Vascongadas, creada en Real Orden de 6 de Noviembre de 1815. Madrid: Oficina de Tomás Jordán, Impresor de Cámara de S.M., 1839.

Decretos del rey don Fernando VII. 19 vols. Madrid: Imprenta Real, 1816–1834. By Fermín Martín de Balmaseda (1814–1823) and by Josef María de Nieva (1833). This has been abbreviated as *CD*.

Diario de las actas y discusiones de las Cortes, legislatura de los años de 1820 y 1821. 23 vols. Madrid: Imprenta de Diego Campoy y compañía, vols. 1–18; Imprenta Nacional, vols. 19–22; Imprenta de la Minera Española, vol. 23, 1820–1821. (This series also contains an appendix entitled *Apéndices al diario de las actas y discusiones de las Cortes. Legislatura de los años de 1820 y 1821*. Madrid: Imprenta Nacional, 1820–1821.)

Diario de las sesiones de Cortes. 16 vols. Madrid: Imprenta de J. A. García, 1858–1885. (Volume for April–December 1823 has the imprint Madrid: La Imprenta Nacional, 1858.) This is abbreviated *DSC*.

Ferrer y Jou, Narciso. See *Guía de la Real Hacienda*.

González, Tomás. *Colección de cédulas, cartas-patentes, provisiones, reales órdenes y otros documentos concernientes a las Provincias Vascongadas, copiados de orden de S.M. de los registros, minutas y escrituras existentes en el Real Archivo de Simancas, y en los de las Secretarías de Estado y del Despacho y otras oficinas de la Corte*. 6 vols. Madrid: Imprenta Real (vols. 1–4) 1829–1830. The next two volumes have a different title: *Colección de privilegios, franquezas, exenciones y fueros, concedidos a varios pueblos y corporaciones de la Corona de Castilla copiados de orden de S.M. de los registros del Real Archivo de Simancas. Sirve ce continuación a la 'Colección de documentos concernientes a las Provincias Vascongadas'*. Madrid: Imprenta Real (vol. 5), Imprenta de Miguel de Burgos (vol. 6), 1830–1833.

Guía de la Real Hacienda. Parte Legislativa. Reales decretos y órdenes de S.M. que producen resolución general en materias de su real Hacienda expedidos desde el 6 de Abril de 1823, en que se restableció el gobierno del rey N.S. hasta fin del mismo año. Por Don Narciso Ferrer y Jou. 12 vols. Madrid: Imprenta de Miguel de Burgos, 1828–1834. (I have also used the *Guía* in its *Parte Legislativa* [there is also a *Reglamentaria*] for the years 1823–1833. [2 vols. for 1824]. The volume for 1827 is: Madrid: León Amarita, 1828.)

Guía Oficial de España. See *Calendario manual y guía de forasteros en Madrid*.

Informe de la Comisión del Territorio español, leido en la sesión de las Cortes en 19 de Junio de 1821. Impreso por orden de las Mismas. Madrid: Imprenta de I. Sancha, 1821.

Plan de Iguala. N.p., n.d. (Full title: *Informe evacuado con fecha 14 de Agosto de 1832 por la comisión permanente de Caminos [de Vizcaya] creada en Junta general de 12 de Julio de 1831, compuesta de los*

Señores D. Pedro Novia de Salcedo, D. Agustín de Ventades, D. Pedro María de Albiz, D. Juan Luis de Goxeascoechea, D. Domingo de Zabala, D. José Joaquín de Arguinzoniz, D. José María de Lambarri, Don Juan de Tellitu y Antuñano, y D. Casimiro de Lóyzaga.)

Polo y Catalina, Juan. *Censo de Frutos y Manufacturas de España y sus Islas.* Madrid: Imprenta Real, 1803.

Propuesta de ley que el Rey hace a las Cortes sobre la división territorial de la península. Madrid: Imprenta que fué de García, 1821.

Reglamento criminal para la sustanciación y determinación de las causas de robos, hurtos, muerte en despoblado o de noche, en el M.N. y M.L. Señorío de Vizcaya, aprobado por S.M. en 18 de Diciembre de 1799. Bilbao: Eusebio de Larumbe, 1815.

Reglamento para los cuerpos de voluntarios realistas del reino. Madrid: Imprenta de José del Collado, 1826.

Report from the Select Committee of the House of Lords, appointed to take into consideration the state of the British wool trade, And to report to the House, together with minutes of evidence taken before the said committee, and an appendix and index thereto. Ordered to be printed 27th June 1828. N.p., n.d. (Front page notation: *Ordered, by* The House of Commons, *To be printed,* 8 July 1828.)

Representaciones elevadas al Soberano Congreso Nacional para que digne declarar a Bilbao por Puerto de depósito de primera clase. Bilbao: Eusebio de Larumbe, 1820.

Books and Articles

Acedo, José F.; Ferrer, Melchor; and Tejera, Domingo. *Historia del tradicionalismo español.* 30 vols. Sevilla: Editorial Católica Española (vols. 1–2), Ediciones Trajano (vol. 3), 1941–1942.

Adorno, Theodor W. et al. *The Authoritarian Personality.* New York: Harper, 1950.

Alonso Tejada, Luis. *Ocaso de la Inquisición en los últimos años del reinado de Fernando VII. Juntas de Fé, Juntas Apostólicas, Conspiraciones Realistas.* Algorta: Zero, 1969.

Aranguren y Sobrado, Francisco de. *Demostración del sentido verdadero de las autoridades de que se vale el Doctor Don Juan Antonio de Llorente, Canónigo de la Catedral de Toledo, en el Tomo I, de las 'Noticias Históricas de las Provincias Vascongadas,' y de lo que verdad resulta de los historiadores que cita, con respecto solamente al Muy Noble y Muy Leal Señorío de Vizcaya.* Madrid: Imprenta de Vega y Compañía, 1807.

Areilza, José María de. "La economía vizcaína a fines del siglo XVIII." *Boletín de la Real Sociedad Vascongada de Amigos del País.* Año II, Cuaderno 2°: 1946, pp. 131–147.

Areitio y Mendiolea, Darío de. *El Gobierno Universal del Señorío de Vizcaya. Cargos y personas que los desempeñaron. Juntas, Regimientos y Diputación.* Bilbao: Junta de Cultura de Vizcaya, 1943.

Artola, Miguel. *La burguesía revolucionaria (1808–1869)*. Madrid: Alianza
   Editorial, 1973.
———. *La España de Fernando VII*. In *Historia de España* directed by
   Ramón Menendez Pidal, vol. 26. [Introduction by Carlos Seco Serrano].
   Madrid: Espasa-Calpe, 1968.
Bacon, John Francis. *Six Years in Biscay: comprising a personal narrative
   of the sieges of Bilbao, in June 1835, and Oct. to Dec. 1836, and of the
   principal events which occurred in that city and the Basque Provinces,
   during the years 1830 to 1837*. London: Smith, Elder and Co., Cornhill,
   1838.
Baines, Edward. *Account of the Woollen Manufacture in England*. New
   introduction by K. G. Ponting. New York: A.M. Kelley, 1970.
Balparda, Gregorio de. *Don Martín de los Heros y el Progresismo
   Vascongado de su Tiempo*. Bordeaux: Feret & Fils, 1925.
Barahona, Renato. "Basque Regionalism and Centre-Periphery Relations,
   1759–1833." *European Studies Review*. Vol. 13, no. 3: July 1983.
———. "Histoire d'une révolte en Biscaye: Bilbao, 1631–1634." Diplôme
   d'Études Supérieures, Paris: École Pratique des Hautes Études, 1971.
——— [Arévalo]. "*The Making of Carlism in Vizcaya (1814–1833)*." 2 vols.
   Doctoral dissertation, Princeton University, Department of History,
   1979.
———. "Politics, Ideology and the Fueros in Vizcaya During the Initial
   Phase of the Liberal Triennium (1820)." In *Basque Politics: A Case
   Study in Ethnic Nationalism*. Edited by William A. Douglass.
   Associated Faculty Press, Inc., and Basque Studies Program: University
   of Nevada, Reno, Nevada, 1985.
———. "Regional Attitudes and Conflicts in Ancien Régime Spain:
   Basques and Castilians Revisited." *Journal of Basque Studies*. Vol. 4,
   no. 1: 1983.
[Bayo, Estanislao de Kotska.] *Historia de la vida y reinado de Fernando VII
   de España*. 3 vols. Madrid: Imprenta de Repullés, 1842.
Bell Stephens, Edward. *The Basque Provinces: Their political state,
   scenery, and inhabitants, with adventures amongst the Carlists and
   Christinos*. 2 vols. London: Whittaker & Co., 1837.
[Boislecomte, Charles Joseph Edmond Sain de.] *Ensayo histórico sobre las
   Provincias Vascongadas, (Alava, Guipuzcoa, Vizcaya y Navarra), y
   sobre la guerra que actualmente sostienen*. Translated by Pedro
   Martínez López. 2 vols. Bordeaux: Cl. Dulac, 1836.
Bordas, Luis. *Historia de la revolución y guerra civil de España, o sea
   hechos memorables acaecidos desde la última enfermedad de
   Fernando VII hasta la conclusión de la guerra en los campos de
   Vergara*. Barcelona: Librería de Manuel Sauri, Imprenta Hispana, 1847.
Bosc, Louis. "Voyage en Espagne, à travers les royaumes de Galice, Leon,
   Castille vieille, et Biscaye." *Magasin Encyclopédique, ou Journal des
   Sciences, des Lettres et des Artes* (Paris). VI Année, tome premier: 1800.
Bourgoing, Adolphe de. *L'Espagne, souvenirs de 1823 et de 1833*. Paris:
   P. Dufart, 1834.

Bowles, Guillermo. *Introducción a la Historia Natural, y a la Geografía Física de España*. 2d edition. Madrid: Imprenta Real, 1782.

Bramsen, John. *Remarks on the North of Spain*. London: Printed for G. and W. B. Whittaker, 1823.

Burgo, Jaime del. *Bibliografía de las Guerras Carlistas y de las luchas políticas del siglo XIX*. 5 vols. Pamplona: Diputación Foral de Navarra, Institución Príncipe de Viana, 1953–1966.

———. *Origen y fundamento del régimen foral de Navarra*. Pamplona: Diputación Foral de Navarra, Institución Príncipe de Viana, 1968.

Canga Arguelles, José. *Diccionario de hacienda, con aplicación a España*. 2 vols. Madrid: Imprenta de Marcelino Calero y Portocarrero, 1833–1834.

Capefigue, Jean Baptiste Honoré Reymond. *Récit des opérations de l'Armée en Espagne, sous les ordres de S.A.R. Mgr Duc d'Angouleme. Accompagné de notices biographiques et géographiques et suivi de considérations sur les résultats politiques de cette guerre*. Paris: E. Gide, 1823.

Carles Clemente, Josep. *Los origines del carlismo*. Madrid: Ediciones EASA, 1979.

Carné, Louis de. "De l'Espagne au dix-neuvième siècle." *Revue des Deux Mondes*. 4th series, no. 8: 1836, pp. 5–33, 377–406, 641–673.

Caro Baroja, Julio. *Los Vascos*. 2d Edition. Madrid: Ediciones Minotauro, 1958.

Clavero, Bartolomé. *Mayorazgo, propiedad feudal en Castilla (1369–1836)*. Madrid: Siglo XXI de España Editores, 1974.

Carreras y Candi, Francisco, director. *Geografía General del País Vasco-Navarro*. 6 vols. Barcelona: Editorial Alberto Martín, n.d.

Comellas García-Llera, José Luis. *Los primeros pronunciamientos en España*. Madrid: Consejo Superior de Investigaciones Científicas, 1958.

———. *Los realistas en el Trienio Constitucional (1820–1823)*. Pamplona: Universidad de Navarra, Colección histórica, no. 1, 1958.

———. *El Trienio Constitucional*. Madrid: Rialp, 1963.

Condiciones y semblanzas de los diputados a Cortes para la legislatura de 1820 y 1821. Madrid: Imprenta de Juan Ramos y Compañía, 1821.

Condiciones y semblanzas de los Sres Diputados a Cortes para los años de 1822 y 1823. Madrid: Imprenta del Zurriago, 1822.

Corcuera Atienza, Javier. *Orígenes, ideología y organización del nacionalismo vasco, 1876–1904*. Madrid: Siglo XXI de España Editores, 1979.

Cruz y Bahamonde, Nicolás de la. *Viage de España, Francia, e Italia*. Vol. 10. Cádiz: En la Imprenta de Manuel Bosch, 1812.

Delmas, Juan Ernesto. *Viaje pintoresco por las Provincias Vascongadas. Obra destinada a dar a conocer su historia y sus principales vistas, monumentos y antiguedades, etc., en láminas litografiadas copiadas al daguerrotipo e del natural*. Bilbao: Imprenta y Librería de N. Delmas, 1846.

Diccionario geográfico-histórico de España por la Real Academia de

Historia. Seccion I. Comprehende el Reyno de Navarra, Señorío de Vizcaya, y provincias de Alava y Guipuzcoa. 2 vols. Madrid: Imprenta de la Viuda de Joaquín Ibarra, 1802.

Diputados por la peninsula, para la legislatura de los Años de 1822 y 1823. Sevilla: Por la Viuda de Vázquez y Compañía, 1822.

Domínguez Ortiz, Antonio. *Sociedad y estado en el siglo XVIII español.* Barcelona-Caracas-Mexico: Ariel, 1976.

Duvergier de Hauranne, Jean-Marie. *Coup-d'oeuil sur l'Espagne.* Paris: Baudouin Frères, Libraires, 1824.

Encima y Piedra, Victoriano de. *De los sucesos del Real Sitio de San Ildefonso, o La Granja, a fines del año de 1832; de las disposiciones tomadas por le ministerio que se nombró en el 1 de Octubre del mismo año, y de las causas inmediatas del estado actual de España.* Paris: Librería de Rosa, 1837.

Espronceda, José de. "El Ministerio Mendizabal." *Biblioteca de Autores Españoles.* Madrid: Atlas, 1954. Vol. 72, pp. 573–579.

Fernandez Albadalejo, Pablo. *La crisis del Antiguo Régimen en Guipuzcoa, 1766–1833: cambio económico e historia.* Madrid: Akal editor, 1975.

Fernández de Pinedo, Emiliano. *Crecimiento económico y transformaciones sociales del País Vasco (1100–1850).* Madrid: Siglo XXI de España Editores, 1974.

———. "La entrada de la tierra en el circuito comercial: la desamortización en Vascongadas. Planteamiento y primeros resultados." *Agricultura, comercio colonial, y crecimiento económico en la España contemporanea.* Edited by Jordi Nadal and Gabriel Tortella. Barcelona: Ariel, 1974. Pp. 100–128.

Fontana Lázaro, Josep. "Colapso y transformación del comercio exterior español entre 1792 y 1827. Un aspecto de la crisis de la economía del Antiguo régimen en España." *Moneda y crédito.* No. 115: December, 1970, pp. 3–23.

———. *La crisis del Antiguo régimen (1808–1833).* 2d edition. Barcelona: Editorial Crítica [Grupo Editorial Grijalbo], 1983.

———. *Hacienda y estado en la crisis final del Antiguo régimen español: 1823–1833.* Madrid: Instituto de Estudios Fiscales, 1973.

———. *La quiebra de la monarquía absoluta (1814–1820). La crisis del Antiguo régimen en España.* Barcelona: Ariel, 1971.

Galería militar contemporanea, o sea colección de biografías y retratos. 2 vols. Madrid: Sociedad Tipográfica de Hortelano y Compañía, 1845–1846.

Gambra, Rafael. *La primera guerra civil en España (1821–1823). Historia y meditación de una lucha olvidada.* 2d edition. Madrid: Escelicer, 1972.

Gaminde, Benito Felipe. *Memoria sobre el estado actual de las lanas merinas españolas y su cotejo con las extranjeras, causas de la decadencia de las primeras y remedio para mejorarlas.* Madrid: Imprenta de E. Aguado, 1827.

Gaminde, Victor Luis. *Intereses de Bilbao. Ecsamen de lo perjudicial que sería la permanencia del sistema foral en el siglo XIX al comercio e industria del país, y a los liberales de Vizcaya.* Bilbao: Imprenta de Adolfo Depont, 1837.

Goicoechea, Sotero de. *A Luminous Guide for the British Cooperative Forces in Spain on the Principal Subjects connected with particular information relative to the Basque Provinces.* Bayonne: [Lamaignère], 1836.

González Portilla, Manuel. "La población en la zona minera y la Ría de Bilbao en el siglo XIX. Daracaldo, un ejemplo del paso de una demografía de Antiguo régimen a la Revolución industrial." Master's thesis, Universidad de Valencia [Spain], 1969–1970.

———. "Una primera aproximación al estudio de las rentas de la tierra en Vizcaya y de los alquileres de Bilbao en el siglo XVIII." Presented at the Congreso Internacional de Santiago de Compostela [Spain], 1975. Typescript.

Guiard Larrauri, Teófilo. *Historia de la Noble Villa de Bilbao.* 4 vols. Bilbao: Imprenta de José de Astuy, 1905–1912.

———. *Historia del Consulado y Casa de Contratación de Bilbao y del Comercio de la Villa.* 2 vols. Bilbao: Imprenta y Librería de José de Astuy, 1913–1914.

Hechter, Michael. *Internal Colonialism. The Celtic fringe in British national development, 1536–1966.* Berkeley and Los Angeles: University of California Press, 1977.

Henningsen, Charles Frederick. *The most striking events of a twelve-month's campaign with Zumalacárregui in Navarre and the Basque Provinces.* 2 vols. London: John Murray, 1836.

Herr, Richard. *The Eighteenth Century Revolution in Spain.* Princeton: Princeton University Press, 1958.

———. *An Historical Essay on Modern Spain.* Berkeley: University of California Press, 1974.

Hirst, William. *History of the Woollen trade for the last sixty years.* Leeds: Printed by S. Moody, 1844.

Hochené [A. Duverine]. *Essai historique sur l'esprit de réforme politique en Espagne.* Paris: Ledoyen, 1840.

Honan, Michael Burke. *The Court and Camp of Don Carlos; being the results of a late tour in the Basque Provinces, and parts of Catalonia, Castile, and Estramadura.* London: John Macrone, 1836.

Hormaeche, Francisco de. "De las causas que más inmediatamente han contribuido a promover en las Provincias Bascongadas la guerra civil." *Revista de Madrid.* Second series, no. 1: 1839, pp. 338–361.

[———]. *La célebre década de Bilbao: o sea, Memoria de los festejos con que su Muy ilustre Ayuntamiento ha procurado obsequiar a SS MM. los Reyes Nuestros Señores, D. Fernando Séptimo y Doña Josefa María Amalia, durante su permanencia en esta M.N. y M.L. Villa de regreso para la Corte.* Bilbao: Imprenta de Basozabal, 1828.

Inglis, Henry. *Spain in 1830.* 2 vols. London: Whittaker, Treacher and Co., 1831.

Iturriza y Zabala, Juan Ramón de. *Historia General de Vizcaya y Epítome de las Encartaciones.* Edited by Angel Rodríguez Herrero. 2 vols. Bilbao: La Gran Enciclopedia Vasca, 1967.

Kirk, Russell. *The Conservative Mind from Burke to Santayana.* Chicago: Henry Regnery Co., 1953.

Labayru y Goicochea, Estanislao Jaime de. *Historia General del Señorío de Biscaya.* 6 vols. Bilbao: La Propaganda, 1895–1903.

Laborde, Alexandre. *Itinéraire descriptif de l'Espagne et tableau élémentaire des différentes branches de l'administration et de industrie de ce royaume.* 5 vols., plus atlas of map. Paris: Chez H. Nicolle et Lenormant, 1808.

——— . *A View of Spain Comprising a Descriptive Itinerary, of Each Province, and a General Statistical Account of the Country.* 5 vols. London: Printed for Longman, Hurst, Rees, and Orme, 1809.

Larra, Mariano José de. "Publicaciones nuevas. Ministerio de Mendizabal, folleto por Don José Espronceda." *Biblioteca de Autores Españoles.* Madrid: Atlas, 1960. Vol. 128, pp. 214–216.

Lasala y Collado, Fermín de. *La separación de Guipuzcoa y la Paz de Basilea.* Madrid: Fontanet, 1895.

Lemonauría, Pedro de. *Ensayo crítico sobre las Leyes Constitucionales de Vizcaya.* Bilbao: Imprenta de Nicolás Delmas, 1837.

Lesur, Charles Louis. *Annuaire historique universel ou histoire politique pour 1818–1861.* Paris: A. Thoisnier-Desplaces and others, 1821–1866.

Lista, Alberto. "De los Fueros de las Provincias Vascongadas." *Revista de Madrid.* First series, no. 2: 1838, pp. 3–22.

Llauder, Manuel. *Memorias documentadas del teniente general don Manuel Llauder, Marqués de Valle de Ribas.* Madrid: I. Boix, 1844.

Llorente, Juan Antonio. *Noticias históricas de las tres provincias vascongadas, en que se procura investigar el estado civil antiguo de Alava, Guipuzcoa y Vizcaya, y el origen de sus fueros.* 5 vols. Madrid: Imprenta Real (vols. 1–4), Imprenta de Don Luciano Vallín (vol. 5), 1806–1808.

Luna, Julián de. *Memoria que contiene una Estadística sucinta de Vizcaya.* Bilbao: Imprenta y Litografía de Nicolás Delmas, 1842.

Madoz, Pascual. *Diccionario geográfico-estadístico-histórico de España y sus posesiones de ultramar.* 16 vols. Madrid: Establecimiento tipográfico de P. Madoz y L. Sagasti, 1845–1850.

Madrazo, Francisco de Paula. *Historia militar y política de Zumalacárregui, y de los sucesos de la guerra de las provincias del Norte, enlazados a su época y a su nombre.* Madrid: Imprenta de la Sociedad de Operarios del Mismo Arte, 1844.

Mémoires et Correspondance Politique et Militaire du Roi Joseph, 10 vols. Paris: Perrotin, Libraire-Editeur, 1856.

Miñano y Bedoya, Sebastián de. *Diccionario geográfico-estadístico de España y Portugal.* Vol. 10. Madrid: Imprenta de Pierart-Peralta, 1828.

[———]. *Examen crítico de las revoluciones de España de 1820 a 1823 y de 1836.* Edited by Angel Calleja. 2 vols. Madrid: Imprenta de Cipriano López, 1858.

[———]. *Histoire de la Révolution d'Espagne de 1820 à 1823. Par un Espagnol témoin oculaire.* 2 vols. Chez J. G. Dentu, Imprimeur-Libraire, 1824.

Miraflores, Marqués de. *Apuntes histórico-críticos para escribir la historia de la Revolución de España desde el año 1820 hasta 1823.* London: Impreso por Ricardo Taylor, 1834.

———. *Documentos a los que se hace referencia en los Apuntes histórico-críticos sobre la revolución de España.* 2 vols. London: Impreso por Ricardo Taylor, 1834.

———. *Memoria histórico-legal sobre las leyes de sucesión a la corona de España.* Madrid: Imprenta de D. L. Amarita, 1833.

———. "Memorias del Reinado de Isabel II." *Biblioteca de Autores Espanoles.* Edited, with a preliminary study, by Manuel Fernández Álvarez. Madrid: Atlas, 1964. Vols. 172–174.

———. *Memorias para escribir la historia contemporanea de los siete primeros años del reinado de Isabel II.* 2 vols. Madrid: Imprenta de la Viuda de Calero, 1843–1844.

Montevilla, Barón de [Orbe y Vives de Cañamás, Jaime de]. "El Armamento General del Señorío de Vizcaya (1804–1833)." *Revista Internacional de Estudios Vascos.* No. 22: 1931, pp. 420–435.

Montoya, Pío de. *La intervención del clero vasco en las contiendas civiles (1820–1823).* San Sebastián: Txertoa, 1971.

Moral Ruiz, Joaquín del. *Hacienda y sociedad en el Trienio Constitucional (1820–1823).* Madrid: Instituto de Estudios Fiscales, 1975.

———. "La presión fiscal en el Trienio Constitucional (1820–1823)." *Hacienda Pública Española.* No. 27: 1974, pp. 47–72.

Mugártegui, Juan J. de. *La Villa de Marquina.* Bilbao: n.p., 1927.

Múgica, José. *Carlistas, Moderados y Progresistas (Claudio Antón de Luzuriaga).* San Sebastián: Biblioteca Vascongada de los Amigos del País, 1950.

Muriel, Andrés. "Historia de Carlos IV." Edited, with a preliminary study, by Carlos Seco Serrano. 2 vols. *Biblioteca de Autores Españoles.* Madrid: Atlas, 1959. Vols. 114–115.

Muruaga, Domingo de. *Colección de lo más indispensable y preciso para cultivo de la viña. Y modo de hacer y governar el vino por D . . . Dedícala a los honrados Labradores del M.N. y M.L. Señorío de Vizcaya a quienes demuestra en un discurso preliminar la necesidad de aplicarse al cultivo de la vid si se ha de evitar la ruina del País.* Bilbao: Eusebio de Larumbe, 1830.

Novia de Salcedo, Pedro. *Defensa histórica, legislativa y económica del Señorío de Vizcaya. Contra las Noticias históricas de las mismas que publicó D. Juan Antonio Llorente, y el informe de la Junta de reformas de abusos de la real hacienda en las tres Provincias Bascongadas.* 4 vols. Bilbao: Librería de Delmas e Hijo, 1851–1852.

Observaciones sobre la necesidad de examinar el régimen administrativo de las Provincias Vascongadas, para fallar con aclerto en esta materia. Madrid: Imprenta de Miguel de Burgos, 1834.

Otazu y Llana, Alfonso de. *El "igualitarismo" vasco: mito y realidad*. San
     Sebastián: Txertoa, 1973.
Palacio Atard, Vicente. *El comercio de Castilla y el puerto de Santander en
     el siglo XVIII notas para su estudio*. Madrid: Consejo Superior de
     Investigaciones Científicas, Escuela de Historia Moderna, 1960.
Pirala Criado, Antonio. *Historia de la guerra civil y de los partidos liberal
     y carlista, escrita con presencia de memorias y documentos inéditos*.
     5 vols. Madrid: Establecimiento Tipográfico de Mellado, 1853–1856.
Presas, José de. *Cronología de los sucesos más memorables ocurridos en
     todo el ámbito de la Monarquía Española desde el año de 1759 hasta
     1836*. Madrid: Imprenta de M. Calero, 1836.
Quadra Salcedo, Fernando de la. *Economistas vascongados y artículos
     varios sobre problemas destacados de la economía vizcaína*. Bilbao:
     Editorial El Pueblo Vasco, 1943.
Quin, Michael Joseph, trans. *Memoirs of Ferdinand VII, King of the Spains,
     by Don *** advocate of the Spanish Tribunals, translated from the
     original Spanish manuscript by Michael Joseph Quin*. London: Hurst,
     Robinson, and Co., 1824.
*Relación de los festejos con que han sido obsequiados los Reyes y Señores
     Don Fernando Séptimo y Doña María Josefa Amalia, en el M.N. y M.L.
     Señorío de Vizcaya, desde el dia 4 de Junio de 1828, en que pisaron su
     suelo, Hasta el 26 del mismo en que salieron para la Ciudad de Vitoria*.
     Bilbao: Imprenta de Basozabal, 1828.
Restaurador, El [Gómez de Negrete, Manuel, Father]. *Demostración del
     incontestable derecho que el Sr. D. Carlos de Borbón tiene al Trono de
     Espana*. Bilbao: n.p., 1833. (In *Fastos españoles*, vol. 1, pp. 536–546.)
"Reflexiones sobre el sistema agricultor del país bascongado." *Extractos de
     las Juntas generales celebradas por la Real Sociedad Bascongada de los
     Amigos del País en la ciudad de Vitoria por Setiembre de 1777*. Vitoria:
     Tomás de Robles y Navarro, [1778?]. Pp. 19–25.
Rocca, Albert Jean Michel. *Memoirs of the War of the French in Spain*.
     London: J. Murray, 1815.
Rodríguez Ferrer, Miguel. *Los vascongados, su país, su lengua y el Príncipe
     L. L. Bonaparte*. Introduction by Antonio Cánovas del Castillo. Madrid:
     Imprenta de J. Noguera, 1873.
Rodríguez Garraza, Rodrigo. *Navarra de Reino a Provincia (1828–1841)*.
     Coleccion histórica, no. 21. Pamplona: Universidad de Navarra, 1968.
Roscoe, Thomas. *The Tourist in Spain. Biscay and the Castiles*. London:
     Robert Jennings and Co., 1837.
Ruiz de Morales, Joaquín. *Historia de la Milicia Nacional desde su
     creación hasta nuestros días*. Madrid: Prats y Ruiz, 1855.
Sagarmínaga, Fidel de. *El gobierno y Régimen Foral del Señorío de Vizcaya
     desde el reinado de Felipe segundo hasta la mayor edad de Isabel
     segunda*. 8 vols. Bilbao: Tipografía Católica de José de Astuy, 1892.
Salvandy, Narcisse Achille de. *Du parti a prendre envers l'Espagne*. Paris:
     Baudouin Frères, Libraires, 1824.
San Martín y Burgoa, Antonio de. *El labrador vascongado, o antiguo*

agricultor español. Demostración de las mejoras de que es susceptible la Agricultura en las Provincias Vascongadas, y de las grandes ventajas que se podrían lograr en todo el reyno observando las reglas de la antigua labranza. Madrid: Imprenta de Benito Cano, 1791.

Sanz Cid, Carlos. *La Constitución de Bayona. Labor de redacción elementos que a ella fueron aportados, según los documentos que se guardan en los Archivos Nacionales de Paris y los papeles reservados de la Biblioteca de Real Palacio de Madrid.* Madrid: Talleres Tipográficos de la Editorial Reus, 1922.

Sarrailh, Jean. *La Contre-Révolution sous la Régence de Madrid (mai-octobre 1823). Étude faite d'après les papiers de la Surintendance de Police.* Paris: E. de Boccard, 1930.

Schuettinger, Robert Lindsay, ed. *The Conservative Tradition in European Thought, An Anthology.* New York: Putnam, 1970.

[Suárez, Juan Antonio.] *Fastos españoles o efeméridas de la guerra civil desde Octubre de 1832.* 2 vols. Madrid: Imprenta de Ignacio Boix, 1839–1840.

Suárez Verdeguer, Federico. *La crisis política del antiguo régimen en España (1800–1840).* 2d ed. Madrid: Rialp, 1958.

———. "Los Cuerpos de Voluntarios Realistas. Notas para su estudio." *Anuario de Historia del Derecho Español.* 1956, pp. 47–88.

———. *López Ballesteros y la hacienda entre 1823–1832.* 5 vols. Documentos del reinado de Fernando VII, no. 6. Pamplona: Universidad de Navarra, 1970.

———. *Martín Garay y la reforma de la hacienda.* 2 vols. Documentos del reinado de Fernando VII, no. 4. Pamplona: Universidad de Navarra, 1967.

———. *Los sucesos de La Granja.* Madrid: Consejo Superior de Investigaciones Científicas, 1953.

Swinburne, Henry. *Travels through Spain, in the years 1775 and 1776. In which several documents of Roman and Moorish architecture are illustrated by accurate drawings taken on the spot.* 2d ed. 2 vols. London: J. Davis for P. Elmsly, 1787.

Torras Elías, Jaime. "En torno a la política tributaria de los gobiernos de los gobiernos del Trienio Constitucional (1820–1823)." *Moneda y crédito.* No. 122: September 1972, pp. 153–170.

———. *La Guerra de los Agraviados.* Barcelona: Publicaciones de la Cátedra de Historia General de España, 1967.

Uhagon, Pedro Pascual de. *Informe evacuado por Don . . . sobre los crímenes cometidos en el aciago alzamiento de 3 de Octubre de 1833.* Bilbao: Imprenta de los Hijos de R. Martín y Cortázar, 1871.

Verduin, Arnold R. *Manual of Spanish Constitutions, 1808–1931. Translations and Introductions.* Ypsilanti, Michigan: University Lithographers, 1941.

Vicens Vives, Jaime. *Approaches to the History of Spain.* Translated and edited by Joan Connelly Ullman. Berkeley: University of California Press, 1970.

Viel-Castel, Louis de. *Histoire de la Restauration*. Vol. 12. Paris: Michel
    Levy Frerès, Libraires-Éditeurs, 1869.
Vilar, Pierre. "Quelques aspects de l'occupation et de la résistance en
    Espagne en 1794 et au temps de Napoleon." *Occupants-Occupés, 1792–
    1815*. Actes de Colloque que s'est tenu a Bruxelles les 29 et 30 Janvier
    1968. Brussels: Université Libre de Bruxelles, Institut de Sociologie
    [1969]: pp. 221–256.
Villavaso, Camilo de. *La Cuestión del Puerto de la Paz, y la Zamacolada.
    Exposición Histórica acompañada de la Memoria justificativa de uno
    de los actores de aquellos sucesos, de documentos inéditos y del plano
    de este importante proyecto*. Bilbao: Imprenta de Juan E. Delmas, 1887.
Walton, William. *The revolutions of Spain, from 1808 to the end of 1836.
    With biographical sketches of the most distinguished personages and a
    narrative of the war in the peninsula down to the present time, from
    the most authentic sources*. 2 vols. London: Richard Bentléy, 1837.
Widdrington, Samuel Edwards [S. E. Cook]. *Sketches in Spain during the
    years 1829, 30, 31, & 32 containing notices of some districts very little
    known of the manners of the people, government, recent changes,
    commerce, fine arts, and natural history*. 2 vols. London: Thomas and
    William Boone, 1834.
Wilson, Glen D., ed. *The Psychology of Conservatism*. London: Academic
    Press, 1973.
Ybarra y Bergé, Javier de. *Datos relativos a Simón Bernardo de Zamacola y
    la Zamacolada*. Bilbao: Imprenta Provincial de Vizcaya, publicación de
    la Junta Provincial de Vizcaya, 1941.
Zaratiegui, Juan Antonio. *Vida y hechos de D. Tomas de Zumalacárregui*.
    2d Spanish ed. San Sebastián: Escelicer, 1946.

Newspapers

El Bascongado. Bilbao, 1813–1814.
El Constitucional. Madrid, 1820.
El Correo, Periódico Literario y Mercantil. Madrid, 1828–1833.
Gaceta de Madrid. Madrid, 1823–1833.
Gazeta de Oficio del Gobierno de Vizcaya. San Sebastián-Vitoria,
    1810–1812.
El Liberal Guipuzcoano. San Sebastián, 1821–1822.
Miscelanea de Comercio, Artes y Literatura. Madrid, 1820.
Le Moniteur Universel. Paris, 1823–1833.
El Patriota Bilbao. Bilbao, 1823.
El Verdadero Patriota. Bilbao, 1822.

Index

Abando, 157, 212
Absolutism, 70, 98, 183, 190, 218–
    20, 241n. 71; change and, 78–79;
    Fernandine, 76–77; Portuguese, 79
Abuses, 184, 199, 223, 289n. 91
Accord (*acuerdo*), 15
Administrator (*ferrón*), 10
Afrancesados, 33, 34, 235n. 57
Agraviado uprising, 90, 104, 147
Agriculture, 4–5, 51, 168–76, 208;
    increase in, 8–9, 35; problems for, 34–
    35, 55; promoting, 128; subsistence,
    169. *See also* Food shortages
Alava, 111, 146, 256n. 85; economy of,
    12–13
Alcalde mayor, 22
Alonsotegui, 157
Alzaá, 165, 219
Amnesty, 182, 202, 204, 206, 225. *See
    also* Reincorporation
Ancien régime, 5, 186, 220, 231n. 9
Animal husbandry, 9
Annexation, 27–28
Anti-Carlists, 144, 171
Anticentralism, 82, 135, 199
Anticlericalism, 60, 62–63, 77–78, 222,
    247n. 162, 296n. 181
Anticonstitutionalism, 52, 54, 68, 75, 98
Antireformism, 98, 181, 203
Antuñano, Miguel de, 31
Apoderado (delegate), 14
Apostólicos, 78, 95
Archbishop of Toledo, 103
Aréchaga, Cándido de, assassination of,
    214–15
Armamento General del País, 73, 136
Arms, 144, 153, 246n. 147; controlling,
    138, 273n. 39

Arratia, 37
Artiñano, Miguel de, 145, 211
Artisans, 199, 214, 222, 224; class
    conflict and, 196–97
Assembly of Bayonne, 23
Asturias, rebellion in, 24
Avril, General, 24
Azaola, Gregorio González, 176–77, 180

Bacon, John Francis, 93–94, 96, 144, 145,
    160, 171, 184, 193–95, 198, 199, 205,
    215, 216
Ballesteros (minister of finance), 102,
    105, 106, 120, 124, 132, 256n. 80
Bankruptcies, 173
Barcelona, uprising in, 90
Batallones de Vizcaya, 73
Batiz, Francisco Javier de, 45, 210, 217,
    280n. 102, 280n. 103
Bayo, Estanislao de, criticism of, 120
Bayonne, 12, 62, 63, 129, 248n. 179
Begoña, 157, 163, 203, 206, 212
Bermeo, 4, 48
Bessières uprising, 78
Bilbao, 4, 8, 11, 12, 14, 28, 44, 47, 49,
    72, 114, 116, 118–21, 125, 129–31,
    139, 140, 142, 148, 169, 194, 235n. 57,
    253n. 42, 295n. 171; census in,
    271n. 11; evacuation of, 66; insurrec-
    tion in, 22, 296n. 178; occupation of,
    xiv, 24, 32, 230n. 6; population of, 6;
    as *puerto habilitado*, 187
Blacks, 161–62, 173, 202, 294n. 151
Blake, General, 24
Boislecomte, Baron of, 219–20,
    293n. 126
Bonaparte, Joseph. *See* Joseph I (Intruder
    King)

Bordeaux, 12, 49, 129
Bourbons, 20, 23
Bourgeoisie, 12, 84, 171, 186, 187,
    192, 195, 198, 220, 225, 243n. 106,
    294n. 151
Brandies, 175; import ban on, 174. *See
    also* Wines
Brigadas de Paisanos Armados, 136–37,
    144–66, 170, 184, 185, 190, 205–6,
    210, 224, 275n. 64, 278n. 89, 278n. 91,
    280n. 102, 280n. 104, 280n. 106,
    292n. 120, 300n. 69; arming, 159;
    Carlism and, 164–65; charter of, 135,
    153–54, 156–60; criticism of, 162;
    liberalism and, 162; numbers of, 154,
    159–60
Bruny, General, 74
Buquet, General, 25

Cádiz, 12, 63; Constitution of, 29, 34
Calderón, Gregorio, 161–62
Campuzano, Francisco de, appointment
    of, 39
Canga Argüelles, José, 56, 244n. 125
Cantabria, 129
Cantaló affair, 210
Cantonnements (quarterings), establish-
    ing, 24
Capitalists, 189, 196; class conflict and,
    194, 198–99
Carlism, 137, 147, 167, 189, 195, 196,
    198, 202, 205, 211, 214, 216–18, 220,
    223, 229n. 6, 258n. 114, 291n. 102,
    297n. 2; conservatism and, 97–98;
    disentailment and, 170; landowners
    and, 196; liberalism and, 204, 206,
    210; Paisanos Armados and, 164–65;
    peasantry and, 192, 194; religion and,
    218; roots of, xi–xiv, 75, 199–200,
    204, 206, 216, 222, 224, 225, 282n. 5
Carlist War, xii, 63, 134, 145, 159, 177,
    195, 199, 221. *See also* Insurrection
Carlos, Don, xiv, 78, 95, 97, 165, 202,
    203, 209, 212, 213, 215–17, 219, 220,
    226, 252n. 32, 294n. 137, 297n. 2
Caro Baroja, Julio, 5
Carranza, 178
Caserío (traditional Basque farm dwell-
    ing), description of, 4
Castañón, Federico, 205–6

Cavanilles, José de, 96, 121, 127–28, 162
Ceballos, Pedro de, criticism by, 41
Celadores, 119, 139, 143
Census, 139, 271n. 11. *See also* Inverse
    Indexes (*Indices Inversos*)
Centralism, 18, 59, 90–91, 102, 136,
    146, 167, 189, 196, 223, 225; clerics
    and, 190; liberalism and, 98; opposi-
    tion to, 138
Chacolí, 9–10, 169, 195, 232n. 25. *See
    also* Wines
Chancilleria de Valladolid, 18, 59
Charcoal, 8, 10, 113, 178
Charity, church-dominated, 69–70
Charles IV, 21, 23
Checkpoints, 47–48. *See also* Customs
    houses
Chief magistrate (*juez mayor*), role of,
    18
Class conflict, dynamics of, 189–200
Clergy, 60–62, 77–78, 140, 196, 197,
    199, 222, 223, 235n. 57, 245n. 137,
    247n. 147; aid from, 216; centralism
    and, 190; class conflict and, 189–91;
    as guerrillas, 190; number of, 6–7;
    peasants and, 190
Colección, 92, 93, 95, 104, 110,
    256n. 59, 257n. 101, 263n. 52;
    publication of, 88, 91
Collaboration, 21, 24
Colonies, 41, 79, 126, 172, 178, 192,
    240n. 61; loss of, 30, 37, 225; trade
    with, 131, 175–76
Comercio de mala fé (illicit or fraudu-
    lent trade), 119. *See also* Smuggling;
    Trade
Comisión del punto de armamento, 156
Comandante general, 22
Commerce. *See* Trade
Commerce interlope (fraudulent trade),
    175. *See also* Smuggling; Trade
Commission on Tariffs (Junta de Arance-
    les), 124. *See also* Tariffs
Comunero, 140
Concejo de Sopuerta, surveillance of,
    143
Conscription. *See* Military service
Conservatism, xiii, 78–81, 84, 98, 189,
    218, 222; Carlism and, 97–98; tenets
    of, 76; traditionalists and, 76
Conspiracies (*conspiración*), 34, 158,

212, 247n. 173. *See also* Intrigue
(*asechanza*)
Constitution (1808), 24
Constitution (1812), 43–45, 47, 55–56,
  198, 219, 241n. 69
Constitutional government, 45, 62, 220,
  251n. 21
Constitutionalism, 44, 50, 52, 58, 65,
  67, 70, 84–85, 155, 170, 183, 241n. 68,
  249n. 193; end of, 75–76; fear of, 136;
  merchants and, 51; opposition to, 60–
  61, 248n. 173, 248n. 188; reemergence
  of, 182
Constitutionalists, 34, 45, 46, 53, 61,
  63–66, 71–72, 171, 173, 176, 182,
  196, 207, 215, 245n. 129, 250n. 2,
  250n. 3, 250n. 11, 251n. 21, 271n. 13,
  271n. 22, 271n. 23, 295n. 165; control
  of, 138–42, 72–73, 143–44, 161–
  62, 272n. 25, 272n. 29; criticism of,
  86; death of, 73; detente with, 174;
  foreign affairs and, 79; *gaditano*, 33.
  See also Amnesty; Reincorporation
Consulado, 20, 36, 41, 42, 48, 50, 72,
  125, 126, 151, 173, 187, 188; defense
  of, 243n. 103; description of, 16–18;
  transformation of, 188
Consuls (*consules*), 16
Consultas, 15, 54–55, 108–9, 127,
  267n. 124
Contraband. *See* Smuggling
Contrarregistros (checkpoints), 47;
  opposition to, 48
Contribution (*donativo*), 100, 101, 103–
  5, 111. *See also* Donation
Convent of San Mamés, 203
Corps of Coast and Border Carabineers,
  formation of, 120
Corregidores, 14, 17, 20, 139, 202
Corregimiento, 21, 22, 72
Corruption, 11, 14, 17, 206, 210
Cortes, 24, 28, 45, 47, 48, 50–52, 54,
  56, 59, 60, 69, 76, 83, 98, 125, 131,
  140, 142, 149, 168, 173, 245n. 137,
  249n. 195, 251n. 21, 297n. 2
Cosmopolitanism, opposition to, 80–81
Council of Castile, 127
Council of Ministers, 87, 88, 90–95,
  102, 109–11, 127, 133, 206
Council of Navarra, 147
Council of State, 56, 87, 90–94, 102,

103, 108, 111, 114, 116, 117, 120, 124,
  161, 257n. 99, 262n. 42; consulta of,
  54–55; military service and, 110
Criminality, 214; curbing, 7–8, 32–33
Cristinos, 202, 207–8, 222, 294n. 151.
  See also Maria Cristina; Isabel
Customs, 18, 39, 40, 223; inland, 49;
  reforms in, 194, 269n. 148
Customs houses, 48–49, 72, 85, 118,
  130–35, 193, 225, 269–70n. 163;
  abolition of, 75, 130; 1812 Constitution and, 47; criticism of, 193;
  establishment of, 47, 56, 126. *See also*
  Checkpoints

Defenders of the Faith, 64, 66
Defensa, 82–83, 92, 256n. 85
de la Mota, Juan Modesto, 204–6, 211,
  213, 215, 216
*Demostración del incontestable derecho
  que el Sr. D. Carlos de Borbón tiene
  al Trono de España*, 217
Dependientes, 119
Descalone, Commissioner, criticism of,
  62
Deusto, 157, 212
Diputación, 7, 11, 13, 15, 17, 18, 20,
  22, 26, 27, 34, 36, 39, 41, 42, 44,
  60, 68, 72, 74–76, 78, 80, 82, 86, 87,
  95–98, 101, 103, 107, 108, 115–16,
  118–23, 125–29, 131, 132, 135, 139,
  141, 142, 144–51, 154–59, 163, 164,
  175, 179–81, 184, 193, 196, 198, 206,
  207, 209–13, 215, 216, 223, 233n. 32,
  250n. 7, 258n. 111, 267n. 127,
  270n. 2, 273n. 44, 273n. 45, 274n. 49,
  274n. 58, 275n. 64, 278n. 87,
  278n. 91, 280n. 106, 289n. 88,
  289n. 91, 293n. 136, 295n. 167,
  296n. 178; conservative policies of,
  186; militia and, 160–61; oath of, 19;
  problems for, 31–32
Diputación General, 29; description of,
  13–16; liquidation of, 59; priorities of,
  31
Diputación Provincial, 29, 45, 46, 48, 59
Discipline, 18, 42, 149, 158, 166, 214,
  224
Discrimination, 7, 173, 189
Disentailment, 60, 170, 171, 191, 193,
  195, 222

Donation, 85, 90, 99, 100, 102, 111, 112, 117, 192, 255n. 56; counterproposal to, 101–2, 104; forced, 104; July Revolution and, 105; resistance to, 102–3, 106; trade issues and, 124. *See also* Contribution (*donativo*)
Draft (*quinta*), 41, 107, 109, 262n. 42; July Revolution and, 110–11. *See also* Military service
Durango, 11, 24, 32, 178; bloodbath at, 65–66
Duties (*averia*), collecting, 16. *See also* Tariffs

Echanove, Francisco Antonio de, 180–81, 190n. 100
École des Annales, xi
Economic commissions, establishment of, 184
Economic crisis, 167–69, 171, 173–75
Egalitarianism, 4, 7
Eguía, Francisco, 32, 66, 67
Eguía, Mariano de, 45, 195, 208
"Eighteen Million Reales" (1818), 42
Eizaguirre (artisan), 161–62
El Bascongado, 29, 33
Elorriaga, Juan de, 143
Elorrio, 11, 32
El Verdadero Patriota, 63
Enfranchised ports (*puertos habilitados*), 124–26; Bilbao as, 187
Enfranchisement (*habilitado*), 7, 38, 126, 128–30, 134, 187, 269n. 163
Ensayo histórico, 220
Entail holders (*mayorazgos*), 5, 44
Entrepreneurs, 12, 186, 222
Epalza, Manuel José de, 211; criticism by, 207
Exiles, revolutionary, 92
Exports, 243n. 106; decline in, 171–72, 175–76; iron, 288n. 67, 289n. 88; licenses for, 141; taxes on, 180; wool, 175–76. *See also* Imports; Trade
Extraordinary Military Tribunal, creation of, 25

Farmers (*labradores*), 194; loyal (*leales labradores*), 64
Fastos Españoles, 216
Ferdinand VII, 23, 24, 31, 38, 64, 70, 87–89, 93, 95, 100, 101, 103, 104, 106, 108, 112, 116, 117, 122, 126, 127, 130, 133, 134, 138, 142, 145, 147, 152, 161, 174, 190, 207, 209, 226, 252n. 32, 296–97n. 2; conspiracy against, 34; criticism of, 120; death of, 164, 212; "politics of hostility" of, 40; release of, 76; Valencia decrees of, 29
Fernández de Pinedo, Emiliano, 170, 194, 196
Fernandistas, 202, 204
Ferrerías. See Ironworks
Fixed itinerary (*ruta fija*), 141
Fontana, Josep, 102, 133
Food shortages, 9, 31–32. *See also* Agriculture
Foralistas, 68, 75, 103, 145, 156, 165, 167, 184. *See also* Fueros
Foreign competition, 36–38, 80–81, 140, 168, 172, 176, 190, 196. *See also* Xenophobia
Franciscans, 61, 62, 190, 210
Francophobia, 75, 80, 173, 196. *See also* Xenophobia
Freemasonry, 34, 79, 140, 172, 237n. 21
French Convention, 32
French occupation, 23–26; consequences of, 30
Fuera del término de la jurisdicción del pueblo, 158
Fueros, 11, 15, 20–22, 28, 38–40, 43–44, 46, 52, 55, 57, 58, 64, 72, 77, 80, 81, 83–85, 90, 95, 97, 102, 103, 108, 118, 122, 123, 128, 132, 134, 137, 152, 156, 172, 174, 184, 185, 188, 189, 191, 194, 196, 199, 205, 218, 219, 223, 224, 233n. 35, 249n. 191, 258n. 111, 263n. 52, 277n. 74, 277n. 80; abuse of, 87; attacks on, 88–89, 109; Carlism and, 220; defense of, 19, 24, 77, 87, 167, 197; description of, xiv, 18–19, 88, 226; invoking, 41, 75, 220; July Revolution and, 93–94, 96; lawyers and, 197–98; military service and, 107; violation of, 121, 179, 187. *See also* Foralistas; Privileges

Galdácano, property sales in, 35
Galería militar contemporanea, 202, 214, 216
Gambra, Rafael, 68
Gaminde, Victor Luis de, 145, 172, 193, 194, 255n. 58, 299n. 35
Garay, Martín, 42

General Assembly (*junta general*), 13, 148, 162, 163, 177, 180, 181, 183, 184, 198, 205, 236n. 1, 288n. 70
General Direction of Public Revenue, 47
General Direction of Revenue, 104
Godoy, Manuel ("Prince of Peace"), 21–23, 26, 58, 88, 191, 234n. 43, 256n. 69
González, Tomás, 88, 90–93, 95, 104, 110, 256n. 59, 257n. 101
González Portilla, Manuel, 195
Gordejuela, 162
Government of Biscay, 26, 34
Grain, 8–9, 32, 35; import of, 168, 282n. 3; shortage of, 168–69
Guard of Honor (Guardia de Honor), 73, 143, 145, 147, 157, 212, 250n. 7, 280n. 104, 300n. 69; charter for, 276n. 69; membership of, 148–49
Guardia de Honor o Paisanos Armados, regulations for, 150
Guecho, 141, 271n. 22
Guernica, 206
Guerrillas, 190, 235n. 56, 247n. 169
Guerrilla warfare, 25–26, 30, 66
Guezala, Domingo de, 61, 64, 65, 248n. 178
Guilds, 16, 17, 173, 197
Guipúzcoa, 111, 119, 130, 131, 147, 155, 161, 205, 212, 215, 217, 247n. 163, 256n. 85, 274n. 55; economy of, 12–13; uprising at, 21, 160
Gurbista, Antonio de, 145, 202, 204
Gutierrez de Cabiedes, Toribio, banning of, 34

Habilitación, 125, 126, 130, 131
Hapsburgs, 20
Holy Company of Elders (Compañía Sagrada de Ancianos), 53, 65
Home rule, 19–20, 59. *See also* Self-determination
Hormaeche, Francisco de, 163–64, 210, 212, 216, 219, 258n. 113, 269n. 163
Hunting, licenses for, 144

Ibargoitia, Juan Martín de, 156, 279n. 102, 280n. 103
Ibarrola, Colonel, 217
Identity cards (*cartas de seguridad*), issuing, 140
Imports, 9, 100, 243n. 106; banning, 168, 174; curbs on, 51, 114, 116,

209n. 88; grain, 282n. 3; iron, 176–77; protesting, 36. *See also* Exports; Trade
Impoverishment, 192, 282n. 5
Income, distribution of, 12
Incorporationism, 83, 223
Inglis, Henry, 271n. 21; observations of, 169–70
Inquisition, 77, 78, 202, 205, 251n. 19, 252n. 34
Insurrection, xiv, 20, 22, 24–26, 64–66, 104, 185, 296n. 178; description of, 212–16; fear of, 136; motors of, 217–21; preparing for, 61; size of, 213–14. *See also* Carlist War
Intendancies, establishing, 56
Intereses de Bilbao, 172, 255n. 58
Interventionists, 70
Intrigue (*asechanza*), 158. *See also* Conspiracies (*conspiración*)
Intruder King. *See* Joseph I (Intruder King)
Inverse Indexes (*Indices Inversos*), 140. *See also* Census
Iron, 12, 85, 99, 129, 174, 186, 196, 263n. 64; contention over, 112–18; curbs on, 113–14, 116, 180, 289n. 88; exploitation of, 179; export of, 180, 288n. 67; import of, 176–77; output of, 176–77
Ironworks (*ferrerías*), 10–11, 100, 180, 181, 225, 232n. 26, 264n. 79, 286n. 64, 287n. 65, 289n. 80, 290n. 96, 290n. 100; foreign competition for, 36–37; modernization of, 177–78; pilot school for, 178–79; problems for, 29, 34–37, 176–77
Isabel, 206, 209, 226, 297n. 2. *See also* Cristinos

Jáuregui, León de, 150
Jefe de sección o Brigada, 157
Jefe político (provincial governor), 43, 241n. 69
Jesuits, 33
Joseph I (Intruder King), 23–26, 191
Judges of contraband (*aduanas*), 131, 132, 265n. 88, 265n. 90, 269n. 163
Juez de primera instancia, role of, 59
July Revolution, 128, 143, 161, 174, 183, 187, 200, 257n. 87, 257n. 99; donation and, 105; draft question and, 110–11; fueros and, 93–94, 96

Junta de Jefes de Hacienda, 105, 133
Junta de reforma de abusos de Real Hacienda en las Provincias Vascongadas, 55; creation of, 39–40, 113
Junteros, definition of, 14
Jusué, José María de, 68

Laborde, Alexandre de, observations of, 1, 3
La Granja, 202, 203, 225; crisis of, 296–97n. 2
Landa, Pacho, 64
Landaida, Manuel de, 190
Landeza, Juan Bautista de, 78
Landowners (*propietarios*), 5, 6, 84, 189, 198, 222; absentee, 6, 170, 195; Carlism and, 196; class crisis and, 194–96
Lands: commercialization of, 193, 195; disentailment of, 60; distribution of, 191; redistribution of, 222; sale of, 35, 170, 238n. 26; tenure on, 191; transfer of, 195
La Rioja, 3
La Romana, General, 24
Larreátegui, Josef Colón de, 8
Larumbe, Eusebio de, 210
Lasagabaster, Juan de, arrest of, 203
Lausagarreta, 104, 160, 281n. 112
Law enforcement. *See* Police
Lawyers, 199; class conflict and, 197–98
Legitimism, 68, 83, 217–18
Lemona, property sales in, 35
Lequeitio, 48, 238n. 23, 271n. 11
Letona, Antonio Leonardo de, 45
Leveling, 113, 120; universal (*nivelación universal*), 81–82, 223
Lezama, José de, 45, 61, 161
Liberalism, xiii, 29, 44, 45, 70, 170, 183–85, 189, 190, 193, 199, 200, 204–6, 209, 220, 223–24, 269n. 163, 290–91n. 102, 292n. 113, 293n. 126, 297n. 2, 303–4n. 122; Carlism and, 206, 210; centralism and, 98; controlling, 140; influence of, 167, 186, 188–89; opposition to, 192–93, 197; Paisanos Armados and, 162
Liberals, 182, 184, 188, 192, 195, 206, 212, 214, 219, 222, 294n. 151, 295n. 171; attacks on, 173, 204; Carlists and, 204; controlling, 205,

272n. 29; reincorporation of, 176, 202, 225
Liberal Triennium. *See* Trienio
Licenses, 120, 141, 144
Llauder, Manuel, 164, 202, 205
Llorente, Juan Antonio, 21–23, 88, 91, 256n. 59
Loans (*empréstitos*), resisting, 41–42
Lóizaga, Casimiro de, 42, 45, 149
Longa, Francisco de, 25, 40, 61
Longue durée, xi, xv
Luna, Julián de, 177, 178

Machinada (1718), 20
Magistrates (*síndicos procuradores*), 15, 16
Mallagaray, José Apoita, 62
Manufactures, 10, 20, 35–36, 51, 85, 99, 125, 134, 141, 172, 174, 198, 225, 243n. 106, 286n. 53, 286n. 64; duties on, 11; problems for, 29, 37–38, 55, 112–18
Maria Cristina, 164, 207, 209, 217, 226, 297n. 2. *See also* Cristinos
Memoria, 102, 105, 106, 115, 116, 124, 133, 179, 288n. 70
Memoria (1827), 178
Memoria (1840), 178
Memoria de la Diputación General sobre el punto de Minería, 177
Mendizabal, Gabriel de, 27, 28
Merchants, 189, 196, 222, 248n. 186; class conflict and, 198–99; constitutionalism and, 51; political power of, 186; resentment of, 194
Merlin, General, 24
Miguelistas, 79
Military service, 10, 41, 59, 69, 85, 89–90, 92, 99, 100, 101, 112, 125, 128–29, 134, 223, 250n. 8, 259–60n. 14, 261n. 32, 263n. 60, 263n. 63; resisting, 107–12, 117; training for, 157, 159, 167, 224. *See also* Draft (*quinta*); Substitution (*reemplazo*)
Militias, 136, 160–61, 244n. 116, 250n. 7, 275n. 60, 276n. 72; arming, 153–54, 159; autonomy of, 278n. 92; controlling, 146–47; disarming, 205–6, 213, 224; forming, 52–53, 154–56; importance of, 224; royalist, 151, 216; training for, 157–59, 167; voluntary, 52–54, 65

Mina, 25, 96, 97, 160, 161, 162, 183,
    235n. 56, 257n. 87, 280n. 104
Mining, 100, 113, 289n. 91; guidelines
    for, 179–80
Ministry of Finance, 39, 48–50, 54, 86,
    105, 112, 114, 116, 118, 123–24, 126,
    132–34. *See also* Supreme Council of
    Finance
Ministry of Trade, 122
Ministry of War, 164; draft issue and,
    108–9
Miqueletes, 73, 149, 215, 216, 275n. 64;
    reestablishment of, 74
Monastic orders, suppression of, 60
Mondragón, 89, 126, 132
Money, scarcity of, 172–73
Monopolies, 18, 130, 197
Morality, 33, 78
Moral Ruiz, Joaquín del, 69
Muruaga, Domingo de, 169

Nantes, 49
Napoleon, 3, 11, 26
Nationalism, 27, 81, 218
National Voluntary Militia (Milicia
    Nacional Voluntaria), 65; enrolling in,
    52–53
Naturalization papers (*vizcainía*), 208
Navarra, 41, 49, 50, 55, 57, 66, 96,
    97, 109, 119, 131, 132, 160, 220,
    244n. 120, 247n. 163, 257n. 87,
    280n. 104, 286n. 53
Negrete, Manuel Gómez, 191, 210, 212,
    217
Nivelador (leveler). *See* Leveling
Northern Castile, 66
Notaries public (*escribanos*), 222,
    295n. 172; class conflict and, 197–98
Noticias históricas, 88, 91, 256n. 59;
    publication of, 23
Novia de Salcedo, Pedro de, 45, 53, 68,
    77, 79, 81–83, 85, 87, 92, 114–16,
    122, 149, 151, 153, 156, 177–79, 195,
    211, 254n. 52, 278n. 89, 280n. 103,
    288n. 70, 288n. 76

Observaciones, 212
Obstructionism, 92, 126
Ochandiano, 11, 36, 203
Old Castile, 3
Ombudsman (*juez de conciliacion*), 198
Ominous Decade, 72, 80, 83, 86, 87,
    98, 100, 106, 113, 118, 134, 142, 159,
    172, 174, 185, 186, 189, 195, 198, 207,
    223, 225, 250n. 8, 259n. 14, 263n. 63,
    272n. 29, 291n. 102, 293n. 126,
    295n. 171
Oñate (Guipúzcoa), 219
Orbegozo, Gabriel Benito de, 23
Ordenanzas, 17. *See also* Consulado
Order, preservation of, 72–74
Ordinance of Andújar, 74
Orduña, 24, 251n. 23, 260n. 14

Padres de provincia, 150, 233n. 32
Paisanos Armados. *See* Brigadas de
    Paisanos Armados
Pamplona, 153
Particularism, 82, 251n. 19
Pase foral, description of, 18–19
Passports, 138, 158; issuing, 140–41
Patiño Convention (1727), 122, 124,
    266n. 107
Patriotic Junta, formation of, 24
Peasantry, 171, 185, 192, 193, 195,
    197, 199, 214, 222; bourgeoisie and,
    294n. 151; Carlism and, 192, 194;
    class conflict and, 191–94; clerics
    and, 190; resentment by, 194; royalists
    and, 80–81; smugglers and, 296n. 181
Pereyra, Luis Marcelino, 17
Permanent Commission, 156–57,
    280n. 103
Permanent Commission for the Im-
    provement of Iron Fabrication,
    180–81, 288n. 64
Pilot school (*escuela normal*), creation
    of, 178–79
Pinedo, Fernández de, 35
Pinilla, José López Juana, 104–5
Pirala, Antonio, 93–94, 145, 210, 212,
    219
Plasencia, 153
Plencia, 48, 141, 271n. 22
Pluralism, 81
Police, 85, 101, 136, 151, 224, 272n. 35,
    273n. 45, 274n. 49, 285n. 45; conser-
    vatism of, 145; creation of, 135; use
    of, 137–46
Police of the Kingdom, 137
"Politics of hostility," 40
Porlier, Commander, 25
Port of Peace, creation of, 22
Portugal, absolutism in, 79

326

Index

Portugalete, 44, 48, 141, 142, 271n. 22
Prebostad, right of, 16
Presas, José de, 218
Primogeniture, 6
"Prince of Peace." See Godoy, Manuel
 ("Prince of Peace")
Priors (priores), role of, 16
Privileges, 11, 15, 20, 31, 39, 46, 55, 68,
 72, 76, 81, 83–88, 91, 93, 132, 133,
 197, 199, 219, 223, 225; description
 of, 18–19; losing, 52; modification of,
 128; violation of, 137, 187. See also
 Fueros
Proletarization, 171, 192
Property. See Lands
Protectionism, 36–37, 51–52, 69, 169,
 196
Provisional Junta of Government (Junta
 Provisional de Gobierno), 71–72
Public debts, 54, 56, 57
Public funds, handling, 184, 208
Public safety, 32–33
Public works projects, 14
Punishment. See Discipline

Quesada, Vicente, 66, 164

Reason, revolt against, 81
Rebellion. See Insurrection
Reductionism, 134
Reform, 18, 30, 33, 96, 136, 184, 187–
 89, 191, 206, 209, 220, 222, 223, 225,
 258n. 105, 296n. 181; customs, 194;
 liberalism and, 167
Regency (Regencia), 71–72
Regidores capitulares, 15–16
Regionalism, 82, 199, 251n. 19; signifi-
 cance of, xiv–xv
Reglamento Criminal, 32
Reglamento Provisional, 119
Regnaudin, Auguste, 43, 47, 49, 60,
 61, 75, 77, 78, 81, 84, 118, 131, 145,
 169, 171–76, 180, 182, 203, 205,
 215, 241n. 66, 243n. 103, 251n. 18,
 253n. 40, 292n. 120, 303n. 116
Regular Militia (Milicia Reglamentaria),
 formation of, 53–54, 60, 64–66
Reincorporation, 176, 202, 225. See also
 Amnesty
Renovales, Mariano de, 25, 28, 34
Rents, 34, 35, 170, 191, 192, 195,
 295n. 171

Repression, 137, 223, 224
Restoration: (1814), 29, 33–38; (1823),
 80–81, 145, 147, 168, 171, 182, 224,
 249n. 2, 259n. 14, 293n. 126
Revolution. See Insurrection
Riot of Aranjuez (1808), 23
Road building, 187
Rocca, Albert J. M., 25–26
Rotaeche, José Ramón de, 156, 160, 165,
 203, 279n. 102, 280n. 103
Royalism, 75, 84, 156, 198, 203, 204,
 223, 258n. 111; artisans and, 196–97
Royalists (realistas), 60, 64, 65, 69,
 71–72, 74, 144, 165, 176, 184, 188,
 202, 204, 210, 213, 220, 248n. 186,
 248n. 187, 251n. 23, 295n. 171,
 299n. 22; clergy and, 62; controlling,
 146; detente with, 174; foreign affairs
 and, 79; makeup of, 66–67; peasantry and, 80–81; problems for, 72;
 surveillance of, 143; vendettas of, 73
Royalist volunteers (voluntarios realistas), 143
Royal Tribunal of Commerce (Real
 Tribunal de Comercio), 188

Safe-conducts, 138, 141, 144; issuing,
 140
Sala de Vizcaya, 18
Salazar, Ceferino, 142, 144
Salazar, Luis de, 86–87, 151–52
Salt-Tax Revolt (1631–1634), 20
Salvatierra, insurrection in, 61
Sancho, Ildefonso de, 34, 272n. 29
San Juan, Benito, 58
San Sebastián, 108, 114, 116, 120, 125,
 129, 131, 205, 259n. 14; enfranchise-
 ment of, 130, 134
Santander, 12, 49; insurrection in, 24
Santoña, 153
Santurce, 141, 271n. 22
Sarsfield, General, 216
Secciones o Brigadas, 157
Secondary offices (aduanillas), 47
Self-determination, 179, 193, 225. See
 also Home rule
Señor, 19
Señorío (seigniory), 29, 34–35, 121, 154,
 185, 205
Señorío de Vizcaya (Seigniory of Viz-
 caya), 3–4
Seoane, Antonio de, 63

Separatism, 82, 199, 251n. 19, 254n. 52
Serviles, attack on, 66
Shipbuilding, 198
Silver, 172–73
Simincas, 90, 91
Smuggling, 5, 11, 37, 60, 64, 67, 85,
    100, 113, 117–24, 129, 131, 193, 222–
    24, 247n. 169; curbing, 40, 48, 123;
    increase in, 74, 112, 175–76; peasantry
    and, 296n. 181. *See also* Trade
Sobry (assistant), 57, 243n. 103
Sociedad Vascongada de Amigos del
    País (Basque Society of Friends of the
    Country), 5, 8, 9, 21
Somorrostro, 10, 37, 150, 179
Sons of Saint Louis, 70
Speculators, 49
Storm, Elias, 143, 272n. 35
Sublime Code, 46
Substitution (*reemplazo*), 107, 109–11,
    261n. 32, 262n. 42. *See also* Military
    service
Subversives, 21, 143–44; controlling,
    139–40
Supreme Council, consultas of, 108–9,
    127
Supreme Council of Finance, 91, 126–
    27, 267n. 124. *See also* Ministry of
    Finance
Surveillance, 143–44, 158, 272n. 35
Swinburne, Henry, observations of, 1
Sympathizers (*adictos*), 140

Tariffs, 11, 36, 38, 39, 49, 116, 124, 129,
    175, 193, 223, 286n. 53; abolition of,
    112; collecting, 16; export, 40, 180;
    iron, 289n. 88. *See also* Trade
Taxation, 7, 14, 17, 26, 27, 34, 35, 42,
    54–57, 59, 69, 90, 100, 106, 108, 125,
    192, 197, 223, 224, 231n. 4; abolition
    of, 75; forced, 103; protection from
    85; relieving, 208
Tenants (*arrendatarios*), 5, 195, 222
Thouvenot, General, 26, 27, 34, 46,
    235n. 55
Tolosa, 117
Trade, 12, 17, 38, 85, 99, 118, 119, 123–
    30, 134, 168–74, 187, 193, 222, 223,
    243n. 106, 286n. 53; barriers to, 50–
    51, 123, 129; colonial, 131, 243n. 103;
    decline in, 175–76, 284n. 15; fraudu-
    lent, 175; free, 12, 52, 122–23, 129–30,

193–94; wool, 284n. 5. *See also*
    Exports; Imports; Smuggling; Tariffs
Traditionalism, 28, 33, 38, 44, 46, 48,
    60, 62–64, 76, 82, 84, 125, 163, 185,
    187, 188, 190, 204, 208, 218, 220, 224,
    225, 245n. 129, 254n. 46, 254n. 50,
    269n. 163, 278n. 92, 287n. 64,
    296n. 178
Transportation, 187, 289n. 91; maritime,
    49
Travel, controlling, 140–43, 158
Treasurer (*tesorero*), 15
Trienio, xiii, 33, 45, 50, 58–59, 62–
    63, 67–70, 72, 76, 77, 100, 140, 149,
    169, 170, 173, 177, 182, 191, 207,
    248n. 186, 250n. 3
Trucios, 178

Ubidea, 36
Ugarte, Hilarión José de, 38
Uhagon, Guillermo de, 141–42
Uhagon, Pedro Pascual de, 96, 97, 122,
    126, 142, 144, 162, 164, 183–85, 190,
    195, 204, 205, 208, 210–16, 271n. 22,
    272n. 25, 294n. 151, 301n. 81,
    302n. 107, 303n. 119; criticism by,
    127; unpopularity of, 209, 269n. 163
Unceta, 202, 204
Unemployment, 52, 67, 69, 191–92
"Universal nobility," 4
Urquijo, Mariano Luis de, 23, 165

Valde-espina, Marquis de, 68, 115, 116,
    151, 153, 156, 160, 165, 177–79, 185,
    195, 202, 217, 278n. 89, 280n. 103,
    280n. 106, 288n. 70, 288n. 76,
    303n. 121
Valdenebro, Eladio Alonso de, 278n. 89,
    280n. 103
Valencia decrees (Ferdinand VII), 29
Valladolid, 8, 59
Vallaro, 36
Valley of Carranza, 44
Valmaseda, 11, 24, 36, 44
Vedia, Lorenzo Antonio de, 43–45, 47,
    58, 61, 178
Velasco (lawyer), 208, 210
Vendettas, 73, 208, 214
Ventades, Agustín de, 280n. 102
Ventades, Pedro Antonio de, 160, 165,
    280n. 102
Verastegui, 219, 303n. 121

Villarías, Marquis de, 149–50
Vitoria (Alava), 108, 169, 219, 303n. 119
Vizcayan Battalions, demobilization of, 32
Vizmanos, Manuel Leonardo, 161
Voting, 14, 16–17

Wage laborers (*jornaleros*), 5, 191, 222
War of Independence (1808), 3, 29, 51, 54, 63, 170, 190
Wheat, 31–32, 168, 238n. 23
Whites, 173
Widdrington, S. E., 165
Wines, 8–10; production of, 169–70. *See also* Brandies
Wool, 12, 174; merchants (*laneros*), 172; trade of, 171–72, 175–76, 284n. 5

Xenophobia, 75, 80–81, 85, 98, 196, 218. *See also* Foreign competition; Francophobia

Yandiola, Juan Antonio, 50
Yandiola, Juan José María de, 23, 45, 46, 49, 243n. 103
"Year of hunger," 3

Zalvide, Clemente de, 211
Zamacola, Simón Bernardo, 22
Zamora, Francisco de, 21
Zaratiegui, Juan Antonio, 217
Zavala, Fernando de, 65, 68, 195, 210, 215; defection of, 216; election of, 209
Zone franche (free zone), 52, 193. *See also* Tariffs
Zornoza, 178
Zorroza, 11